'A searing new biography . . . a very powerful work of difficult truth-telling. It is always easier to deceive yourself about how you would do the right moral thing than ever actually doing it. Most of us, like Frister, would selfishly choose life'

Kevin Tollis, *Guardian*

'Roman Frister is one of the few who have refused to draw a veil over the moral breakdown induced by Nazi violence. A fascinating and disturbing book which raises more questions than it can answer'   Hyam Maccoby, *Evening Standard*

'Roman Frister's story, and how he tells it, make his book utterly unputdownable . . . Frister's is not yet another chronicle of the mass murder of innocents, but an excruciatingly honest portrayal of human beings under deadly duress'   *Jewish Chronicle*

'An entirely new perspective on life in the camps . . . truly remarkable. Written without sentimentality or passion, it is a searingly honest account. Frister does not spare himself, for this is no hero's autobiography. Nor does he play the part of a neutral observer. Just the reverse. It is a very personal exploration of Hell'

Noreen Taylor, *The Times*

'Staggering in its honesty, Frister's memoir of his life in Poland as it was shaped by WWII has been deservedly praised in the international press . . . The precise depiction and abundance of detail yield a taut and compulsively readable narrative that makes fresh again horrors that have become familiar' *Publishers Weekly*

'*The Cap* is both brutal and beautifully written. Frister offers a life without defence. He seeks no applause and deserves none'

Boston Globe

'The book has been both heralded and criticised for its "brutal honesty". Frister may be aggressively candid, yet it is hard to argue that honesty is as brutal as repression'

San Francisco Examiner & Chronicle

Roman Frister was born in Bielsko-Biala, Poland, in 1928. He survived concentration camps and death marches. After the end of the war Frister worked as a journalist in Poland, until he was arrested by the communist authorities. In 1957 he emigrated to Israel. After many years as an editor and reporter on the leading Israeli daily *Ha'aretz*, Roman Frister took over running the School of Journalism in Tel Aviv in 1990. His books – novels, plays and non-fiction – have been translated into several languages. His autobiography caused a great sensation in Israel as a result of its unremitting frankness, and spent many weeks on the bestseller lists there, as it did in Poland and Germany.

THE CAP
or the Price of a Life

ROMAN FRISTER

PHŒNIX

A PHOENIX PAPERBACK

First published in Great Britain by Weidenfeld & Nicolson in 1999
This paperback edition published in 2000 by Phoenix,
an imprint of Orion Books Ltd,
Orion House, 5 Upper St Martin's Lane,
London WC2H 9EA

First published in Israel in 1993 as *Self-Portrait with a Scar*
by Dvir Publishing House
P.O. Box 149, Tel Aviv

A CIP catalogue record for this book
is available from the British Library.

ISBN: 0 75381 096 4

Printed and bound in Great Britain by
The Guernsey Press Co. Ltd, Guernsey, C.I.

Contents

PART I

The Taste of Bread

If cedars are in flames,
What is the moss to do?
(A Tamuldic saying)

1

We were permitted to move about the camp till 8 p.m. In summer, when the days grew long, the guards allowed us a limited freedom while dusk gathered slowly and the sky and earth joined on the horizon. It felt good to stand with my back to the perimeter fence, looking at the parade grounds in the middle of the camp. By glancing up I could see that the sky was still there, as blue and eternal as ever. It was good to look down, too, away from the stares of the guards behind their machine guns in the watchtowers. The prisoners strolled as casually among the barracks as if visiting old neighbours. A lively trade in staples went on behind the closed doors. No one knew how all the loaves of bread or sacks of rice and buckwheat were smuggled in, or where anyone obtained the dollars and diamonds to pay for them. Sometimes a fight broke out; sometimes, a friendship. It was just like the real life beyond the barbed wire – except that no one thought of tomorrow. We lived by the minute, the secret of our modest happiness being the ability to plod like cattle around our pen, oblivious of the slaughter house.

The camp was located in the upper town of Starachowice, in the Kielce district of Poland. The lower town, founded by Cistercian monks, had been inhabited for centuries by Jews. Its main landmarks were a ramshackle synagogue; a marketplace paved with cobblestones; a sleepy old well in the middle of the square; the dilapidated stores surrounding it; and the more spacious houses of the well-to-do in the nearby side streets. Years afterwards, in an old-age home in Tel Aviv, I met a woman who wanted to know if the alley cats still basked in the sun by the well in Starachowice. She had the naive faith that time can be stopped, frozen, and thawed out again at will.

The work camp stood on top of a hill, not far from a working-class neighbourhood that was lived in largely by men who worked in a nearby iron mine. Other, similar camps were scattered throughout the vicinity, their prisoners a mixture of Poles and Jews. Designed to keep the wheels of the Nazi arms industry turning, each was a patch of life and death in a crazy quilt that only the historians of the future, perhaps, will know how to decipher. Ostensibly, these were not death camps with their cloying smell of the crematorium. No selections – *Left! Right! You will live! You to a mass grave!* – were held in them. You were even allowed a natural death. Despite the brutal work, the punishing discipline, and the cruelty of the Latvian and Estonian guards, our daily nourishment was a food called Illusion. We played at make-believe – the belief that it wouldn't happen to us.

Was I blind? Impervious to the truth? Looking back today, I can see that being able to repress an apocalyptic reality was a prerequisite for survival. Like everyone, I had to struggle to forget all that had happened to me from the beginning of the war. Every painful experience that might have sapped my will to live became a blank spot in my memory. The one thing I couldn't banish was my dying father's face. It accompanied me everywhere like an inner weight, an inner barb.

It was still light outside when I returned from the steelworks. At fifteen, I was the youngest of the workers in the Siemens-Martin plant, whose blast ovens were as obsolescent as the rest of it. Built at the turn of the century by a Jewish magnate named Solomon Frankel who believed in the future of the industrial revolution, its furnaces were idled in the 1930s when it was deemed unprofitable to invest in their modernization. But the Nazi invaders of Poland breathed new life into the cold chimneys. Paid workers and forced labourers scraped the rust from the cars of the internal rail system, removed the warts of petrified concrete from its tracks, and drove out the rats that had taken over the empty workspace. New lathes were delivered from Germany. Now part of the Hermann Goering Werke conglomerate, the plant produced badly needed steel from ore and old scrap metal and cast it into bomb casings and howitzer barrels. The ovens worked around the clock. It was reassuring to know that as long as they kept operating, we had an exemption from death in our pockets.

My father lost his on the day he fell ill. For months he had pushed the cars carrying the sand-tempered steel moulds from the foundry to the quality control room. Each weighing half a ton, the cars screeched on every curve and constantly threatened to jump the rails. Whenever they did, the German supervisors beat the prisoners with iron bars until the cars were back on their narrow-gauge tracks. Even those Germans who were not born sadists became them. They were in a panic of productivity, as if the slightest delay might decide the war against them. A defeat, they knew, meant the end of the Nazi dream of a Volkswagen for every pure Aryan.

I could see my father's strength giving out. He slipped and fell even without being struck. 'Stop smoking,' I scolded. I knew he was secretly exchanging his daily bread ration for roaches of cigarettes and shreds of low-grade tobacco. If he didn't want the bread, why not give it to me? I couldn't bear having to listen to his smiling apologies that he needed the nicotine to live. I was less ashamed of his addiction, or even of wanting the bread myself, than of his need to justify himself. Today I would say that this was the last straw of his paternal authority. Morally, I was on my own long before he breathed his last. Without knowing how or when it happened, I had stopped looking up to him. My only god was the god of survival.

By the time I realized my father was sick, it was too late.

Too late! An absurd thought. As if there was anything I could have done had I known earlier. There was no possible way I could have helped him. Would acknowledging this have made it worse? I don't know. A psychologist would have said that I had strong defence mechanisms. Since the start of the war I had wrapped myself in a thick layer of callousness. It was suicidal not to detach yourself from the human suffering around you. The path to freedom from self-destructive qualms ran over the corpses of those nobler than you.

The typhus fever epidemic that killed my father was as devastating as the plague in medieval Europe. In anti-Semitic posters that I had seen in the streets of Poland before my internment, Jews were portrayed as a germ-infested people. Now the Nazi propaganda proved right.

I can't say when my father was infected. As long as he was able to stay on his feet, he hid it from me. Perhaps he wanted to believe that he was only under the weather and could cheat his fate by denying it.

One morning his legs buckled at the daily roll-call. I tried supporting him. The prisoner on the other side of him paid no attention. No one was prepared to waste energy on such things. It was best to steer clear of others' misfortunes.

My father doubled over. His hand slipped from my proffered shoulder. There was no point in pretending any longer. He fell as soundlessly as a sack of absorbent cotton. Although my first instinct was to help him to his feet, I straightened up and stared at the German officer on duty. I was experienced enough to know better than to involve myself with a hopeless case. Bad luck was contagious, too.

The kapo stopped counting heads. The officer striding alongside him stepped back and barked:

'This is all we need! Get him to the infirmary!'

Two prisoners whose job it was grabbed my father's limp arms and hauled him off. Was he conscious? Did he know what was happening? I never asked. His legs dragged along the sandy ground, the trail behind them progressively fainter. I didn't want to look. Perhaps I realized unconsciously that the sight would always haunt me. But as though hypnotized, I kept my eyes on the receding pair of shoes that were attached to my father. The kapo waited for him to disappear behind a barracks and divided us into work teams. Men collapsed like that every day. It was no big deal. Five minutes later I was marching in line as usual along the dirt path that led down the hill to the steelworks.

One of the barracks had a sign that said, Infirmary. A wooden shack with a tin roof, it was otherwise no different from the others. No doctor, Jewish or Christian, had ever set foot in it. The job of the prisoners who worked there consisted of removing the corpses to an open space in the back. Both the dead and the living were tallied at roll-call. Not until the figures matched did the SS officer permit the dead bodies to be trucked away to a mass grave on the outskirts of town. I never asked where it was. I didn't want to know.

I visited my father every day after work. The shift ended at 6 p.m. Evening roll-call took another hour. It was a great effort just to climb the hill after a day's work, passing through the gate under the searching eyes of the sentries. Sometimes we were searched for smuggled food. Anyone caught with it was shot.

After roll-call we were free. All I wanted was to lie down in my bunk and let the leaden fatigue run out of my legs. Had I given in to this desire, though, I could never have forced myself to rise again and go to the infirmary. Stronger men than myself were wiped out by the end of the day. The Siemens-Martin blast ovens had a temperature of sixteen hundred degrees centigrade and gave off poisonous vapours that assailed us each time their doors were opened to expel their molten contents. Years later, while reading Jean-Paul Sartre's play *No Exit* in which a character remarks that 'Hell is other people', I was struck by the profundity of the remark. But such a hell was nothing compared to our daily immolation in the steelworks of Starachowice. I still felt scorched by it as I approached the infirmary.

The infirmary door was kept closed. For a moment I put off turning its handle. Beyond it, where life met death, there was no more room for lies.

It took a moment to get used to the darkness. The shutters had been nailed shut to keep even a ray of sunlight from penetrating. By the dim light of a bulb that hung from a rafter, the sick men's faces looked like wax dolls'. A few still had the strength to pick the lice from their hair. Most lay without moving. Death crawled slowly forwards here, out of sight, beneath a cover of darkness that hid the final parting from the world.

My father's cot was the last in its row. I passed the other patients without giving them a second's thought. I had no sense of sharing a common fate with them. While they were already waiting in line for the next world, I was still in this one. A sour stench of urine and disinfectant filled the air. Someone stuck out a hand, his dry throat wheezing incomprehensibly. Perhaps he was thirsty and wanted water. I pretended to see and hear nothing. Although I was not afraid of physically catching anything, I was terrified of the slightest connection with these people, who had the power to drag me down into their lost, dark world.

'Father, it's me,' I whispered.

There was no reply. His silence did not fool me. The slight tremor of his fever-chapped lips told me he had heard. The awkward angle of his head on the straw mattress, together with his bulging Adam's apple, sagging mouth and bony hands that opened and clenched, seemed to be sending me some signal that I could not decode. I asked:

'Are you thirsty, Father?'

No answer. Nothing.

'Father, are you with me?'

I bent down to him: not to listen for a heartbeat but to gently crush the lice that had taken up residence between his eyelashes. Most of the sick men lay silently, some in grotesque positions as if embalmed halfway through an epileptic fit. The lice alone stirred. I wondered what would happen to them when the body that nourished them grew cold. Would they die, too, or would they migrate to the next cot and begin life all over? Carefully holding them between my fingers, I looked at them before crushing them with a thumbnail. They popped with the sound of a small cap pistol.

It took a while to do my father's lashes. I ran a finger over his brows.

'Open your eyes, Father,' I urged.

Did he know me? I badly wanted him to. But to know what? That I had honoured him to the last? That I had stayed by him even though abandoning those you loved was taken for granted in a place like this? Damn all that empty moralizing! Couldn't I see that his stupor had passed beyond comprehension or suffering, that his meaningless existence was sputtering like a candle flame that no longer gave light? One touch and it would go out. Deep down I knew that I wasn't even seeking his recognition. That was just an excuse. Beneath his louse-ridden straw mattress was hidden half a loaf of bread. He hadn't eaten that day. I was hungry.

'Father?' I whispered. 'Father, is there . . .?'

I started to ask if he needed anything, then realized the absurdity of it. My voice was so low that I could hardly hear it. Was I trying to keep him from hearing, too? What would I do if he asked me to put him out of his misery?

He wiggled his fingers. It was a sign – but of what? My hand froze on its way to the bread. I sat on the edge of the cot, waiting for him to die so that I could take it with a clear conscience.

For a week now I had watched the Angel of Death with his bag of tricks. I had seen him slowly, cunningly, reach out to take men's lives. The son of a bitch! First he drained the colour from their cheeks. Then he soaked their brows with cold sweat, flooded their bodies with exhaustion, set them trembling with fever, paralysed their brains. A master craftsman.

I was a veteran. I had seen sudden death at work many times. I had seen Wilhelm Kunde of the SS Special Forces smash my mother's skull with a pistol butt. It would take forty years to bring him to justice in West Germany. I had seen people shot like kewpie dolls, kapos murder prisoners with clubs and pitchforks, desperate men throw themselves on high-tension wires. Sudden death was the chequerboard on which we inhabited a few temporary squares. Stunned by it at first, you soon came to regard it as routine. Slow death was a hundred times more frightening. It was death at its most intimate. My father's death went on and on. There was no way to overlook it.

And while it lingered, all I could think of was that half a loaf of bread. I was afraid it might crumble before he stopped breathing. That it would be eaten by the rats or discovered by the orderly who was now telling me to leave. The clock over the door said a quarter to eight. There were fifteen minutes until the curfew. I laid a hand on my father's shoulder. 'I'll be back tomorrow,' I promised. He didn't hear me. Not that it mattered. It was just to make myself feel better.

The orderly slammed the door behind me. The last prisoners were hurrying back to their barracks. The guards were taking out the watchdogs from their kennel by the front gate. We heard their short, staccato yelps every night, the barking of sated beasts who would gladly kill for the pleasure of it.

The next evening the orderly, who had been drowsing on the chair by the infirmary door, told me my father had 'given up his soul'.

'Who are you kidding?' I said. 'There's no such thing and no one to give it to.'

He shrugged, not in the mood for a philosophical conversation. 'Go on, beat it,' he told me. But I went to have a look. On the last cot in the last row lay a new typhus patient waiting for another death. I felt furious. I had lost both my father and the bread. The last umbilical cord to my childhood snapped right then. From that moment I was entirely on my own.

2

Childhood had its own smells and colours. In the yard of the house that we lived in until World War II stood two spreading lilac bushes, one white and one purple. Although they grew in the shade of giant chestnut trees, they had taken over most of the garden. In May and June, when they were in full blossom, I went to bed with the window open and fell asleep to their intoxicating sweetness.

Fifty years later I returned. The house was as gloomy and neglected as an uncared-for old man. I glanced up at my window. Half-open, it dangled from warped, rusty hinges like a wounded bird's wing. Only the stumps were left of the felled chestnuts. The lilacs had perished of thirst, stripped of the earth around them. And yet it all has remained. Each time I smell lilacs, forgotten pictures from a past before the past emerge from the depths of oblivion.

I never knew why my parents chose to settle in Bielsko-Biała, a textile centre in the region of Southern Schlesia where Polish and German culture met and clashed. Although environmentalism was not yet the fashion, the polluting mills and looms were kept on the outskirts of the city, whose air remained clean. A peaceful place, Bielsko-Biała nestled in the Beskid Mountains – which did not thrust sharp granite peaks at the sky like the nearby Tatras but ran softly down to gentle valleys that were green in summer and white in winter. It seemed obvious that such beauty and serenity would last for ever. I was born and raised in a stage set designed for a happy childhood.

Outwardly, our house was no different from the others in the neighbourhood. The wealthy burghers of the early years of the century had built in the ornamentally rich and architecturally poor style of the late Austrian baroque. Their homes expressed the outward solidity rather than the inward spirit of the times. They were like the city itself, whose municipal charter was granted in the late eighteenth century when Count Josef Alexander Sulkowski, a protégé of the Polish king Augustus II, added 'Prince of Bielsko' to his titles. Bielsko's great period of prosperity followed later, when it became a linchpin of the wool industry. An influx of German and Jewish capital spurred its development and helped make it one of the wealthiest towns in Poland.

The Sulkowskis, who preferred metropolitan glitter to provincial life, frittered away their fortune in Paris and the Côte d'Azur and lost their economic standing. Like many Polish aristrocrats, they were unable to adjust to the industrial age. By the end of World War I, when southern Poland parted company with the Austro-Hungarian empire, their holdings were reduced to five hundred unbuilt acres in the city centre. In the 1930s these were sold to a group of contractors. Foundations were dug for a new development on the grassy space that I once had played in under the eyes of Hilde Baron, my German governess. Perhaps because its tenants were mostly well-to-do Jews, its white Bauhaus buildings were known as 'Tel Aviv'. Many of my parents' friends, especially those desiring a fashionable address, moved there. My parents stayed put. We went on living in the same grey, characterless house in which I was born in January 1928, a winter said to be the hardest of the century. Thousands of homeless people froze to death in it.

We lived on the second floor. Most of the windows faced the street. My father received his guests in the smoking room, which had easy chairs, a mobile bar, and walnut bookcases. I liked to sneak into it, climb on a chair, and browse through the books on the top shelves. Their distinguished but frayed bindings testified to a history of having been read and not merely looked at.

The brightest room was my parents' bedroom with its rosewood furniture. Running across the waxed parquet floor from the sofa, a carpet made by a local craftsman spun a warm intimacy that contrasted with the severity of the dark foyer, whose heavy brocade curtains kept out the sun. Not even the Persian rugs, loved so much by my mother that she would not flee the Nazis without them, could soften the stiffness of this room that was my parents' pride and status symbol. I sometimes wondered what it felt like to be one of the porcelain ballerinas who danced for ever behind the glass doors of the corner cabinet. Along one wall stood a huge mahogany buffet, its compartments crammed with silk tablecloths, fine china, and solid-silver Viennese cutlery. I called it 'the coffin'.

A table for twelve stood in the room's centre like a black mushroom. At least once a month my father's most important clients met around it for dinner. Dressed in a tie and jacket, I was allowed to sit up with them until nine, mainly for Mother to take pride in my table manners, my European education, and my precocious knowledge of literature. Sometimes the spoiled brat in me tried my parents' patience. Then my father sent me an ominous glance and reached for the bell, shaped like a fairytale dwarf, that hung from an antique crystal chandelier above the table. One squeeze of the fawning dwarf's head summoned our housemaid Paula from the kitchen.

'Take him to his room,' my father would say severely. Paula gave me her hand and I followed her, outwardly rebuked and brimming with malicious pleasure.

The fragrant view of the backyard was Paula's and mine. She lived in an alcove behind the bathroom, a big, ageless woman with a large behind that could have been sculpted by Maillol. Descended from generations of German peasant stock, she seemed to me the foundations on which my family had rested long before I was born. Indeed, she remained in place even when we were uprooted by the winds of war. I still see her standing motionlessly by the door through which our exodus began, promising that she would wait for our return even if it took a whole year. My father laughed, waved goodbye, and promised to be back before autumn.

After I was born my father moved his study from our home to his office in the commercial district. He was doing well. Bielsko was prospering. Its thriving businesses needed good lawyers to deal with corporations and banks. His firm expanded and took on assistants. Its receptionist, whom I thought of as its Paula, was Miss Mila. She ushered visitors into the waiting room and spent her spare time at a machine on which she hand-rolled the eighty Turkish-tobacco cigarettes that my father smoked every day.

The ordinary customers fell to the assistants. Only the most important were invited into my father's office and offered a seat in its old leather chairs whose venerable age bespoke respectability, pomp, and tradition.

I didn't care for my father's office, perhaps because I felt that he never had any time or patience for me there. The Venetian blinds of this sanctuary were always lowered halfway, the dim light casting a spell of mystery, especially when my father and his clients talked in low voices by the light of the green-shaded desk lamp while smoking and studying documents from the safe, a hefty and ancient steel box.

I never understood my father's attraction to the things that towed one back into the past. I myself was drawn to what was new and bright. But the ex-study that I inherited, which not even my parents ever called 'the children's room', had nothing cheerful about it. A white bed was the only new furniture to join the huge desk, which sailed out of one corner like a steamship towards the black oak bookcases that looked like a cross between Biedermeier and art nouveau. My toy soldiers now camped on the same shelves that had housed my father's law books and files. Pitilessly sending them into battle, I played at war until I was eleven. The toy stores of the city had entire reserve battalions waiting for a call-up from me.

Besides faultless manners, my mother's ambitions for me included musical proficiency. A woman of culture, she could not imagine a boy from a good Jewish home unable to play the piano. All my pleas and explanations that I had no talent for music, a genetic defect passed down to me from her, fell on deaf ears. 'It's merely a question of will-power,' she insisted.

For my seventh birthday I received a piano. Black and wingless, it stood in my room like a hostile beast that threatened to devour my play time with its white teeth. Luckily, two or three lessons were enough for 'Mrs Mozart', as I called my piano teacher, to decide that I couldn't tell a C-flat from an E-sharp and put an end to the torture. The piano was donated to the gym of the Maccabee Athletic Club, where I happily worked out twice a week to its music with my classmates.

Shortly before the same birthday Hilde Baron, whom we called *das Kindermädchen* as though she had no name of her own, was dismissed and I was registered for the local Jewish school. Although Bielsko had an active and influential Jewish community, this was my first contact with it. In those years it was controlled by the Zionists, Zionism being an abstract notion that meant nothing to me. Only after World War II did I learn of the culture wars fought between them and the Orthodox, many of whom attended the Great Synagogue, a building with a medieval women's gallery and a modern organ. It was only then, too, that I discovered we had had Orthodox neighbours.

Most of the religious Jews lived in Biala, on the southern bank of the Bialka River that divided the town. Theirs was a voluntary ghetto, a distant and off-limits world for the children of the non-observant. Not until we fled the Nazis to the rural regions of eastern Poland, which I had previously known about only from the stories of Sholom Aleichem, did I see my first Jew with a gaberdine, beard, and ear locks. I didn't even know that the landlord who rented us our apartment was a Rappaport, a family claiming descent from the famous Hasidic rabbi Itchik Meir of Gur. The Rappaports had owned textile plants in Lodz, before their expulsion from that city by the Tsarist authorities in the 1880s made them move to Biala. Linked by marriage to leading rabbinic families, they had grown wealthy and prominent without surrendering their religion and without my having heard of them. It was not merely a small river that separated the religious Jews from us. It was a wall so high that no ladder could have helped me to peer over it.

No doubt wishing to spare me friction with the Polish and German boys who studied there, my father declined to send me to the local public school. The Kraszewski Hebrew Elementary School that I attended was named for a nineteenth-century Polish intellectual who believed in Jewish-Polish brotherhood, which he espoused in the pages of the *Gazeta Codzienna*, a liberal daily financed by the Jewish magnate Leopold Kronberg.

Appropriately for an institution bearing the name of a Polish author and historian, the Kraszewski School's language of instruction was Polish. Although starting with the fourth grade we also studied some Hebrew and the Bible, this was little more than a sop to tradition. My father himself sought the golden mean between the two worlds – or perhaps among the three of Polish, Jewish, and German culture. He was typical in this respect of his generation, which found no contradiction between religious, national, and universal values. From childhood on I was accustomed to three literatures. By the time I was ten I was reading both Jewish and Polish books, whilst even before discovering the German adventure novels of Karl Mai I was familiar with Emil Ludwig's biographies of Bismarck and Napoleon, and Arnold Zweig's *Sergeant Grisha*.

I haven't mentioned my riding lessons. God, how I cursed my father's love of the cavalry, especially each time I fell off a horse! Twice a week I had to pay the price of his nostalgia for his years in Marshal Józef Piłsudski's mounted legions. Although no doubt tame and tired from their dull rounds, the horses I rode seemed like wild mustangs to me. The master of my riding school, a retired Polish officer, regarded his job with reverence and saluted each time he passed the equestrian portrait that hung by the entrance to the stables of a blue-uniformed Piłsudski gazing up at the sky. This earned him the respect of my father, who was also a great admirer of the hero of modern Polish independence. Our whole house was plunged into mourning at the time of Piłsudski's death in 1935. When his coffin was brought by special train from Warsaw to Cracow, Poland's ancient capital and the traditional burial place of her kings, my parents rented a balcony along the route to have front-row seats for the funeral cortège that made its way to the tomb in Wawel Castle.

I myself knew nothing at the time about the uproar caused in aristocratic circles by the decision to bury Piłsudski with Polish royalty or of the wars of succession fought in Warsaw's Belvedere Palace. If my father took an interest in such things, he never spoke of them. Nor did he share any anxieties he may have had about the new government's revocation, one after another, of the freedoms granted by the Piłsudski regime or its opening of the floodgates to a tide of anti-Semitism. I lived on a protected island. My political awareness went no further than the portraits of Piłsudski's successor in our classrooms with their caption, made in response to Hitler's demands for a territorial corridor to Danzig: 'We won't give back a single button!' This slogan accompanied the Polish people to their collapse in September 1939.

Although my father, who spoke perfect Polish, insisted that I read the Polish classics, these did not keep me from falling under the sway of the writings of the militant Zionist leader Vladimir Jabotinsky. But it was not Jabotinsky's dream of a Hebrew army in Palestine that most enticed me. It was rather the thought of the British boarding school that would, for a fee, make an English gentleman of a Jewish boy from Eastern Europe.

To this day I sometimes enjoy playing 'What if?' What if my life had gone according to my parents' wishes? Most likely I would have ended up a wealthy conservative like my father, a man with refined taste, a loathing for the mob, and a wife from a good family who eased his life with a handsome dowry and enveloped him in dismal boredom. This is not someone that the person I am today would have liked. Should I be glad that it turned out differently and that the Holocaust, whose unhealed scars I mean to bare in these pages, shaped me more than did my father? Perhaps such questions are better not asked. Still, if I must answer it, I have to say: yes.

As far back as I can remember it was taken for granted that I would receive the best education money could buy, starting with the English school I would be sent to after my bar mitzvah. No one ever explained to me where this idea came from or why my parents preferred Eton to Vienna. The plan was obviously a long-standing one, since I was required to study English from the age of six. I hated its grammar long before I knew what hatred was and managed to absorb what I did of it thanks solely to my private tutor, Mr Rosensztyn. How a Jew like himself, a native of Buczacz in Galicia and a great admirer of his fellow townsman, the future Nobel Prize-winning Hebrew author S.Y. Agnon, developed an affinity for British culture was beyond me. Sometimes, when I grew exasperated with my lessons, he read to me from a German translation of Agnon's picaresque novel *The Bridal Canopy*. Since my father was not paying him the princely sum of two zloty per hour for me to study Agnon, this remained a secret between us.

To the best of my memory, I was ten when Jabotinsky came to Bielsko and delivered a fiery oration on the subject of his 'Repatriation Plan'.* My father was completely won over. No doubt this was why I was sent for my next vacation to a summer

---

This was a plan to transfer 1.5 million Jews from Eastern Europe to Palestine within ten years. The Jewish community opposed it because it feared legitimizing the anti-Semites' contention that the Jews were a foreign presence in Poland. The Polish government, on the other hand, supported the idea and even instructed its delegation to the League of Nations to request Palestinian visas for the prospective immigrants from the British.

camp of Betar, the youth movement of Jabotinsky's Revisionist Party. It was located in the fairytale village of Szczyrk, at the foot of Mount Klimczok, a majestic peak fabled in poem and song. Returning to it in the summer of 1980 in search of the Goplana Boarding House, the site of my first sexual experience, I found a wooden villa with strange wooden towers like an exotic mosque's. On the ground floor, where our counsellors had taught us to be little Revisionists, was a bar selling alcohol to all ages.

The unforgettable part of the Goplana was my intimate encounter with Rita, the ten-year-old daughter of a perfumery owner from Dziedzice. Pulling me into the thick bushes that grew by a stream, she offered to demonstrate the difference between the male and female of the species. 'You'll feel me and I'll feel you,' she proposed. I didn't dare. Soon after, however, when I masturbated for the first time, her flashing eyes and petite figure with its flowery dress raised to the waist were my inspiration. After the war I tried tracking her down, hoping to resume our little game in adult fashion. In vain. Little Rita had been buried in life's ruins.

Let us return to my childhood room and to the desk on which I did my homework. Neither it nor I got very far, the desk because of its great weight and I because of my attitude. I was (and still am) one of those insufferable pupils who find everything easy and think they know ten times more than the teacher. More interesting than my homework were the desk's many locked drawers and compartments. Unable to restrain my curiosity, I broke the locks and found bundles of love letters written by my father to my mother when he was still a cavalry officer, first in the days of Kaiser Franz Joseph and then under Piłsudski. My mother's replies were there, too, the blue and pink envelopes arranged in perfect chronological order, each batch tied with a white silk ribbon. Tearing off their stamps with no respect for their privacy, I pasted these in an album given to me by an aunt.

Two years later I took the step of reading them. My mother had a clear, round hand; my father's gothic lines stood perfectly straight and at attention like my toy soldiers at morning roll-call. The more I read, the more astonished I grew. My father's letters were totally at odds with both his handwriting and his character. It was beyond me how this man, the most serious in the universe, could have written such nonsense about his uncontrollable longings for my mother's body and his dreams of a life together. Nor could I fathom how my mother, a self-centred woman obsessed with her appearance, could have been so limitlessly devoted. I may have known Polish, German, and despite myself some English, but I still knew nothing of the language of love.

Today my father's photograph stands on my desk in a brass frame. His face looks stern; the brow is high, the hairline receding, the moustache clipped, the gaze directed straight at me. *No, don't look at me that way, Father. Your stare no longer intimidates me. The eyes of the dead don't scare me. You were a great proponent of order, discipline, and routine, but all that belongs to the past, from the scattered bricks of which I'm free to build my story. Had you known I would write about you like this, you would no doubt have gone straight to the bathroom for your leather shaving strop and given me one of your whippings. But I intend to hold you to your word. It was you, after all, who once said to me that if there is no God, everything is permitted.*

I find it hard to picture his impressive features. Without the photographs I could probably not remember them at all. It is as though they have faded with the rest of him. But I do remember the rod he refused to spare whenever he thought I misbehaved. He was a firm believer in its educational properties, and strange as it may seem, I accepted his chastisement as part of his paternal love. It was always to the point. Never once was I whipped for something I had not done. Never once did crying or begging help. Forbearance was a word absent from my father's vocabulary. He always insisted that the punishment fit the crime. To this day I believe that this approach, which would shock any contemporary pedagogue, taught me the laws of moral retribution. To them I owe a sense of justice that not even the Nazi concentration camps could eradicate.

On Sunday mornings, when the offices and factories were closed and the eternal Paula betook herself to church to share her secret yearnings with the Divinity, my parents stayed in bed until nine. It was the only time I was allowed under their blanket for a hug and perhaps even a ride on my father's hairy chest. Such rare moments of indulgence brought a brief but intense pleasure. Although it may seem that it took little to make me happy, it was really a question of expectations. Neither my expensive toys and clothes nor my regular allowance had anything to do in my mind with love. They were simply things I took for granted, although I felt deprived when denied them.

When the Sunday weather was good, I was permitted to accompany my father on a nature walk. While my mother preferred to loll in bed, his spartan principles dictated a hike through the woods. After breakfast we took the tram to its last stop and climbed narrow paths to a hill on which stood an inn with a restaurant that served wild game. There, in a side room, he met his cronies for a few rubbers of bridge. The walk took forty minutes and gave us a chance to talk. Did he listen? Did my problems interest him? I still don't know. Once he told me: 'You're old enough to master your feelings.' I was a fourth grader at the time, newly in love with a slim, smiling girl named Lili Carter. Perhaps this had something to do with her parents owning a bicycle store and my wanting to trade my horse for a bike; in any case, the relationship remained platonic. The one time I touched her was to cut off her braid.

This was not a rash or spontaneous decision. Everything about it was well planned. Even the scissors were brought from home, hidden in the bottom of my school bag. Taking advantage of Lili's sitting in front of me, I waited for her to lean back in a moment of concentration and wielded my weapon with manly determination. It was not easy to cut a thick braid and I must have caused her no little pain. She burst out crying, my plot was discovered, and I was suspended for three days. Although this did not distress me in the least, my father's strop kept me from sitting on my behind for a week.

Now, on our walk up the hill, I tried explaining to him the need I had felt to express my passion for Lili. But such impulsiveness was foreign to his nature. The conversation on which I had pinned such hopes ended with a rebuke.

I sometimes wonder if my father ever played such pranks himself. Can there be a happy childhood that does not occasionally kick over the traces? But I knew nothing about his younger years. He never talked about his parents, or the rural estate he had grown up on, or the schools he had attended. Our relationship had no roots and dissolved after his death. To this day I can't imagine him tossing a rotten egg into Mr Hahn's sweets shop the way we did.

The shop was on The Third of May Street, Bielsko's main thoroughfare, named for the day Poland received its constitution. One of the city's fanciest, it had a sign with a rooster, which was the meaning of *Hahn* in German. On our way back from school, we first hid our bags in a next-door stairway for a quick getaway. Then two or three of us entered the shop and studied the wares on its counter like connoisseurs while waiting for Erik, our class's best throwing arm, to appear in the doorway and fling against the rear wall an egg we had buried until its stink was unbearable. As soon as Mr Hahn, a short, bald German with a paunch, ran outside to catch *den Kleinen Bandit*, we swung into action. By the time he returned huffing and puffing, our pockets were full of cupcakes and chocolates.

I never knew Erik's mother, who killed herself when he was an infant. Although none of us knew why she had done it, we did know that Erik's father shared a bed with his *Kindermädchen*, a German like Hilde Baron. When the Nazis arrived, it was she who helped the family to escape.

Erik's father had businesses in Poland and abroad. He dealt in international trade, owned a large number of breweries, and was a partner in a run-down movie house in Bielsko's south end that showed films produced, as he put it, 'for housemaids and their lovers'. Erik received free tickets and we went to the cinema at least once a week, less for its Grade C Hollywood movies than blushingly to watch the couples necking in the back.

I didn't believe that my father ever committed such breaches of conduct when young. I never saw him hug or kiss my mother. He must have mastered his own feelings as a foetus. His daily schedule was rigorous. At 7.30 sharp Paula served him his breakfast – always the same cup of coffee with milk and the crisp, brown, four-sectioned roll that was called for some reason 'a Kaiser roll'. Perhaps old Kaiser Franz Joseph had breakfasted on it in the Schönbrunn Palace in Vienna. Anything Viennese, no matter how old-fashioned, was considered chic in Bielsko.

We breakfasted together. Much to the chagrin of my mother, who considered it bad manners, my father dunked his roll in his coffee and ate it with relish. My mother made do with some dry crackers and a glass of milk while I was forced to down a drink called Ovomaltine, which tasted like cocoa but cost twice as much because it was enriched with vitamins 'to fortify your child against illnesses and physical weakness'. My only comfort was that other children had to drink cod liver oil.

At 7.55 my father left for work, first depositing a ten-zloty coin on his night table to cover the day's household expenses. (The coin was solid silver. If I remember correctly, it had a bust of Piłsudski on one side and a Polish eagle on the other.) At 2 p.m. he returned for lunch and lay down for an hour's nap. Not even the flies were allowed to buzz while he slept. At 4.00 he returned to his office, at 7.00 he went to his bridge club, and at 9.00 he came home for supper. He ordered all his suits from the same tailor and spent all his vacations in the same hotel with the same people, all his social equals, in the resort town of Krinice. Dull and unimaginative as all this may have been, it gave me a strong sense of stability. Everything seemed as eternal as the earth's orbit around the sun. Even as the clouds were darkening over Europe and thunder rumbled on the horizon, we went on seeing starry skies. If there was anyone who read the writing on the wall, it was not my parents.

I know that it is easy to be wise in hindsight. More knowledgeable people than ourselves guessed wrong, too. While the pages of *Mein Kampf* were being rewritten as operational manuals in the *Reichsführer*'s office in Berlin, the leaders of enlightened Europe looked the other way. In March 1938 Hitler's troops entered Vienna. Jewish music was barred from the opera, the decadent works of Bartok and Mahler were banned, and the gates of the Mauthausen concentration camp were opened to receive prisoners.

The English protested weakly. The French were too involved with their political crises to react. In September the great powers sacrificed the Sudetenland at Munich. Forgetful of the proverb that appetites grow with eating, the British prime minister Neville Chamberlain boasted of 'peace in our time'. The Polish army crossed the Olse River and seized a piece of moribund Czechoslovakia. The Polish newspapers reported this act of historic justice with patriotic enthusiasm; the postal service issued a special stamp in its honour. I was one of the first to buy it. It remained behind in its album with other heroic stamps when we had to flee our home less than a year after the dismemberment of Czechoslovakia was celebrated with drums and fifes.

But I am getting ahead of myself. October 1938 was a cold, rainy month. The autumn leaves were falling when a trainload of deportees from the Third Reich was shunted to a side track at the little border station of Zbaszyn in the Poznań district. Thousands of Jews with Polish citizenship were being returned to their Polish motherland. The train stood in the no-man's land between the two countries, neither of which wanted its passengers. The days passed with no solution. A collection was taken up at school and we donated food and clothing to the unfortunates. That evening, as my father was washing down his meal with a glass of cherry liqueur, he glanced at the newspaper and remarked:

'It says here that those poor people are selling their valuables to the local farmers in exchange for food.'

My mother nodded in commiseration. Suddenly she said:

'Jewellery, too? Maybe we should take a trip to Zbaszyn.'

My father gave her an annoyed look.

'Well, then, of course not,' she said. The conversation was over.

At the other end of Europe, in the City of Light, a Jewish student named Herschel Grynszpan read about the same refugees. His elderly parents were in one of the cars. Distraught at the world's indifference, he sought to shock it by an act of desperation, shooting and killing Ernst vom Rath, a junior German diplomat serving in Paris. The Nazis retaliated with Kristallnacht.

3

Bielsko had had its own pogrom a month earlier, right after the Munich agreement. For the first time since its annexation by Poland, its German inhabitants openly flew the swastika and called for expulsion of the city's Jews. A Polish mob quickly joined in. Rumours spread of anti-Jewish riots planned for the following Monday. My parents and their friends decided to cross the Olse and wait things out in the Czech border town of Cieszyn.

Our small convoy of five cars left Bielsko early Sunday afternoon. I regarded it as a pleasure excursion and wanted badly to sit in the front seat of Dr Frankel's MG. A colleague of my father's, Dr Frankel liked sports cars and elegant women. He was the only man in Bielsko to have twice divorced and thrice married the same woman, which did not keep him from having affairs on the side. Now, too, the seat I desired was occupied by an unfamiliar young lady in a light, tight-fitting raincoat and a long silk scarf wound around her neck. 'Isadora Duncan,' mocked my mother. As much as I would like to remember her face, it has been erased like those of the others on that trip. Sometimes, unsuccessfully racking my brain to rescue someone from oblivion, I am overcome by a feeling of sadness and loss. One more piece of my childhood is gone for ever.

The drive took less than an hour. The road rose and fell like the folds in the tail of a Chinese dragon alongside green fields and orchards heavy with unpicked fruit. Peasants sat in front of whitewashed houses, smoking their Sunday pipes. In one village we heard church bells, late for the hour. The roar of our motors alone disturbed the tranquillity. Even the customs officials at the border were lazier than usual. No one liked working on a Sunday. Glancing casually at our passports, they omitted their usual question about the purpose of our visit. By four o'clock we were parked in the main square of Cieszyn, in front of the Korona Hotel.

'How long will you be staying?' asked the desk clerk politely. 'We don't know yet,' replied Dr Frankel. The clerk nodded understandingly. Lowering his voice, he said: 'You'll no doubt want to place a call home tomorrow morning.' Without waiting for an answer he summoned a bellboy to take us to the third floor, where five rooms were reserved for us.

A conspiracy of silence surrounded the pogrom. Just as some people are careful never to utter the word 'cancer', so the impending events in Bielsko were referred to by such euphemisms as 'the disorders' or 'the irresponsible actions'. The topic soon became tiresome and was changed. The ladies regretted that it was Sunday and that the stores were closed. Czech shoes were said to be as chic as Viennese ones and cheaper.

After washing and resting, we met for tea in the Four Seasons Salon on the mezzanine. Here, between the hours of five and seven, a young pianist in a bow tie played Vivaldi, Dvořák, Czech polkas, Viennese waltzes, and Mozart's *Eine Kleine Nachtmusik*, a repertoire favoured by the hotel's regular patrons. Waiters in billowing frock coats served tea from antique silver and poured coffee in paper-thin porcelain cups.

I stopped to look at myself in the huge mirror in the lobby. Still too young for long pants, I wore a tailored wool suit – made in Bielsko, of course. My blue blazer, gathered at the waist, was in the latest juvenile fashion. A bright red necktie adorned my white shirt. My shoes gleamed like the copper pots in Paula's kitchen. As though their social standing would be judged by it, my parents paid great attention to my appearance. They had no idea that I kept an old jacket and beat-up pants in the basement apartment of our building's janitor and put them on each time I sallied forth with Erik. Once home again I changed back into my good clothes and was complimented for taking such fine care of them. The janitor was rewarded for his silence with a few coins from my weekly allowance.

The men saw to it that the cars were parked in the hotel's courtyard and arranged for a game of bridge after dinner. This was played on two green-felt card tables beneath lamps shaded by translucent green glass. Local residents occupied the other tables.

Given permission to remain in the card room until late, I sat by the side of my father and followed the game. It was less the game itself that enthralled me than the money passing from hand to hand. I liked watching the faces of the men, who didn't utter a superfluous word. Serious and concentrated, they were masculine and mysterious at once. Gradually the room filled with cigarette and cigar smoke. A splendidly uniformed bellhop emptied the ashtrays from time to time. A waiter refilled the coffee cups and liqueur glasses.

My father was a master at bridge. Half jokingly and half in earnest, my mother liked to say that he earned more from it than from his law practice. Although I knew she wasn't serious, I felt a thrill each time he raked in another pot. He was so engrossed in the game that he failed to notice the Czech coin that rolled off the table and fell soundlessly on the carpet. Carefully I covered it with a polished shoe and waited. The seconds stretched to eternity. My heart pounded. A minute or two passed before I dared to bend down. Pretending to tie a shoelace, I palmed the two crowns with a premeditated movement. Then I nonchalantly slipped them into my pocket, trembling with fear and pleasure.

On Monday evening my father called his office and spoke to Miss Mila, a tall, flat-chested, sombre-looking spinster, as ageless as Paula and efficient as a robot, who wore high-necked, dark dresses or black skirts with grey blouses buttoned to the neck. Her husky voice was so deep and masculine that I could hear it through the receiver.

The whole pogrom, Miss Mila told my father, had turned out to be a farce. A few shop windows were broken and some drunken hooligans had shouted slogans against Jewish exploiters. In her opinion, there was no reason not to come home.

'I told you there was nothing to worry about,' said the woman who had usurped my seat in the MG. My mother gave her a scathing look. That morning Dr Frankel's mistress had bought a pair of alligator-skin shoes with a matching bag. 'In the most horrid colour,' whispered my mother to my father.

The next day we packed our bags and returned to Bielsko, arriving in time for our dinner. The pogrom had not spoiled our appetites.

4

Two days before he died, my father asked me to sit by his cot. Although his physical strength was exhausted, his mental vigour had returned and he was clear-minded. I knew this was only temporary. Many typhus patients had such remissions, from which they plunged even deeper into an insensate abyss.

In the calm tones of a man who knows that he has reached the end of the road, my father discussed my life after the war.

'There won't be any after the war,' I said.

The words were uttered more belligerently than I had intended and without taking their effect into account. I could not have accounted for my anger. The Nazis had surrounded us not only with barbed wire but with a wall of orders, regulations, and prohibitions that demanded blind obedience. Perhaps with my father alone I felt free of all that and able to let off steam. It never occurred to me that a man's approaching death might make him idealize the future, or that it was easier to die hoping than despairing. I was too tired from the day's work to think of such subtleties. My empty stomach was like a pump that sucked me into it.

'As long as there's a God above . . .' my father started to say.

It was a strange remark from a man who had never prayed in his life. I checked the temptation to say something sarcastic about those who believed in the Omnipotent Bastard called God only to be abandoned by Him when they most needed Him.

My father signalled me to come closer. He was so weakened by his illness that a few sentences were enough to drain him and force him to rest. His cheeks were grey, his breathing shallow. Death was knocking on the chambers of his heart. I bent to listen.

'When it's all over, go see Kruczek in Garlica Duchowna. You remember him, don't you? He's the man in whose house we hid in 1942. He'll give you a small suitcase. There are twenty thousand dollars' worth of Polish Bank shares in it. It's a rock-solid investment – you'll have no trouble getting cash for it. You can kill a man, destroy a house, wipe a city off the map, but banks last as long as air, water, and land. Yes, I've invested in land, too. We own part of a lot in Bielsko and some properties in Cracow. Next to the bank shares you'll find a blue cardboard file with a list of these. It will be enough to start you off on your new life. Don't let the money go to waste. I want you to finish your studies. Go to England, pick the best college there is, and come home with a diploma.'

'What home are you talking about?' I interrupted. 'Do you really think Paula is still waiting at the door?'

'For you,' he whispered. 'She's waiting for you.'

I didn't argue, although perhaps I should have. Like a runner getting his second wind before the finish line, he waited for his lungs to fill again. His fingers twitched nervously. The orderly napping by the door rose and walked between the rows of cots, checking for fresh corpses to dispose of before the curfew.

'Are you listening?' asked my father as if returning from an exhausting journey to a far place.

'Of course.'

'Good. Perhaps you won't go to England. Perhaps that's just a dream. You may not want to study and you may even waste the money. But there is one thing I insist on. One thing! Be a man. A decent human being. Don't take the morality of the concentration camps with you. The law of the jungle mustn't be yours. Forget all you've learned here – the lying, the cheating, the taking advantage, the contempt for rules and honesty. Promise me you'll never . . . Are you listening? . . . Promise me you won't steal.'

Had he guessed that I was thinking about the bread beneath his mattress? I said:

'You musn't tire yourself out.'

'Promise!'

'I promise.'

My voice was not convincing. He asked me to repeat it.

'I promise,' I said more forcefully, uncertain what was bothering him.

'Is something the matter, Papa?'

'I want you to be an honest man.'

It wasn't the place to tell him that here, in the concentration camp, honesty was suicidal. I wasn't going to argue with a man on his deathbed. I nodded to let him know that I had heard. He grabbed my hand.

'Do you remember the money you stole in Cieszyn? How much was it? Five crowns?'

'You saw me?'

'Yes.'

'It was only two,' I murmured in self-defence. My father raised himself slightly on his elbows and summoned what strength he had left:

'It makes no difference. None!'

The prisoner dying on the next cot looked at us wonderingly. My father fell back on the filthy mattress. I gently freed my hand from his grasp. It was bathed in cold sweat.

'All this talking isn't good for you. Why bring all that up now?'

'Because there won't be any other time.'

'But why did you never mention it until now?'

He fixed his eyes on the ceiling and talked into space:

'It's haunted me all these years. I don't know myself why I kept silent. Today I see things more clearly. You can understand that, you're not a child any more. When you picked up that coin and put it in your pocket I had a terrible feeling of failure. I asked myself what had I done wrong, what had I neglected in your education. But no matter how much I thought about it, there was no answer. Now, though ... Now I can admit I was too weak. There's no one to judge me any more.'

I said nothing.

'Are you still there?' He continued to stare at the ceiling.

'Yes.'

'It will be a different world, the one that comes out of all this chaos. Everything will start all over. Mankind will have learned its lesson from the catastrophe it brought upon itself. It will be wiser and better. Honesty will be a supreme value. It's a shame that I don't believe all the nonsense about life after death. How I'd like to look down on it all from above!'

'Father!'

'Shhh, don't interrupt. All good people ...'

'There are no more good people, Father. They've all been exterminated.'

'Who taught you that? You're still a child. You talk as though life has disappointed you. Why? You're only twelve.'

'Fifteen.'

'Twelve! The war years don't count. They should be erased from your biography. Forgotten ... unless I'm wrong and even they have good memories. Memories of men who refused to give in to evil, like Kruczek or Krol. Think of Witold Krol and his wife. And now go to bed. Come back tomorrow. Think of Krol.'

'I will,' I said for his sake.

'And don't forget you owe me two crowns.' Was he trying to show me that he hadn't lost his sense of humour or simply to end on a gentler note?

I squashed a few lice crawling on the blanket, covered his bare shoulders, and left. The searchlights shone from the watch-towers, their glare vying with the sunset. Guards with leashed watchdogs emerged from the SS barracks. The staccato barks of the dogs, trained to tear you apart, sent a chill through me. I cut in front of them across the parade grounds, taking a short cut to my barracks.

Fredek Minz was waiting for me there. We were the same age. We had been sent to Starachowice in the same car of the same train and had become friends. Not until our transfer to Auschwitz a year later did our ways part. Of our friendship, which had seemed immune to time's ravages, all that remains today are a few bright synapses in the cells of memory. The product of circumstances, it vanished when they did.

Fredek Minz was a slum child, the son of a Jewish house painter who supported his large family from odd jobs and lived a meagre, uncomplaining life. Like his father, Fredek had an undemanding nature and an admirable ability to cope. Flattered by his unquestioning acceptance of my leadership, I secretly envied his talent for wishful thinking. There was no situation too hopeless for him to dream his way out of or to imagine an escape from. I, on the other hand, had learned to be rational about everything. I analysed each situation with the precociously adult logic of a bookkeeper while Fredek was turning bowls of hot water into meat soups, rotten potatoes into gourmet meals, his barracks bunk into a royal four-poster. Although he sometimes tried including me in these daydreams, it never worked. I had lost the gift of fantasy.

Not that he was detached from reality. Once he ran out of veils to cover it with, he accepted it. That April his father had been caught smuggling a small sack of rye flour into the camp. A Latvian guard shot and killed him by the gate. I never talked about this to Fredek, the rest of whose family, a mother and two sisters, were murdered in the Cracow ghetto. I wouldn't have known how to console an orphan my age. Nor did he ask for my sympathy. He simply hugged me, said, 'Well, that's that,' and never mentioned it again.

Until now, when he said to me: 'Now that your father is gone, you can sell the blanket you shared with him and share mine.'

'What are you talking about?' I said. 'He's still alive.'

'He's still breathing. That doesn't make him any more alive than my own father.'

'That isn't so. I just talked to him.'

'Don't kid yourself. It's pointless. The truth is written all over your face. You buried him the day he was taken to the infirmary. Don't pretend, Roman. You know as well as I do that he won't need his blanket any more. Why play games?'

He was right. I just hadn't wanted to admit it. It was easier to lie to myself.

'Well?'

'What's the rush?' Deep down, though, I knew he was right.

We sold the blanket for two loaves of rye bread and half a kilo of beet jam with ersatz sweetener. I didn't tell my father. Only once, when our glances met, did the terrible thought cross my mind that I was glad he wouldn't live to discover my perfidy. I felt no pangs of conscience. The brave new world he dreamed about was still unborn.

Fredek and I now slept under one blanket. As the autumn grew colder, we lay pressed together like two spoons. First I breathed on his neck; then we turned over and he breathed moistly on mine. Our physical closeness, while consisting of no more than a craving for warmth, strengthened our tie even more. But while I was prepared to share my blanket with him, I was not prepared to share my thoughts. Nor, despite his skill at gauging my emotions, was he tactless enough to ask unwelcome questions.

The kapo shut the door. From now until morning no one could leave the barracks. There was still half an hour to lights-out. I lay beneath the blanket with Fredek, thinking of Witold Krol as my consciousness slowly faded. I didn't know if I was asleep or not. My body had slipped its gravitational moorings and was floating – or, rather, falling slowly into an infinitely deep chasm. Or perhaps it was drifting down the dark shaft of memory, on the bottom of which I landed.

I had never told Fredek about the Krols. I had a good reason not to. I remembered them well: Witold, his wife Helena, and their daughter Judwiga. They lived near the apartment we had moved to in Lvov after the Nazis invaded Poland. Witold Krol was a quiet, unassuming man who had worked all his life as a small-time railway official – 'one with full pension rights', as he liked to remind people. His wife, who never enjoyed a free moment, supplemented his income by cleaning houses and taking in washing. Judwiga was six years older than me and did not interest me. 'I'm going to be an actress,' she told anyone willing to listen, while her mother waved a dismissive hand and her father smiled apologetically. Meanwhile, she was taking a secretarial course in the hope of getting a job with the railway through her father.

I had never thought of our relations with the Krols as being more than one of polite hellos. It was only several months after being sent to Starachowice that my father revealed that he had entrusted part of his savings to them. Now the time had come to put their honesty, never doubted by him, to the test.

Apart from its forced labourers, the steelworks employed many townsmen. Most had worked in the plant before the German occupation, which treated them decently because they were skilled workers. All intercourse with them was strictly forbidden. Since the punishment for a casual conversation was a flogging for us and a docked salary for them, all were careful to obey the rule. Nevertheless, my father had managed to contact the Polish maintenance chief, a man allowed by his job to move freely about the complex, which was spread over a large, barbed-wired area through which ran a nameless stream and a railroad line. Familiar with all the nooks and crannies of its various wings, which were connected by thick, snakelike pipes, the man easily found a hideaway where he and my father could talk in concealment from probing eyes. There they agreed that the maintenance chief would mail a letter written by my father to Mr Krol in Lvov, telling him to sell our holdings; would keep half of the remittance for himself; and would buy us bread and milk with the other half. To judge by his ruddy nose he was a heavy drinker, and heavy drinkers were always in need of cash.

Still, I didn't believe that he would keep his share of the bargain. Why should he? There was nothing we could do about it if he kept all the money. Whom would we complain to – God? God did not employ fraud inspectors. The maintenance chief could always say that he hadn't heard from Lvov or that he had never mailed the letter for fear of informers. There were plenty of potential rats in the steelworks. Plenty of taverns in town, too, for him to spend the loot in.

I was wrong. Two weeks went by and the maintenance chief informed us that he had heard from the Krols. 'You see,' said my father happily. 'There are saints even in Sodom.'

From that day on the man left us a loaf of bread and a bottle of milk every day in a pile of junk near a point on the railway line where the cars slowed down to take a curve. This gave my father a pretext to bend down, ostensibly to make sure that the wheels were on the tracks, and retrieve the package.

A sip of the milk and a bite of the bread were all he took. 'I'm not hungry,' he would say, urging me to finish the rest as quickly as possible. If discovered by the Germans, we would have been tortured to reveal our benefactor; if by our fellow prisoners, compelled to share the food with them.

I dutifully obeyed. Only a halfwit would have believed he wasn't hungry. The sticky bread tasted like paradise.

Unlike my father, Fredek Minz's father was a believing Jew. He liked to talk about the afterworld, heaven, and hell, subjects he had strong opinions on. Hell, he said, was not a place but a spiritual absence, a vacuum devoid of human thought. Heaven had neither sorrow nor pain because nothing corporeal existed there.

I found it odd that a simple house painter had such thoughts. Finding them incomprehensible, I said to him brashly:

'What fun would such a heaven be? All our pleasures, such as food or love, or even resting after a hard day's work, are physical. How could a disembodied soul enjoy anything? How could it even know it wasn't sad or in pain if it didn't know what pain or sadness felt like?'

'Your intellect has grown up too fast,' Fredek's father replied. 'The child in you has been killed without your noticing.'

'My father says that it's best to forget the past.'

'Those are just words. Replacing the pages of the Bible with Darwin doesn't change how the world was created.'

'You can't tell me you don't care whether you're alive or dead.'

'I do care. But I cling to my existence because I love life, not because I fear death. There's a big difference, my boy, though I doubt if you can understand it.'

'I wouldn't even try, Mr Minz.'

He didn't deign to answer that. Never having studied a page of the Talmud every day, or learned all of the answers of the rabbis by heart, I was not a worthy conversation partner. Still, the alcoholic maintenance chief's bread and milk taught me I was right about one thing: food tasted better when you were hungry.

Without that extra food I would probably not have survived the ordeals of the foundry. With it my father might have overcome his illness. I hope I was right in my theological arguments with Mr Minz, because I would not want to have to give an accounting of myself if death is not the end of everything.

These pages are the first time I have ever mentioned the bread and milk to anyone. That included Fredek. We were partners in a blanket, no more. I never gave a moment's thought to the maintenance chief either, although the Nazis would have shot him and his family on the spot had they discovered what he was up to. My life revolved around my own needs and problems.

The food package continued to be left in its daily hiding place even after my father's death. It didn't stop until I was sent to Auschwitz following an unsuccessful attempt to escape from Starachowice. I never met the maintenance chief during this whole period. It was an elementary precaution not to.

5

Five years after the war I ran into Witold Krol's daughter Judwiga. I was working at the time as a journalist for a supposedly apolitical paper called *Polish Word*, published in Wrocław. In charge of its various local editions, I was in line for promotion to the post of assistant editor. It was less my talent than my being an ex-concentration camp prisoner and a Jew that had enabled me to advance so quickly. The Communist regime helped people like me to get ahead because it didn't trust the Polish-Catholic intelligentsia. Christianity and Marxism did not go together in its opinion. I would have been foolish not to take advantage of this. I was not costing anyone else his job and my conscience was clean.

At the time that I met Judwiga my new life absorbed me completely and I was determined not to be dragged back into the past by her. Without consciously realizing it, I had repressed every memory that might cast a shadow on my present life. By now I had a second, more recent past that began in the summer of 1945 with a train trip from Austria to Czechoslovakia followed by an escape from a tuberculosis sanatorium in the Tatra Mountains; a marriage that collapsed after a brief period of illusory happiness; and various other adventures undergone by a young man of twenty-two who felt exhilarated to be breathing the heady draught of big-city pollution instead of Zyklon B in a gas chamber or mountain air prescribed for consumptives.

The first summer after the war, the trains did not run on time. In fact, there were no timetables at all.

Twice, in the stationmaster's office in Enns, a typical Austrian town on the Danube, I asked the Russian lieutenant sitting next to me when the train for Vienna would arrive. Twice he shrugged indifferently, reeking of alcohol. He was as helpless as the hundreds of other passengers waiting outside on the platform.

34

The Allied bombers had destroyed most of the tracks, on which only one east- or westbound train could travel at a time. Besides this intractable bottleneck, there was also a shortage of locomotives, drivers, and coal. Dozens of boxcars loaded with war booty, prisoners, soldiers, and passengers stood marooned on Enns' sidetracks. The buffet had run out of drinks and sandwiches, the toilets were filthy, and the entire station stank of urine.

I had arrived there early that morning in a wagon drawn by a team of horses. As I was stepping down from it, the coachman handed me a package wrapped in brown paper. 'It's from Bertha,' he said. Bertha was the German nurse who took care of me for several months after my release from Mauthausen.

I opened the package. It contained some American canned goods in dark green tins. On each tin was written: 'K-Ration for One Soldier – Chopped Beef and Two Cigarettes.' Feeling the envious glances of those sitting next to me, I quickly rewrapped it all, put the package beneath me, and sat on it. I wasn't at all hungry. I was simply weak.

The platform was roofed. The steel beam above me had an electric clock whose hands moved around a white dial, jumping a black numeral every minute. I had patience. I was in no hurry to get anywhere. Tomorrow could wait.

'Where are you from?'

The man asking the question wasn't Austrian. His accent was familiar, Polish. I glanced up at him. He was older than me, a tall, thin man with short-clipped hair that told his history. All of us ex-prisoners had hair like that. Hands in the pockets of his army fatigues, he wore a stained, wrinkled jacket that was too small for him. I instinctively clutched at my package.

'Don't worry,' he said, flexing his shoulders to show me his backpack. 'I have enough food here for a week.'

It was more natural to ask a waiting passenger where he was going, not where he was from. But although asking me my origins was a clear attempt to strike up an acquaintance, I answered anyway. 'Henryk Leiderman,' the man introduced himself, shaking my hand. His callused grip scraped like a file. He turned out to be a compulsive talker who did not shut his mouth from the moment he first opened it. In a rough mixture of simple Polish and folksy Yiddish, he regaled me with selected stories from his life while we sat waiting for our train. He was born in Cracow, an only son with three sisters, all perished in the Holocaust. Trained as a mechanical electrician, he had preferred working before the war as a pedlar, selling Jewish religious artefacts in the Stradom quarter of Cracow and rosaries to the Catholic peasants in the nearby villages. Eventually he found a job in a butcher's shop and became its owner upon marrying the butcher's daughter. Having discovered that the meat he sold weighed more when injected with water, he was well on his way to becoming a wealthy and respected member of the community when the accursed war came along.

After the liquidation of the Cracow ghetto Henryk Leiderman went from concentration camp to concentration camp, ending up at the time of the liberation in Steyr, not far from the station we had met in. For a while he made a living from shady deals on the black market, buying cigarettes and instant coffee from American soldiers and reselling them to Austrians. Part of this merchandise was paid for with Austrian women, a form of barter terminated by the threats of 'local hoodlums' to murder him. Rescued by an Austrian widow, he lived with her on a barge on the Danube until she informed him that he was about to become a father, at which point he set out for greener pastures. Now he was returning to Poland to look for the butcher's daughter ('if she's alive') and the butcher's shop ('if it isn't a whorehouse by now').

I listened without being able to distinguish what was true from pure fabrication. Leiderman's chatter helped pass the time. When our train pulled in at last and the crowd of passengers rushed to board it, he cleared a path for us both while helping me up the steps of the car. Every seat was taken. We had to stand in the corridor. As the train began to move, I said:

'Listen, I don't have a ticket.'

'Don't make me laugh,' said Henryk Leiderman. 'Just stick with me.'

He didn't have to tell me that twice. I stuck as close as I could and let him take me under his wing. I was still in need of someone to tell me what to do and when to do it and Leiderman was a gift from the blue. Seeing I was tired, he gave me his backpack to sit on; realizing I was thirsty, he let me have a sip of grape juice from a bottle kept in his jacket pocket. I liked its sweet taste. He laughed and said: 'You're on the way to becoming a wino.'

A few kilometres before the Melk Forest we halted at a small station at which our locomotive quite literally ran out of steam. The driver and his assistant went to look for coal. Hours went by without their returning. Perhaps no coal was to be found and perhaps they were drunk in some tavern. Towards evening we decided to step outside and stretch our limbs. Taking our bags, we headed down the main street of the town towards a park in which some Russian soldiers were bivouacked. As we approached, we saw long tables made of boards laid across sawhorses. On them was spread what looked like wallpaper. On closer inspection, it turned out to be Hungarian money.

I still remembered some of the Russian I had learned in school and starting a conversation was no problem. Although most of the Soviet soldiers I had encountered since the war travelled with regimental flags and plaster statues of Lenin and Stalin that resembled the church icons and portraits of the Tsar paraded by their ancestors, the soldiers in the park were a different breed. On their way through Budapest they had hijacked dozens of rolls of freshly printed money from the government press – some sheets of which, having subsequently been soaked in a rainstorm, were now spread out to dry in the sun. Leiderman fingered them and murmured to me appreciatively:

'Baby, it looks real.'

'It's probably wartime currency that has no value,' I said.

'Don't be so sure. Let's try to buy a roll or two. They're crazy about American canned goods. You said that nurse gave you some.'

'Don't even think of it.'

'Why not? We could return to Poland as millionaires.'

'If it were legal tender they would have spent it on booze long ago.'

'You're being too logical,' he objected. 'What made you so cynical so young? Where's your faith in fortune?'

'What are you two talking about?' asked a Russian with sergeant's stripes.

'About how you're wasting your time with all this,' said Leiderman.

The Russian was offended. 'These are real hundred-pengö notes,' he said.

'Don't make me laugh. They're worth shit. All they're good for is wallpapering my apartment.'

'The idiots in this town don't believe us either. But it's good money. We used it all through Hungary. Want to buy some?'

Leiderman shrugged. 'What for? I don't have an apartment.'

'Consider it an investment in the future,' grinned the Russian.

'Who says there's a future?' countered Leiderman.

'A roll for a bottle of vodka. How about it, comrade?'

'We're all out of vodka. All we have is some American army rations.'

'No, we don't,' I said.

'You keep out of this,' said Leiderman, poking me in the ribs.

'Do they say, Made in USA?' asked the soldier.

'You bet. You can forge money but not a can of food.'

'Let's see.'

Before I could protest Leiderman had snatched the package from under my arm and opened it on the table. The sergeant examined its contents. He seemed satisfied.

'Two cans for a roll of money,' Leiderman said.

'Four.'

'Three and not a can more.'

'It's a deal.'

I couldn't hide my chagrin as my cans disappeared into the sergeant's knapsack. Leiderman rolled up five metres' worth of pengös and said in Yiddish:

'Let's get out of here before he changes his mind.'

The next morning the train resumed its journey. Twenty hours later we were at its last stop of Bratislava, the capital of Slovakia. From there we would have to find northbound transportation to Poland. We stepped into the station's buffet.

'You wait here,' said my guardian.

'Where are you going?' I asked worriedly. I was afraid of being abandoned. Leiderman didn't answer. Carrying his roll of money, he disappeared in the crowd. A quarter of an hour later he returned, flashed a hundred-pengö bill, and announced:

'I cut them with a razor in the bathroom. Come on, let's get something to eat.'

He pushed me ahead of him to the counter and ordered two cheese sandwiches and two beers. The counter-woman took the money, held it up to the light, folded it in four, and gave us change in Czech crowns. Leiderman scooped the coins off the counter, slipped them into his pocket, and said triumphantly:

'What did I tell you? We're rich!'

I ate my sandwich in silence. The cheese had no taste. The bread was like glue.

'Don't worry. Pretty soon we'll be having champagne and caviar.'

'I've never tasted either.'

'It's time you lived the good life.'

'Right now we don't even have a place to sleep.'

'Don't make me laugh. You think this burg has no hotels?'

We hailed a taxi. 'Take us to the ritziest hotel in town,' Leiderman told the driver.

The desk clerk at the Palace Hotel regarded our worn clothes suspiciously. 'I'm sorry,' he said with a lordly air. 'We're full up.'

Leiderman laid a hundred-pengö bill in front of him. The condescension yielded to an apology:

'Oh my, excuse me. I didn't notice. We still have one room left.'

'We generally take a suite,' declared Leiderman as if we had just hit the jackpot at Monte Carlo.

'A suite? Of course. We have just the one for you. It was once reserved for the Kaiser. I'll have your bags sent right up.'

'We have no bags,' said Leiderman, pulling out another hundred-pengö bill.

'Of course. Some people like to travel light. It's on the fourth floor, Room 401. The elevator is out of order. They've promised to fix it but you know how it is. Nothing works nowadays. I'm at your service if you need me. My name is Waclav.'

Leiderman thought for a moment. Then he said:

'You look like you know your way around, Waclav.'

'I do my best, sir.'

'Good. Send us up a bottle of champagne. And two girls. With big boobs, if possible.'

'Count me out,' I said in alarm.

Leiderman looked at me disdainfully. 'Don't make me laugh, son. Weren't we just talking about the good life?'

'I'll live it another time. I don't . . . I mean, I can't . . . Please, don't make me,' I pleaded.

'Have it your way. One bottle and one girl, then, Waclav. But one who knows which end is up.'

The whore knew which end was up. Her giggles annoyed me. Leiderman's grunts were embarrassing. I couldn't shut my eyes until she had left.

It was late when I awoke. The royal suite turned out to be two rather shabby rooms, although it was fancy enough when compared to other places I had slept in over the past years. We had breakfast in bed. Later in the day we went to have a look at the city and ate a big meal in a restaurant. I bought five shirts, a suit, and a pair of shoes. Leiderman was stingy with my pocket money. 'You don't smoke, you don't drink, and you don't screw,' he explained. 'What do you need money for?' Not wanting to argue, I refrained from pointing out that the money was bought with my cans. I had lost the quick wits that had so often saved me in the camps – and besides, what was I complaining about? Life was looking up.

I put on weight. My face grew round and my ribs stopped protruding. Yet I remained short of breath and every walk about the city wore me out. I had coughing fits, too, and constant blood in my saliva. Although I realized I had TB, I refused to see a doctor. I feared being hospitalized against my will while Henryk Leiderman ran off with our money. I didn't want to be left alone, either. In the end things took their own course.

I was unconscious when brought in an ambulance to Dr Simko's sanatorium in Stary Smokovec. Nothing short of passing out in the streets of Bratislava could have induced me to enter that white prison in the Tatra Mountains of Slovakia. By the time I came to in a soft bed in a sun-drenched room – surroundings I was only too familiar with from Thomas Mann's *The Magic Mountain* – it was too late to do anything about it.

Until the Communist coup in 1948, Czechoslovakia still permitted free enterprise. Private hospitals were a boom field and Dr Simko was a well-known expert in pulmonary diseases. No sooner had I regained consciousness than it was explained to me that Mrs Rubin, the American director of the Bratislava bureau of the Joint Distribution Committee, had sent me to him for 'the very best care'.

The war had skipped over this renowned doctor's Shangri-La. The castle of his little kingdom, a jewel of Alpine architecture from the 1920s, blended perfectly with the enchanting landscape. Its verandas faced south towards a hillside thickly forested with fir trees that ran like a thick bolt of green fabric down a slope to stop abruptly by the banks of a stream. All day long the air was scented with fir needles; only at night did the alien odour of disinfectant invade the rooms. Yet although I felt like a wilted flower that had blossomed again after a long winter in defiance of all natural laws, putting back flesh on my bones and colour in my face, this could not fool the X-rays. I was gravely ill. Lying on the veranda on doctor's orders beneath a light woollen blanket while filling my lungs with the dry air that was supposed to cure me, I tried to calculate when I had caught the disease. It was impossible to pinpoint the time or place in which Koch's bacilli had seized control of my lungs, devoured their membranes, and left behind 'cavities the size of plums', in the words of the head radiologist.

Up to my last day as a Nazi prisoner I was convinced that I was merely suffering from malnutrition, nor did I want to know the truth afterwards. Now, despairing of finding out where the disease had come from, I passed the time counting the whistles of the train that passed every ninety minutes carrying nature lovers to Strbske Pleso Lake. In the deathly, vacuous silence, the blasts of the labouring locomotive were a sign of life.

The Joint had sent me to Dr Simko after I was found bleeding in the street by some pedestrians, who called for an ambulance. Only my extreme state of debilitation prevented me from putting up a fight. And yet had I been at all logical, I would have gone for help long before. For weeks I had ignored the blood in my saliva, the fever that racked my body every morning, the choking feeling in my throat. It didn't need a doctor to make a diagnosis. I had simply refused to face up to it.

Once I opened my eyes in Dr Simko's sanatorium, however, reality could no longer be denied. It was enough to watch the whispered consultations of the doctors after listening to my chest through a stethoscope and see the averted glances of the nurses each time I tried to read their eyes. The discovery of streptomycin was still five years off. Meanwhile, Dr Simko's patients pinned their hopes on calcium shots, the healthy climate, and the intervention of a merciful God.

As far as God was concerned, I had a bone to pick with Him that precluded any faith in His salvation. I struggled against the calcium injections, too, hating the waves of heat that washed over me as soon as I felt the needle's jab. My only companions were the fresh air and my own idleness. *The Magic Mountain* indeed! But I bore no resemblance to Hans Castorp and was not compelled like him to be awoken by a cruel war from reveries of time, life, and death. The order was reversed in my case, as were the conclusions. My stay in the sanatorium struck me as one long, passive preparation for a clean and discreet end. For aesthetic reasons, the dead were removed by Dr Simko's staff overnight. In the morning we pretended not to notice the missing places at the breakfast tables.

My greatest fear was of dying without having tasted real life. And yet I had not the slightest idea of what real life was. I did not miss my parental home, whose routines did not strike me as worth returning to. I dreamed of great, never-ending adventures that I couldn't define. I longed for dangers, challenges, a life filled with content – but I could not have said what I wanted these to be. Eventually, convinced that time was working against me, I made Dr Simko a proposal he couldn't refuse.

The director of the sanatorium did not like talking to his patients. Mostly he stayed secluded in a small, second-floor room guarded by a secretary in a white nurse's smock who had endless excuses for turning away unwanted visitors. Pretending to have been invited for a chat unrelated to my health, I took advantage of her momentary confusion to walk into the doctor's room before she could block my way. Dr Simko looked up from the document he was reading to regard me with unconcealed wonder.

'Don't worry, Doctor,' I reassured him. 'I haven't come to complain. Or to beg. I have a business proposition.'

Imperfect as my Slovak was, he appeared to grasp its meaning. At any rate, he arched an eyebrow and raised a hand as if to ward off a conversation that had not commenced on his initiative. Determined not to arrive at an understanding, however, I plunged ahead.

'The Joint,' I said, 'pays you two hundred and fifty dollars a month at the rate of . . . no, wait, Doctor, let me finish. I'm sick and tired of this sanatorium. The problem is that you're not tired of the money you get for me and would like to continue getting it.'

'You can't leave. You're sick.'

'So what? Are you going to bring in the police to make me stay?'

'I'm not used to such talk, young man.'

'What would you say,' I went on, ignoring his remark, 'if I were to leave the sanatorium without informing the Joint's office in Bratislava. The money for me would keep arriving and we could split it like good Christians, half-and-half.'

'I've never in my life heard such an impudent suggestion.'

'A little bird tells me that you take your time reporting the deaths of patients and illegally pocket the money that keeps coming for them. Don't think you can do that with me. I'm not about to croak while you go on counting those nice, crisp dollar bills. On the contrary.'

'You can't be serious.'

'I've never been more serious, Doctor.'

'You're making a grave and baseless accusation.'

'I'm making a proposal.'

'You Jews are an obstinate, dangerous race.'

'That's a quote from the writings of Jozef Tiso.'

'Tiso was the president of Nazi Slovakia. I've never been involved with politics. I'm a physician.'

'I'm waiting.'

'I will accept your proposal, young man, but only under protest. You still have an active case of tuberculosis. You won't last a month once you're discharged. Two months at the most. And not even two weeks without some means of support.'

With the regularity of a Swiss watch, Dr Simko was forced to share with me poor Mrs Rubin's monthly stipend until my last day in Czechoslovakia. I soon realized, however, that half of the Joint's money was insufficient to pay for all my whims.

As so often in my life, blind chance came to the rescue. One day there was a knock on the door of the apartment that I rented in one of the loveliest villas in the area. My caller, a Mr

Herskovic, introduced himself as a small businessman from Kezmarok, a nearby town with a large Hungarian Jewish population. He had barely opened his mouth when I realized that he was the answer to my financial problems.

'I've heard you have TB,' he began without beating around the bush or even being invited to take the seat he settled into. I nodded.

'You're in a position to do a rare good deed,' he said.

'Good deeds don't interest me.'

'Then you're my kind of person,' smiled Mr Herskovic. 'I'll tell you what it's all about. My son has just turned eighteen and wants to go to Palestine. All that's keeping him here is his army duty. His one chance for an exemption is to have an infectious disease. I see you're beginning to catch on ...'

'You wouldn't be here if you took me for an idiot.'

'Precisely. The tailor in Smokovec told me you were a clever fellow. I'm sure we'll have no difficulty finding a common language. That's the same tailor, by the way, who was never paid for the two suits you ordered from him. I've taken care of the bill. I never realized he was so expensive.'

'Expensive but first rate. I once heard a saying that I decided to be guided by. *Life is too dear to be lived cheaply*. What's your opinion of that, Mr Herskovic?'

'That's not a businessman's philosophy.'

'I'm not a businessman. I just happen to have something you're interested in buying. All that remains is to set a price.'

'Based on what?' asked my visitor with a touch of irony.

'Supply and demand,' I replied.

'There's no lack of people with TB.'

'Who are of draft age? And have pulmonary cavities the size of plums? And are willing to run the risk?'

'And you say you're not a businessman!'

6

Equipped with a forged ID card, I was sent by the Herskovices to Prague. In Kezmarok, where everyone knew everyone, the deceit would have been discovered in no time. As Czech law required draftees to report for duty in the place of their last three-month residence, I filled out a change of address form in a government office and spent the next three months happily waiting for my call-up in a hotel – or, more precisely, an inexpensive boarding house – paid for by Mr Herskovic. My lodgings were near the centre of town, a five-minute walk from Waclaw Square, where most of the cafés and cinemas were.

My room and board were covered in advance. My gentleman's agreement with Herskovic also left me a reasonable amount of pocket money and I lived quite well at the expense of the young immigrant to Palestine, whom I never had the pleasure of meeting. On the day of my call-up I told the draft board, with more enthusiasm than competence in Slovak, that my greatest desire was to serve the Czech motherland and to die for it. While the board's chairman hastened to reassure me that World War III was not imminent, the doctors poked and prodded me, took my temperature, and peered into my lungs. The X-rays astonished them. What was someone like me doing out of the hospital? Then and there they wrote me the exemption that the Herskovices were eagerly waiting for.

For the first time in my life I was independent, with neither parents nor prisons to run my life. My new freedom was intoxicating. Having jumped into the water without knowing how to swim and been kept afloat, I made straight for the highest diving board. I stopped worrying about my health and lived extravagantly, spending large amounts on clothes, as befitted

45

someone starting a new life, and patronizing fancy pubs, restaurants, and resorts. Large sums also went to my unsuccessful wooing of the wife of a Czech diplomat fifteen years older than me.

Forty-two years later I was asked in an interview on Israel Radio whether the hedonism that (so said the interviewer) characterized me was an attempt to compensate for my suffering in the Holocaust. 'I think not,' I replied. 'I've just returned from a very pleasant vacation in Hawaii. In my hotel I met many people. Most owned faster cars and more stylish clothes than me and some had even been married more often. All were seeking to live life to the fullest without ever having been through the Holocaust. To what do you attribute *their* hedonism?'

But although not even Freud could psychoanalyse himself, I can safely say that I was not telling the whole truth. Back in 1946 I definitely felt that I was in a cruel race with death in which I had to run my fastest to drain life's nectar. And now that I was no longer being generously supported by Mr Herskovic, I had what bankers call a 'liquidity problem'. I was in urgent need of a new source of income.

Thus it was that I remembered my grandfather, who had emigrated to the United States a quarter of a century before I first saw the light of day. As a child I had heard no end of stories about him. Feeling cooped up in Austrian Galicia, Solomon Rosenwiesen had abandoned his wife and two children, my mother and her brother Max, a year before the First World War. He was already heading west when my grandmother discovered that the oil rigs near Borislav for which he had left her to seek a livelihood sat on wells that had long ago run dry.

Grandfather Solomon's first stop was Switzerland, where he learned the art of watchmaking. From there he proceeded to America and made a killing from the sale of cheap watches to blacks and unfortunates. Once a year he sent me ten dollars for my birthday. How, I now innocently asked myself, could he possibly refuse to help his only surviving grandchild, a Holocaust victim? For the first time in my life I thanked my old English teacher Mr Rosensztyn, without whose persistence I never would have managed to compose the touching English letter I now wrote.

I had devoted three whole pages to prying open the heart and pockets of a man I didn't know before realizing that I didn't have his address. Although many people found missing relatives through the Red Cross, the money owed by me to tailors, bartenders, restaurant owners, and my Prague landlady left no time for an extended search. The clamours of my creditors were mounting and I might have ended badly had I not recalled my old habit of rummaging through my father's drawers. Apart from old postage stamps and love letters, I had also found in them envelopes from a bank whose name was chiselled in the grey cells of my memory: the First National Bank of Wisconsin.

I mailed my letter care of the bank. In a separate enclosure addressed to the conscience of the bank manager, I pointed out that every year, in the month of January, Mr Rosenwiesen had sent me a cheque for my birthday. Based on the logical assumption that he was a First National Bank of Wisconsin customer, I would therefore, I wrote, 'appreciate it greatly, Mr Manager, if you would forward my desperate plea to him'.

By return mail I received a cheque for one hundred dollars. Not from my grandfather. My letter had so moved the manager that he had decided to bail me out at his own expense, even though 'We no longer have the honor of servicing Mr Rosenwiesen, who has moved to one of our southern states.' He would do his best, he promised, to locate him and, failing that, some other relative.

A month later the postman surprised me again with another letter from America. This one came from Mr Ben Levenauer, a bank client and owner of Stewart's Department Store in Milwaukee, who wrote emotionally of the ancient blood ties between us. (His father and my grandfather, I believe, were second cousins.) Needless to say, this would have interested me as much as last year's snow had not Mr Levenauer promised to support me for as long as my precarious health prevented me from standing on my own two feet. From that day on cheques arrived from him at regular intervals. Added to my monthly allowance from Dr Simko, they provided a quite satisfactory income.

In the end Grandpa Solomon was traced to Biloxi, Mississippi, from where he assailed me with long letters lamenting my parents' frivolity, which they paid for with their lives, in not heeding his advice to leave Europe. However, apart from detailed instructions regarding my behaviour, my wardrobe in summer and in winter, and the diet I should follow for an optimal metabolism, I received not a thing from him. I later found out that he had just married a young American lady of twenty-five, who no doubt left little time for a pesky grandson spared from death by an unfortunate quirk of fate.

My life in Prague was prematurely curtailed by the Czech authorities. In April 1947, during a routine check at a roadside restaurant that I was dining in, the police discovered that I was in Czechoslovakia without a permit. Having destroyed the papers identifying me as young Herskovic immediately after my discharge by the draft board, my only ID was an American army certificate saying that I had been liberated from Mauthausen, which failed to impress the Czech authorities. After an abortive attempt at bribery and my failure to persuade an immigration official who sneered at Dr Simko's affidavit that my state of health forbade me to relocate, my request to remain on Czech soil was turned down. Two policemen accompanied me on a train to Cieszyn, pointed to the bridge over the Olse, and ordered me to cross it. Carrying two suitcases with all my worldly possessions, I walked under their gaze to the banks of the river, where a customs shack flew the red and white flag of the People's Republic of Poland.

Ten years had elapsed since I had last crossed that bridge into Poland. Then I was a boy with two stolen Czech crowns in my pocket. Now I had a bulging wallet in my tailored sports jacket and Koch's bacilli in my ravaged lungs.

My father had a brother and four sisters, each of whom raised a large family. But the Holocaust had taken its toll and left alive only my Uncle Marian, his wife Niusia, and their son Edouard.

It was only natural that I should head for my uncle's after being deported from Czechoslovakia. I didn't know another living soul in Poland. But the reception given me, to put it mildly, was not a warm one. A chill wind blew from Aunt Niusia in particular. In vain I tried finding out what made her so unfriendly. I had no idea that an old grudge against my father was now being directed at me.

Marian and his family were an illustration of the caprices of fate. When the KGB combed Soviet-occupied Lvov for illegal refugees from the Nazis, my father and Edouard hid in an attic while Marian, for reasons that were never clear to me, decided to turn himself in. He and his family were arrested and sent to a semi-penal colony in the Urals, from which they were released after the war and allowed to return to their native Cracow. There they regained possession of the pharmacy they had owned before the war.

Uncle Marian was an excellent pharmacist and his business flourished until its nationalization by the Communists, when he emigrated to Israel with his wife and daughter. I had known vaguely of his plans to leave Poland, of which he informed me in a general way. At the time I was in another sanatorium, this time in Lower Schlesia, from which I travelled to Cracow once a month on brief visits whose main purpose was to dispose of my father's estate – an apartment building that had belonged to my grandparents. 'Cracow is a place I would like to live in,' I said to my uncle, offering to buy their one-bedroom flat if they left it. 'I'll pay the going price,' I added, not wanting them to think I was expecting a discount.

'We'll let you know when the time comes,' promised my aunt.

But they didn't. On one of my periodic visits to Cracow I found their home lived in by strangers. They had departed without a trace. I never received so much as a postcard from Israel and lost all contact with them.

Although the Polish bank shares that were supposed to guarantee me a respectable income were not worth the paper they were printed on, the new regime having refused to honour its predecessor's financial commitments, I was far from economic distress: Ben Levenauer continued to mail me his generous cheques. The one thing I lacked, if only unconsciously, was a home. I was looking for a family.

It was only after my aunt and uncle had passed away at a ripe old age that my mother's brother Max revealed Niusia's secret. As a young woman, he told me, she had been spurned by my father, who married my mother instead. Niusia married my father's brother – and refused to forgive my father until her dying day. 'Hell knows no fury like a woman scorned,' Max quoted. Although I had no way of verifying this, my appearance at Niusia's door was in all likelihood a reminder of unrequited love. Perhaps I had retriggered her youthful trauma. And she had other reasons for wanting me out of her house, too. She was quite frank about her fears of being infected by my tuberculosis.

The sanatorium in Lower Schlesia – a region annexed after the war by Poland, which expelled most of its German inhabitants – was found for me by my Uncle Marian soon after my arrival in Cracow. It was housed in an attractive convalescent home that was expropriated property given by the government to the Jewish community, whose institutions the authorities had not yet co-opted. Despite its beautiful surroundings, and my uncle's repeated warnings not to repeat my error of rejecting medical assistance, I had no intention of staying longer than necessary. The place reminded me too much of Stary Smokovec. Perhaps that was why I wrote to Mrs Rubin on my first day there and told her to stop the payments to Dr Simko.

The next day I met Gita.

Gita was six months older than me. Good-looking and friendly, she had an openness that I liked. She worked as an auxiliary nurse and lived nearby in a small apartment that consisted of two rooms and a kitchen. A narrow path from the back gate of the sanatorium's garden wound uphill past raspberry bushes and heather straight to her front door. It took a week of smiles and furtive body contact for me to follow it. Even then the idea wasn't mine.

Gita was one of those women accustomed to giving free rein to her desires. I could tell from the start that she liked me, something that she made no attempt to conceal. Looking at my old photographs, I try to understand what she saw in the tall, slender, half-boy-and half-man that I was. My hair in these pictures is dark with a curly cowlick and the large, brown, curious eyes are graced by long lashes that were not the least of my charms. The lips are thin, not sensual, expressing determination and perhaps obstinacy; the smile, forced and disdainful. In a studio portrait in which I have one jaunty hand on my hip and the other on a balcony, I am wearing cavalry pants and high riding boots – outward symbols, it would seem, of a masculinity I was still unsure of. All this had its effect. Losing patience with my lack of initiative, Gita said one day:

'Why don't you come around for a drink tonight? And bring your pyjamas.'

Although I didn't tell her it was my first time with a woman, her female intuition guessed as much. 'Relax, all of life is ahead of us,' she whispered as I wildly embraced her to hide my bashfulness.

We had a drink. The smell of beer mingled with the scent of lavender perfume. I felt dizzy. I wasn't used to so much alcohol.

Gita set the pace. She took me to her bedroom, undressed me, laid me down on the bed, and rode me in slow motion. My body revelled in the loss of its virginity. The scent of lavender yielded to that of sweat. As my passion burst and exploded, a surge of fulfillment came over me.

I kissed her. 'Stay for the night,' she said. It was an order, not a request.

In the morning, I inspected her naked body by the first light of dawn with the wonder of a child discovering a new world. All I wanted was to wake up like this every day for the rest of my life. I forgot that there are dreams that remain in our consciousness for only a few seconds after waking – after which, despite all our attempts to hold onto them, they vanish like birds freed from a cage.

Gita – short for Margarita – was born in the east of Poland, the daughter of a non-commissioned officer and a local country girl. Her father disappeared at the beginning of the war when the Red Army invaded Poland and took most of its soldiers prisoner. Although she had no proof of it, Gita was sure he had been murdered by the Bolsheviks in the Katyn Forest massacre. Her mother was banished to Siberia as an enemy of the Revolution. She and her younger sister Theresa, now a student in a boarding school near the sanatorium who came to visit us once a month, were left all alone. One evening, as we were cosily chatting, the two had a madcap idea:

'Why don't you write to Comrade Stalin and ask him to free our mother?' asked Theresa.

'Yes. Why not?' Gita chimed in.

It seemed to me like pure lunacy. 'Do you really think Stalin has nothing better to do than help little girls find their mothers?'

'You know Russian. What do you care? Write a letter for us,' Theresa urged.

There was no point in arguing. I wrote a long, heart-rending letter. As my written Russian left much to be desired, it was full of mistakes. Gita and Theresa signed it without understanding a word.

'It's a waste of a postage stamp,' I said. The letter was sent by registered mail. The postal clerk gave me an astonished look when I laid it on the counter and said casually, 'Airmail, please.' He must have thought I was off my rocker. No one in his right mind in Poland wrote a letter addressed to Generalissimo Iosif Vissarionovich Stalin, The Kremlin, Moscow.

That summer I took my leave of the convalescent home and moved into my lover's apartment. Being the head of a family was a new situation for me and one I liked. An acquaintance of ours who had just been appointed manager of a porcelain plant offered me a job as his assistant. The plant was in Mieroszow, some ten kilometres away, which was a reason to buy a bicycle. For eight hours a day I was an important man who sat behind a huge desk and signed documents of whose import he had no idea. 'Good morning, Manager,' the guard at the gate greeted me each morning. The workers tipped their hats when I passed through the yard and the mayor of Mieroszow asked me to be his guest on Independence Day. I preened myself like a young peacock.

Early that autumn the unbelievable happened. The days had grown short and it was already dark when I returned from work. I liked the time of day when light yielded to darkness and the lamps, switched on despite the early hour, doled careful dollops of domestic warmth from beneath their shades. Gita had dropped in on a neighbour and I was in a brave new world with Aldous Huxley when the doorbell rang. Grudgingly I laid the book down and went to the door. It was the postman.

'Special delivery for your wife,' he said, handing me a long, brown envelope in the upper left corner of which were a hammer and sickle with the return address: 'Office of Generalissimo Stalin, The Kremlin, Moscow'. 'Sign here,' said the postman. My hand shook as he handed me a sheet of paper. He waited motionlessly while I went to get a pencil and remained standing in the doorway after I had signed, as though seeking to share the glorious moment with me. Only when I gave him a generous tip did he salute me by touching two fingers to his cap and depart.

I locked the door, slit the envelope with the pencil, and opened it. Comrade Stalin's secretary, whose signature was illegible, had the pleasure of informing the daughters of Maria Fisola that instructions had been given to locate her and repatriate her to her homeland as part of a humanitarian programme of family reunification.

Later that evening we went to bring the good news to Theresa. The letter had to be translated for her three times before she grasped it. Then she blurted:

'Mama will kill herself when she finds out you're living in sin.'

'She hasn't even been located yet,' I said. 'We'll cross that bridge when we come to it.'

But Theresa was worried. 'Will you tell her Roman is a Jew?' she asked her sister.

'What an idea!' Gita snapped. 'You'd better keep your big mouth shut.'

'All the neighbours know it. You can't shut their mouths.'

'There's nothing to do, sister dear. I'll just have to live with it.'

'But what about Mama? How is she going to live with it?'

'I have no idea.'

'Why don't you get married? I'm sure the priest in Mieroszow won't ask any questions.'

'I thought I was a Jew,' I said.

Theresa smiled. 'The priest needn't know.'

'If we have to, we'll do it,' I decided.

Gita's jaw dropped. Years later, when we ran into each other after the wounds of our divorce had healed, she confessed to never imagining that I might propose marriage. The minute I did, she said, she knew it stood no chance. She grasped better than I did the differences between us. She knew the boundaries of her world, which extended no further than the walls of her home. Unintrigued by life's mysteries, she did not number intellectual curiosity among her traits. I, on the other hand, was constitutionally unable to lie sunning myself like a cat. I longed to set sail for uncharted waters, to taste the fruit of the Tree of Knowledge.

Two brief years after the war, however, I was too inexperienced to make use of what I knew. I had no appreciation of the commitment demanded by marriage, which seemed no more than a demonstration of my manhood. As soon as a telegram arrived with news of the impending arrival of Gita's mother I went straight to the priest, who sympathized with my plea to waive the traditional banns. The problem wasn't so much the town's Catholics as its Jews, who would hasten to tell him I didn't qualify for a Catholic sacrament.

'I'm a Party member,' I lied to him. 'We're not allowed to participate in religious ceremonies. You have to understand, Father, that I can lose my job if the authorities find out.'

'I understand and so does the merciful Jesus,' the priest replied. 'For special cases like yours we make allowances.'

He married us in a modest ceremony, in a little alcove that served as a dressing room. As he handed us our marriage certificate, Gita snatched it and put in her handbag. I asked:

'How much do I owe you, Father?'

The priest rubbed his palms on his black robe as if to clean them of avarice and said quietly, his face turned toward the crucified figure on the wall:

'Generally I take twenty thousand zlotys from Jews. But for you I'll make it ten.'

To celebrate the great change in our life, I bought a six-room villa from the government bureau in charge of abandoned property. It was a decorated mountain chalet with three rooms on the bottom floor and three more on top, each with a fretted oak balcony. The ground floor was set aside for Gita's mother and we took the top one for ourselves. While renovating, I found an old sign on the roof that said: 'Monika's Inn'. I took it and flung it on a pile of refuse, oblivious to its secret message that my first great love would be a woman named Monika.

In the end, Gita's mother stayed out of our affairs. Her years of solitude in the steppes of Siberia had made her a silent and unobtrusive woman. Accepting me unreservedly as the household head, she took my side against her daughter each time we quarrelled. 'The man is always right,' she scolded Gita. 'He's right even when he's wrong. That's married life.'

Did she realize that our marriage was on the rocks? I think she must have, long before it was obvious. She had a peasant's nose for ferreting things out and keeping them to herself. I kept silent about my own thoughts, too, but for a different reason. Gita and I had simply run out of conversation topics. Her interests seemed trivial to me; mine were foreign to her. All that bound us was our arguments. Gita thought of our relationship as a flat coin to be gripped tightly; I thought of it as a round one to let roll freely. Eventually, even the delights of passion failed. Once sex became routine, it was time to part. Any illusion of happiness I might still have had was abruptly ended by Theresa.

Having graduated from boarding school at the age of eighteen with no plans for the future, Theresa came to live with us on Gita's invitation while deciding what to do next. For the first time I noticed that she was no longer a high-school girl but a sexually provocative young woman. It didn't surprise me when she took advantage of Gita's going shopping with her mother to come to our bedroom one day and offer herself as if it were the most natural thing in the world.

'Who taught you this?' I asked as she went to work on me with the hands of an experienced milkmaid.

'The nuns,' she giggled, pulling me towards her. I was entering an unlocked gate. To my knowledge of sex was now added the realization that its pleasures were not limited to one woman. What I had gotten from Gita was available elsewhere.

That evening I announced that I was leaving. Gita's mother kept her usual silence. Theresa helped me to pack. Pressing down on the bulging lid of my suitcase, she whispered:

'Where will you be? I'll come to you anywhere.'

'I don't know yet,' I answered. I wasn't eager to jump from the frying pan into the fire. The world was full of exciting women. Why commit myself?

The suitcase clicked shut just as Gita burst into the room, threatening me with a horrible revenge. She wept, cursed, flung sobbing accusations, choked back a last cry, and fell silent, shattered and uncomprehending.

She had left out the most important thing of all. I didn't know that she was pregnant. Nor did I notice the disappearance from my belongings of a photograph taken in the streets of Cracow shortly before my arrest by the Nazis. I never dreamed that it would lead to being charged with crimes against the state by the Polish secret police.

A year after leaving Gita, a journalist in Wrocław, I met Monika, the first woman to guide me through the delightful and torment-ing labyrinth of true love. But I am getting ahead of myself. For the time being, I was living from day to day. Fitting easily into the company of the journalists, artists, and writers my age who met in the Artists Café, a glass-paned establishment behind the Opera, I came there regularly to stalk its lively night life – generally dancers from the local ballet troupe who came for a drink after the show. Usually, they ended up making breakfast for us the next morning. One affair followed another in a long series of casual liaisons that made me feel as though I were riding a magic carpet whose flight would never end. We all wanted to make up for the lost years of the war and not miss any of the pleasures around us. Who knew if there would be a tomorrow?

I never found out what brought Judwiga Krol to the Artists Café. It certainly was not to pick up a man. I recognized her at once despite the great change in her. She seemed wrung dry. Her appearance was weary, unkempt. Her eyes had lost their lustre and she no longer had the gay laughter I remembered from the stairwell of our building in Lvov, where she had flirted with her boyfriends in 1939.

I invited her to join me. There was no need to worry that the person she had become would evoke a past I preferred to forget. She sat on the edge of her chair, ill at ease and unconvinced that I really wanted to talk with her.

'How are things?' I asked. It was just a polite question. Her nod told me things could have been better. A quick reckoning established that she couldn't have been more than twenty-eight. God, how she's aged, I thought. I said, 'What are you doing these days? You wanted to be an actress.'

'The act is over,' she answered cryptically.

'And now?'

'You look good. You must be doing well.'

'You too,' I lied.

'Bull.'

'Would you like something to drink? They have real French cognac here.'

'I'll take a glass of tea.'

I ordered her tea and honey cake. Judwiga surveyed the other customers. 'It's nice here,' she sighed.

'Are you in some kind of trouble? Is there any way I can help?'

'Why on earth would you want to help me?'

'Because I'll never forget what your family did for us.'

'When?'

'When we were in the camps.'

'What are you talking about?'

'Your parents never told you?'

'No.'

I explained about the letter, the money, the bread, and the milk.

She interrupted me. 'That's all a fairytale. We never received any such letter and we never sent you a thing. You're imagining it.'

'Believe me, I've only had a glass or two to drink. I'm perfectly sober and I'm telling you it's true,' I said, adding a few more dates and details to convince her. But Judwiga continued to insist I was mistaken. Shortly after we left Lvov, she told me, the Germans had arrested and executed her father for collaborating with the underground. Left without means, she and her mother went to live with cousins in the country.

'We sold your things to stay alive,' she confessed awkwardly, adding in a defensive tone: 'I hope you won't try to get any of it back. I'm broke.'

I said nothing.

'Does that shock you?' My silence had been misunderstood.

'Shock me? Not at all. A person's first duty is to himself.'

'That's not what the maintenance chief in Starachowice thought,' she said.

'No, it isn't,' I agreed. 'He risked his life for people he didn't know. I'll never understand him. Can you? Can you explain to me why he helped us?'

Judwiga glanced hastily at her wristwatch. 'Not now,' she said. 'It's late. I have to go. Maybe some other time . . .?'

'Let me have your telephone number.'

'I don't have a phone.'

'Then write down mine.'

She wrote it on a napkin, folded it, and stuck it in her handbag. It was clear to us both that she never would call. She left without shaking hands. If not for her untouched glass of tea on the table, I might have thought I had hallucinated her.

That weekend I borrowed a car from the photographer of my newspaper and drove to Starachowice. I hadn't been there since my days in the camp. I was surprised to see that the place had changed. The steelworks were on the verge of closing and a huge truck factory was under construction in the upper city, where the Germans had manufactured ammunition.

A low-income project stood on the site of the mass grave in

which my father was buried. The houses were sad, grey concrete blocks. I walked among them as though among tombstones in a giant cemetery. No one looked at me and I looked at no one. There was no chance of running into the maintenance chief. I wouldn't have recognized him anyway. All I remembered was his ruddy, bulbous nose. Simple man that he was, I would never have the chance to thank him. I couldn't ask where he lived because I didn't know his name. What was I doing here?

In the evening I returned a wiser man to Wrocław. My father thought Witold Krol was a saint. I thought the maintenance chief was a greedy drunk. Both of us were wrong. People were not what they seemed. All you ever saw was a reflection of your own image of them. And even if you could get at the truth behind that image, there was absolutely nothing you could do with it.

7

The investigator had a lock of reddish hair, round, freckled cheeks, and light blue eyes. Brimming with zest, he was not how one pictured a cog in the machinery of evil. He laid a small photograph on his desk and asked with an almost friendly smile:

'Do you know this man?'

I nodded. 'It's me.'

'In the uniform of the Hitler Youth?'

'Yes. The Hitlerjugend.'

'Can you explain that?'

'Where did you get this photograph?'

'I'm the one asking the questions. You'll answer them, comrade.'

I nodded again. Although it had begun innocently enough, the rules of the game were perfectly clear to me. I had not been arrested at dawn by secret agents, the way it was done in the spy books. An elderly man with the face of a retired school janitor had appeared in my office at 8 a.m. He carefully wiped his shoes on the entrance mat, nudged it back in place, and asked if he was disturbing me. Only when assured that he wasn't did he ask me for my name without taking the seat I offered him. My identity confirmed, he pulled a brown, unaddressed envelope from a tattered briefcase, handed me an ordinary notebook, and told me to sign for the letter.

'Who is it from?' I asked.

'I'm only a messenger,' he replied, waiting patiently for me to sign. He shut one eye when I returned the notebook, studied my signature with the other, nodded with satisfaction, hesitated by the door as if wanting to say something, bade me a polite goodbye, and went his way.

I tore open the envelope. On the stationery of the Public

Security Service was a laconic summons. Citizen Roman Frister was requested to report at ten o'clock to the district office and show this notice to the guard. No one was to be told about its contents, which were confidential. I could not make out the signature at the bottom.

The summons took me by surprise. In its upper left-hand corner was an empty line beside the word 'Re'. Nothing told me why the Public Security Service was looking into my affairs. I was not a spy. I did not belong to the anti-Communist underground, if indeed there was such a thing. I had never sought to subvert the regime. I had written nothing against the official line. But the Public Security Service did not believe that a man was innocent until proved guilty. More than once I had laughed at the joke that went: 'Bring me the man and I'll find the crime that fits him.' Now it no longer seemed so funny.

The hands of the clock pointed to 8.20. The offices of the PSS were a five-minute drive away. I had plenty of time to think. My first reaction was to regard the whole thing with an almost nonchalant disdain. With every minute that ticked by, though, my self-confidence faltered and my morale began to sink. True, I had done nothing wrong. I was not a child of the Revolution to be devoured by it. But the Revolution had a healthy appetite. It ate its stepchildren, too. I could easily have fallen victim to a plot I was ignorant of. The Party's power was based on an endless struggle against the enemies of the working class; when real enemies were not available, imaginary ones would do. Thousands of citizens had received brief letters like mine, had reported for questioning, and had disappeared – for a month, for a year, or for ever.

The Communist regime had sought to establish itself in a soil that rejected its abolition of private property and its atheism. The Polish peasant was tied umbilically to his plot of land. Although the newspapers spoke of the enthusiasm with which the agricultural collectivization campaign was received, journalists returning from the countryside bore blood-curdling tales of the brutal methods used to impose it. I knew from my own experience that no magic wand, or even gun barrel, could eradicate a thousand years of Christianity. And though it could be excised from the textbooks, the hatred of a Russia that had thrice brought Poland to its knees could not be eliminated from the mentality of a people. Every Polish child knew that now, too, for all the Polish eagle's flaunting of the feathers of independence, the Russians pulled the strings from Moscow.

On the Olympus of Polish politics, the gods changed frequently in those days. Sometimes this happened in silence and sometimes to the blare of propaganda. No one was above arrest, imprisonment, and trial. The element of uncertainty was both an accelerator and a brake, causing people to fight tooth and nail for their positions while leaving them vulnerable and exposed. Tens of thousands of informers who had infiltrated every nook and cranny obediently reported to their superiors, kneading a dough of their own imagining when there was nothing to bake the bread of slander from. The Poles accepted it passively. Post-war Europe had been divided into zones of influence and all hopes for a change perished with the Western capitals' ratification of the Yalta Pact.

Perhaps this was why it never occurred to anyone to disobey ominous summonses like the one I had just received. As in the days of the Nazi occupation, people deluded themselves that it couldn't happen to them – that they would easily explain their innocence, be given a pat on the shoulder and an apology for the unfortunate misunderstanding, and get sent home. Quickly calculating all my possible and impossible misdeeds, I, too, concluded that it was all a mistake, a human error, perhaps a question of mistaken identity. Such things had been known to happen.

The moment I crossed the threshold of the Public Security Service's waiting room, however, all illusions vanished. The building, an old, Crusader-like castle made of red bricks, plunged me into gloom. Everywhere else a journalist was an important person. Not here. The doorman, or more precisely, the guard, cast an indifferent glance at my summons and said:

'Sit on that bench. Your name will be called.'

I sat. The benches ran along walls that had not seen a coat of fresh paint for years. The floor was filthy. A brightly coloured poster showed a worker with a hammer calling for stepping up the struggle for a socialist homeland. The windows were barred. Ten other people sat on both sides of me. All were silent, withdrawn, careful to avoid each other's eyes. Perhaps they were afraid to reveal their thoughts, which could cost them long years in prison. From here on, it was every man for himself. Who I was or what I had done meant nothing in this place. The Moloch wanted to be fed and had picked me at random.

I was made to sit for a long time. In the argot of the interrogators, I later learned, this was called 'the softening-up wait'. The more time passed, the more helpless I felt. I rose to stretch. The guard barked:

'Sit down and keep still, comrade. This isn't a boardwalk.'

It doesn't take much to humiliate a person. I remembered how I felt when the Nazis shaved my head and pubic hair; although objectively speaking this had no significance, it took away my self-respect at once. Now, too, with the sentry's rebuke, I felt the same degradation. Now, too, it was illogical. I could easily have put his remark down to pure rudeness. What other satisfactions did a little man like him have?

From time to time the room was crossed by men in leather coats. Their assertive gait made it clear who they were. I wondered where secret service agents' fondness for leather came from. Felix Dzerzhinsky's Chekists had worn it after the Bolshevik Revolution, as had the top brass of Hitler's Gestapo.

It was almost a relief to hear my name called. I was led to the room of the interrogator.

'You don't have to tell me. I already know,' I said. Before my eyes flashed a picture of Gita on the day I left her. 'You'll be sorry,' she had said, blocking my path. I pushed her roughly aside and walked off.

My freckled interrogator was surprised. Curious, too. 'You do?'

I smiled. 'This photograph comes from my ex-wife.'

'Its source doesn't matter. I asked you to explain it.'

He opened a drawer, took out a Belvedere cigarette, the most expensive brand there was, lit it, threw the match on the floor, and ground it out with his shoe. Then he gave me a hard look. It was no doubt a look he had learned to give in some interrogators' course. The whole thing, I now realized, was a simple misunderstanding. Gita had found the photograph in my album. I now understood what she had meant when she screamed as I descended the stairs: 'You'll rot in jail! No one will want anything to do with you. I'm the only one who will visit you. I'll bring all you need and you'll be mine. That's when you'll understand what true love is!'

The logic of a jilted woman.

'Well?' asked the interrogator. He was getting impatient.

I picked up the photograph. A Cracow photographer had memorialized me in the black uniform of the Hitler Youth, a swastika on my lapel. I was grinning broadly.

I put the photograph back on the desk. 'I'm afraid you may not understand,' I said.

'I'd better.'

'It's a long story.'

'We have all the time in the world.'

'Fine, if that's what you want. You'll have to use your imagination, because I'm taking you all the way back to the summer of 1942. I was working then as a messenger boy for Count Potocki . . .'

'What does that have to do with it?'

'To tell you the truth, the story begins in September '39, on the day the Nazis took Cracow . . . You're not really going to write down all I say, are you?'

'Of course. We'll need a protocol. Maybe one day, when you get out of prison, you'll read it like a novel. Everyone we question has some tall tale.'

I never did go to prison. The episode ended after a few days of questioning. My story struck the interrogator as too fantastic for disbelief, just as Marxism was for a good Marxist. 'Nobody could ever invent such a thing,' he laughed when he was done with me, calling his assistant to tell him I was free. The assistant walked me to the door. I never met my interrogator again.

The protocol was preserved in the archives. It goes:

Record of the Accused's Statement

Place: Wrocław. Name of Accused: Roman Frister. Date: 3.5.1952. The following is the statement of the accused:

Jan Bialecki lived in my grandfather's house at 20 Szlak Street in Cracow, corner of Dluga Street. The building is there to this day. Back then there were horse-drawn carriages standing in front of it, a form of transportation that still competed with taxicabs. My grandfather was a man who hated the internal combustion engine and all other technological innovations. He claimed that they disturbed the delicate balance of nature. He liked to sit at his window, elbows on the windowsill, and stare for hours at the top-hatted coachmen and their horses lazily munching hay from the canvas feed bags slung around their necks. When the municipality decided to move these *fiacres* to a sidestreet (that was the French word they were known by, just like in Vienna), my grandfather wrote the mayor a letter of protest. It was filed away without being read.

My grandfather could not stop the flow of progress. Taxicabs replaced carriages. Jan Bialecki couldn't have cared less. He couldn't see the horses anyway. His apartment was entered from the courtyard and his windows faced a blank wall; the sour odour of garbage pails assailed him when he opened them ... But of course you know, Comrade Investigator, what people lived like under the old regime. Bialecki was hard-up and often late with his rent. Each time that he was, my grandfather announced that this was the last time: Bialecki would be evicted and thrown into the street with his family despite all his pleas for mercy. But in fact, there were no pleas for mercy at all. Bialecki was a poor but proud man and my grandfather never carried out his threats. Each time Bialecki told him that he had no money for the rent, he granted him an extension with an impatient wave of his hand. My grandmother Adele (who, to put it mildly, was tight with her money) had a soft spot for her ground-floor tenant. Before Christian holidays she would even press a few coins into his children's fists and tell them to go buy some candy.

Have patience, a little patience, Comrade Investigator. The picture will soon be clear. My fate became intertwined with Bialecki's on the day the Nazis entered the city, although neither of us were initially aware of it ... But wait, I've forgotten the most important thing: Jan Bialecki drove an engine for the fire department. On the Wednesday morning on which the first troops of the Wehrmacht appeared on the west side of Cracow, Bialecki's brigade was sent to put out a fire on the east side. When the fire was out, he did not return his truck to the fire department. He drove it home, parked it where the *fiacres* used to stand, removed its licence plate, and repainted its bright red with a thick coat of venomous green. The next day he hung a sign on it which said: Bialecki Movers. Thus, thanks to the war, the general confusion that enabled him to obtain new licence plates, and his own wits, Jan Bialecki became the owner of a moving company.

How Bialecki met Count Potocki remains a mystery. One way or another, the two men became acquainted. Potocki owned many fish ponds in the faraway Lublin district; Bialecki had a truck that could transport live carp (a few holes in the roof, which were then covered with mesh, were enough to ensure the fish had oxygen); and a fat carp not only made excellent gefilte fish, but it was considered a delicacy by the Nazi top brass. Although Potocki was a Polish nobleman, he had a Jewish head for business. He once even used those words with me in a moment of high spirits after concluding a successful business deal.

That first autumn of the war, the count hired Mr Bialecki to bring fish to the commanders of our conquerors. Business was good. The following year, when my grandparents were sent to the ghetto, the Bialeckis moved into their big apartment. Deciding to buy new furniture that suited his changed status, Bialecki shipped my grandparents' old furniture to the ghetto, too, for which my grandfather heartily thanked him. The Germans were highly satisfied with the partnership of Potocki & Bialecki that supplied them with all the fresh fish they could eat. Twice a week the green truck made the six-hundred-kilometre run to the Lublin district and back. The road ran through thick forests in which the Polish resistance movement had its bases. As I was later told by Bialecki himself, in his picturesque style:

'In early November, or maybe it was late October, I was driving my regular route from Lublin to Cracow. The fish were quiet, the motor buzzed like a horsefly, and I was humming an old song to keep awake. I drove slowly because the autumn rains had begun and the road was slippery. My headlights could barely pierce the thick darkness.

'Luckily, I have good vision. Otherwise I never would have seen the tree trunk laid across the road. I slammed on the brakes. That locked the rear wheels and made me skid, but I managed to stay on the road. Three masked men wearing capes leaped out of the night. Two had sub-machine guns. They climbed into the driver's cabin and told me to follow the third man, who walked ahead and directed me onto a muddy path leading into the forest.

'We drove deeper into the trees. That's what you get for being so greedy, Bialecki, I thought. But no. The partisans weren't out to kill me. They only wanted the fish. I told them who I worked for and they said: "Please pay our respects to the Count." Then they asked me to empty the truck. I let the water run out, opened a back flap, and sent those fish slithering into all kinds of baskets and crates. God knows where the partisans got them from.

'One of them, apparently their commander, saluted and handed me a note. "What's this?" I asked. "Read it," he said. I switched on the cabin light. On some paper torn out of an arithmetic notebook he had written that the carp were confiscated by the Free Polish Army, which would reimburse the owner in full at the war's end. At the bottom of the page was the emblem of the Polish republic, a crowned eagle with spread wings.

'I stuck the note in my jacket pocket. "Forget where you've been and have a good trip," said the commander, ordering one of his men to guide me back to the main road. I was soaking from the rain and my own cold sweat.

'I reached Warsaw at dawn. The Germans questioned me for hours. They spread a map in front of me and asked me to show them where the fish had been hijacked. What did the bandits look like? What kind of weapons did they have? Although I answered as best as I could, it didn't satisfy them. There's no knowing how it would have ended if not for the intervention of a high-ranking officer who was friends with Potocki. I felt like a condemned man when the hangman's rope snaps at the last second. The Count himself took it calmly. "It's nothing to be upset about; the shipment was insured," he reassured me. Maybe he was also reassuring himself.'

That nocturnal incident, Comrade Investigator, changed Jan Bialecki's life. Getting hold of an arithmetic notebook and a rubber stamp like the partisans' was no problem. Every few weeks he sold his fish on the black market in Lublin and returned to Cracow with a confiscation receipt. It worked so well that by the the time I arrived in Cracow with my parents, Bialecki was a rich man. He invested his profits in a canning factory and the chain of Potocki & Bialecki Fish Stores, Inc.

We found a place to live, Comrade Investigator, a mouldy basement belonging to an old woman with the same wrinkles in her clothing and her face. For a modest rent she let us have her bed and moved to a faded sofa in the far corner of our shared room. We didn't tell her we were Jews. Perhaps she suspected it. It wasn't every day that an educated family asked to rent such a room. In any case, she asked no questions. She sat for hours on a little stool without moving like a snail in its shell, or else lay napping on the sofa. She went out so rarely that I wasn't sure if she even knew there was a war on, although she did take our papers to the local police station when we first moved in. The police suspected nothing. The forger had done a first-rate job.

My father preferred to stay indoors. The walls of the houses had bounties posted on them for every Jew caught outside of the ghetto. The city was full of informers out for the money. After a while my father's old housekeeper Miss Sziwek put him in touch with Mr Bialecki. Bialecki, who still felt grateful to my grandfather, offered me a job. 'He can work as a special delivery boy,' he said to the Count, introducing me to his partner. 'I assume you know what you're doing,' said Potocki. Although I was dying to know if Bialecki had told him I was Jewish, I didn't dare ask.

My deliveries really were special. Most likely Bialecki knew exactly what he was doing when he hired a Jewish boy who would have to keep his mouth shut. Every day I rode my bicycle to the best neighbourhoods of Cracow and delivered fresh fish to high-ranking Nazis. Courtesy of Potocki & Bialecki. The bored wives of the SS and Gestapo officers were glad to talk to a Polish boy who knew German. Sometimes they asked me what I was doing delivering fish. I had a convincing story about being a refugee from Schlesia, from which my Polish family was expelled, and in most cases I was treated well. Sometimes I was granted a word of casual sympathy and almost always I received a large tip. One woman even made me a gift of a Hitler Youth uniform. 'It's too small on my son,' she said, advising me to find a tailor to make a regular suit of it. I brought it home and tried it on. It fitted perfectly.

That gave me an idea, Comrade Investigator. Delivering fish for Potocki & Bialecki and rubbing elbows with all those high-ranking Nazis had made me over-confident. I didn't listen to my father's warnings. Walking the streets after work was far better than being shut up in a mouldy basement with an old woman. Are you beginning to get it . . .? Not yet? . . .

All right, I'll spell it out for you. In the summer of 1942 Hitler's armies were besieging Moscow and Leningrad and had driven as far south as the Crimea. A German victory was imminent; at least that was how it seemed to readers of the *Krakauer Zeitung*, a daily paper published with the blessings of the occupation authorities. Cracow was far from the front. The Allied bombers left it alone, whether because it was out of their range or because the British air marshals wished to spare its historic buildings. The royal chambers of the old castle of the kings of Poland built on a cliff overlooking the Wisla River now housed the headquarters of Dr Hans Frank, the governor of occupied Poland; their vaulted halls were home to the offices of the Nazi government. Sometimes I brought Potocki's gift packages there. The ticking of the typewriters, the click of Prussian heels, the spotless dress uniforms, the pennants of the Reich stuck in maps of Russia in the hallways, and most of all, those smug Nazi faces: everything created the impression of a well-oiled and invincible juggernaut. It was what we were going to have to live with.

Life in the city went on as usual. People worked, bought and sold on the black market, loved, hated, were born, died. But they were all divided into the two tiers of occupier and occupied. By the entrances to the best restaurants and movie theatres signs went up saying: Germans Only. The studios of the Polish film industry, that huge factory of rosy dreams, fed the public love stories and comedies designed to wash away the war with a wave of sentimentality. And I didn't want to think of the war either; I wanted to laugh, too. One day I took my black Hitler Youth uniform from the closet without telling my parents, put it on in the stairwell, and went downtown. What a marvellous feeling! A Storm Trooper on a corner gave me a Hitler salute. Automatically I Heil-Hitlered him back.

The Polish auxiliary police directing the sparse traffic had always frightened me. Now they seemed harmless, pathetic creatures.

What I most wanted was to buy an ice cream in the 'Germans Only' Italian ice cream parlour on Florianska Street. Does that seem strange to you – that at a time when we Jews were hiding in every hole we could crawl into, a Jewish boy's greatest dream was a double scoop of chocolate and strawberry ice cream? When I tell you all this now, Comrade Investigator, it occurs to me that perhaps I was out of my mind. But on second thoughts, I'm convinced of the opposite. It was a sign of mental health. In spite of everything I had maintained a spark of childhood innocence that not even the greatest horrors of the occupation could destroy. The ice cream melted in my mouth. I licked my lips to keep from losing a single drop of its cold sweetness.

You may wonder how I could have enjoyed myself when my father, marooned in a basement, was waiting helplessly for me to come home. How I could have walked all the way across the bridge to Podgorze and looked curiously back at the walls of the ghetto in which my grandparents were imprisoned. I can't answer that. I'm not a psychologist. Human motives are not my field. I only know that I couldn't wait for each work day to end so that I could walk again through the city streets, protected from all harm, practically a member of the Master Race. If gendarmes closed off a street to check ID cards and arrest suspects for deportation to forced labour camps, I walked right up to them without a qualm. As time went by, I grew more confident – or perhaps I should say more impudent. After a month I began going to the 'Germans Only' cinemas. The cashiers were mostly *Volksdeutsche*, Polish women of German descent whose status, although higher than that of ordinary mortals, was not that of a citizen of the Third Reich. They came to know me and appeared to like me, because they always gave me a good seat in a centre row. I came to know German movie stars like Erich von Stroheim and Sara Liander and even collected programmes with their photographs.

All of which brings us to the unfortunate photograph on your desk, Comrade Investigator. A street photographer snapped me in my uniform on the corner of Florianska and Market

Square. You don't see the ice cream because I've just finished the last of it. Why am I smiling? Most people smile at a camera. You see the uniform and the swastika, Comrade Investigator, and you think: Hitlerjugend. But it wasn't. It was simply the black armour that protected me from danger ...

8

I had told Investigator Rieger the truth, but not the whole truth. The German woman who gave me the Hitler Youth uniform had not told me her son had outgrown it. She was too young to have a son my age. She had said her brother had outgrown it – her older brother, who had been drafted. Or, rather, who had volunteered for a secret unit that could not be talked about, an elite corps serving the Führer on the eastern front, perhaps even deep inside Russia. All she knew was his military address.

Her brother, the woman had told me enthusiastically, was a hard-working, disciplined boy for whom no task was too hard. With a bit of luck he would come home with his officer's stripes. Doing what you were told to, her husband liked to say, was the best way to get ahead. Experience was the best teacher, too, and her husband was a high-ranking officer – not at the front, but with a paunch and a cushy job in the quartermasters corps of the SS. There wasn't much glory in being responsible for meat and fish supplies, she laughed, pointing to the still-breathing carp that I held wrapped in a newspaper.

'Why are you standing in the doorway?' she asked. 'Come in.' She ushered me into her foyer.

I was startled. Although I had been in German houses before, I had never gotten beyond the hallway or, at most, the kitchen.

'Sit down, sit down,' she urged, pointing to a deep armchair upholstered in leather. I sank into it as though it were a bathtub full of fluff.

The sight of my rough shoes on the polished parquet floor made me shove my feet beneath the chair. The woman noticed my embarrassment, plucked a sprig from a wilted bouquet of flowers in a vase, and sat facing me on a high stool.

'My name is Grete,' she introduced herself. 'What's yours?'

'Roman.'

'Very romantic,' she smiled. 'Have you ever drunk Drambuie?'

'No.'

'It's divine. French, of course. Those frog-eaters know a thing or two about liqueur. How clever of the Führer to conquer Paris.'

I sipped my drink. The sweet, sticky liqueur burned my throat and coated my lips. Grete (a name that I would never have dared call her by at our first meeting) surveyed me curiously. I stole an inquisitive glance back at her. She was a good-looking young woman, a tall Nordic type with blonde hair pulled back in a black velvet band who could easily have passed the most stringent Aryan race tests. For a moment, as she shifted position, her bright thighs flashed at me. Her bathrobe was tied carelessly with a pink wool sash. The deep cleft of her breasts bespoke a generous body.

'Another drink?'

'Uh, no. I have to work.'

'What a pity that that's what a boy like you must do.'

'I'm not a boy.'

'No, you aren't.' Grete moved her stool closer to me and put a hand on my knee. 'You aren't a boy at all.'

My head was spinning from my drink. How old was she? Twenty-five, at least. A grown-up. Why was she playing cat and mouse with me? Was she out to seduce me? That made no sense. Even if bored to death by her husband in bed, what could she see in me – a teenager too old to bring out the mother in her and too young to come on as a man? I knew my place. I was a delivery boy for a fish company.

But Grete? Did she know her place? Perhaps she only wanted someone to talk to. Why else would she have invited me in, drunk more than she should have, told me about her happy childhood on the shores of a Bavarian lake, bared her heart to me each time I came with a delivery of fresh fish? Life in occupied Poland, she complained, was strange and foreign. She was lonely. The pitcher of Time failed to fill her empty days. Her husband was unable to get her pregnant.

During one of my visits she complained bitterly about this husband, who was too involved in his work to pay her any attention. On another she didn't stop praising her brother. His elite unit, she finally revealed to me, was assigned to the liquidation of the Reich's mortal enemies, the Jews. After downing half a bottle of Drambuie, she confided her greatest worry. It was her brother's homosexual tendencies, which endangered his career.

'If you can keep a secret,' she said, 'I'll show you something.' Without waiting for an answer she opened a drawer full of gold rings, pins, brooches, and pendants.

'You see? It's all from him.'

'It must be worth a fortune,' I said.

'A big one. Not even my husband knows about it. It's for a rainy day.'

Gretchen – after a few visits I summoned up the nerve to call her by a pet name that won her heart – even trusted me enough to read me letters from her brother describing the shooting of peasants accused of helping partisans. The partisans, wrote her brother, were unattackable because: 'The bandits hide deep in forests we don't control, where it's dangerous to pursue them.' In the same letter he described at length an enticing Belorussian boy who was his personal valet and bed partner.

Eventually, Grete's brother's relations with the Belorussian were discovered and the affair was ended with the brother shooting a bullet in the boy's head. 'Now I'm alone again,' he wrote grievously to his sister. Gretchen pitied his misfortune. I, too, sympathized more with the murderer than with his victim.

These conversations bolstered my self-confidence. Obviously, Gretchen had no idea of who I was. Only once did she send a tremor of uncertainty coursing through me by giving me a hard look when I wiped my liqueur-sticky fingers on my pants, as if to say: *Just a minute – no German boy would do a thing like that*. This happened during a conversation about eternity, or, more precisely, about immortality. Little did I know that soon I would be discussing the same subject in the camp in Starachowice – and in a less theoretical context.

Grete was not a believer. The fleeting present meant more to her than a thousand years of paradise. I agreed with that. But whereas I was sure that the final heartbeat spelled the end of everything, she thought that the soul went on existing after death.

'In that case,' I joked, 'I hope you won't be reincarnated as an ugly old man.'

'The body I'm given doesn't interest me,' she said. 'I'm sure I'll end up in paradise despite my sins.'

She poured us each another drink, lifted hers high, and toasted: 'To paradise!'

'I wonder if paradise has a paradise,' I mused out loud.

She set her glass down and said with sudden seriousness:

'That sounds too much like Jew-talk.'

'Jew-talk? Why?' I was instantly on guard.

'Because the Jews make everything sound so complicated.'

I never told anyone about her, not even my parents. I also kept to myself the details of the death camps worked in by her brother. I doubt that I grasped their full significance. The strange relationship between us made me forget that I was talking to and drinking Drambuie with the wife of a Nazi officer. I never thought of Grete as belonging to the people that wanted to kill me. When she sent me home for the day with her regards to His Excellency Count Potocki, or with her brother's old uniform, I kissed her hand in the best tradition of the Cracow people.

My Hitler Youth uniform fired the imagination of Mishka Szindler.

My first instinct is to write that Mishka and I met in St Mary's Cathedral in Cracow. I could have made an intriguing scene of it: two hunted Jewish youths becoming acquainted to the strains of an organ at the feet of the crucified Jesus.

But this is not another police interrogation and I intend to stick to the truth – which is that, while Mishka Szindler and I did go to mass together each Sunday, I met him because he and his parents were living in the apartment of my Uncle Marian, who was off somewhere in the Ural Mountains of Russia.

On these Sundays my mother made sure I dressed nicely and checked to see if my shoes were shined, my fingernails cleaned, and my hair properly combed. At seven in the morning Mishka and I met by the entrance to the church. St Mary's stood in the centre of the old city of Cracow, its two towers a familiar landmark ever since its construction in the thirteenth century. Full of old statues lit by a bluish light that filtered through the stained-glass windows, it conveyed a sense of majesty. Doing our best to blend in with the parishioners, we sat, kneeled, and prayed demonstratively in a back pew with our black, leather-bound missals, surrounded by pious women and adolescents in their Sunday best like ourselves. This went on for a few weeks until a boy from the neighbourhood stopped me at the end of a mass and asked pointedly:

'Hey, are you a baptized Jew or what?'

If only I had been wearing my Nazi uniform! Lacking its armour, I felt a sudden dryness in my throat.

'Are you out of your skull or something?' I answered in the same style. I sounded so sure of myself that only Mishka noticed the slight tremor in my voice. He rushed to my defence, glaring at the little Catholic and giving him a shove.

'Hey, what's with you, you little shit? You look like a kike yourself. I'd like to know who fucked your mother.'

The Polish boy turned his cap sideways to indicate that he wasn't looking for a fight. 'Hey, it's no big deal,' he said. 'I didn't mean anything. It's just that all the other guys play cards in church while you only sit and pray. You want to be priests?'

'Not exactly,' grinned Mishka. 'We were afraid you'd fink on us to the Father, so we pretended to be extra-religious . . . you get me? Or do I have to make myself clearer?' He waved a fist in front of the boy's nose.

'No need for that. I'm no dummy.' Retreating to a posture of friendship, the boy stuck out his hand. 'I'm no fink, neither. My name's Bolek. So starting next week we deal you in?'

'Right. Deal us in.'

'Bring money. We play for high stakes,' Bolek boasted. Happy to have made peace with us, he swivelled his hat back in place, yanked down its brim, and went his way.

We learned our lesson. We learned to play poker, too.

Mishka was a year younger than me, intelligent, quick, and rotten to the core. It took me a few weeks to gauge the astounding depths of his cynicism, so very different from my own nonchalance. Meanwhile, we became friends.

Mishka liked to join me on my strolls around the city. He called them our 'Hitlerjugend walks'. Once he asked me to lend him my uniform. Since he was short, we had to roll up the pants and sleeves. This was risky because the Germans took great pride in their appearance and any sloppiness might arouse suspicion.

Mishka, however, returned beaming. He startled me by pulling a wad of money from his bulging pocket and handing it to me to count.

'What did you do, rob a bank?'

'You jerk,' he laughed. 'You work like a donkey and don't have a penny. Your biggest dream in life is a scoop of Italian ice cream. I made this whole wad in one shot.'

'How?'

'You know the Podgorze bazaar, the one near the ghetto? It's full of dumb clucks just asking to be taken. I went there in your uniform and shouted something in German. I can't even remember what it was. It was just a lot of words – my German's not as good as yours. But it was enough to scare them into letting me walk off with a few cartons of cigarettes. I sold them to some operators in the Zwiezeniec market. The whole thing took twenty minutes.'

I admired his guts. It wasn't the only time. We now had enough money to play poker in church and to spend on whatever else we wanted. I hid the bills in the fuse box in the stairway. I never asked my father if he needed them. There was no way to explain where my sudden wealth came from.

Mishka was a distant relative. I had never heard of him until the war. The Szindlers had lived in a small town near Cracow and were apparently too unimportant for my parents to acknowledge them. Mishka's father was named Jakob – Koba for short. An amiable man who was quick to make friends, he was willing to work at anything, including petty fraud. I liked the way he dressed in the latest 'Occupation style' with gleaming boots, woollen riding pants, and a checked, broad-lapelled jacket. His blond hair and blue eyes were a passport to safety. No one would have suspected him of being Jewish. With the help of his two hobbies, drinking and women, he cultivated contacts with the Polish auxiliary police that soon turned to active collaboration. Mishka told me about it a few months after we met.

In my Uncle Marian's apartment, at 10 Holy Cross Street in the centre of old Cracow, Koba Szindler hid Jewish escapees from the ghetto. Word spread until more and more people were knocking on his doors. But he chose his customers carefully. Meriting his mercy meant first passing a means test. 'I'm running a business, not a charity,' he told those he rejected. His apartment was particularly in demand each time the Germans purged the ghetto of its 'non-productive elements' by shipping the elderly and unskilled to camps from which no one returned to tell of the horrors that were whispered about.

The day I visited it, Koba Szindler's apartment was in a turmoil. Mishka's mother was busy cooking for dozens of mouths. Nervous women ran back and forth, small children played in the hallways, infants bawled. The men said nothing. The whole place stank. Although the sewage pipes were blocked and the toilet was overflowing, the windows were kept closed for fear of the neighbours.

Koba Szindler charged a large sum for each day's accommodation. The tenants paid without raising an eyebrow. For staying alive, any price was a bargain. They remained there for as long as it took to obtain the false papers that enabled them to go their separate ways. Koba knew a clerk in the population registry bureau who was bribed to produce these documents. If I am not mistaken, my own family's papers came from the same source.

But the apartment on Holy Cross Street was less a shelter than a blackmail trap. Once its tenants ran out of cash, they paid their rent with valuables. Koba was an expert at telling a pure blue-white brilliant from a diamond smudged with coal stains, could estimate what carat gold he was being shown at a glance, and was familiar with the most exotic gems. Nothing, Mishka told me, enraged his father more than a tenant who tried cheating him with a counterfeit coin or a fake piece of jewellery. A swindler himself, he brooked no competition.

Koba's tenants never caught on to his deception. Each time they complained about the long wait for their documents, he had some new story of bureaucratic obstacles to tell them. 'Do you think I like your company enough to want to keep you here?' he would ask with a wink. Blessed with a good sense of humour, he polished off many a meal with a racy story and made himself liked in the worst situations. Mishka worshipped him. I, too, found him entertaining. Not until Mishka told me the truth did I realize that he was a loathsome murderer.

Generally, Koba's tenants stayed with him until, never suspecting that this spelled their doom, they informed him that they had run out of means of payment. As soon as he had no more use for them, he turned to his friends in the Polish police.

In the middle of the night, when curfewed Cracow was a ghost town, a police van would drive up to 10 Holy Cross Street. Its uniformed occupants climbed to the second floor and hammered with their fists and pistol butts on the door. While the neighbours pretended to hear and see nothing, the police burst inside, pulled the blankets off the frightened sleepers, and dragged them from their beds. 'You're under arrest, you filthy kikes!' they shouted, kicking the women and children to make them get dressed and hurrying them downstairs to the waiting van.

Koba would hide in a closet, where the commander of the force had no trouble finding him. 'You too! You too!' he would shout, shoving Koba outside with the others. Only Mishka and his mother Zelma were allowed to remain behind. Once everyone was gone they tidied up the house, aired the mattresses, and cleaned the smelly bathroom.

Meanwhile, the police van sped off into the night, quickly outdistancing the suburbs and last houses of Cracow and lurching along a bumpy road that led to an abandoned flour mill. Sooner or later, emerging from his shock, a passenger would ask: 'Where are we going?' 'To the last place you'll ever see,' he would be told.

This was Koba's cue to stage his crowning performance. Making his way forward to the commanding officer, he would beg for his life and the lives of his fellow Jews in a tearful voice. For a while the two men whispered while everyone fell silent. Even the children stopped their screaming. Then Koba announced timidly:

'He's willing to let us go, but it will cost. I have a thousand dollars. That's not enough, though.'

With a trembling hand he extended a wad of green bills to the officer, who counted the money by the light of the roof bulb, stuck it in his pocket, and waited for more. From the heels of shoes and other hiding places the passengers produced the last cash and valuables that they had managed to shield from Koba's avarice for their future existence. Diamond pins and gold coins dropped into the officer's cap.

When the collection was concluded, the driver was told to stop. The doors were opened and the bewildered passengers were pushed outside, having no idea of where they were. 'Run that way,' Koba would tell them, pointing out an escape route. Panic-stricken, they ran across a field towards the silhouette of the old mill. Koba would try to run also but would be forcibly restrained by two policemen. 'Not you, pal,' they yelled. 'You'll stand trial for this.' The driver turned the van around and started back. By the time the lights of Cracow were visible again, the loot had been divided up.

'Isn't your father afraid that someone will be caught and squeal?' I asked Mishka.

'Where are your brains?' he asked, insulted to the depths. 'My father's no idiot. There's another police squad waiting in the mill. No one gets out of there alive. Each body is checked to make sure it's dead. Who the hell is going to squeal?'

Mishka told me all this as though it had nothing to do with us. The Jews involved were not our friends or relatives. They were strangers. *A la guerre, comme à la guerre*. 'What's it to you?' he asked. In fact I must have failed to grasp its full monstrousness, since otherwise how could I have gone on being his friend? We continued to take our 'Hitlerjugend walks' and to play cards with the boys in the neighbourhood. At least once a week I had a talk with Grete. Consciously or not, I was doing everything to flee our gloomy basement. I lied when scolded by my father for my frequent absences. Mr Bialecki, I told him, insisted that I work overtime. Although, skilled liar that I was, I wasn't sure that he believed me, he preferred to say nothing – perhaps to avoid tearing the delicate fabric of our relationship. The work, the money, and my contact with the seamy side of life had given my character a new dimension that (or so it seems to me today) I was not prepared to cope with. My father and I rarely talked.

One night, though, he broke his enforced silence by informing me: 'Mishka has been taken away.' It was then that I realized he had known all along. He had never had any illusions.

What had happened was that Koba had decided to get rid of his wife. Zelma no longer met his standards. Embittered, her beauty gone, and haunted by the ghosts of Koba's victims, she threatened to turn him over to the Germans upon finding out that he was keeping a young mistress.

That sealed her fate. Koba's mistress was a Gestapo collaborator. The two came up with a simple and easily executed plan that would have permitted them to live happily ever after, were it not for a minor mishap.

Mishka had no idea why his father insisted on his going that same day to visit friends in a small town near Cracow. Against his wishes he packed a bag and boarded the bus. We had no chance to say goodbye.

That evening Koba went to one of his carouses, which was held in a tavern frequented by collaborators who were left alone by the gendarmes enforcing the curfew. In his absence a Gestapo squad burst into his apartment and rounded up all the tenants, including Mrs Szindler. Taken by surprise, she was dragged into the waiting van. So, however, was Mishka. Unlike his mother he kept shouting for his father, but no one paid him any attention.

What had gone wrong? It was simple. Finding the house of his father's friends locked, Mishka had taken the next bus back to Cracow. He arrived at eight o'clock, ten minutes before the Germans. 'They were all shot in the old mill,' my father told me.

9

Mishka swept through my life like a comet with a bright head and no tail trailing after it. Although I sometimes missed him, having no one else to spend my time or share my experiences with, this was a purely selfish emotion involving no real sense of loss. The fact was that I could manage without him. So could my parents, who, disapproving of his rare visits that took place only when he had no other way to contact me, pointedly ignored his remarks about our basement apartment, which he said was as cheerful as a grave. Perhaps they were afraid of his blabbing something to our landlady that would make her wonder who we were. For the same reason, they talked little between themselves.

My father suspected the old woman of being less hard of hearing than she seemed. While pretending to be deaf, he said, she was straining to hear every word that we uttered. Since she never gossiped with the neighbours, however, or asked about our past, there was no way of proving this. Once a month she emerged from her dark corner to count our rent money by the window, her warty, arthritic fingers ticking off each bill. Once convinced that she had not been cheated, she tucked away the treasure in the folds of her skirt.

My father spent much of his time observing the feet of the pedestrians passing before our window, which was level with the sidewalk. Sometimes I did that, too, trying to imagine what people looked like from the style of their shoes or the cut of their pants. My mother sat and read. The three of us led isolated lives, each alone in an uncommunicating world. I had no appreciation in those days of the human need for verbal contact and no awareness that our family was crumbling. It was a long, slow process in which I could not have pointed to the moment at which I ceased to require my parents' company.

But I was not at peace when alone either. I bubbled with energy like young wine. Although I could cage my thoughts, I refused to be kept from the light and commotion of the city around me. Despite their dangers, the streets flowed with life. I continued to roam in them.

The pubs were always full. Through their doors came a clamour of voices, drunken song, the laughter of whores. I came to know my way about the alleys of the old city, in whose courtyards scalpers sold expensive foods. I taunted fate by stopping to watch the illicit trade over the ghetto walls and sometimes, dressed in my black uniform, struck up conversations with the German officers sitting on the benches in the park that surrounded the downtown area. Usually these were soldiers on brief leave from the front. In their faces I saw the other, weary side of the proud Nazi war machine. Had anyone chided me for leading such a life, I would have answered: in what way am I different from the rich Jews in the ghetto who dance every night to the music of orchestras, wining and dining in the depths of their degradation while tens of thousands die of hunger around them? Not that I considered such people immoral. Far from it. They were draining life to the lees while they could. Soon would come the deluge.

Despite all this, Cracow was not a dissolute city. Its solid façade and bourgeois lifestyle persisted throughout the war years, which failed to dent its beauty or ancient grandeur. No bombs toppled its walls. Not a trench was dug in its parks. None of its castles or churches was destroyed. It was a city on which every period had left its imprint, from the gothic quattrocento to the Italian baroque, saving that of the German occupation. The latter remained invisible, carved only in human hearts.

I learned to read the city as a Gypsy reads a palm, mixing reality with wishes. Day in and day out, Cracow woke to the screech of the first streetcars taking the curves of the rails; day out and day in, it prepared for bed with the start of the curfew. But behind its blacked-out windows another life went on, full of sometimes clandestine activity. There were apartments in which underground classes were held after the city's high schools were closed, taught free of charge by unemployed teachers. I was invited to attend a few of these but always found some excuse to beg off. A horse that has tasted freedom can't be returned to the stable. I wasn't prepared to resubmit to that kind of discipline. Nor did I have the least desire to study. I wasn't one of those people who did all they could to preserve an outward semblance of normality.

In the city's shop windows the meagre merchandise available was displayed like fancy goods. Bolts of faded fabric were advertised as the latest fashion; boxes of saccharine said: Sweeter than Sugar; the permanently empty shelves of the butchers' shops bore signs declaring: Temporarily out of Meat. Waitresses, most from down-and-out families that had once formed the Polish intelligentsia, served cakes baked from potato flour in cafés at whose tables men sipped ersatz coffee and whispered guardedly about the approaching fall of Hitler. Just because the Wehrmacht was laying siege to Leningrad and threatening the oil fields of the Caucasus was no reason to refrain from fantasies. It was easier to go on dreaming than to come to terms with the fact that all over Europe, from the shores of the Atlantic to the Urals, the Nazi banner was flying.

Rumour had it that the Cracow ghetto was about to be liquidated and its residents sent to concentration camps. This included my grandparents, my father's parents, who had been among the last Jews to move to the ghetto on Yom Kippur, 1941.

Since then we had lost all contact with them. Their faces grew blurred in my memory. Now that the rumour reached me, my grandmother's frail frame and my grandfather's shock of white hair flashed before me again.

These visions of them began to haunt me. I dreamed of my grandfather constantly. His glance went right through me; his lips whispered that it was time for him to leave. Sometimes he appeared by himself and sometimes with my grandmother, who seemed deceptively full of life. I felt far closer to them in my dreams than I ever had in real life.

It was not in my dreams, though, that I thought of a way of getting them out of the ghetto. The idea was born in broad daylight as I was walking near the ghetto walls and wondering who inside them would survive.

The ghetto drew me towards it like a magnet. At the time I had no idea why. Today it seems obvious that it was more than just curiosity. I took a morbid pleasure in a sight that illustrated better than anything that I was still free while tens of thousands of other Jews waited passively for the Nazis to decree their fate.

The key to saving my grandparents, I now realized in an inspired moment, was the Nazi race laws. These went three generations back. Not only baptized Jews, but even the grandchildren of baptized Jews, were considered Jewish and sent to the ghettos. Yet once dead, these same converts and their descendants could be removed from the ghetto for a Catholic burial. Whilst I never understood the German logic that gave such rights to corpses, it now struck me that I could use it to free my grandparents.

More than once, leaning my bicycle against a lamppost and placing my parcel of fish on the sidewalk, I had witnessed a nun and novice priest enter the ghetto without having to stop for inspection. I knew they were on the way to some Catholic within its walls who wanted the last rites on his deathbed. The Polish police treated them with respect and would never have thought of searching them or asking for identification. Some doffed their caps or crossed themselves at the sight of a priest bearing a candle in a small glass case – a sign that he was on his way to administer extreme unction. At night, under cover of darkness, the undertakers came for the body. Needless to say, the family inside the ghetto was not permitted to attend the funeral.

10

My father was less than enthusiastic. My mother was thoroughly opposed. 'It's madness,' she said of my plan.

'That's just why it will work,' I insisted.

'Don't you dare. I refuse to let you risk your life for nothing.'

'Saving Grandfather and Grandmother is nothing?'

'Don't get smart with me. I said no and that's that.'

'Stop shouting,' my father intervened. 'The old woman is listening.'

'Let her.'

My mother had not been shouting. For all her agitation, she was whispering. Clearly, that was no way to make me abandon my plan. Who could be convinced by a whisper?

'I don't understand you. I've worked it out down –'

'I don't want to hear another word.'

'– to the last detail. The risk is tiny. The chances of success are good. It will be harder without your help, but I'll still do it.'

My father intervened again. 'Let's hear him out,' he told my mother. 'Then we'll decide.'

'All right,' I said. 'I'm sure I can get you to see it my way. I've staked out the gate to the ghetto many times and I know exactly what the procedure is. Entering isn't a problem. The best time would be the night before. I know where all the openings in the wall are. I'll crawl through one of them with a cassock and a habit. I'll have the lace cape of a novice, too. The next day Grandfather and Grandmother will come back out with me, dressed as a priest and a nun. No one will stop us.'

'I can't believe how innocent you are. What makes you think that the policemen at the gate won't see through you? They'll know that the three of you didn't enter.'

'I've thought of that, Mother. I know when the guards start

their shifts. We'll cross soon after a new shift has started. They'll think we entered during the previous shift. What do you say?'

'I say you haven't thought it through. What will you do with them? Bring them here? Do you want us to tell the old woman that they're my lost brother and sister who have come to live with us in this stinking cellar?'

'Father will write to Aunt Matylda in Slomniki. She'll be glad to take in her own parents.'

'How will I get a letter to her?' asked my father.

'By ordinary mail.'

'It's not so simple.'

'It's very simple. All it takes is paper, an envelope, and a stamp.'

'Where will you get a priest and nun's clothing?' persisted my mother. 'Where will you find a novice's cape?'

'I'll steal a cape from the wardrobe in St Mary's. I can buy fabric on the black market. You'll sew it to Grandmother's and Grandfather's size.'

'I will?'

'Yes. You will.'

'What made you so sure I'd agree?'

My mother sewed the nun's habit from black cloth that I bought on the cheap. She tried making a cassock, too, but seeing that she was an inexperienced tailor without a sewing machine, I was forced to steal one along with the cape.

That proved easier than I had thought. After mass I waited for the priest to change his clothes and leave the wardrobe. His sermon about Judas Iscariot was still echoing in the vaults of the cathedral when I entered the room. Although the chest with the silver chalices was kept tightly locked, the closet was open. What would anyone want with a priest's old gown? In no time it was in the knapsack I had brought. So were a glass candle case, a little bell, and a censer – all required for shriving the dying. I planned to slip into the ghetto with them the following day.

I knew all the gaps in the wall. They were used by smugglers, who employed small boys to wriggle through them. The goods were supplied by Polish black market operators and purchased by wealthy Jews and officials in the ghetto. None of this was very secret. Nor was the plight of the tens of thousands of poorer Jews packed into the ghetto's streets. And yet what I had heard was nothing compared to what I saw with my own eyes after crossing over.

I had no trouble finding my grandparents' address. We had kept it from the days when it was still possible to correspond with them. They had written to Miss Sziwek, their loyal ex-house-keeper, and she had passed their letters to my parents.

The house was a dilapidated two-storey building. The front gate was gone from its hinges and the filthy stairway smelled of sauerkraut and urine. A woman dressed in rags came towards me from the courtyard. With an amazed look at my clothes, she asked in Yiddish:

'Where are you from? The other side?'

Although I spoke no Yiddish, I understood enough to nod. There was no point in pretending. No ghetto child looked as I did.

'It's dangerous,' said the woman in broken Polish, tapping my jacket sleeve. 'You don't even have a yellow star.'

Damn! I had thought of everything and forgotten the most important thing of all. No Jew was allowed in the ghetto's streets without a yellow star of David on his sleeve.

'It must have fallen off on the way,' I murmured.

She shook her head at my carelessness. 'Do you what you must and God help you,' she said. She switched back to Yiddish: 'Who are you looking for?'

I didn't want to mention names. She didn't pursue it. I climbed to the second floor. A long list of tenants was posted on the door. My grandparents lived in one of three rooms that they shared with a large family. Pieces of Bialecki's furniture stood disman-tled against the wall.

The family stared at me suspiciously. My grandmother was sitting on a bed board with her back to me. My grandfather saw me first and grabbed my jacket. His long, thin fingers were tremulous from age. He could hardly speak.

'Good God! What are you doing here?'

'I have to talk to you.'

'Is anything wrong? Your father . . .?'

'Everything is fine. Father is well. So is Mother.'

'Then why have you come?'

'Not here, Grandfather. Isn't there somewhere we can talk in private?'

'Outside.'

We went to the staircase, descended half a flight, and stood outside the communal toilet.

'The Germans are planning to liquidate the ghetto,' I told him drily. Not wanting to excite him, I tried sounding unemotional. Despite his seventy years, he took it calmly.

'That's nothing new,' he said quietly.

'You have to get out while you can.'

'That's fine advice,' he mocked. 'There's nothing Jews are better at.'

'First listen to me,' I said, piqued. 'Then you can make fun.'

'You've become quite the cheeky fellow.'

'Cheek is all that keeps anyone alive these days.'

'That may be. Bread helps, too.'

'You'll have as much of it as you want.'

'Don't tell me you've opened a bakery.'

'No. But I'm going to open the gates of the ghetto for you.'

His expression grew serious. Only now did he understand my purpose. 'Talk,' he said.

I laid out my plan while he listened intently. When I was done he thought and said:

'If Grandmother has no objection, we'll do it.'

Grandmother had no objection.

Although my grandmother was a small, frail woman, it was a great mistake to judge her by her appearance. As strong and wound-up as a spring, she ran the household unchallenged. Before the war she had kept the books while Grandfather sat writing protest letters to the mayor. Grandfather, who had failed at running a large farm, was only too happy to let her run the family business. Buying a building on Szlak Street, she turned it into a source of income that permitted them to live comfortably. Despite her stinginess, she had managed to reinvest every zloty wisely. 'A waste of money' was the most pejorative term in her vocabulary.

Back before the war, on each of our visits to Cracow, she would signal me to follow her to the kitchen. There, among her jams and stewed fruits, she kept a jar full of coins. Holding it up to her myopic eyes, which she refused to equip with spectacles, she squinted at its contents, fished out a fifty-groszy piece, inspected it carefully to make sure she hadn't mistaken it for a gold zloty, and said: 'Go buy yourself an ice cream.' She was so fragile that, afraid to hug her, I made do with a kiss on her cheek.

Now, in the ghetto, her body had shrunk even more. She was as energetic as ever, though. And as clear-minded.

'A Purim masquerade,' was her reaction when I took the nun's habit from my knapsack and handed it to her like a saleslady showing a customer a dress.

'Someone might come,' warned Grandfather, suggesting that we go to the toilet. The three of us barely managed to squeeze into the airless, windowless cubicle. The stench was unbearable. I locked the door from inside. While I struggled with the collar of the lace cape, Grandfather stripped off his clothes, threw them behind the toilet, and put on the black cassock.

'You look born for the priesthood,' I declared.

Grandmother rebuked me with a glance. 'This is no time for jokes. And I can't undress in this place.'

'Of course you can. Be quick, before our neighbour with the diarrhoea comes.'

'You and your jokes,' she grumbled almost angrily, taking off her skirt and blouse. As she slipped into the robe sewn by my mother, I glimpsed her protruding shoulder bones. They looked like the wings of a starved bird.

'I'm ready,' she said. 'I was always afraid of ending up in a nunnery.'

I slid open the latch. The rusty bolt squeaked. I listened for sounds from the stairs. There were none. I opened the door, peered outside, and signalled that the coast was clear.

We descended the stairs. I halted by the entrance to the building. Although the entranceway was dark, the street outside was sunny. Reaching into my pocket for a box of matches, I lit the candle in its little lantern case, took out the bell, and rang it lightly by swinging it. I handed Grandfather the censer and we set out.

'I'll go first. You follow me,' I told them.

I began walking towards the ghetto gate. Grandfather followed me with the censer, its fragrant smoke wafting around us. Grandmother brought up the rear with dainty steps, as unhesitatingly as a mother superior. A Jewish passer-by spat at us indignantly. Converts were not popular in the ghetto. Less prejudiced, a rickets-stricken boy held out a beggarly hand. We ignored him. Like a stone, his curse was flung at our backs.

Two auxiliary policeman, a Jewish ghetto policeman and a petty Nazi officer, stood on the corners of Limanowska and Wegierska Streets. I looked straight ahead to keep them from reading my eyes. Until now I had played the hero's role successfully. Now, though, I was afraid. What if the whole perfect plan were to fail? We would all pay with our lives for my folly. Hadn't my mother said it was a crazy idea?

A miserable flop – it was that more than death that I feared. I couldn't bear the thought of hearing my mother snap to my father: 'I told you so, Wilek. Didn't I say it wouldn't work?'

The seconds crept by like hours. Would the guards be suspicious and ask to see our papers? I measured the distance to the gate. The closer we got to it, the more my eyes raced back and forth. Every fraction of a second a new scene flashed before them.

The policemen order us to stop. We ignore them. They cock their guns. A shot echoes between the houses. Dogs bark. (There wasn't a dog in sight.) *We begin to run. Grandmother slips and falls. The passers-by stop to watch with pleasure. Hard-eyed and mean-looking, they shout something at us. I don't understand their language. We're foreigners and they hate us. They cheer as the gate slams shut, trapping us inside.*

Figments of my imagination. The Polish policeman doffed his cap. The Jewish one ignored us. A German officer pointed a camera at us and snapped the shutter. I would have given anything for a copy of the picture.

We advanced with measured steps. Grandfather blessed the soldier and policemen, drawing a cross in the air. (How on earth did he think of it?) The three of us passed through the ghetto gate.

Beyond lay a world of relative freedom. Still, I could feel the stares of the guards – or was it again my imagination? – boring into my back. I knew I musn't look back. Was this how Lot felt as he fled the doomed city of Sodom?

When the gate was far enough behind us and we had blended into the human landscape of the street, we halted for a brief consultation.

'We'll take a tram now,' I explained.

'A tram?' marvelled my grandmother. 'I haven't been on a tram in two years.'

'All the nuns take them.'

'How do you know?' Grandfather asked.

'I've done my homework.'

'Clever boy.'

'He's not a boy any more,' objected Grandmother. 'He's a young hoodlum.' I wanted to ask if this meant I would no longer be getting my ice cream money but restrained myself.

In half an hour we had reached the central bus station. Dozens of people were waiting in line for tickets. 'Let the priest through,' I called out. No one dared protest.

'Two tickets for Slomniki,' I told the cashier. I paid for them and led Grandmother and Grandfather to the bus platform.

'I'll stay with you until the bus leaves. The driver will tell you where to get off. Aunt Matylda will be waiting for you in Slomniki. She's expecting you. I'll come visit next week if I can.'

There were only two buses a day to Slomniki and the wait was a long one. As he was about to board the bus, I kissed Grandfather's hand as a novice does to a priest. Grandmother caressed me. I stuck a wad of bills in her purse.

She was startled. 'What is this for?'

'Ice cream,' I answered. Did she hear the pride in my voice?

As soon as the bus pulled out with a stream of exhaust I ducked into an apartment building opposite the station, pulled off my cape, and threw it in a garbage pail together with the glass candle case. Then I crossed the yard, jumped over a fence separating it from an empty lot in the next street, and hurried home to tell my father that his parents had been rescued from death.

A year or so later, all the Jews of Slomniki were sent to the death camps. The trap was laid carefully, in the best Nazi manner. First the Judenrat was instructed to compile updated lists of the city's Jewish inhabitants. Only then did the SS special units spring into action. The words 'Final Solution' were still a secret slogan coined at Wannsee; no one had any notion of what lay ahead. The official notice simply requested, as usual, that everyone assemble at the railroad station for transport to labour camps in the East.

Nearly everyone obeyed. Not Grandfather, though. Did he have a sixth sense about was about to happen in the next twenty-four hours? In any event, he and his family decided to stay home.

The Nazis, however, were well organized. Accompanied by Latvian mercenaries, SS soldiers made the rounds of Slomniki's houses to make sure no hold-outs were hiding in them.

There was no one to tell me exactly what happened when Grandfather heard the soldiers' steps on the stairs. When I tried reconstructing it after the war, the neighbours told me that he was bleeding profusely when he came through the door. So were Grandmother, Aunt Matylda, Matylda's husband Jakob, and their eighteen-year-old daughter Kristiana, who all staggered after him. In a moment of desperation – or of foresight – they had decided to take their own lives. The blood from their razor-slashed veins splashed over the stairs and the walls.

This was in April 1947. The stairs had been whitewashed. Nothing was left of the drama that had taken place six years before.

11

As it got to be autumn, the walls of our basement apartment were covered with green mould. We all suffered from the cold, especially my father, who had arthritis. Although the old woman's side of the basement had a stove, there was no coal for sale in the city. We were barely able to buy wood to cook with.

We knew the autumn rains would be followed by frost and snow. It could only get worse. The winter temperature in Cracow often dipped to twenty degrees centigrade below zero.

And it was then that Fortune smiled on us. Perhaps it was a Christmas present from our guardian angels. Actually, our landlady was in the middle of decorating her Christmas tree – God only knew where it came from – when the doorbell rang. She didn't hear the single, short ring. Or perhaps she pretended not to. She had not had a visitor since the day we moved in. We were not expecting anyone either. Uninvited guests were never good news.

My father folded his newspaper, exchanged looks with my mother, and signalled me to open the door. 'There's no need to worry,' he said. '*They* don't ring bells so gently.'

The man standing in the doorway wore peasant's clothes, a long, rough woollen coat, and a sheepskin cap that he removed from his head. About sixty, with a permanently weary look, he strained to see in the sudden darkness of the room. At first I took him for a beggar. I was about to tell him to move on, since we could not even offer him a bowl of hot soup, when he stepped towards my father and asked quietly:

'Dr Wilhelm Frister?'

You could hear a pin drop. Our forged papers had a different, more Polish-sounding name. How did he know our real one?

'I'm afraid not,' said my father. 'You must have the wrong address.'

93

'I'm sure there's no mistake. You have nothing to be afraid of. My name is Jozef Kruczek.'

'I don't believe I've ever had the honour of meeting you.'

'May I sit down? It would be best if that old woman . . .' Our visitor gestured towards our landlady. 'If she were kept out of this.'

'Out of what?' asked my father with a sharp edge. My mother gave the stranger her seat. Jozef Kruczek dropped into it heavily.

'Excuse me,' he apologized. 'I'm a bit tired. I rode my bicycle all the way here. I'm no longer the man I used to be.'

Although he spoke a good Polish, not at all like a peasant's, he showed the signs of a hard life. His face ploughed with deep wrinkles made him look at least ten years older than he was. His hands were callused and liver-spotted. I did not feel suspicious of him like my father. Whoever he was, he seemed sincere.

'My name is Jozef Kruczek,' he repeated.

'You've told me that. But mine isn't Wilhelm Frister.'

'You've told me that, too,' said the man. 'But there's nothing to be afraid of. I haven't come to harm you. I've come to help.'

'We don't need any help.'

'I have a farm in Garlica Duchowna. That's a small village about an hour's ride from here by carriage. Before the war I worked in the Szapiro silos.'

'I never heard of any Szapiro.'

'I was given your address by Zofia Sziwek. I believe you know her.'

There was no longer any point in denials. 'Yes. I do.'

Kruczek glanced around the room. 'That woman . . . this place . . . it doesn't look safe to me. Not for long, anyway. Why don't you come live in my cottage? It doesn't have the luxuries you may be accustomed to, but I can see that this, too, is no palace.'

'No, it isn't,' my father agreed.

'I worked for Mr Szapiro for twenty-five years. I own a small farm, twenty acres all in all, and not the best land either. Some of it is irrigated. It's all pasture, not enough to support a family. We would never have survived without the silos. Twenty-five years of them. We came a long way together, Mr Szapiro and myself. I began as a simple workman and ended up his foreman. A hundred zlotys a month, that was my pay. It was a fortune for a peasant like me. And that wasn't all. You know how it is: we farmers live from one natural disaster to the next. What would I have done without him? Whenever we were hit by a drought, or lost a field to a flood that rotted the wheat, Mr Szapiro helped out. He was a good man.'

'Is he dead?'

'Not at all. He's with his family in Hungary. When the persecutions started and the Jews were made to wear the yellow star and looked headed for more plagues than in the Bible, I invited the Szapiros to stay with me in my village until things blew over. This insanity can't go on for ever, can it? It has to end some time. It does. He didn't need my help, though. Mr Szapiro knows how to get along, in good times and in bad. He's as strong as an oak tree. A smart, strong man.

'When all the other Jews went to the ghetto, he didn't go with them. He got hold of some passports and visas and whatever else was needed for Budapest. The whole family left in 1940. I went to the train to see them off. A minute before boarding it – he had reserved seats in first class – Szapiro took me aside and said: "Listen, Kruczek, we're safe now. But if you ever run into a Jew in trouble, please think of him as though he were me."'

My mother asked:

'Would you like a glass of tea? We have real tea. Sugar, too.'

This was a vote of confidence in our surprise guest.

'A hot glass of something would do no harm,' answered Kruczek.

My mother went to the stove to make tea. The old woman rose, opened a faucet, and filled the kettle. Perhaps she was really not deaf after all. Kruczek took off his coat, hung it on the back of the chair, and sat with his legs straight out in front of him.

'I'm bushed,' he sighed. 'I'm getting old.'

'Take your time,' said my father.

I brought cups and put them on the table. 'What will we tell Bialecki?' I asked worriedly.

Kruczek's cottage in Garlica Duchowna had a thatched roof of the kind I had seen only in children's books. Its clay walls were painted sky-blue. The peasants believed that this colour repelled evil spirits, just as a horseshoe above the door brought good luck and a girl finding a four-leaf clover would marry rich. A combination of superstition and devout Catholicism was their handbook to life – from which they asked nothing more than God's blessing on their fields, health for their families, and misfortune for their enemies. Beneath its pastoral serenity, the existence they led was one long succession of feuds handed down for generations. At bottom, most of these were about the lust for land.

Kruczek lived with his family in a cottage built by his great-great-grandfather. Not much had changed over the last century. There was no electricity, no running water, no plumbing. The toilets were in the farmyard and water came from a well.

As in the other farmhouses in the village, people and animals lived together. Behind the kitchen, on the other side of a narrow entranceway that led to the cottage's two rooms, was a barn for two cows and a small pigsty. The night-soil was used to fertilize the fields. Chemical fertilizer was unheard of.

Fetching water was the job of the eldest daughter. Turning the crank that raised the bucket from the well built strong muscles, in which the girls of a peasant family took as much pride as a boy flexing his arms before a fight. They were unforgettable, the village girls, particularly Bronka, who sought to introduce me to the pleasures of the flesh. But more than anything, I remember the taste of the well water. Cold and clear, it went down the throat like the purest elixir.

The cottage stood at the foot of a hill exposed to the autumn winds. Nothing grew on its slopes but wild grasses. Now, at the end of the dry summer, even these had faded to a few sparse patches that only the goats took an interest in.

At the other, northern end of the farm, where it met the road that was the village's main thoroughfare, ran a winding stream. The road was unpaved and sent up thick clouds of dust each time a vehicle passed over it. This was useful for the peasants, who were warned that the Germans were coming. No one else had cars or motorcycles – and these, too, left the road to horse-drawn wagons once it was turned to a muddy porridge by the first rains. But the danger grew again, Kruczek told us, with the winter snows because the Nazis were fond of sleds. 'The sons of bitches take the bells off the harnesses and drive as quietly as ghosts,' he said.

The stream was too swift to ice over. Ever since the plank laid across it by Kruczek had been used by some boys for a bonfire, it was uncrossable even on the coldest nights. It stood, so I felt, between us and the rest of the world. The land beyond it was a forbidden country, a great minefield best avoided. Although there was nothing visible to bear out this impression, both sides of the stream being equally peaceful, the far bank· was occupied territory for me. There alone were the ghettoes, prisons, concentration camps. The near bank was mine, safe.

Jozef Kruczek had prepared a perfect hideout for us. Beneath a bale of hay tossed with deliberate carelessness on the floor of the barn was a hidden trapdoor that descended to a cellar as big as the cottage. Before we came this had served as an abattoir. The screeching of the slaughtered pigs remained within its walls – a big help in avoiding German confiscations and getting the meat to the black market. Kruczek's wife had cleaned this space for us, furnished it with three beds, a closet and a table, and even hung a picture of the Virgin Mary on the wall before her husband brought us in a wagon piled with hay. 'She'll protect you even though you're Jews,' she said of the Virgin. She was as religious as her husband. My father took this in good spirits and replied:

'Why not? Her son was Jewish, too.'

The pig cellar, as I called it, was for emergencies only, in case of a visit by gendarmes or police. We never used it in the course of our stay. For our everyday use the Kruczeks gave us the room belonging to their three daughters, who moved in with them. The hardest part about it for me was having nothing to do. After my busy life in Cracow, I couldn't put up with the idleness. I had no notion of how to 'kill time'. My mother's endless games of solitaire made me want to scream. My father spent the days hunched over a home-made radio, from whose tubes he tried to coax the BBC out of a constant chatter of static. He rarely succeeded. Usually, the crystals in the tubes passed on nothing more than the latest victory announcements of the German high command. Sitting in our room behind a curtain drawn for privacy, I counted flies. It was Kruczek who first noticed my predicament. He said:

'Perhaps you'd like to read something.'

'I'd love to. But what? You don't even have a newspaper.'

'What would you like?'

'The longest novel ever written,' I joked and promptly forgot about it. Kruczek, however, did not. A few days later he returned from Cracow with the collected works of Tolstoy in twelve fancily bound volumes.

'Here, son,' he said, laying the books on my bed.

'They must have cost a pile,' I murmured.

'Not at all,' he answered disdainfully. 'I bought them all for a pitcher of milk. Books don't fetch much these days.'

I could only read in the daylight hours. As the days grew short, night dropped its black veil on the village by three o'clock. The peasants lit their homes with carbide lamps, but like everything else, the fuel was rationed and expensive. Light was at a premium.

'I wish I were a bear and could hibernate,' I complained half-smilingly to my father. Still as withdrawn as he had been all summer when we lived in the basement in Cracow, he wasn't listening. The most he ever said was a word or two to Kruczek.

I had no choice but to spend my time with Anna Karenina and Prince Vronsky. Although I thrilled to the epic action of *War and Peace* and tried in vain to fathom the profundities of *A Confession*, I was too young to understand Tolstoy's search for meaning in life.

At night I was allowed out into the fresh air. Wearing a warm coat and a fur hat that came down over my ears, I circled the cottage in ever-widening spirals as my confidence grew. On one of these walks, which took me further than most, I met Bronka. She, too, had gone out to enjoy the enchanted evening that hung like a bright velvet drape from the starry sky to the snowy earth.

Although Bronka was the daughter of peasants who eked a difficult life from the rocky soil, the poverty she was raised in had not crushed her natural spirits. On the contrary: it had only heightened her hunger for life. We liked each other from the start. I was as curious to learn from her about local customs as she was to hear about the big city that I came from.

'Why did you leave? What made you come to a dump like this?' It was more than she could fathom.

I made up such a long, complicated story that I lost track of my own lies, but Bronka was so guileless that she swallowed every bit of it avidly. Familiar with every path and house in the village, she led me on our second meeting to a deserted hayrick. The stubbly straw jabbed our behinds.

'Do you want to neck?' she asked.

'Sure thing,' I replied, glad she couldn't see me blush in the darkness. We embraced. Bronka put her lips to mine. Her tongue slid into my mouth. I had never kissed like that before and closed my eyes. I could hear her breathing in the tense silence.

'Did you like it?'

I said nothing.

'What are you thinking about?'

'Nothing.' Could I have told her I was thinking of Grete?

'I know what you're thinking about. So am I. But we can't do it tonight.'

She was not only older than me – she had just turned fifteen – she was also a woman while I was not yet a man. Without the slightest embarrassment she told me she had her period and explained when we would be able to make love safely.

There was no telling what it might have led to had not my parents gotten wind of it. The Kruczek girls, who sniffed everything out like little mice, discovered our trysting place and told their father and mother. That evening, returning in the elated mood of a boy who had finally learned to kill time, I was told by my father that he wanted to have a talk with me. His face was stern as he questioned me.

'Is it true that you've been seeing a village hussy?'

'She's not a hussy, Father,' I said, defending Bronka's honour.

'Where are your brains?' he scolded. 'Have you forgotten who we are and what can happen to us? All we need is for that girl to find out we're Jews.'

'There's not a chance of that. It would never cross her mind.'

'It has nothing to do with her mind. There are other parts of the body. Have you forgotten you're circumcised?'

12

Goodbye, Bronka. Goodbye, Anna Karenina. My little adventure with both of you is over. It wasn't either of you who made us leave the village. It was the neighbour's horse. A dappled brown one, stolen overnight.

The thefts started at the end of the winter time. 'It's the same story every year,' lamented Kruczek. 'All winter the thieves stay away. They know their tracks in the snow will lead us to them and that nothing can keep an angry farmer from spilling their guts with a pitchfork or bashing in their brains with an axe. And every spring the bastards come back, because they know they can't be caught then.'

He had a particularly low opinion of horse thieves. Without his horse no farmer could plough, and without a plough there was no bread. Every farm's mainstay was its work animals.

The theft caused us to pack our bags in a hurry. The stolen horse was listed with the village registrar, who was responsible for every animal that might aid the German war effort. Although my father offered to pay the owner to buy a new horse, the man feared the heavy hand of military law if his failure to report the theft was discovered. Since no partisans were involved, it was strictly a matter for the Polish police, with whom the peasants got along. Yet the very appearance of police in the village was a risk. Testimony would be taken and someone might talk. Although Kruczek thought it was safe for us to take cover in the cellar until the investigation was over, my father disagreed. 'It's too dangerous,' he said. 'God Himself can't help us if we're discovered. The police will tell the Nazis and they'll have no mercy. It's not just our problem, either. You and your children will pay for it, too. There's no choice. We're going back to Cracow.'

We reached Cracow that afternoon and by evening had a new home: a rented two-room apartment at 76 Dluga Street. The documents we used were the same forged papers we had gotten from Koba Szindler – papers, as he put it, that were 'better than real'. I appeared in them as Roman Wrzesniowski. The original Roman Wrzesniowski had been killed with his parents in an automobile accident a year before the war and Szindler claimed that a clerk had been bribed to destroy the death certificates. Let the Nazis investigate all they liked. We were one hundred per cent kosher Catholics.

The next day I showed up at the office of Bialecki & Potocki and asked for my old job back. Count Potocki was on vacation at the country estate of his uncle Antony. Mr Bialecki wavered.

'I need the Count to help me decide,' he said.

'We have no other income. My father was sure you wouldn't let us down,' I lied.

'All right, then,' he said reluctantly. 'When do you want to start?'

'Now.'

I didn't know that, while we were in Garlica Duchowna, my father had also arranged a hiding place for his sister Sydonia and her daughter in a house at the other end of the same village. What had inspired my grandfather to give his six children their names? My father presumably was named for Kaiser Wilhelm, who defeated the French and united the Germans under Prussian rule. But why call his brother, any connection between whom and the Virgin Mary was dubious, Marian? And as for the four girls, Hermina, Zofia, Matylda, and Sydonia, all sounded to me like the heroines of a romantic nineteenth-century novel.

Sydonia was the eldest. I had liked visiting her in Cracow before the war not because of any feeling of kinship but on account of the juicy pears that grew on the boughs of an old tree in her yard. More than one pair of my pants was torn climbing it.

Sydonia's husband, Uncle Leon, was drafted by the Polish army at the war's start and took part in its long eastward retreat until taken prisoner by the Russians, who had invaded western Ukraine and Belarus to 'liberate' them from the imperialists. A less successful lawyer than my father, Leon was interested only in his stamp collection. Aunt Sydonia often grumbled to my father that he neglected his work and family for the insane passion of philately. Although he died in Omsk, on the Siberia –Kazakhstan border, my only association with his round, myopic face and thick glasses was the magnifying glass through which the two of us peered at his albums. Every page of them was devoted to a different series of stamps from a different country. I learned more about the globe from Uncle Leon than from all my geography teachers.

Exactly how Aunt Sydonia died was a mystery. I never even found out how she reached the village, where she and her seventeen-year-old daughter Hedi lived with neighbours of the Kruczeks, decent people who didn't know she was a Jew. The story told them was that she and Hedi were Poles forced to leave their home when her husband, a captain in the army, was taken prisoner by the Germans. Such cases were common and the story was plausible.

The peasants who took in Sydonia and Hedi were not profiteers. My aunt paid them very little for a hideout that included room and board. Had it not been for the stolen horse, she could probably have lived out the war there. She and Hedi, too, however, had to clear out before the arrival of the police, which could have brought ruin on the family that sheltered them.

But at this point things took an unexpected turn, because Aunt Sydonia fell ill and could not be moved. Kruczek and my father improvised a stretcher of willow branches and carried her to the abandoned hayrick in which Bronka and I had played our forbidden games, hoping that even if she was discovered it would be impossible to trace her and Hedi to any particular house.

Aunt Sydonia was delirious with fever and babbled senselessly. Hedi, who had been left to look after her, heard policemen approaching, panicked, and fled by a back way. After wandering for a few days in the forest she joined a band of partisans, lived through the war, and moved to Australia when it was over.

All we knew about Aunt Sydonia was that she was taken by the police for interrogation. I only learned of it when, back in Cracow, I heard my parents condemning my cousin. 'How could she go and leave a sick mother like that?' stormed my father. Although it wasn't worth an argument, I couldn't agree. Why be selflessly heroic for no purpose? Had Hedi remained with her mother, she, too, would have died at the hands of the Nazis. I was reminded of my old Bible teacher in Bielsko, Bruno Kalter, who had liked to flavour his lessons with Talmudic stories. One was about two Jews stranded in the desert with a single bottle of water between them. Divided equally, it would have saved neither from dying of thirst. The sacredness of life demanded that one of them drink it all.

I only met Hedi one more time, when she visited Israel with her husband. The subject of her mother did not come up. We both preferred to consign it to oblivion.

I hadn't forgotten Grete. Nor had she forgotten me. When I reappeared in her home with two fresh carp, she welcomed me like an old friend who has been away on a long vacation.

'Where did you disappear to? Well, what difference does it make! I'm glad to see you back. You look good. And . . . I don't know how to put it . . . more grown-up.'

'It's been a while,' I said, taking the carp from their basket. Despite a hammer blow to their heads, they had refused to die and were still flopping in the newspaper that stuck to their wet scales.

'Have you started shaving?' she asked.

I blushed and ran a hand over my cheek. It was as smooth as a baby's bottom.

'No,' I answered. 'Not yet.'

'Would you like some liqueur? Like in the old days? I still keep a bottle of Drambuie.'

I nodded. Grete went to the bar to fetch the bottle. My glance followed her attractive figure, then roamed around the room. The foyer had been refurnished. Only the leather armchairs remained. Modern pieces and antiques stood side by side – rather tastelessly, I thought. Some oil paintings were hung on the walls. Grete saw I was curious, handed me a large glass of clear, aromatic liquid, and explained:

'More of the ghetto has been liquidated. Kurt managed to salvage a few things. He's good at that, my lazy husband. Shall we drink a toast to my new possessions?'

I downed the liqueur in one gulp.

'That's no way to drink Drambuie,' she protested. 'A liqueur should be drunk slowly, in small sips. You have to savour each drop. Watch me.'

Grete showed me how to drink Drambuie, throwing back her head and shutting her eyes as it trickled down her throat.

'Did you see?'

'Yes.'

'Next time we'll practise together.'

Bialecki & Potocki expanded. It acquired more fish ponds, opened more branches, and widened its clientele. There were more deliveries to the homes of German officers. Cynically referred to by Mr Bialecki as 'greasing the wheels', this was the work I was now assigned to. Nearly all the higher-ups in the military government were on his gift list.

The gift packages were prepared under Bialecki's watchful eye, each according to the recipient's rank and importance. I quickly learned the names and addresses of all the important SS and Gestapo officers – names the very mention of which would have made most people shudder. Many later turned up on the Allied lists of Nazi war criminals. In Cracow, however, these men, still at the height of their power, were invariably nice to me. Bialecki was satisfied with my work and its results. His gifts were rewarded with the removal of bureaucratic obstacles, and a blind eye was turned towards the sale of his fish on the black market and the inferior produce that went into his cans of battle rations.

The firm's greatest period of prosperity commenced when the Potocki estates were released entirely from their obligation – mandatory for all farmers under the Nazi occupation – to supply the military. Count Potocki himself pretended to know nothing of his able junior partner's accomplishments. The scion of a family renowned in Polish history, the exploits of which filled long pages in encyclopaedias and history books, he often left Cracow for his country residences. Perhaps this was why I had such contempt for him. It was only after the war that I found out that, on one of these estates, he had sheltered the Jewish lawyer Bronislaw Szaten and a young Jewish woman named Liebeskind.

The Cracow ghetto shrank steadily. The Nazis emptied more and more of its quarters, until there were only two left, known as Block A and Block B. Those deported vanished into the wilderness of the death camps.

It was Bialecki who informed me of the ghetto's final liquidation. 'Watch out,' he said casually one day, handing me a package of fresh carp, the weekly delivery for Wilhelm Kunde, one of the most notorious of the SS's top brass. 'The city is crawling with police looking for escaped Jews.' I had no idea that Kunde and I would soon meet again under different circumstances.

Grete had never told me that the ghetto's last inhabitants were about to be transferred to a barbed-wired camp recently erected on two Jewish cemeteries in the suburb of Podgorze. Perhaps she knew nothing about it. My father did – how, I'll never know. Although he read all the Polish and German newspapers published with the permission of the authorities, none of these devoted a line to such things.

My father agreed with Mr Bialecki that the situation was more dangerous than ever. There had been all kinds of terrible cases, he told me, in which the Nazis and the Jewish ghetto police had torn parents from children, wives from husbands, the elderly from younger protectors. Mothers seeking to smuggle babies to safety had been beaten and shot. The heads of children had been smashed on the cobblestones. Hundreds of wretched ghetto dwellers, whole families with their children and possessions, had made their way through the filth and excrement of the sewer pipe leading to the Wisla Bridge only to run into extortioners at the exit. Whoever lacked the money to pay them off with met his death in the foul sewers. Most of those who paid were also quickly caught and shot by SS firing squads. A mere fifty families – members of the Judenrat and of the Jewish police, and professional informers used to round up stray Jews – remained in the ghetto under Nazi protection.

The Jews sent to the camps were marched in long columns to the railway station. Did they know what awaited them? Many years after the war, as a man of sixty, I read for the first time an astounding memoir written by a Pole named Tadeusz Pankiewicz, the owner of a pharmacy abutting the ghetto walls. An inadvertent witness, he wrote:

> The hour for departure has arrived. We can tell by the confiscations. Everyone has been ordered to leave his possessions behind. This time the Germans have left no room for illusion. There are no longer any lies or superfluous deceptions. We are witnessing the end of the ghetto. SS men have been taking even wallets and briefcases and throwing them on

a growing pile. Here and there someone screams that important documents are in them, clutching one last time at the belief that he will still need them. Such people resemble a hanged man whose body goes on twitching after death.

Cracow became one huge hunting ground. It was open season on whoever fled the ghetto. But Jews were willing to pay such high prices for their blood that it was foolish to shed it for nothing. The most loathsome types climbed out of the human gutter of Cracow to make a profit from this. Polish blackmailers lay in wait in the city's streets. Their ultimatums of 'Your money or your life' did not have to be backed by a weapon; the threat to turn their victim over to the Gestapo was enough. My friend Mishka, who had access to the stencilled flyers put out regularly by the partisans, had told me all about it. He also passed these publications on to me, which I read behind the locked bathroom door. When I was done I flushed them down the toilet. Some stuck in my memory. One, typical of that Cracow spring whose logo was the finger of the informer, went as follows:

One Gram of Courage

I'm safe! A short while ago I escaped from the sealed Jewish ghetto, in my coat pocket a fake passport with my photograph, on my lips a fake smile. Next to the passport, in the same pocket, was my courage – bought for a bargain from a man whose name I don't know. He wore thick glasses, had the high forehead of an intellectual, and went by the name of 'The Druggist'. Every afternoon from two to four he sat in the Café Ziemianska, where he retailed and wholesaled, between one sip of tea and the next, courage and death.

Although life was not worth much at the time, the price of death, subject to supply and demand, varied from one hundred and fifty to two hundred dollars a gram. I was not a great hero. It wasn't that I was afraid to die. But I was terrified of dying slowly and nastily. I feared the interrogations of the Gestapo, walls covered with the graffiti of the dead, the whistle of the descending whip, a bullet narrowly missing my heart, the benches in the corridors outside the torture chambers. The Druggist, who was also an experienced psychologist, saw through me at a glance. He put my fear at one hundred and seventy five dollars. I paid it without batting an eyelash. It bought me a capsule that gave off a strong smell of bitter almonds and was known by the commercial name of cyanide.

This gram of courage bought on the cheap was the best insurance policy in the world. It stood between me and death by torture and protected the forgers who had given me my new name – a name carefully checked three generations back. Undaunted, I walked about the city. Posters screamed at me from the walls, promising a bounty for the heads of escaped Jews. I wasn't fazed by them. They could just as well have been leaves from the Tree of Knowledge or pages from the Encyclopaedia of Culture – according to the latest edition of which, even the law was no longer legal.

I walked with my head held high. The drops of sweat pouring off me were solely due to the overhead sun and my old winter coat, beneath which my clothes were stitched with a yellow star like the mark of Cain. Suddenly I heard my name called: 'Avrum!'

Now Avrum means Abraham, and Abraham means a Jew, and a Jew means ... instinctively I stuck my hand into my pocket. *You can breathe easily, Avrum, it's still there, your little pill – your gate of gates to the ultimate haven.* Just touching it restored my confidence. Slowly, trying to appear calm, I turned around. There on the sidewalk, his legs outspread, was Piotr. He beckoned to me.

Piotr and I had shared a desk all through high school. He was gifted at copying my algebra homework, and I was happy to help him pass the quizzes of our Polish literature teacher, who was equally hated by us both. We saw each other every day until the ghetto wall rose between us.

'Hello, Piotr,' I said, sounding almost cheerful.

'Hello, Avrum,' he answered.

'Shhh, don't call me that. It's dangerous.'

Piotr gave me an inquisitive look. It was both cold and clammy. I tried explaining my situation. He interrupted by asking:

'Have you escaped from the ghetto?'

'Yes. Everyone was killed. I'm the only survivor.'

'Survivor?' he repeated. He smiled. 'Don't be so sure. Life is full of surprises.'

I nodded. He brought his face close to mine. I could smell the beer on his breath.

'You know that Poland lost its feelings together with its independence. The times are hard. We all have to manage. Me too. Do you get me?'

The lurking suspicion I had was now a certainty. I took a step back. Piotr grabbed my lapel.

'All right,' he said. 'Let's not play hide-and-seek. Our conquerors are doing well and I'm working for them. History never judges the victors. Still, deep down in my conscience there's something left of our old friendship. Let me have a thousand dollars and we'll shake hands one last time. A thousand is all I'm asking for.'

'You've got to be kidding,' I said. 'If I had a thousand dollars, I'd have been over the border long ago.'

A taxi was parked nearby. Piotr hailed it. It drove slowly over to us and stopped. Piotr pushed me inside, sat beside me in the back, and slammed the door. What a sound! 'Where to?' asked the driver. Piotr gave him an address that made me shiver.

'You've got three minutes to think it over,' he whispered.

'Believe me, I don't have a cent.'

'Jews always say they have no money and always find some when they need it.'

'Piotr, what's happened to you?' I asked. I knew perfectly well what had happened to him. He was both the hero and the victim of the Era of the Pointing Finger. A few seconds went by. I clocked them by the pounding of my pulse. The taxi was heading for Gestapo headquarters. I saw people through the window, a young woman out for a walk with her little blond boy, a coachman drowsing in the seat of his carriage, pedestrians hurrying nowhere for no reason I could think of. Piotr said:

'Two more minutes.'

The two minutes before my death were a long time. A lot could have happened in them. The war might have ended. There might have been a sudden earthquake, or even the apocalypse. In two minutes Piotr could have had a heart attack

or a stroke, the driver could have had an accident, Allied
bombers could have destroyed Cracow. Partisans could have
blown up the Gestapo building.

'One minute,' said Piotr drily, like an experienced businessman. The absurdity of hoping on the scaffold that the
hangman's rope will tear in time! I stole a glance at him. My
fate was written on his blank face. The Druggist had promised
that my stomach acids would dissolve the capsule in thirty
seconds. I slowly reached into my pocket. The poison went
down quickly. My only sensation was bracing myself for a
bitter taste that never came. The driver stopped at the corner.
If I were to open the door and make a run for it . . . but no,
there was no longer any need for that. I was no longer in Piotr's
power, no longer in the Gestapo's. I was a ghost with nothing
more to lose.

'You bastard!' I shouted. Those two words contained all my
hate for the friend who had betrayed me, depriving me not
only of my life but of my last faith in humanity. The dam
burst. I broke out in a flood of quick, contemptuous sentences.

It was then that the miracle happened. I must have wounded
Piotr to the depths of his soul – if he had one. He told the
driver to stop and said in a friendly voice:

'Stop shouting, you idiot. I was only joking.' Before I could
say anything he was out of the taxi and gone in the passing
crowd. We were five hundred metres from the Gestapo
building. Only now did I realize that thirty seconds had gone
by with nothing happening. I didn't need a PhD in chemistry
to understand that The Druggist had cheated me shamelessly.
He had sold me life instead of death. Fighting to conceal my
emotion, I gave the driver the address of the Café Ziemianska.

It was a quarter to four. The Druggist was sitting in his usual
spot. I approached him quietly, so as not to attract the
attention of the customers at the next tables. The psychologist
in him did not let him down. Taking one look at me, he
extracted one hundred and seventy-five dollars from his
wallet, handed me the bills, and murmured:

'Your satisfaction or your money back.'

I wondered what had happened to the author of this story in the
end. Unsuccessfully I tried picking out the Druggist from the

clients of the Café Ziemianska. How would I have reacted had it been me in the taxi? Would I have had the courage to swallow the cyanide? Deep down I was forced to admit that I could never, no matter how hopeless the situation, take my own life. It seemed too precious to willingly give up. Even after reading 'One Gram of Courage', and although no longer protected by my black armour (I had burned my Hitler Youth uniform in a neighbour's yard before boarding Kruczek's wagon for Garlica Duchowna), I did not feel threatened. No blackmailer seemed likely to waste his time on me. I felt no fear when passed by the police patrols that were combing the city more and more intensively. I even felt a tinge of condescension as I watched them march along the sidewalks, their bodies as stiff as if they had swallowed a broomstick, their heads encased in odd, brown helmets. Stamped in metal on their chests was an eagle with outspread wings, the symbol of their position and authority. Pedestrians crossed the street when they saw them coming. Not me.

Today I am one of the lucky survivors who isn't haunted by nightmares of the Holocaust. Still, it may be that my shell of confidence in those days was thinner than I thought, that I, too, had unconscious doubts. My dreams at night were exhausting. In one, recurrent one I found myself on a narrow precipice between a mountainside and an abyss, running to escape an unseen danger. My panting lungs made me feel that I was choking; that a heavy stone was pressing on my chest. One night my father woke me to ask if I was all right.

'I'm fine,' I answered with an angry defensiveness. I didn't like to seem vulnerable.

'You're drenched with sweat,' he said, pulling the blanket over my shoulders like Hilde Baron, my governess when I was little. My tossing and turning must have disturbed him. Often he didn't sleep at all. Was he preoccupied? Afraid? Thinking of the future? Wondering if we would perish or be saved? He never spoke about such things. I never asked him. The more time we spent together within walls, the more we retreated into ourselves.

Although it was not a deliberate decision, I stopped roaming the streets of Cracow. I visited Gretchen less, too, after she remarked one day, between one glass of liqueur and the next, that she liked my dark complexion. 'I'm not crazy about light German skin,' she said. That evening I stood for a long time before the mirror studying my prominent ears, my dark eyes, my curly hair. Yes, I had a Semitic face. Someone else might notice what Gretchen had missed.

I registered for the public library and hurried home after work to read the new books I took out. The librarian liked me. I was one of her few remaining clients. Who had the patience to read these days? A student of Polish literature before the war, she thought highly of my verbal skills and choice of reading matter. I was happy to be instructed and let her guide me through the French classics and the Polish novel, listening eagerly to her explanations of Rabelais' language in *Gargantua and Pantagruel* and to her analysis of the romantic influence on late nineteenth-century Polish nationalism. Sometimes, when the spirit moved her, she pulled from her desk a book of poems by Julian Tuwim, whose works were banned because of his Jewish ancestry, and discoursed about the Jewish contribution to Polish culture. She had no idea who I was and never dreamed that I was a Jew myself. I devoured the books that I borrowed by the bushel. I read until the early hours of the morning, stopping only when my father or mother made me put out the light. Yet as opposed to the days in Kruczek's cottage, I no longer identified with the heroes I read about. Their fates had ceased to touch me. My reading was devoid of emotion, mere information gathering. My mind recorded what it read as if taking inventory in a stock room.

'This will interest you,' said the librarian, giving me a heavy volume, a book about Colonel Redl, a Russian spy on the Austro-Hungarian general staff during World War I. I tucked it under my arm and left. It was 5 p.m. Not many people were in the street, a narrow one in an old neighbourhood of Cracow dating from the last century. The plaster was peeling from its mildew-covered walls. On the corner was the optometrist's shop of Mr Kulke, who always waved hello when I stopped to look at the brightly lit Zeiss lenses in his display window.

Now, too, I stopped to study them. In a playful moment I even winked at the electric eye that was blinking at me. Maybe this was why I failed to notice the patrol behind me. A policeman barked:

'Your papers!'

I turned around. A tall German, towering two heads above me, was standing there. I handed him my papers unhesitatingly. Unable to pronounce my forged Polish name, he handed the ID to a companion, who shrugged as if to say that he couldn't read the damned thing either. It was all perfectly routine. Without being asked for it, I handed them my work permit, too. It bore the symbol of the Reich and said in plain letters that I was employed by a firm enjoying high priority in the Nazi war economy.

A few men turned into the street. To judge by their overalls, they were workers on their way home. Spying us, they quickly ducked around a corner. One man alone, whom I had paid no attention to, was left in the middle of the sidewalk some ten metres from Mr Kulke's shop. There was something shiftless about the way he stood, as if waiting to see what would happen next. He was about fifty, a short, thin fellow in an unfashionable grey suit and black hat. You rarely saw such types in the streets of Cracow. I wondered why he didn't move on. There was never any telling what the Nazis might do next. In a second he might be asked for his identification, too, especially since the shabby, uncertain look of him could make anyone suspicious.

I suddenly recalled Bialecki's warning. Could the man be a Jew himself? I dismissed the thought at once. He didn't look at all frightened. I was not afraid either. I had been asked for my papers many times and was always sent on my way in the end. The connection between the strange onlooker and the police only dawned on me when the policeman holding my ID turned to look at him. The man nodded with a slow, accidental-looking movement of his head that must have been a pre-arranged signal. Yet even now I didn't get it.

'*Jude?*' asked the policeman.

'Of course me no *Jude*,' I replied in the broken German spoken by most Poles.

He repeated the word. This time, however, it was a statement of fact:

'*Jude!*'

'That's crazy,' I said. My confidence was still unshaken. 'I work for Hauptsturmführer Kunde. For Sturmbannführer Haase. For Herren Hujar and Frummer of the Gestapo.' Like rabbits from a hat, I produced all the names on Bialecki's gift list. Every one of them except Grete's. The policemen hesitated. The tall one's arm hung limply with my papers. In a second, I felt certain, he would hand them back to me and the whole thing would be over. I had no idea what went wrong or passed through the second policeman's mind to make him say:

'Just a minute. Let me ask about this.'

'What's there to ask about?' I said boldly.

'Shut your mouth!' ordered the tall policeman, stuffing my papers into the pocket of his uniform. His companion went over to the man in the hat and exchanged whispers. I watched them closely, beginning to feel uneasy. Although still not realizing that I was trapped, I had an ominous feeling. Justifiably, for the policeman returned to us, stuck a fist in my back, and propelled me toward a nearby building.

'In there, through that gate!'

I blinked my eyes in the dark, cobblestoned corridor. At one end of it was a stairway leading to the upper floors. The three-storey building was ancient, a historic landmark such as Cracovians were proud of. The policeman tried turning on the hall light. Whether because the switch wasn't working, or because the tenants had disconnected it to save electricity, nothing happened. The policeman swore. I could hear the grin in his companion's voice as he said:

'Save the curses for your wife. Let's finish with this Jew-bastard and have done with it.'

Were they about to shoot me and go their merry way? In my mind's eye I saw my body sprawled on the floor. I knew that the danger was real now and that only a miracle could save me. But I didn't believe in miracles.

'Pull down your pants,' ordered the shorter of the two men.

'I don't understand,' I said in an absurd attempt to gain time and ward off the inevitable.

'Hurry up, let's go,' the policeman prodded me, showing me with his hands what to do. Colonel Redl was still under my arm. I laid the book on the floor. The policeman picked it up, glanced at it, and threw it down again without interest.

The overhead light came suddenly on. At the end of the hallway a door creaked. It opened a crack, enough to catch a glimpse of a woman in a flowery house robe. She had an aquiline nose and curious eyes in a round face. For a second our glances met. Did she realize what was happening? I unbuckled my belt.

She stepped into the hallway, smiling at the Germans. They paid her no attention. I dropped my pants to my ankles.

'Your underpants, too.'

I did as I was told. I didn't know which was worse: my fear of inevitable detection or my shame at being stripped naked before a strange woman. Humiliated, I stood with my lowered underpants locking my legs, my private parts covered with my hand. The short policeman drew his pistol and pushed my hand away with the cold barrel. He took off his helmet, asked his companion to hold it, and bent over my shrunken member, which was as soft as an old rubber tube. He inspected it at length like a collector studying a new specimen, then straightened up and exclaimed angrily:

'The devil only knows!'

I felt a wave of relief. He didn't know a circumcised penis when he saw one. But my relief was premature.

'Go get our Jew. He'll know,' the short policeman told the tall one.

The man in the hat came quickly. He paused for a moment in the gate, his long shadow falling on me.

'What are you waiting for?' scolded the tall policeman.

'I'm coming, I'm coming,' the man apologized. His rubber soles rendered his steps soundless. 'What an idiot,' he mumbled in Yiddish. He didn't need to look at me for long. He straightened up immediately, his expression telling the police that I was the genuine article. The tall policeman pulled out my papers and read the address in them.

'Is this where you live?'

'Yes.'

'Who lives with you?'

'No one. I live alone.'

'Tell that to your grandmother.'

'My grandmother is dead.'

'We'll soon see about that. Let's go!'

The door at the end of the hallway swung shut, this time without a creak. Out of the corner of my eye I saw the woman disappear into her apartment. The man in the hat was gone, too. No one bothered to switch off the light. As we emerged in the street I remembered my book. *The librarian will be angry*, the ridiculous thought flashed through my mind.

The policemen ordered me to walk two steps ahead of them. I obeyed, knowing that my father would open the door not for me but for his own death. I hoped that my mother had not yet come home from work. Perhaps she might still get away. I prayed that if she did she would never find out how her husband and son had been caught.

The site of my arrest was a fifteen-minute walk from our apartment. None of the passers-by in the street associated me with the policemen. I walked ahead as if having nothing to do with them. I knew that their rifles were cocked. The slightest false move and they would shoot. It gave me no advantage to be faster than them or know the area better. I was already in invisible chains, a guide leading his executioner to the scaffold. Low in the west, the sun tinted the city a ruddy hue. I had a horrible feeling of guilt.

PART II

The Taste of Love

There be three things which are too wonderful for me,
yea, four which I know not:
The way of an eagle in the air;
the way of a serpent upon a rock;
the way of a ship in the midst of the sea;
and the way of a man with a maid.

Proverbs XXX, 19

13

The Swissair plane took off from Kloten Airport with the punctuality of a Swiss watch. It was 4.30 p.m. on Saturday, 17 July 1967. I planned to spend the night in Hamburg and take the hour's train ride the next day to Kiel, where I was to appear on Monday in the Federal German Court of the state of Schleswig-Holstein as a witness for the prosecution in the trial of ex-Gestapo officer Wilhelm Kunde.

It struck me as symbolic that this trial was taking place in the capital of a state that had been the last holdout of the Nazis. Some three weeks after the suicide of Adolf Hitler and sixteen days after Germany's final surrender, Schleswig-Holstein was still being governed by officials of the Third Reich. Its president was Admiral Karl Doenitz, the former chief of the German navy, an expert in submarine warfare who had enjoyed the full trust of the Führer. During his short term of office, he outlawed the Nazi Party in the hope of ingratiating himself with the Allies. On 26 May 1945 all the members of this bizarre government were arrested and Doenitz was tried and sentenced to ten years in prison.

There was a measure of historic justice in Kunde's being brought to trial in this remote corner of Germany. This was the only justice that interested me, although his long face still lurked in my memory and his polished boots were the last thing I saw from where I lay on the floor of his office while waiting for a bullet to put me out of my misery.

I had first encountered Kunde's name on the gift list of Bialecki & Potocki. Like most of his colleagues, he had no qualms about receiving little perks. But when our paths met again in a detention centre established in the emptied Cracow ghetto,

Wilhelm Kunde was fishing for something larger. He was out to hook my parents' assets, valued at tens of thousands of dollars.

The ghetto was evacuated of the last of its inhabitants in March 1943. Kunde took part in this action and was responsible for the transfer of the deportees to Plaszów, a concentration camp outside the city. His office was located in a building that had served as the headquarters of the Ordnungsdienst, the Jewish police. On paper this force was under the jurisdiction of the Judenrat, the Jewish committee that ran the ghetto's daily life, but inasmuch as the latter was a puppet of the Nazis, so were the Jewish police. They dressed in khaki uniforms and berets with yellow ribbons; their families enjoyed special privileges and their children were spared deportation. They also received special rations, which they supplemented by plundering the ghetto's poor. Some remained in the ghetto's ghost streets after the final evacuation to help mop up its last Jews; together with the Jewish informers, most were put to death later that summer. Many of these killings resulted from jurisdictional disputes between the Gestapo and the SS. While the Gestapo was in charge of Cracow, the SS ran Plaszów and both vied for the property of the murdered Jews.

The detention centre was in Nazi headquarters. Its original function had been the incarceration of escaped Jews caught on the 'Aryan side' of the city. Occasionally, Poles accused of looting were brought to it, too. These looters tried to keep a step ahead of the work teams sent from Plaszów every day to take stock of the ghetto's abandoned property. Cataloguing each item, piece of furniture, and article of clothing, they compiled lists of pots and pans, works of art, Persian rugs, medical equipment, and so on. Everything was recorded with German precision and shipped in sealed boxcars for storage in the warehouses of the Reich. Whoever sought to help himself to any of it was putting himself in mortal danger. Yet greed proved stronger than prohibitions. All kinds of adventurers risked their lives to get hold of what evaded the work teams. Rumours circulated of fabulous wealth hidden in cellars and attics. Night after night men stole into the ghetto and burrowed like rats through its remains. They went from one empty house to another, rummaging through dark lofts, slicing open mattresses, prying loose floor tiles, digging shafts in cellars, drilling holes in walls in search of strongboxes, ripping pictures from their frames. The lucky ones took their booty home. The luckless were brought to the Ordnungsdienst building and shot without trial. These executions were usually carried out in the early morning. Sometimes they woke me like an alarm clock.

In front of our prison, a long, one-storey structure, was a narrow space that we were allowed to walk in. It was a paved section of yard, an unroofed hallway adjoining the cell doors. We called it 'the pergola', since it was enclosed by rusty barbed wire on all four sides and overhead. The cells themselves were small and of concrete, with neither windows nor air vents. Each had three tiers of bunks and almost no room to stand. We relieved ourselves in a bucket that filled and overflowed every night, permeating the cell with a stench like a poisonous cloud that we came to smell of, too, having no opportunity to change our clothes. Although this kept the Germans out of our cells, its advantages were limited, since each cell had a kapo who ruled it ruthlessly. The more veteran prisoners had learned to get along with him. The newer ones were at the mercy of his whims.

It was this man who assigned me my place in an upper bunk. The ceiling was scant centimetres above me. Sometimes, forgetting its existence, I banged my head against it. The air was worse up here, smellier and with gases unknown to science. It lay on my chest like a millstone while I slept and drove nightmares up into my brain. One of these – the old, familiar dream in which I ran along a precipice pursued by a vague, half-human and half-bestial creature – kept coming back. Not daring to turn around, I ran for my life, knowing that the minute I was caught I would be ... but *what*? In the dream, my feet and heart racing with fear, I did not know. Panting breathlessly, I awoke into a daymare. This never happened quickly or easily. My waking senses refused at first to function. Even after opening my eyes I kept running as fast as I could while fighting off the thought that a new day of imprisonment was dawning. I hovered between two worlds, convinced I was really awake only when assailed by a powerful smell of excrement.

At 6 a.m. Jewish policemen opened the cell's doors, which remained unlocked until twilight. Whoever wanted could go out to the 'pergola' and stare like a caged bird at the rectangular, unpaved yard that lay between the cells and the Gestapo's offices. Most of us chose to do this.

The offices hummed with activity around the clock. On the second floor, where the senior staff had its rooms, Kunde of the Gestapo and SS Plaszów commander Amon Goeth conducted their private confrontations. Whenever Kunde murdered one of Goeth's Jewish agents, Goeth retaliated by killing one of Kunde's informers. Reports of the power struggle between them filtered down to us prisoners from the guards, whom we had bribed into a fairly friendly relationship. Some of us followed this conflict round by round, seeking guidance on how to behave. During a long interrogation, every bit of knowledge could be crucial. Although both Kunde and Goeth were seeking all the information they could get, telling the wrong one of them the wrong thing was sticking one's neck in a noose.

The ground floor was for more ordinary pursuits: the bookkeeping department, the intelligence section, the archives, the vehicle division, the statistics department so beloved of the Nazi bureaucracy, its data devoured hungrily in Berlin and by the offices of General Frank, the military governor of occupied Poland. Yet all this feverish activity, which occupied dozens of officers, NCOs, and adjutants, came to a halt when Wilhelm Kunde had guests. As though coming to see the exotic animals in a menagerie, VIPs in uniform and civilian dress flocked to Kunde's installation. As soon as we saw them stepping out on the balcony that overlooked the yard, we knew we were in for an ordeal. When the weather was good (all that May, not a single drop of rain fell) Kunde's visitors had an outdoor show put on for them. Ensconced in leather armchairs brought from abandoned apartments in the ghetto, they first listened to nostalgic songs played on an old gramophone. From behind the barbed wire of the 'pergola', I could easily recognize the faces of Bialecki & Potocki's regular customers – one of whom, although I could not have identified him, might have been Grete's husband. Kunde's one-armed adjutant, Rottenführer Ritschak, changed the records, and then drinks were served and the guests broke into song themselves. A favourite was 'Lily Marlene'. This was all a prologue to the main act.

Kunde was a talented and bloody director. At an order from him, Jewish policemen dragged into the yard a group of Orthodox Jews. 'They're simply too picturesque to resist,' I once heard Kunde say of them. Brought from various ghettos, the wretched men had spent their last night in the cellar of the building, ignorant and in isolation cells. Now, their moment on stage at hand, they were lined up in a row with their backs to the balcony and their bearded faces towards the walls of a ruined structure that bordered the yard to the north. Kunde addressed them in a quiet, almost fatherly voice:

'Someone else would kill you without mercy. But I am prepared to give you a chance to live. Do you see that wall facing you? The distance to it is no more than thirty metres. When you hear a gunshot, run. Whoever reaches the wall first will be spared. Show us you're as fast as Jesse Owens. Show us you deserve to live.'

The officers cocked their pistols, pulled their armchairs to the railing of the balcony, and leaned their elbows on it. They held their weapons with both hands as they were taught in target practice, fingers expectantly caressing the trigger. An ominous silence descended as Ritschak removed the gramophone needle from its record. The script was the same every time. Motionlessly watching the preparations for the massacre, we knew exactly what would happen next.

Kunde fired his pistol in the air. The Jews sprang forward, their black gaberdines flapping in the wind. The Nazis took aim and shot, rarely missing. The dead and wounded were dragged by their feet to the other end of the yard by the policemen, where they were waiting to be piled into a wagon. In the absence of a crematorium, they were buried in a mass grave in Plaszów. Sometimes the wagon was too heavy for the horses, who were whipped brutally by the policemen as if to vent their frustration on them. The few Jews who reached the wall unharmed were returned to the cellar to await the next performance.

'Once they finish off the ones with the beards, they'll start on us,' said the prisoner on my left.

I shuddered. His logic was impeccable.

But it remained an unfulfilled prophecy. Perhaps because most of us were still being interrogated, or perhaps because we weren't picturesque enough. A mere supporting cast, we washed the bloodstained yard with water.

I was summoned to Hauptsturmführer Kunde's office many

times, sometimes alone but generally with my mother. At first Kunde tried being pleasant. He wanted to know where we had hidden, who had helped us, where we had gotten our forged papers, who else was hiding outside the ghetto and where. 'I don't know,' I answered every question, a reply that sent him into a frenzy. He slapped my face, kicked me in the stomach and testicles, hammered my head against the table top. My mother looked on in silence. 'Talk,' he shouted at her, 'or I'll kill your son!' When his threats had no effect on her he reversed them, beating her viciously while asking if I wanted her to die. 'What's this, don't you Jewish children love your mothers?' he taunted when I still didn't talk. It was pointless to explain that I had no idea how my parents had obtained our papers and knew no other Jews living under an assumed Catholic identity, even though this happened to be the truth. And I would sooner have been torn to pieces than give away Jozef Kruczek or Zofia Sziwek.

Whenever we met in the 'pergola', my mother told me to keep mum and not be frightened by the beatings. She was sure Kunde would never carry out his threats. He had no interest, she said, in killing us. On the fateful day that I was asked to testify about in Kiel, the exact date of which I didn't know because I had no calendar or watch, my mother was waiting for me in Kunde's office. She sat in a chair in the middle of the room while he strode irritably back and forth, the polished wooden floor squeaking beneath his weight. My mother was wearing the tight green woollen dress she had been arrested in two months earlier; her usually groomed hair was unkempt, her skin was the colour of wax, and the lustre was gone from her eyes. In sixty days she had aged by ten years. A quick glance was all she cast at me before turning away. If she was seeking to transmit a message, I failed to get it. Kunde said nothing. Familiar with the procedure, I went and stood by the wall. He continued to pace, hands behind his back, face flushed from anger or alcohol. (Although he had good reason to be angry, he was also a man who liked to drink.) My mother had just accused him of not keeping his promise. They had had an agreement, she said: my life and hers in return for the family's valuables.

'I stuck to my half of it and you welshed on yours,' she flung at him.

Ritschak sat at a little desk in the far corner, typing one-handedly. He had lost his left arm in battle and its stump was concealed by a sleeve folded at the elbow and pinned to his uniform. Rewarded with a desk job, he did his best to please his master. Now he was taking down a protocol of the conversation.

'Where is a German officer's word of honour?' my mother went on as if she had forgotten whom she was talking to.

Kunde stopped pacing. Her boldness only stoked his fury.

'We've heard that story of yours. I have no idea what you're talking about.'

'I'm talking about my karakul fur, my jewels, and six thousand dollars in gold coins.'

'What Jewish nerve!' Kunde roared.

'It's you who have nerve for not keeping our agreement,' my mother shot back.

'I would never dream of making an agreement with a Jewess.'

'But you did.'

'That's a Jewish lie!'

'I'm not a Jewess. You know that.'

'Shut up.'

'Not until you keep your promise.'

Kunde struck his leather gloves against his boot. 'You're making it up!' he shouted. 'You'll pay dearly for your lies.'

'Are you denying that we went to Cracow, that I took you to neighbours of ours, and that you searched their house and found what I had left with them?'

'Of course I'm denying it. It never happened.'

'As God is my witness . . .'

'The only God here is me. And I've told you to shut up.'

'Not as long as I live.'

I watched astonishment mould his face, which quickly yielded to anger. Kunde was not used to prisoners answering back. Kunde was not used to being crossed. Kunde was the master. Kunde did not like the idea of my mother's words being in the protocol. Kunde knew what was done to an officer guilty of embezzlement. Kunde knew that his SS rivals were just waiting for him to slip. Kunde could not afford a living witness to his blunder. Kunde drew his pistol. Kunde stood behind my mother. Kunde raised the pistol above her head. Kunde brought it down butt-first. With one savage blow it split open my mother's skull. She didn't let out a sound. She crumpled and slid from the chair, her body thudding on the floor.

Ritschak sprang to the centre of the room.

'Stay where you are!' ordered Kunde.

Ritschak snapped to attention. 'Yes, Hauptsturmführer, sir!'

'Return to your place.'

'Yes, Hauptsturmführer, sir!'

Kunde turned to me as though noticing my presence for the first time.

'It's your turn, you little Jew pig.'

I braced myself against the wall. He saw this and said:

'Lie down.'

I obeyed.

'Closer to your stinking Jew mother.'

I moved closer until I felt my mother's warmth. Although she was no longer breathing, her body was deceptively hot. 'Mama,' I murmured, only realizing I would never hear her voice again when she failed to respond. Her body lay on one side, the face turned towards me. The only sign of violence was a bit of blood on her ashen cheek. Kunde nudged me with the tip of his boot as one does a whipped dog. His boots were so polished that they gleamed. He stood above me, legs apart, a fearful picture of authority. Cast in bronze, he would have made a classic Nazi sculpture.

'Did you see what happens to liars?'

His voice was calm.

I didn't dare open my mouth.

'Are you deaf?'

'I saw.'

'And you'll remember?'

'Yes.'

'As long as you live?'

'As long as I live, Hauptsturmführer, sir.'

He placed a foot on my stomach and pressed to test my reaction. My eyes popped from their sockets. He smiled with satisfaction.

'Did that hurt?' he asked with feigned concern.

I nodded. He aimed his pistol at me.

'I'll make it stop,' he comforted me.

I shut my eyes. The seconds passed. I felt them pulse like the artery in my wrist. I had just seen my mother die without a scream. Without even a groan or grimace. Death, it struck me unexpectedly, did not hurt. I opened my eyes. Kunde weighed the pistol in his hand, put it back in his holster, and burst out laughing.

'You're all a lot of dirty rats. Get up!'

As I rose on all fours he kicked me in the behind. I sprawled on my mother's corpse. Losing interest in me for some reason, he left the room with hasty steps. The door slammed behind him. I lay without daring to move. My mother's body grew cold beneath me. I could not say how much time passed before the telephone rang on Ritschak's desk. From the other end of the line came an order to return me to my cell. 'You've got more luck than brains,' Ritschak jeered as he handed me over to two Jewish policemen. My mother was buried that same day. I never found her grave.

On the train to Kiel, reclining in my soft, upholstered seat, I thought about that scene twenty-four years previously. Time is said to heal all wounds. Perhaps it does, because I felt no hate for the murderer. My only sensation was anger. Not at Kunde. At myself, for feeling no desire for vengeance. All I wanted was to see Kunde as scared on the defendant's bench as I had been on the floor. And this, too, was a minor satisfaction I could have done without.

I knew I would recognize him right away. Would he know who I was? I wondered if he would look me in the eyes when I took the witness stand to tell the judges of the day he split my mother's skull with his Parabellum, the standard weapon of a German officer. It was idle curiosity. The answer had no significance.

The train stopped for a minute at one of the quiet stations that were scattered along the line. A few passengers got off. A few got on. Ordinary people with unfamiliar, apathetic faces. None took any notice of me except for the ticket puncher. He took my ticket and we exchanged polite words.

The ticket puncher shut the door of the compartment behind him. His monotonous voice receded and was drowned out by the sounds of the train. I could make out the dialect of northern Germany. It was hard, different from my mother's Viennese. I found myself asking whether our fates are determined by pure accident. Does what happens to us have any relation to our desires, plans, and decisions, or do we blindly turn left or right at each crossroads with no understanding of what we are doing? And how much of life is the result of decisions made by others? I wondered what would have happened if my mother had not spoken German. It was her knowledge of the language of Goethe and Hitler that enabled her to establish a relationship with her murderer and talk her way to her death.

My mother had studied German as a girl in order to attend school in Vienna. She was fourteen when she left for the capital in the middle of the First World War, shortly before the death of the Emperor Franz Joseph. People like her mother, my grandmother, still believed in those days that the Austro-Hungarian empire would last for ever. Vienna was the eternal capital of culture, art, and manners, its opera and *Sachertortes* the epitome of civilization. It was only natural to seek to find Franya, as my mother was known at home, a suitable place to study and live. She was registered for a commercial high school and domiciled in a room in the 19th District, the petty-bourgeois neighbourhood of Doebling. A fifteen-minute tram ride from there, in the town of Grinzig, in one of the many taverns whose bartenders served cheap local wine, she met the handsome lieutenant on leave from the Italian front who was to become my father.

Franya had not been sent to a commercial high school unthinkingly. The decision was a practical one made by my grandmother, who had learned the hard way that a woman must be able to support herself.

The same year that the Tsarist army was routed by the divisions of Japan – that is, in 1904 – my grandfather, Solomon Rosenwiesen, staged a private flight of his own, packing his bags in the town of Borislav in eastern Galicia and unpacking them only when he reached Zurich. The wide world was beckoning and he had decided to conquer it without the help of cannon and machine guns. As I have observed, he left behind a wife and two children – my mother, named Franciska for Kaiser Franz Joseph, and her brother Max, named after the Hapsburg prince Maximilian, the hapless king of Mexico. These royal names were unable to help, however, when the promissory notes meant to support the family in my grandfather's absence turned out to be worthless. My grandmother was left without an income. Were it not for the modest help of some distant relatives, she could never have sent my mother to Vienna.

None of this, it must be said, affected my grandfather's entrepreneurial spirits or kept him from seeking his fortune far from home. For a year he studied and practised the art of watchmaking until Switzerland too grew too small for him and he journeyed to the Land of Unlimited Opportunities and opened a small jewellery store in Milwaukee. Soon his business sense told him to go south. He made a mint selling cheap watches and costume jewellery to poor blacks in Alabama and Mississippi and invested his profits in human capital, leaving behind an American heiress of thirty-three when he died at the age of nearly ninety in 1954.

My grandfather's story would not be complete without a brief word about Uncle Max. Two years younger than my mother, Max was educated in Poland. In 1930 he moved to Warsaw, where he obtained a good job as manager of the Polish branch of Meinl, an Austrian firm that was the biggest European importer of coffee beans, cocoa, and oriental spices. Following the Nazi *Anschluss*, the firm's Jewish employees were fired and Uncle Max went on an extended vacation to Italy. In Florence he met a certain Alice Schwartz. Together they admired the view from the Ponte Vecchio and crossed the bridge they had come to, parting with the vow to live the rest of their lives together.

Alice, a teacher from Chicago, returned to America, and Max went back to Warsaw to apply for a visa. The wedding was set for the autumn of 1939. On 30 August of that year Max boarded the Warsaw–Paris express, in his pocket a ticket for a New York-bound ship that was sailing from Le Havre in mid-September. Early on the morning of 1 September, while his passport was being checked at the German-French border, a French gendarme informed him of the invasion of Poland. The outbreak of hostilities caused the United States immigration authorities to cancel Max's visa and he was stranded on French soil.

The following summer, in June 1940, Max crossed the Pyrenees to escape the Nazis, who were at the gates of Paris. After wandering through Spain for a year he reached the Portuguese capital of Lisbon. There was no work there for illegal immigrants.

Only Alice's love letters, with their remittances that kept him from starvation, maintained Max's spirits in his cheap hotel room near the harbour. The appeals for help sent to his father went unanswered. Solomon Rosenwiesen saw no reason to help his son get to America. 'When I was your age, dear Max,' he finally wrote back, 'I learned to manage on my own.' This letter was shown to me by my Uncle Max when I first visited him in New Orleans. A quarter of a century had passed between the days in Lisbon and the muggy Louisiana summer night on which we sat on a bench in his garden while his American wife Louise poured cold lemonade into our tall glasses. Max told me:

'Lisbon during the war was an international centre of espionage. An illegal immigrant without money, a valid passport, or anyone to protect him was an obvious target for blackmail and extortion. Worse yet, the long months of idleness had frayed my nerves. I wrote long letters to your parents, all of which were returned with the stamp "Addressee Unknown". My father refused to take responsibility for me. I was desperate to reach America at any price – except that of taking further advantage of Alice, who was regularly sending me money from her meagre salary. Although the American authorities issued visas to applicants with affidavits from US citizens pledging to keep them off the public dole, my father's repeated refusals to sign such a form forced me to act on my own. In 1941 Cuba joined the Allies and opened its gates to refugees. A Jewish organization paid for my passage to Havana and underwrote my stay on a Cuban farm. After a year Alice missed me so much that she sent me the affidavit herself.

'Well, there I was, a straw hat on my head and nothing in my heart, on the deck of a ship being tied to a New York pier on which a slim figure was waving the brightly coloured silk kerchief that I had bought her in Florence. During the hard times I had lived through, I had fallen out of love with her. I can't tell you whether my feelings for Alice were left behind when I crossed the mountains into Spain, or whether they went down the drain in that flophouse in Lisbon. I can only say that if I hadn't gotten up the courage to tell her the truth on the taxi ride to my hotel, I would have ended up a bitter, unhappily married old man.

'Alice understood. We parted that day with a peck on the

cheek. I promised to pay her back from my first earnings. It took a few years before I could. I didn't stay in New York long. After seeing to a few pressing matters, I took the train to New Orleans. My father was waiting for me at the Roosevelt, the swankiest hotel in the South. I found him in high spirits. Although I didn't remember him, having been a baby when he left home, he greeted me as naturally as if we had parted the day before, settled into a red, upholstered chair, kicked off his shoes, handed them to me, and said: "Here, polish these. The bellboy gets five cents for them. I'll give you the special rate of a dollar." At first I thought this was his peculiar sense of humour. But he was far from joking. I took his shoes to the electric polishing machine in the corridor, feeling ashamed for myself and for him.

'There's not much more to tell. That dollar was the most I ever got from him. He didn't even come to my wedding when I married Louise or visit me in the hospital when I had a kidney removed. He was afraid he would be made to pay for the operation if it was discovered that I had a wealthy father.'

My grandmother did not live long enough to witness this, thus sparing her additional heartache. But she had been prescient enough to realize that her daughter needed financial independence. A profession, she believed, was the best nest egg for a rainy day. In the commercial high school in Vienna my mother learned ancient Greek and German stenography, Latin and touch-typing. She graduated cum laude, although it took a second world war to put her education on trial.

It was tested after we left Kruczek's cottage and moved back to Cracow. I suppose that what made my mother look for work was less the monthly salary than the certificate affirming that she had a steady job – and not just any job, but one deemed vital for the Nazi war effort. Such a document from the Bureau of Employment was valuable protection against the police squads that hunted down 'vagrants' in the streets and sent them to munitions plants in the Third Reich or to farms whose owners had been drafted.

My mother came across the opportunity quite by accident one day when her eye lit upon an ad placed by the occupation authorities in a Cracow newspaper:

> Military Organization Needs
> Secretary. Perfect Knowledge of
> German Required. Shorthand
> Desirable. All Applicants are
> Referred to the Officers' Club,
> Cardinal Sapieha Street. Morning
> Hours Only.

'It's made to order for me,' said my mother.

'I'd never let you take such an irresponsible risk,' my father objected. 'Wasn't that awful adventure in Lvov enough for you?'

My mother shrugged as if to say that she had stopped listening to him long ago. She jotted down the address and said, 'I'll go tomorrow.'

'Do as you wish,' said my father. 'But . . .' The word dangled like a warning, qualifying his capitulation.

He said nothing when my mother went for an interview the next day. His only reaction was to snort behind her back as she stood before the mirror putting on make-up and combing her hair.

'Women,' he murmured with a wry face.

'And don't make faces,' my mother said coyly, kissing him on the forehead before leaving. Three hours later she returned smiling blissfully and waving a piece of paper.

'What's the celebration?' my father asked. 'Have you won the lottery?'

'Better. I got the job.'

My father put on his glasses, examined the paper, and asked: 'Are you sure you can handle this?'

'I have experience, motivation, and, I hope, luck. Does that answer your question?'

I gave her a hug.

'Congratulations, Mother. I'm sure it's the start of a great career.'

'Just like Lvov,' grumbled my father.

'That wasn't so terrible, Wilek. We had a few good months there, have you forgotten?' She stroked his unshaven chin. 'You'll see, everything will be all right,' she reassured him. My father nodded unconvinced. He knew that from now on he would spend long hours by himself within the walls of our home that was not a home.

My mother quickly became the darling of the officers' club. Her Austrian accent gave her speech a special charm and she was complimented on her looks by more than one German who wooed her like a fellow countrywoman. Unaware that she was only deepening my father's depression, she told him of these conquests with pride.

My mother's job gave her a renewed sense of independence and created an illusion of normality. As she was sometimes asked to work overtime, she was given a pass allowing her to break the curfew. She even grew friendly with officers who bared their hearts to her and told her news of the front. Much of it cast a new light on things. General von Paulus' divisions had just surrendered at Stalingrad and von Paulus himself was taken prisoner by the Russians. In North Africa, Rommel was on the run. On 3 November 1942 he had retreated from Tobruk; on the 17th Derna had fallen; and on the 20th he had evacuated Benghazi. And while the British were turning the tide against him, the Americans had landed at Casablanca and the Free French had captured Tunis.

My father's annoyance gradually dissipated as my mother brought home more good news. It was just the shot in the arm that he needed. Every evening the two of them sat hunched over the newspapers that my mother brought home from work, struggling to decode the propaganda of Minister Goebbels. When the official Nazi paper spoke of a 'redeployment of forces', my mother was able to explain where and why the German armies had retreated. My father marked the shifting lines of the front on a map and read the progress of the fighting with the expertise of an ex-Austrian officer. Every communiqué announcing the appointment of a new general or field marshal was connected by my mother to the latest gossip about who had fallen out of Hitler's favour. The tongues of the officers at the club grew particularly loose when they had had one drink too many. As infantry commanders they did not have a high opinion of their colleagues with the skull insignia of the SS. But the SS was still firmly in control. Even German officers were afraid of it.

It was not just at the club that my mother was liked. Kunde, too, told her one day while in a good mood that he enjoyed having her at interrogations because 'it's a pleasure to hear your German.' At his trial he was to claim that he had never intended to murder her and was merely punishing her for her ties with the Polish underground. His attorneys stuck to this line of defence throughout.

My mother's interrogation took the form of private sessions with Kunde. Returning to the 'pergola', she would tell me about them. She was convinced that he was still fond of her and believed her story. A sophisticated enough lie to be credible, it was that she, the daughter of a good Christian family, had fallen in love with a Jew and sacrificed her social status for him and their child. Whereas my father could not deny his Jewishness because he was circumcised, my mother possessed the papers of a real Catholic woman whose death had been expunged from the records. Mixed children, according to the Nazi race laws, had the right to live outside the ghetto if this did not jeopardize the security of the Reich. Since the Gestapo's opinion was crucial in my case, everything depended on Kunde.

My mother made him an offer: her and my freedom and my father's life in return for our hidden property. Kunde accepted. My father was sent to Plaszów, from which we received a sign of life from him a few days later. It was now my mother's turn to keep her side of the bargain. 'Tomorrow Kunde and I are going to our Dluga Street apartment,' she told me upon returning from her next-to-last meeting with him.

Kunde took my mother in his official car, a black Mercedes with a Gestapo licence plate. He even gave her the quick tour of the city that she requested and invited her for a snack at a restaurant. From there they proceeded to Dluga Street. I hadn't known that just as she had left things with the Krols in Lvov, so in Cracow, too, she had deposited items with the neighbours. Her jewellery was hidden beneath the coal bin in our neighbour's basement and all her furs were in their closet.

The appearance of a high-ranking Gestapo officer was a shock to them. 'Don't worry,' my mother reassured them. 'He's only looking for property.' The neighbour's wife handed everything over while murmuring under her breath: 'They say no one comes back from Plaszów alive.'

Kunde put the valuables in a briefcase, draped the furs around my mother's shoulders, slapped the frightened neighbour's face, and snapped: 'Enough of this nonsense, let's go!' Back in the street, he opened the car door for my mother like a gentleman. Now, seeing me in the 'pergola', she whispered:

'I've bought our lives for a bargain.'

14

And just as lives could not be bought or sold like merchandise, wars were not won or lost on the battlefield. The taxi ride from the airport to downtown Hamburg made this clear to me. I had seen dozens of photographs of Hamburg in ruins. Gallons of crocodile tears had been shed for the destruction wreaked by the Allied bombings. Seen through the car window, however, Hamburg seemed a lively, prosperous, victorious place.

In Israel the Six Day War had just ended. I had followed it stage by stage as a prize-winning journalist, starting with Gamal Abdal Nasser's threat to destroy the Jewish state and ending with the intoxicating Israeli triumph. Dozens of war albums had been rushed into print and devoured by the public. Yet the distinguished Schwimmer Award for Journalism that was awarded me was for reporting the dark, other side of the six days that had stunned the Middle East: the story of the war's Israeli casualties.

Was it sheer coincidence that I took an interest in the suffering of victims whose physical injuries were secondary to their psychic ones? Most of them were not aware of the latter. The men I wrote about were soldiers and officers who had performed heroically on the battlefield and then fallen apart in bed with their wives; pilots who had penetrated deep into enemy airspace and cracked up after a safe landing. One, a man who had lost both legs, now sat in a wheelchair looking out at a different world from the one seen from his tank turret. Consumed by jealousy each time his wife left the house, his fears of betrayal swelled to monstrous proportions. In the end he locked her up in the villa given him as government compensation until she walked out on him one day, unable to bear it any more.

By contrast, there was the story of the devoted wife whose marriage hit the skids when her husband returned from an army hospital to embrace her with his prosthesis. His original arms had been shot off while storming a position near El-Arish and the same woman who had loved him to distraction was now overcome with disgust every time he took her in his metal ones. 'The stainless steel makes me nauseous,' she told a friend two days before entering a mental hospital. Haunted by delusions and frustration, her husband became a drug addict. He was not the only person I wrote about who failed to adjust to a new reality.

Was not this true of we Holocaust survivors, too? Here I was, dressed in a stylish suit, wearing a Givenchy tie, and smoking a Davidoff cigar, a blasé look on my face and a cruel scar in my soul. It was frozen, this soul. It had lost the ability to register emotion. Something had gone wrong with its metabolism. In twenty-four hours I would be facing my mother's murderer and it meant nothing to me.

The taxi driver spoke into his two-way radio and asked me politely if this was my first time in Hamburg. I didn't answer him. He strongly recommended St Pauli, he said. I would find it interesting. I didn't reply to this either. What, apart from the address of my hotel, did I have to tell this stranger?

He broke off his small talk and lost interest in me. The fact was that I was not really in Hamburg. It was as if someone had borrowed my exterior to make this trip while my thoughts remained far away.

Neither the trial ahead of me nor the war freshly behind me were on my mind. I was driving to the hotel in the shadow of a death. Not my mother's. Shula's. The woman I had left behind in Tel Aviv. Although she was only thirty-four, both of us knew that her condition was hopeless. Her illness was one of the many evils that had grown from World War II like a weed that the most skilful gardeners were unable to uproot.

Europe was under the boot of the Nazi conqueror when Shula's kidneys were first infected. It was a time of *sauve-qui-peut* when the long finger of the informer was the most feared weapon and Shula and her mother were in hiding in a God-forsaken Polish town. Calling the doctor meant putting one's life in unknown hands that could not be trusted. The Hippocratic Oath was in abeyance. A Jew handed over to the Gestapo was worth at least a kilogram of sugar. The infection gnawed at Shula's body like a worm at an apple.

In the 1950s, the Café Nitza on Tel Aviv's Allenby Street was a hang-out for new immigrants from Poland. Polish reigned so supreme there that even the Moroccan waitress learned to speak it. Only Herr Deutsch, the bald, paunchy old German-Jewish proprietor, insisted on speaking German. Herr Deutsch was an avid collector of our experiences, perhaps because he had few of his own. Not only did he keep track of all our little adventures, he shared them with everyone else. It was he who told me that Elisabeth, the good-looking Hungarian who for some reason frequented the Nitza, too, was not averse to casual affairs with young men. Before long I discovered that this tip was accurate. Although I was no longer the amateur at love that I once had been, Elisabeth took me down a few new paths to pleasure.

She was a married woman. Although her husband, an engineer, worked in Safed, far away in the Galilee, she had an apartment in north Tel Aviv that was paid for by a wealthy industrialist whose mistress she was. To explain her frequent stays there, she had invented a cover story about working as a model for a well-known fashion firm. Since her sexual appetite was unsatisfied by her ageing patron, she varied her lovers with people like me. Of course, I, too, had no exclusive rights over her love-hungry body – which was what ended our passionate relationship early in 1959.

Knowing that her industrialist would spend New Year's Eve with his wife, Elisabeth had decided to usher in the new year with a man from Haifa she was attracted to. Informing her husband that an important fashion show kept her from returning to Safed, she packed her nightgown (black silk, of course), toothbrush, and make-up kit, and took a cab to her new lover's home town.

What followed was a comedy of errors. Elisabeth's husband, stricken by longing, journeyed to Tel Aviv; opened the door of his wife's apartment with a key he had; found it empty; innocently concluded that she was still at work; undressed, got into bed, and fell asleep. Meanwhile, the industrialist, having brought his wife home from a party, made some excuse and headed straight for Elisabeth's flat. Opening the door with his own key, he slipped out of his shoes and tiptoed to surprise his sleeping mistress. The ensuing row was loud and violent. The angry neighbours summoned the police. 'I have to leave Tel Aviv,' Elisabeth told me a few days later. 'It's all over between us, but it was worth every minute.' What a woman!

It was in the Nitza that I also met Shula. Far from being an adventurer like Elisabeth, she was a serious intellectual looking for someone to help her translate the philosophical essays of Leszek Kolakowski, a Polish thinker with a reputation in the West. I volunteered. We became friends. Before the translation was done we were living together.

It was now some two years since I had arrived in Israel with my wife Mira, my five-year-old son Avigdor (who was named Witek as a baby), and my adopted eleven-year-old daughter Ariella (born as Frania). Mira had not wanted to leave Poland. Looking back, it was unfair of me to tear her away from it, especially since I was tired of our marriage and should have realized it was coming to an end. This wasn't Mira's fault. She was blameless. So was Shula, who was only the trigger.

The crisis was worse than I had imagined. At first Mira asked no questions when I began coming home late or not at all. One night, however, returning with Shula's perfume still on me, I found her unconscious in bed. It was impossible to wake her. I called for help. A doctor friend who hurried over took a look at her and said: 'I'm sorry, but this is one mess I can't get you out of. You'll have to call an ambulance. Your wife has overdosed on sleeping pills.'

I took Mira to the hospital. Her stomach was pumped at 2 a.m. At 3 a.m. she opened her eyes, saw me standing there, and murmured:

'Leave me and I'll do it again.'

A nurse and doctor were standing by the window. I bent down and spoke softly to keep them from hearing:

'I don't believe in marriage at gunpoint.'

It was a cruel answer. I knew, though, that I could no longer go on feeding Mira lies and deceptions. It was too critical a situation for promises I couldn't keep. The nurse excused herself to the doctor and came over. Her angry look told me she had heard all.

'Please, we'd like to be left alone,' I said.

'Your wife is a wounded woman,' she answered sternly. 'She needs to be left alone by you. She needs rest.'

I left.

A week later Mira and I sat down to agree on a divorce. Whilst still agitated, she had sobered up considerably. She had drawn up a balance sheet of my sins and estimated the damage at five thousand Israeli pounds – a sum, slightly greater than my annual income, that it did not seem possible to pay. She also wanted our apartment minus our children, who she insisted remain in my custody. Although our lawyer, a mutual friend, was taken aback by her decision to surrender them, I knew her background and could understand it. The lawyer wrote the agreement on a sheet of paper. I was to put five thousand pounds in escrow and transfer ownership of the apartment to Mira. The bank would release the money to her when she brought them our final divorce papers.

Although Shula had a two-room apartment, her parents were adamantly against my moving into it. A provincial couple, they disapproved of their only daughter living out of wedlock with an older, married man who had two children and no money. I had no choice but to rent a modest flat. A few days later Shula moved in with me.

Shula's parents could not stand the disgrace. Rosa, her mother, asked to have a talk with me. It was to be a secret, she said. Not a word was to be breathed to her husband or daughter. We met on a park bench, like two secret agents. She handed me a package wrapped in newspaper and tied with twine.

'What's this?' I asked. 'A bomb?'

'You might call it that,' answered Rosa. 'The whole town is gossiping about Shula. It's too much for us. Like any good Jewish housewife, I had some money put away. You're holding it now. Five thousand pounds in cash. Put it in the bank and get your divorce as quickly as you can. If my crazy daughter wants a man like you, let her at least have a proper wedding.'

'Thank you.'

'By the way, my husband wants you to know that he'll double the sum if you give Shula up entirely. How about it?'

We were married early in 1961. Although we had wanted a modest ceremony, we found ourselves in a large hall with an orchestra, cocktails, and a meal for two hundred guests. Had Shula's parents given us half of what the wedding cost them, we would have gotten off to a good start in our new life. But Rosa and Bernard were more concerned with making an impression.

That same night we set out in a rented jeep for our honeymoon by the Sea of Galilee. On our return, we had to start supporting four people. But the biggest problem was not financial. Avigdor and Ariella did not understand the legal steps taken by their mother, could not comprehend their separation from her, and openly rebuffed all Shula's attempts to be a loving stepmother.

This was long before we found out that Shula could never have children of her own.

The truth about Shula's physical condition came to light in Switzerland during the second, delayed part of our honeymoon several years later. The trip had been planned to begin in Europe and end in Canada, to which we had been invited by Shula's Uncle Henry. Unlike Shula's mother, Henry was a man with broad horizons who had made a great deal of money and believed in living and letting live. My friendship with him, commenced on my wedding night, has lasted through all the ups and downs of my life. The secret knowledge that Shula had a fatal disease had been kept from him as it had been kept from us.

I can only guess why Shula's parents never told her the truth. The psychological barrier that they faced, I believe, was composed of equal parts of shame and guilt. Perhaps they feared being blamed for her condition, or perhaps they simply lacked the courage to tell her what she could expect. It was only on the eve of our departure for Europe, when Shula had finished packing, that her mother said casually:

'Do you remember Professor Schaffhausen from Zurich? I've spoken with him on the telephone. He's expecting you on Friday, at ten o'clock.'

'What for?' snapped Shula, who had a quick temper that rarely lasted long.

'Just a check-up. You know how it is. It's always better to be safe.'

Thus I discovered that Shula, who did not even have a medical file in Israel, had already been to see a renowned Swiss kidney specialist. Until now, however, she had not been told her true condition. This time, after an intensive examination, the doctor said to her:

'Mrs Frister, you must under no circumstances get pregnant.'

It was impossible to get more out of him. He was as committed to confidentiality as a Swiss banker. 'I'll send the diagnosis by mail to Israel,' he insisted. 'And don't worry about the bill, young lady. Your parents have already taken care of it.'

Shula left the doctor's office nervously biting her lower lip. I was sitting outside in the large waiting room. The receptionist, a well-groomed woman with a white smock, curly, copper-coloured hair, and a neck long enough to model for Modigliani, had helped me pass the time with small talk about the weather, the superior quality of handmade Swiss watches, and the shameless Japanese invasion of a market that had been a Swiss preserve for centuries. Noticing Shula's pallor, she offered her something to drink with professional, emotionless concern. Shula looked right through her. I hurried out after her. By the elevator I asked:

'For God's sake, what is it?'

The elevator arrived, a modern machine that descended in silence. We leaned against opposite sides of it, in a cage detached from the world. Shula stared in the mirror.

'I'm no longer a woman,' she said.

'You don't look like a man,' I tried joking.

'That isn't funny.'

'What did the doctor say?'

'That I can't have children.'

'So what? You'll take pills.'

'You don't get it. Or else you don't want to,' she answered and fell silent.

The elevator dropped to a gentle stop on the ground floor. I held the door for her. We crossed the lobby and stepped into the street. A light drizzle was falling. Its thin drops wet Shula's hairdo. I opened an umbrella. She pushed it away as though to make no more concessions to her feminine looks. She walked at a distance from me. Soon her eye shadow began to melt too. I couldn't tell if the rain or her tears were washing it onto her cheeks.

There was a smell of autumn in the air. We passed a yellowing chestnut tree. I thought of the wonders of nature, which allow a tree to lose its leaves and blossom again undiminished. Shula tightened the belt of her coat. To this day, whenever I think of her, it's making that movement, next to the chestnut tree.

Being a woman meant being a mother. And being a woman was everything for her. Not in a feminist sense. She needed a man by her side. But now that the centre had dropped out of it, life had lost all significance. This didn't mean that she had to put an end to it, she said. But from now on it would be like food without salt. Tasteless.

How differently we looked at things! An expert at rationalizing, I could always explain that if I stumbled this was better than falling, and that falling enabled me to get more firmly back on my feet. Had my first and second marriages failed? This was only in order to make a third, better one possible. The belief in luck was built into my character.

Shula was not like that. She did not have the convenient knack of calling black white, or at worst grey. She was a woman incapable of self-deception and she paid dearly for her honesty. Now, too, she objected to my suggestion that we continue our trip. 'How long can we make-believe?' she asked. 'How many times will you have to pretend that you don't see my mood?'

It was pointless to argue. We sent Uncle Henry a telegram saying: 'Sorry we won't be coming,' and took the first flight back to Israel. Shula's parents were waiting for us at the airport. My father-in-law sat silently behind the wheel of his beloved Opel. My mother-in-law chattered nonsensically without once referring to the fact that we had unexpectedly cut short our second honeymoon.

The next day Shula was examined by an Israeli specialist who told her everything. Not only could she never give birth, her situation would only get worse. In all seriousness she suggested: 'We'll have to get divorced.'

'Don't be ridiculous,' I said. 'I have children from my first marriage. That's enough.'

'It's not the same thing.'

Intellectually, I understood her distress. Emotionally, I didn't feel it. Perhaps this was because I had never paid much attention to my own children. Once I wrote to my daughter that I wouldn't even win a bronze medal in an Olympic competition for fatherhood. I can remember how, after the war, watching blissful young mothers walk their babies in the park and bend lovingly over carriages to arrange a pillow or return a pacifier to a mouth, I felt no happiness for them. All I could think of was the nights they had made love while I lay in some concentration camp, never knowing what the morning would bring.

We met to talk in a small Tel Aviv café whose tables spread out on the sidewalk. Shula ordered fresh orange juice. I asked for an espresso. The crowds of people at the nearby tables and in the street created a paradoxical sense of privacy. No one took the slightest interest in us. Shula spoke almost in a whisper, without emotion. Her voice was drowned out by the din around us. I had trouble making out the words.

'I can't hear you,' I said. She knew that in the camps I had lost the hearing in my right ear.

'It's pointless to go on,' she said more loudly. 'Even if you can accept me as I am, I'll always feel that I've cheated you. I'll never be at peace.'

'But I don't feel cheated,' I said.

'You're an idiot.' She put a finger to my lips. 'One day you'll wake up and think badly of me. I know you. I can take it. It's you who can't.'

'You're insulting me.'

'No. I just want you to be realistic. If you want to run away from the truth, you'll have to run away from me.'

'We'll live through this phase together,' I declared.

'It's the only phase there'll ever be.'

'I love you,' I said.

But as soon as I said it, I wasn't sure that it was true. The one thing that was clear to me was that I was never going to abandon her, no matter how rough it became. Or so I thought. I had yet to experience married life as a long term on death row in which only one of the condemned believes in a pardon.

Shula walked towards her death with open eyes. If she was afraid, she never showed it. She made a point of carrying on with her daily routines, doing her translation work and housework, and entertaining friends as if nothing were the matter. Once the last of them was gone, she would collapse exhaustedly in bed.

She wasn't beautiful. It was her charm and intelligence that enamoured me. If such a thing is possible, I was in love with a personality. Yet the sicker she grew, the more sexual she became. Soon this became a nightmare for both of us. Even on those days when her blood pressure rose so high that her heart was literally in danger of shattering, she gauged life by my wanting to make love to her. High-strung and obsessive, she demanded proof from my body that she was still desirable. If she couldn't arouse it she would say:

'You think I'm a corpse already.'

No rational argument could substitute for the moments when my spontaneous passion still testified to her being the queen of her own bed. My tension and fear made these rare, however. No amount of manual stimulation could bring about the miracle. Her desperate attempts to coax sex from the void poisoned the atmosphere. Her doctors had warned me that the slightest physical exertion could prove fatal for her. The thought immobilized me each time she came close to me. My impotence sent her into tantrums of rage and tears. We were torturing each other. I suppose this was why I didn't have a guilty conscience when another woman appeared on the scene. But no woman on earth could make me leave Shula. The worse her health became, the stronger our bond grew. Invited to testify in Kiel, I was loath to leave her. I didn't know if she would be there when I returned. It was she who insisted: 'You have to help convict that man. It's your duty to your mother. Nothing can excuse you from that.'

She could fool everyone but her own body. Within a year she had reached the point where her doctor, an honest man who admired her courage, recommended dialysis. Unlike Professor Schaffhausen of Zurich, Professor Yosef Rosenfeld of Tel Aviv believed that his patients should know the whole truth. This alone could make them, as he put it, 'masters of their fate'. Without mincing words he explained that he could not refer Shula to a public hospital. The dialysis machines were in such short supply that he was obliged to give priority to patients with better prospects of recovery.

'Just what are my prospects?' she asked.

There were four of us in his office: Shula, her mother, Uncle Henry who had come from Canada, and myself. After a good ten seconds of silence, the professor's words were like stones dropped down a well:

'Dialysis won't save your life. It can prolong it, though.'

'By how much?' Shula asked.

'I'm only a doctor, not God.'

'Don't play games with me, Doctor. By how much? A month? A year?'

'Medicine is not mathematics. I can't answer that. I can promise you several reasonably good months.'

'In your terms. Not in mine.' That was the end of it. Shula

patted Uncle Henry's hand while turning down his generous offer to pay for private treatment and abruptly cutting short her mother's pleas:

'Cut out those phoney tears,' she said harshly.

'How can you talk to me like that?'

'Everyone has his style. Mine may be crude. But at least it's not fake.'

'You're unfair.'

'So are you, Mother.' The conversation lapsed into a long silence.

Shula's relations with her mother had never been smooth. Her bouts of belligerence were met by Rosa's evasive reactions. Always on the defensive, her mother played the injured party. Deep in Shula's unconscious, I suspected, behind all her talk of a generation gap, were sadness, resentment, and anger at not having been given the medical attention that might have cured her when she was young. Her conflict with her parents had made her leave home at an early age and lead an independent life. She had bought a small apartment in Tel Aviv with German reparations money and furnished it according to her own taste. After our marriage, she forbade her mother to visit us uninvited. Each time that Rosa called to make an appointment, Shula found some reason to put it off.

Her parents were against our relations from the start. Married; with small children and no means; a new immigrant living in a rented apartment; a correspondent for a low-circulation left-wing paper: I was not the son-in-law of their dreams. True, had it not been for Rosa's money we would probably never have gotten married. But this did not soften Shula's attitude. Only when she was bedridden and no longer had the strength to oppose them did she begin to agree to her mother's visits.

By then I had ceased to be an embarrassment. I was now assistant editor of the weekend supplement of *Ha'aretz*, a prestigious liberal daily, and a member of the board of directors of the Journalists Association with several awards to my name. For someone who had been unable to read the Hebrew alphabet ten years earlier, this was no mean achievement.

Two days before the Jewish New Year, I was going over the proofs of our holiday edition when Rosa called my office with a clipped announcement: 'I'm afraid Shula has had a heart attack. I've called the doctor.'

I hurried home. Shula died before either the doctor or I could arrive. Her mother covered her head with a sheet. Her face, despite the ravages of her illness, was lovely and serene.

15

If not for Shula's insistence, I might never have flown to Germany for Kunde's trial. Was she right? Although I was already on the plane from Zurich to Hamburg, I still failed to feel the sacred obligation that she had spoken of so passionately. The longer the flight took, the thicker grew the partition between me and my memories. I was gazing at the fleece of white clouds over which the plane rode when a young woman's voice pricked the bubble of my indifference:

'What would you like to drink, sir?'

A stewardess in a blue uniform was leaning toward me. Her silk neckerchief smelled of expensive perfume. Although Shula always wore Ecisson, I had no difficulty making out the scent of Joy. I glanced up. She flashed a polite smile. Beneath her heavy make-up lurked fatigue.

'Coffee, please.'

'Anything alcoholic?'

'No, thanks. Just coffee.'

She turned to the man in the aisle seat on my left. I had paid him no attention in the twenty minutes that had elapsed since our take-off from Kloten.

'And you, sir?'

'Beer,' the man said curtly. As she was proceeding to the next row he added:

'Pilsen. And make it cold.'

He had a stern face and deep voice that annoyed me. A man of about sixty, he was immaculately dressed except for his slightly askew, brightly checked Hermes tie. His tweed jacket came from Savile Row in London.

The stewardess returned on a cloud of Joy and placed our drinks on our folding tables: fragrant coffee for me and foaming beer for my fellow passenger. He emptied it in one long draught. I watched his Adam's apple bob up and down. He held the container in his left hand. His right hand was missing a finger. Perhaps that was why he wore his wedding ring on his pinkie. When he finished drinking he turned to regard me with the sated smile of a man whose thirst has been quenched. With the back of his hand he wiped a drop of foam that clung to his upper lip. Seeing the weekend *Ha 'aretz* in my lap, he asked in poor, German-accented English:

'That is a Hebrew newspaper?'

'Yes.'

My laconic reply was meant to convey my lack of interest in continuing the conversation. He did not take the hint.

'You come from Israel?'

'Yes.'

'I take off my hat to you.'

'You're not wearing one,' I said rather humourlessly.

'Great work! Great work you have done in Sinai! So many Egyptian tanks I have seen kaput on the TV. Better work has done not the Desert Fox.'

I nodded politely at the reference to Rommel. He took this as encouragement to go on:

'You were at the front?'

'Yes.'

'That is good. That is very good. One must fight. I understand very well battle. In the war I was officer in Waffen SS. The armoured corps. I understand fire and movement. Fire and movement. Like Rommel. Like Guderian. But better. May I shake your hand for admiration? Soldier to soldier.'

Before I could answer he had grasped my hand and was shaking it firmly. The last of the coffee spilled on the table top and dribbled on my lap, wetting my newspaper. I pulled my hand away. Feeling my revulsion, he murmured:

'Excuse me. I think there is not reason for anger. I was just soldier and *mein Herr* was just soldier. I have no feeling against Jews. I have no bad thoughts for them. Never did I injure civilians. Waffen SS was army: only war. Only war. Against Communists. For civilization. Now I make business. Pharmaceuticals and chemicals. For CIBA. *Mein Herr* has heard of CIBA?

It is Swiss pharmaceutical company. So many years have passed.
It is not possible ... not possible ...'

'What is not possible?'

'Emotions, *mein Herr*, are not good. It is not possible to live
only in the past.'

I didn't answer. Although I, too, wanted to keep the past at
arm's length, it kept returning like an unexpected guest. No
psychiatrist can remove on request the memories we would like
to erase. I was not in control of my thoughts. A spring had
uncoiled within me, freeing from one of the millions of cells in
my brain an incident that I wanted to forget – or, rather, that I
believed had been expunged for good. Now – damn its stubborn-
ness! – it was back again.

'Please ...' I said without finishing.

The German nodded understandingly. 'All right, *mein Herr*. I
have not the intention to hurt.'

A minute later he rose and moved to an empty seat at the back.
I tried to return to my newspaper. The letters refused to make
words. The words did not form sentences. The sentences had no
meaning. The jet engines hummed in my ears like a barricade
against reality. They reminded me of the jammed Western
stations we used to get on East European radio. I tried to
concentrate on Shula and our home. Strange drums pounded in
my temples. Kunde, Kunde, Kunde. SS uniforms. A pistol butt. A
blow. Silence. Death.

Damn whoever it was who once said to me: 'You can't always
think what you want.'

The desk clerk in the Prince Bismarck Hotel found my name on
the reservations list at once.

'Welcome to Hamburg, Herr Frister,' he said, handing me a key
attached to a wooden pear and a garish brochure describing the
city's red-light district. 'The elevator is at the end of the hall.' Did
I need any help with my luggage?

All I had was one suitcase packed by Shula.

'Thank you, I'll manage,' I said and went to my room.

It was large and high-ceilinged. The furniture combined the
genteel and the functional; a double bed with a brass bedhead
stood against the wall. All it was missing was a velvet canopy. I
placed my suitcase on a closet shelf; took out my electric shaver,

stowed it beneath the mirror in the bathroom; and sat on the edge of the huge bed whose soft pliancy made me feel that I was sailing over water. I took off my jacket and glanced at the brochure I had stuck in my pocket. The strange symbiosis of this solidly bourgeois hotel and its listings of strippers, X-rated bars, pornographic transvestite shows, and call-girls from all over the world with special discounts for tourists made me smile. Five months ago I had turned thirty-nine. I had never been with a whore in my life. The idea of paying for what should be obtained by the age-old exchange of feeling for feeling, pleasure for pleasure, was repugnant.

The brochure promised a release from every tension; a respite from every worry; total nirvana in the arms of the latest Thai import; the disco-drowning of all inner discord; and, of course, the final purging of the day's problems in an orgiastic jacuzzi. I laid it on the marble night table, undressed, and slipped under the blanket without washing.

The starched sheets were cool and pleasant. I reached for my unfinished newspaper. There were still coffee stains on the front page. I let it drop to the floor. It was early. I was afraid of not being able to sleep. The train for Kiel left at six in the morning. I dialled the operator to ask for a wake-up call. The minute I turned out the light I fell into a sleep in which I dreamed a strange dream:

I was walking in a strange German city. It bore no resemblance to Hamburg or to Kiel as I imagined it. Yet there was no doubt that I was in Germany. The streets, whose houses were for some reason all painted dark brown, were unfamiliar. Each house had rows and columns of windows and every window was decorated with red flowers in white window boxes. An old, toothless woman leaned on one of these boxes, leering at me disgustingly. I didn't know who she was. Our glances met. The leer ceased and she grew serious.

The sky above me kept changing. Like backdrops in a theatre, it was now a brilliant blue, now so grey and sombre that I had to strain to see, although the sun was still shining and there wasn't a cloud. I strolled about the strange city, looking at the crowds. Faces floated towards me. Some were long, some round, some happy, some sad, some good, some bad, some indifferent and expressionless. A hoarse voice whispered to me that all wished to harm me.

I tried to see where this voice was coming from. Looking up, I saw that the speaker was the old woman in the window. Although I tried resisting her words with all the power at my dream's disposal, the toothless old hag refused to desist. *Go away, damn you*, I begged her, *go to somebody else's dream* – but she paid no heed and I knew I would have to put up with her. Just then she pointed to a policeman who was politely stopping traffic for her to cross the street. Only how could she cross the street when she had never left the window? Before this question could be answered the policeman turned into Wilhelm Kunde. The old woman took his hand and they approached me slowly, the policeman in high boots, the woman with crooked legs. The crowds were gone. Only the two of them remained, their arms outstretched as though to embrace me. The woman touched me, scalding my skin . . .

It was dark. What was I doing in a fabrics store? The salesman stroked a bolt of red silk with some tiny pattern. It was the same silk that the German's tie was made of on the airplane. But it was no longer soft and delicate. Thorns grew from it. It pricked the hand of the salesman. Blood flowed. I tried making out his face but it was hidden in mist and the effort exhausted me. I asked him to look at me. He shook his head. The old woman laughed raucously. The houses of the strange city were painted red. An orchestra played in the background. I knew the melody. It was 'Lily Marlene'. Couples danced the tango. A man stood off to the side, observing them critically. It was Wilhelm Kunde. His eyes were set deep in their sockets above a hooked nose that curved to thin lips. I hadn't wanted to see him. Enough! I was weary of so many faces. I didn't want to go on looking for my mother, whose face I could not recollect. It was as if it no longer existed. I sank into a black, bottomless hole. Perhaps it was the abyss of oblivion. Perhaps it was a common grave. I fell and fell. My wake-up call woke me.

I opened my eyes. A frail light shone through the curtains. I picked up the telephone, still half-asleep. A woman's voice said:

'Good morning. It's six o'clock.'

I replaced the receiver, feeling my dream fade. I tried to hold onto it, to gather its pieces that were scattered all over the room.

Not until I had fixed its content in my mind did I emerge from my trance.

Today, I think of it as a dream that I would gladly forget. As something I lost control of, so that it stuck to me like a leech. Now I release it in the pages of this book. Perhaps it will stay in there and die. Perhaps.

The train pulled into Kiel on time. German trains are never late. I stepped onto the platform, its glass roof forming a transparent umbrella above me. I was heading for the exit with my suitcase when a young woman approached me and said:

'I hope you had a good trip, Mr Frister.'

How did she know who I was? Did I transmit some identifying signal that made her act towards me like an old friend? I said:

'Excuse me, but have I ever had the pleasure . . .'

'No. We've never met. Not physically, anyway. But I do know you – or, more precisely, your biography. I'm referring to the period of your life because of which you're here in Kiel. Please don't look so amazed, Mr Frister. I'll explain everything. Is this your only bag?'

'Yes. I didn't pack for a vacation.'

She took exception to that:

'That was unnecessary, Mr Frister. But I understand how you feel.'

'I didn't mean to offend. By the way, miss, I still don't know in what way I can help you.'

'It's I who am here to help you. Or, rather, to take care of your arrangements, such as your hotel, restaurants, taxis, all that. I belong to a charitable organization of the Lutheran Church. The Church has made itself responsible for people like you. So far we have had twelve witnesses from all over the world and we wish to show them that there is another Germany. We view this as part of seeing that justice gets done.'

'Can justice accomplish now what it didn't when it should have?'

'I don't know,' she shrugged. 'I was a girl when all that happened. But if it's pointless to try rectifying the past, it's also pointless to bring Kunde to trial.'

'You may be right. Forgive me.'

'There's no need to apologize. Do you have a hotel reservation?'

'No.'

'I'd like to recommend the Rebs Hotel. We've reserved a room for you there. Of course, you can always go elsewhere if you're not happy with it. There are lots of hotels in Kiel. It's a hospitable city. My car is parked in front of the terminal. Please follow me.'

She had an old Volkswagen, which she drove like a fancy sports car. She was about thirty, with a pretty, make-up-less face. Her dark blue cotton dress had sleeves up to the elbow and a white collar like a high school uniform's. She had a simplicity and innocent charm.

'May I ask what your name is?'

'Good Lord, I've been talking so much that I forgot to introduce myself! You see, I only look quiet and calm. I'm really quite excited. This is the first time I've ever done this kind of thing. I didn't know how you would take to me . . . My name is Trude. Trude Van Gluck. I'm originally Dutch, as you may have guessed.'

We drove down what seemed a main thoroughfare. Blattstrasse, said a sign on the corner. 'It's not far,' Trude said. Without being asked, she began to tell me about her family. Her father, a Flemish doctor and follower of the Belgian fascist leader Anton Mussert, volunteered for the SS and died on the eastern front. How, was unclear. In his last letter he had written that he did not believe he would survive the Belorussian winter. He was posthumously awarded the second order of the Iron Cross.

'I hope I haven't upset you with my story. It's very personal, but I felt the need to tell it. To you especially.'

'That's fine. I'm not a very emotional type.'

'You're not tired?'

'Not at all.'

'I can suggest a short tour of the city. After you're checked into your hotel, of course. Today is Sunday. I like Kiel on Sundays. The weather is exceptionally good today. Usually we never go out without an umbrella.'

'I'll be glad to see the sights with you.'

The tour, by car and foot, took a long while. Although I did not find Kiel as beautiful as my guide did, I kept this to myself. What I liked best was the port area and the North Sea canal. This was much narrower than I had imagined and the ships in transit from the North Sea to the Baltic were much larger. Most flew foreign flags. The downtown buildings, typical of northern Germany, were not to my taste. Their bare, unplastered brick walls made entire streets look like barracks. We stopped before the huge building of the courthouse. It, too, was build of red brick, with neo-classical columns to soften its façade. Across from it, in Shutzgraben Park, young people lounged on the grass. Looking at them reminded me that there was a new generation in Germany.

On the way back to the hotel we stopped to eat at a restaurant. A waiter brought us menus. Trude Van Gluck put hers aside.

'Perhaps it was wrong of me to tell you about my father and his medal,' she apologized.

'I've already told you that it was perfectly all right.'

'I can see you're very polite. Your father was a lawyer, wasn't he? A good bourgeois family. It's no wonder you're so well mannered. And your German is so fluent. For a moment I forgot you were a Jew. I mean, an Israeli. It's not the same thing, is it? Under the circumstances, I shouldn't have said what I did. But I so wanted you to understand me. I mean, to try to understand me.'

'I do understand, Fräulein Van Gluck.'

'Call me Trude. I know what happened to your mother. But what happened to your father?'

'He died in a camp.'

'I'm sorry.'

'So am I.'

'I've done it again! I mean, I've blundered. Please forgive me. Perhaps I shouldn't have taken this assignment. There are many women in Kiel who would never have dreamed of volunteering for it. But I so wanted to help. I wanted to be part of the *Wiedergutmachen* that you look down on. I do hope you'll understand. Every little thing left of my father, even his Iron Cross, is heartwarming for me. It's not that I care about heroism. But I'm told that he risked his life for soldiers wounded on the battlefield. Your own Torah says that the man who saves a single life . . . Do you know that verse?'

'I know it.'

'I must emphasize that there is no connection between my feelings as a daughter and my feelings about the times my father lived in. I'm a Christian and Nazi ideology is abhorrent to me, as it must be to any believer in God. Are you a believer?'

'No.'

'That's too bad. My faith is enormously important to me. It has been a great source of comfort. My mother sees it differently, but that's her business. She lives in a world of memory, cut off from life by an advanced case of muscular dystrophy. If not for the small pension that she gets from the state, I don't know how she would manage. Our house was destroyed in an air raid. We were left with nothing. I mean, with next to nothing. Are you listening, Mr Frister?'

'I'm listening.'

Was she cleverly trying to equate the suffering of the Nazi conqueror with the victim's or simply naively attempting to get close to me? I didn't bother to find out. We parted upon our return to the hotel. My 'thank you' must have made it clear that I did not want us to meet again. I started up the stairs, feeling her standing there with her eyes on me. I wanted to turn around and wave. I didn't. I went to my room and asked for a connection to Tel Aviv. Shula assured me that she was feeling better. I knew she was lying.

He wasn't the Wilhelm Kunde of my dream. He wasn't even the Wilhelm Kunde of the newspaper photograph that Trude showed me in the restaurant between the minestrone soup and the tongue with sauerkraut.

How had I expected him to look? I couldn't have said. I certainly had not expected to find an old man who sat in the dock of the Kiel courtroom like a spectator who had wandered by mistake into the wrong performance. Had he borne the slightest resemblance to the omnipotent Gestapo officer I knew in Cracow, I certainly would have felt something. But the silent, withdrawn man in the grey suit two sizes too big for him seemed little more than a harmless doll. Grown-ups don't get worked up over dolls.

The courtroom attendant called my name and led me to the witness stand. I was not asked to take an oath. One of the two defence attorneys threw me a frozen glance. The other bowed stiffly from the waist. The prosecutor leafed through his brief. The judges sat on a high podium. All I could see of them was their black robes. The next day it was reported in the newspapers that I testified emotionlessly. That was true. Kunde seemed to awaken the minute I began. When I was done, the prosecutor asked:

'Has the defendant anything to say?'

Counsel for the defence rose to answer. Kunde replied before him:

'I remember the woman. The witness may indeed be her son. I don't remember him at all. It's all a mistake. I never harmed the witness's mother.'

'But you did take her possessions?' the prosecutor pressed him.

'I didn't take a thing. I just told you. It's all a mistake.'

'Witness Frester has given a different version,' the prosecutor persisted. Kunde had no further reaction.

Kunde's lies did not upset me. A defendant is entitled to twist the truth. I was more upset by the prosecutor's getting my name wrong. *If a name doesn't matter to you*, I thought, *then neither does the person it belongs to*. I started to correct him, then stopped. What was the point of such details when the entire trial was pointless? I regretted ever listening to Shula.

'The witness is dismissed,' declared the chief judge drily. The attendant escorted me out. I walked down the corridor, my footsteps echoing in the monumental building. 'You can get reimbursed for your trip to and from Hamburg,' said the attendant, pointing out the cashier's office. The cashier was surprised to hear that I had travelled second class. Everyone, he said, travelled first class. I wanted to ask if this was compensation for the cattle cars in which Kunde's victims were shipped to the death camps. But I didn't. The cashier would not have understood. He was a young man, born after the Holocaust. He counted the bills and coins twice before laying them on the counter and requesting:

'Sign here, please. It's your acknowledgment that you received the money.'

16

That evening Fräulein Van Gluck called to tell me that the defence had waived its right to cross-examine me. She offered to drive me to the train station whenever I wanted.

'Thank you, but I'll manage,' I told her.

'As you wish,' she said. 'I don't mean to impose.'

I checked the train schedule and boarded a first-class car in the morning. From Hamburg I flew to Israel, this time via Frankfurt. A month later I received a letter. Trude Van Gluck wrote that the judges had sentenced Kunde to seven years in prison. I never sought to find out if he served his sentence. I am not in the least curious to know if he is dead or alive, although it is perhaps an illusion to think that by forgetting the murderer one forgets the murder, too.

As I write these lines, my mother's photograph is on my desk. Recently I removed it from a family album that had been left with the Kruczeks. Mr Kruczek gave it to me wrapped in an old cloth when I visited him soon after returning to Poland from Czechoslovakia. The village hadn't changed. Kruczek, too, was the same struggling farmer. I asked about Bronka. Kruczek's wife smiled:

'We knew about your affair. She's married to a neighbour and expecting.'

I tried imagining the girl that I had known pregnant. Kruczek told his eldest daughter to bring drinks and food. We sat down at the table.

'It's very kind of you to have remembered us,' he said.

'How could I have forgotten? How could I not remember what you did for us?'

'It wasn't for you. It was for Him.' He pointed upward. 'We were the beneficiaries.'

His daughter brought a bottle of home-made beer and some slices of bread spread with lard.

'I was the beneficiary because I served my Lord,' Kruczek said. He took a sip of beer and a bite of bread. 'Have some, it's good,' he urged. I told him about my parents.

'I'm sorry to hear that,' he said. 'At least the Lord protected you. You're looking good.'

'Thank you.'

'What are your plans?'

'I've sold my grandmother's house in Cracow. I have money.'

'Money is good. If you use it well.'

'That's what I wanted to talk to you about, Mr Kruczek.'

'Me? Who am I to give you advice? I'm sure there are Jews in Cracow who can tell you what to do with it.'

'I know what to do with it. I want to buy you some land in the village. I remember how you always dreamed of land. So that your children wouldn't go hungry. I remember you saying that.'

'You'll have children of your own some day. You have to think of them.'

There was a mild note of reproach in his voice.

'How much do ten acres of land cost here?' I hadn't realized that I had hurt his sense of honour.

'I'm a farmer, not a real estate agent.'

'I want to compensate you. What's wrong with that?'

'I'll be compensated on Judgment Day.' He took another sip of beer.

'I never questioned your motives. But why shouldn't you improve your and your family's lot? That's not a sin.'

'I've told you. My reckoning is with God. And with no one else.'

'You're a stubborn man.'

'That's how it is. We farmers are a stubborn breed.'

He remained as immovable as a rock. We shook hands in parting. He didn't make the gesture of inviting me back. I, too, felt hurt. I was not mature enough to understand him. I returned to Cracow with my parents' documents in my bag, annoyed and disappointed. If not for the photograph given me by Mr Kruczek, I would probably never have remembered what my mother looked like.

Today my favourite hobby is photography. I know that a good photograph reveals not just what is photographed but the photographer as well. My mother had been caught by the camera with the smile of a woman who is aware of her beauty and capacity for pleasure. Her portrait was taken by Nolek, an amateur camera buff and her admirer. It was shot by him during the winter before the war. Despite the snow-covered trees in the background, she is wearing a short-sleeved dress with a looped gold pin on the collar. Her dark, narrow eyebrows bring out the pallor of her complexion. Her brown eyes sparkle with *joie de vivre*. Her long fingers are made for expensive rings.

Nature had been generous with her. My mother, however, was not a woman to depend on nature. She made a supreme effort to preserve the beauty granted her. Her mortal enemy was Time and she fought it with all her strength. Ointments, creams, massages, face packs, and regular naps were her weapons in this war. She was so afraid of every grey hair that she allowed me to swindle her. She would ask me to pull these hairs out. Generally she would sit in a chair by the window, her back towards the light, while I gripped a pair of tweezers and combed her lovely hair in search of the evil omens. Each grey hair I extracted earned me a bounty of five groszy. Sometimes, in my greed, I showed her the same hair ten times.

My father knew nothing about this. My mother took care to conduct our depilatory sessions when he was away. For this I scorned her. I scorned her for being clothed by the couturiers of Vienna rather than by the well-stocked shops of Bielsko; for her closet full of dresses, suits, mink stoles, hats with veils and ostrich feathers, silk underwear, furs, high-heeled shoes, Coco Chanel scarves, and two dozen leather belts. I couldn't understand her fear of ageing and her need to dress like a model in a fashion magazine. I thought it a dreadful waste of time and money.

Her summer vacations were spent in the spas of Central Europe. Winters, she graced the ski resorts. Wherever she went, she proudly bore a face without wrinkles. Until I was six I accompanied her on these travels. The smells and sights of the exotic and voguish places that we visited have faded into oblivion. All that is left is the yellowing photographs given me by Kruczek. Dates and names are written on the backs of them:

Baden-Baden, Karlsbad, Wiesbaden, Como. Once I was older and more aware of my surroundings, my mother ceased to take me along.

No matter where we were, at home or travelling, she never raised a hand to me. If I grew unruly, she asked my father to discipline me. Perhaps this was why I refused to acknowledge her authority. Even now, fifty years later, I find our relationship difficult to describe. The more I think about it, the more I am bothered by the feeling that I never felt the love for her that every mother deserves. I judged her for her weaknesses, real or imagined, and failed to honour her. When I ask myself, however, whether I missed the one period of life in which a child develops in the wondrous glow of its relationship with its mother, I do not believe that I lost anything irretrievable. One cannot regret never having what one was never aware of. My attitude towards my mother only changed when I saw her exhibit, in the most trying of times, a courage and resourcefulness that had remained hidden as long as she had no need for them. The image of her revealed to me then is the crown jewel of all my memories.

My eleventh birthday was 17 January 1939. Nothing told me that it would be the last I would celebrate in Bielsko. That New Year's Day the members of the local German football team had demonstrated in the city's streets for the right to have their language recognized as an official one by the Polish government. They were dispersed by the police.

It was not the only such incident. The Nazi radio station across the border intensified its propaganda. Polish-German clashes broke out all over Schlesia. Although the censored Polish press played down these confrontations, my father had no illusions about them. 'Today it's their language, tomorrow it's their country,' he said at dinner, wagging an ominous finger. Although I knew it was not the time for discussing my birthday present, I couldn't resist. I was dying for a bicycle.

'Out of the question,' my father interrupted before I could finish the long speech I had prepared.

'Do you want to get run over in the streets?' asked my worried mother.

'I want to go riding with Erik in the Gypsy Woods. Erik has a bi—' My father's look silenced me in mid-word.

'Didn't you hear what your father just said?'

'Yes, Mother. I heard. But –'

'There are no buts when your father says no. We've decided no bicycle and no bicycle it is.'

'We've decided,' I repeated sarcastically. My mother always used the first-person plural when hiding behind my father's opinions. Although I was on the verge of tears, I knew that not even a flood of them would change my father's mind. Too proud to flaunt my chagrin for a lost cause, I went to my room to be alone with my sorrow. There I hatched a devilish plan.

I would let Nolek do the work for me.

Nolek's real name was Anatol Lewik. Although as an heir to various family businesses he was a highly eligible bachelor who never lacked for money, he had an inferiority complex due to his short stature. Still, he was a true playboy, the only one of his kind in the petty-bourgeois world of Bielsko.

Nolek was born in Cracow, where he became acquainted with my mother under circumstances that were unknown to me. Eventually they became good friends. At first he came to Bielsko for quick visits once or twice a month. I was always happy to see him because he never neglected to bring me candy or toy soldiers for my collection. Before we knew it, he was one of the family. His purchase of a bankrupt textile plant in Bielsko soon became the subject of gossip in the President Café. Not even my presence could stop the whispers that the textile plant was but a pretext for his increasingly frequent trips to our city. My father, who was genuinely fond him, refused to be affected by this tongue-wagging. Although older than Nolek by fifteen years, he got along with him famously.

Nolek and his Leica were inseparable. He took it everywhere, the way a soldier never parts with his gun, and he particularly liked to photograph my mother. Today it is clear to me that she was never so beautifully and happily radiant for the camera as she was for him. Was my father aware of this? How did he explain it? Was he secretly jealous of Nolek? Did their friendship mask other feelings? Was he upset by the gossip? Did Nolek come between him and my mother? I have no answer for any of these questions. The more I try to remember things that might cast light on my parents' relationship, the more stymied I become. The wall between my room and theirs was a thick one. I never saw them embrace or kiss. I never heard them quarrel. They lived within a shell of etiquette that thoroughly protected their privacy. And perhaps there was nothing to protect and it was all in my imagination, spurred on by the gossip at the President. Perhaps Anatol Lewik was no more than a distraction, a curtain hiding nothing behind it. I never found the key to the black box of my parents' marriage.

It was a Friday the 13th, a day known to the Poles for its bad luck, when Nolek arrived to spend the weekend in Bielsko. The weather was wintry. I returned from school, removed my slush-covered boots, and walked barefoot to my father's study. Nolek was lying on the couch. He didn't notice me until I said hello.

'What's cooking?' he asked uninterestedly, putting down the book he had been reading. He liked to use youthful slang.

'Nothing.'

'What's the matter? Bad marks at school?'

'Since when have I ever had bad marks?' He knew I was at the top of my class. Schoolwork was easy for me. I did most of my homework during recess.

'So what's bugging you?'

I told him about wanting a bicycle and my parents' refusal to buy me one. 'You're the only one who can help,' I said with cunning if childish flattery.

'You know I can't. Not if your parents don't want you to have one.'

'Yes, you can.'

'I said I can't.'

'That's because you don't want to.'

This annoyed him. 'Suppose I don't,' he said impatiently. 'So what?'

'So you better.' My cocky look must have made him suspicious, because he raised an eyebrow.

'What's that supposed to mean?'

'That you'll buy me a bicycle even if my father is against it. You can pretend you didn't know he was.'

'That would be a lie.'

'It might be. But it wouldn't be the first or the last.'

'Watch it, kid. I don't like that kind of talk.'

'You're the last person to talk yourself, Nolek. You may not like it – but you sure like my mother.'

'Are you nuts?' he shouted. The book fell from the couch to the floor. His anger was real. His cheeks reddened, his upper lip trembled, and his little moustache bristled at me. I talked as fast as I could for fear of chickening out before I finished:

'If you don't buy me a bike I'll tell my father that you kissed my mother.'

'That's not true!'

'Maybe not,' I answered with the sudden calm of a man overboard in a stormy sea who discovers that he is still afloat. 'Maybe it's a lie. We'll see who my father believes.'

17

When we packed to leave Bielsko and loaded our things onto our little Czech Skoda, there was nowhere to put the bicycle Nolek had bought me. Perhaps Friday the 13th had really been an unlucky day because the bike – the product of my hard work and wits – remained behind in the attic. Our housekeeper Paula promised to grease it if we weren't back by the autumn rains. It was no comfort to me that the oil portrait of my mother, painted by a fashionable Viennese artist, was wrapped in linen sheets and stored together with the bike.

It was my mother who set the priorities. At her command the concierge of our building, a man called 'Grandpa' although he was childless, took the red Bukhara carpet from the foyer, the Baluchi from the study, and her two favourites, the little Shirwan and the silk Kashan bought at an auction in Vienna, and lashed them with strong rope to the car roof. She preferred, she announced solemnly, death at the hands of the Nazis to a cruel separation from the treasures she had spent her life collecting. Her delicate porcelain ballerinas, packed in shoeboxes padded with thick layers of cotton wool, went into the back seat. The baggage compartment had room for a trunk full of her clothes; her black, patent-leather hat boxes; a special silverware case; and two eiderdown blankets 'just in case we need them'. That left no room for the pillows. 'But you can't go without them,' wept Paula, labouring in vain to squeeze them among the rugs. 'What will you sleep on?' Pillowlessness seemed to her an omen of eternal unrest.

The neighbours leaned out their windows and looked on with interest. 'What's going on?' asked the wife of the surveyor from the second floor. 'The kikes are moving,' he replied. Twenty-four hours previously he had still doffed a submissive hat each time he met one of my parents on the stairs.

Although my father had begged my mother to leave Bielsko a week earlier, she had refused. She had such an obsessive relationship with every little item in the house that abandoning any of it seemed to her like saying farewell to the pleasures of life itself. Her polished parquet floors were the deck of a ship anchored in a safe port, from which she was now being asked to set sail on stormy seas. Even when several of her friends began to depart, she remained adamant. 'Rubbish,' she said dismissively of the news of impending hostilities. On 25 August the Polish foreign minister Jozef Beck and his British colleague Lord Halifax had signed a mutual defence pact in London, which was followed by a treaty with the French. A wave of optimism swept the country, raising morale. We had no way of knowing at the time that these developments had caused Hitler to cancel a planned attack. The sealed battle orders, code-named 'White Incident', had called for an invasion of Poland at 4.30 a.m. of that day. But the news from England meant no more than a brief respite.

In the streets of Bielsko posters went up calling for volunteers for the civil defence force. Blackouts were declared at night and air-raid wardens patrolled the streets and issued summonses to violators. Masking tape to protect windows from bomb blasts was prominently displayed in the stores. Aunt Matylda telephoned hysterically from Cracow to tell us that her husband and brother-in-law, who were partners in a pharmacy, had been called up by the medical corps and taken to an unknown base. 'It's lucky they haven't taken you,' my mother told my father with relief. The thought did not comfort him. On the contrary, he was offended not to have been called to arms. Although his sword from Piłsudski's legions had rusted in its sheath and the uniform issued him by the Kaiser had been eaten by the moths, the age of fifty, he thought, was not too old to rally to the flag. 'You're fifty and ten months, that makes all the difference,' said my mother. Mockingly she added: 'I don't know what the fuss is all about. There won't be any war. You men are always making a great to-do.'

She wasn't alone in her views. The conventional wisdom was that Hitler would back down at the last minute before the military might of England and France. People believed what suited them. War, like natural disasters, had no place in my mother's thinking. The world she had constructed around her was eternal. No earthquake capable of shaking it was permissible. Pressed to the wall by the arguments in our dining room, she retorted that even if Hitler dared cross Poland's borders, as he had done in neighbouring Czechoslovakia, the Polish army would make him rue the day. Around the clock we were assured by government propaganda that our soldiers were waiting to rout the enemy. Even the most sceptical observers never imagined that the army's weapons were obsolete, that the country had no effective air force, and that its famous defence lines existed only in its generals' imaginations.

It was my father, the passionate patriot, who had a more realistic grasp of things. Bielsko was near the frontier; the Germans, in his opinion, would overrun it in the first hours of hostilities. In the end my mother gave in and agreed to go to Chelm, a city on the east bank of the Bug River, where we would wait for things to blow over. Inasmuch as it had been designated a centre for the evacuation of the wounded, Chelm would certainly not be bombed.

The war of nerves had reached its height when we set out on Wednesday afternoon, 30 August. The radio spoke of desperate Italian mediation efforts aimed at forestalling a German declaration of war. A few minutes past midnight, Ambassador Henderson, the British envoy in Berlin, appeared in the office of Foreign Secretary Ribbentrop. The Nazi minister received him stonily. In a monotonous voice he read out loud the German demands, first and foremost the ceding of Danzig to the Reich. Henderson requested a copy of the document for the Polish government. 'The Führer has no more patience. The sands of time have run out,' replied Ribbentrop, who claimed that the Poles had lost their diplomatic chance. Before dawn Henderson met with Hermann Goering and obtained the document he sought. But when Lipski, the Polish ambassador, sought to read it over the telephone to his superiors in Warsaw, he was startled to discover that the phone lines had been cut. There was no longer any denying it. Hitler did not want negotiations. He wanted war.

Our first stop was my grandparents' home in Cracow. My

grandmother was unexpectedly generous. When no one was looking she pressed two zlotys into my hand, told me, 'Sweet dreams,' and kissed me on the head. I slept in Aunt Matylda's big bed, dozing off to the excited voices of the radio announcers through the door. They were still talking when I awoke. Hitler's staff had announced the Polish government's categorical rejection of Germany's legitimate demands. My mother scolded me for not tying my shoelaces. Aunt Matylda's housekeeper burst into the room. 'What will become of me?' she wept. My mother told her to please knock before she entered. I took advantage of the tumult to skip brushing my teeth.

After breakfast we drove on towards Lublin. At noon, near Anapol, we reached the Wisla. We were not allowed to cross the bridge, which was being wired with dynamite by soldiers of the engineering corps. For three hours we waited in a long convoy of vehicles until a major in a faded uniform asked my father for identification. My father gave the officer his reservist's passbook.

'You're a captain?'

'You can see what's written there.'

'Why haven't you been called up?' The officer was openly sceptical. Warnings of German spies were posted everywhere. Suspicions were running high. Poles of German origin were rumoured to be traitors. Every soldier was expected to be alert.

'My unit has been transferred to Lublin. I'm on my way to report there.'

'Your name is Frister?'

'Dr Frister,' said my mother. My father silenced her with a hand on her knee and nodded. 'That's written there, too.'

'That's a German name.'

'What are you talking about?'

'Or maybe a Jewish one.' The major obviously didn't make a great distinction between the two. My father said sharply:

'I'm a Polish officer. Watch your language or I'll file a complaint with the division.'

'All right, let's not make a big deal of it,' the major backed down. 'As soon as the work is finished, you can cross.'

The sappers worked until dusk. It was nine-thirty when we crossed the bridge. In Chelm, my father now disclosed to us, we had a relative, Dr Wilenko, a widowed bacteriologist who was his cousin. She was expecting us.

In the summery sun and fine weather of 3 September, Chelm was a quiet, peaceful place. Its main streets ran up a hill to a park that surrounded the cathedral. The traffic in the streets was sparse. No one seemed to be in any hurry. As in most of the eastern provinces of Poland, time appeared to have no meaning here.

No illusion could have been greater. For the past forty-eight hours fierce battles had been going on between the Polish army and the German invaders. Poland's military inferiority was clear from the first shot. The courage of its soldiers counted for little against two and a half thousand tanks and two and a half million soldiers with modern weapons, airplanes, and mechanized divisions. Within hours whole cities were in ruins. Defence lines toppled one by one. The government prepared to evacuate Warsaw. Although encouraging speeches and marching songs were still broadcast by the radio, the greatest optimists now conceded that defeat was imminent. The waves of refugees, however, had not yet reached the east bank of the Wisla. In sleepy Chelm life went on as usual. Peasants drove into town for supplies and parked their wagons in the main street, their horses stamping impatiently and defecating on the pavement. Vendors hawked their wares in the market. The taverns were open. Women crowded the grocery stores. My mother decided to buy shoes. For the first time in her life, she wanted a pair without heels.

The piles of shoeboxes placed in front of her by the saleslady grew higher and higher. My mother tried on shoe after shoe and complained of their poor quality despite all the protestations of the saleslady that 'this is the best there is.' If it didn't have a designer label, it wasn't good enough. She was trying on yet another shoe with a disapproving shake of her head when the air-raid sirens sounded. First one, then others. Within seconds the air was shrieking with their rise and fall like a pack of wailing jackals.

'Where are you going?' cried my mother.

'I'll be right back,' I answered, racing outside. I wasn't about to miss the air raid. The passers-by scattered in every direction, leaving the nervously pawing horses in the street. They had hardly calmed down, the sirens having stopped, when I heard a muffled sound like the angry buzzing of bees. From the horizon, over the rooftops, a squadron of German planes approached. They peeled off one by one, dived, released their load of bombs, and climbed steeply back into the sky. Columns of smoke rose from near a school, whose roof was painted with a red cross. Batteries of anti-aircraft guns opened up from the other side of the city. The shells flashed far from the planes, trailing plumes of smoke like dull fleece. Someone shouted:

'Hey, kid, get out of here!'

I didn't dream of leaving my observation post. Two soldiers emerged from a gate by the shoe store. One trained his binoculars upwards and called excitedly:

'They're on the run! They're on the run!'

Even I, an eleven-year-old boy, could see how absurd that was. The bombers had finished their destruction and were heading west, back to their home base. When the last of them had vanished, the sirens wailed the all-clear.

I returned to the store. The saleslady looked surprised to see me. 'Are you looking for the lady? She left right after you did.'

An ambulance sped by, frightening the horses. Someone shouted that the hospital had taken a direct hit and that there were casualties. The merchants hurried to close their stalls. Iron shutters clattered down. The saleslady climbed a ladder to return the boxes to their shelves. From the top rung she remembered:

'I think the lady ran out to the yard.'

I went to look for my mother, fearing the smack I would get from my father for abandoning her. A wooden beer keg of the kind used by housewives for collecting rainwater, which was better than tapwater for washing hair, stood beneath a drainpipe by a wall. A broad-brimmed hat rose from it.

'Is it over?' asked my mother.

'Yes, it is,' I said, bursting into laughter.

Auntie Wilenko, who put us up, was a friendly woman. Despite her age, which must have been over sixty, she went all out to make our stay pleasant. She cooked our favourite foods, went to the kiosk early each morning to buy my father his paper, and pampered me with candies and hugs. 'I always wanted a son,' she told me. She and her husband, a doctor like herself who had died of scarlet fever contracted from a patient, had four daughters. The youngest, Malinka, which meant 'Little Raspberry', was just like her name: round, sweet, and red-cheeked. I took a liking to her and felt embarrassed each time she came near me. Thirty years later I met her again in Tel Aviv. Despite her hard life, her troubles had not dulled her charm. This was not the case with her older sister Marysia. 'Marysia is still a Holocaust victim,' Malinka said to me in Tel Aviv. 'She has a wounded soul.'

Marysia's story deserves a digression, if only because of its moral. One of the lucky survivors, she and her husband Icchak returned from the camps to a comfortable life in Communist Poland, where they took Polish-sounding names and shed their Jewish identities. Icchak was a man for all seasons who adjusted easily to the new regime. He joined the Party and quickly climbed the professional ladder. When we met in 1948, he told me his philosophy. Being Jewish, he thought, was a catastrophic burden. It was too much to have to go through life with. All it had ever brought him was suffering and humiliation.

When Icchak and Marysia had a son, they baptized him and even brought him up to be an anti-Semite. Once he reached the age of three and began to take an interest in the world around him, I was requested to stop visiting them. My very existence was too much of a link to the past. They had chosen to live in the closet and were afraid I might open the door.

But although Marysia and Icchak could deny their real origins, they could not rewrite their assumed ones. This oversight cost them dearly. The Polish name borrowed by Icchak happened to have belonged to a man who had worked as a Gestapo agent. Thinking that they had tracked him down, the police arrested Icchak. It was not easy for him to confess his deception to his interrogators. The return to his Jewish identity that this demanded was enough to make him physically ill. And yet to conceal the truth would have meant signing his death warrant. The Polish authorities were ruthless towards war criminals.

Icchak was released but did not go unpunished. Although he and Marysia managed to emigrate to Canada, their son could not bear the thought of belonging to a people he had been taught to despise. When the boy was sixteen he left home, refusing to return even when his father had a heart attack. The rupture was irreparable. Icchak died without seeing his son again. Marysia still lives in Toronto. She has nothing to do with her old friends and does not answer her sister's letters. 'I'm not angry at her,' Malinka says. 'I pity her. The Nazis murdered her soul.'

We were still in Chelm when the Polish defences collapsed and the Germans advanced into the heart of Poland.

The government and its senior officials fled to Rumania. It was time to say goodbye to Auntie Wilenko. We repacked our possessions in the car and set out. Where to? It hardly mattered as long as we put distance between ourselves and the Nazi army. Like hundreds of thousands of other refugees, we headed east. A feverish exodus gripped rich and poor, Poles and foreigners, alike.

The roads in eastern Poland were unpaved. Clouds of dust rose from them. A fine silt filmed the windshield. My father had to manoeuvre between people on foot and in wagons, swing around automobiles marooned for lack of petrol, avoid the potholes that menaced the axles, and watch out for the army trucks that sped heedlessly ahead. Through the grimy windows I watched the long lines fleeing a war that had no intention of letting them get away, as was betokened by the Stuka dive bombers plummeting like hungry hawks. No one returned their fire except a lone soldier who refused to take cover and stood in the road firing his pistol at the sky. The Stukas spattered the road with bullets and left him sprawling, his mouth open in a yawn. His blood seeped into the earth as he twitched his last.

It was my first corpse and I stared at it undismayed from a cement culvert into which I had dived with the appearance of the first planes. It was like looking out from the barrel of a giant gun. These culverts, which connected the drainage ditches on either side of the road, were our only bomb shelters. Each time we heard the buzz of the planes we leaped from the car to look for one. Everyone else did, too. If none was available or had room, we ran into the fields and lay in the ploughed furrows, our heads hugging the ground in the delusion that not seeing the Germans meant they couldn't see us. To this day the smell of ploughed ground makes me think of machine guns.

We spent the nights in roadside inns where farmers met to drown their sorrows in drink. By the light of the kerosene lamps, they looked like characters from a play by Chekhov. While we waited at a side table for a waitress to serve us dinner, which was usually buckwheat porridge, milk, and dumplings, I listened to the conversation of these men. Those who were already tipsy argued loudly about the approaching apocalypse in which the world and their villages would come to an end. Their world *was* their villages. Few had ever been beyond the provincial capital. Abysmally ignorant, they lived bare subsistence lives. The fields they worked were too small to support their large families. As more male heirs accumulated with each generation, the plots of land shrank until they looked like the wheat-cabbage-and-clover-coloured squares of a chessboard. Worse yet, the summer of '39 passed without a rain cloud in the sky. The farmers foresaw a poor harvest.

The dry spell was a double blow, because only torrential rains could stop the invader. At least this was the hope of those Poles who believed that God would stand by His people. Church bells were rung and flowers laid by the statues of the Virgin that served as milestones on the village roads. The mud of the rainy season, so it was claimed, would bog down the German armour and tip the scales of battle to the Polish cavalry. But God had other plans for His flock. The drought continued. The curse of blue skies hung over Poland and hastened its final demise.

Our journey through the East was like an expedition to a far continent. For the first time I saw chimneyless cottages, houses taken from illustrations to the Grimm Brothers, drunken men and barefoot children. Women in rags sat selling eggs and milk by the doors of their wretched hovels. Never again would they have the opportunity to charge prices ten times the normal ones. Although my mother complained that they were 'outrageous', she paid them without bargaining. After a while the farmers stopped accepting Polish money. They only wanted to barter. My mother was happy to exchange a silk blouse for a chicken, a tailored wool suit for a piece of meat.

Our biggest problem was not food but petrol. The few petrol stations around had shut down for lack of fuel. A new class of black-market dealers took their place. With a despairing groan my mother agreed to part with her Persian rugs. The dealers laughed at her. They wanted foreign currency. 'This Kashan is worth hundreds of dollars,' she protested. But the dealers did not know the real thing from a cheap factory imitation – and besides, who needed a fancy rug for a packed-dirt floor? It was a seller's market and fuel went to the highest bidder. No one knew if it could be found at the next stop down the road or what its price might be there.

Coming into one village (I can't remember its name because

they all looked the same to me), we passed a truck with broken axles in a ditch. The driver had five twenty-litre jerrycans of petrol and was willing to take Polish money for them. My father decided that we needed all one hundred litres. 'Where do you think you're going?' I asked him. 'You can get all the way to Moscow on that.' In the voice of an old reserve officer who has taken command of a new squad, he angrily ordered me to throw the rugs in the ditch and make room for the jerrycans.

I started with the dark red Bukhara and followed it with the triple-framed Baluchi with its intricate knots. Next came the turn of the little Shirwan, bought on a trip to Turkey, and the silk Kashan that my mother loved for its figures of Persian hunters. The full jerrycans were loaded onto our Skoda. The truck driver helped tie them to the roof, spat on his fingers, carefully counted the bills, and nodded with satisfaction. Stuffing the money in his pocket, he took a bundle from the truck cabin, gave the door a kick, and walked off without looking back. Several peasants watched the proceedings without interest. None bothered to pick up the rugs.

My mother wept silently.

I took her hand in mine. With appalling innocence I said:

'Don't worry, Mother. My toy soldiers were left behind, too.'

Zdolbonow was such an insignificant town that it had not been mentioned in a single one of my geography or history lessons. The Soviet border was an hour away by horse and buggy. Although no doubt the town appeared as a strategic point on the maps of the German general staff, no German unit was bivouacked there. The first foreign soldier I saw was not German but Russian. Wearing a tattered uniform with a Red Army star on his cap, he suddenly appeared with a big grin on his face and a band of curious children. I didn't find him at all frightening even though he held a tommy gun and addressed me in an unknown language.

'He's saying hello,' a six-year-old translated.

'Where's he from?'

'Over there.' The boy pointed up the street.

'What language is he talking?'

'Russian.'

I turned and ran to tell my parents. My mother listened, scolded me for getting so excited, and declared:

'That's all we needed, Bolsheviks!'

I had no idea that I had witnessed a historic event. We were not yet aware that the German and Russian foreign ministers had signed a secret agreement partitioning Poland. Everything east of the Bug River was apportioned to the Russians. Nor did I know about the diplomatic letter given the Polish ambassador to Moscow by Molotov on 17 September, informing him of the Red Army's invasion of the eastern provinces of Poland 'to protect the inhabitants of the Ukraine and Belorussia'. It took fifty years for the full contents of the Molotov–Ribbentrop Pact to be made available to the Polish public with the fall of the Communist regime in Warsaw.

It wasn't just my mother who detested the Russians. My father considered the Bolsheviks to be even worse than the Nazis. The Russians, for their part, saw their real enemy in our little Skoda, which was parked in the yard of the house that we had rented a room in. They came for it in a group of three – an officer and two members of the local people's militia. A militiaman with a red armband slid behind the steering wheel.

'The keys!' he commanded.

My father handed him a ring of keys. He started the motor, struggled with the gear shift, put the car into reverse by mistake, stepped on the accelerator, and slammed into a brick wall. Our poor Skoda was no match for the wall. Its baggage compartment crumpled, oil poured from the rear driveshaft, and the motor quit. The people's expropriators did not seem concerned. The militiaman stepped from the ruined car and said with a laugh:

'So much for capitalist property!'

The three of them walked off. During the night unknown thieves stripped the car of all its parts, even the seats. The naked chassis was still standing there several days later when we boarded a train for Lvov.

Our temporary home in Zdolbonow was the house of a rich Jew called Reb Shmuel, although his real name was Zalman. We arrived in the town at noon on 17 September. A passer-by directed us to the Krau family. My mother negotiated the complex transaction of renting a room in return for outfitting Reb

Shmuel's wife Shura with clothes. As a gesture of good will, she threw in a mother-of-pearl snuff box. This made a great impression on Reb Shmuel. It was unheard of in Zdolbonow to give away something for nothing.

I myself had never seen such a house. Had I known of the work of Marc Chagall, I would have sworn that it was our roof that his magical fiddler floated above at night while playing deliciously sad Hasidic tunes. But being a child brought up on frightening fairytales, I was more reminded by Reb Shmuel's house of the evil witch's dwelling in *Hansel and Gretel*. There wasn't a straight wall in it. The entrance hall was dark. Fat Shura's strident voice was like the cry of ravens. We settled into a room on the hall's left that faced out on the main street. A flower box with wilted geraniums stood on the windowsill. A smell of cooking clung to the covers of the chairs and couches.

Reb Shmuel had so many children that I never was able to count them. Every few minutes a new one would peer into our room without bothering to knock. We were creatures from another world for them. We didn't wear gaberdines, my father had no beard or ear locks, and my mother's unshaven head was not even covered by a kerchief.

'Are you Jews?' one of Reb Shmuel's daughters asked me.

'Of course we are.'

'I've never seen Jews like you.'

'I've never seen any like you either,' I replied.

'Where are you from?'

'Bielsko.'

'Is that a village or a town?'

'A town.'

'Bigger than Zdolbonow?'

I smiled. 'Much bigger.'

'I thought Zdolbonow was the biggest town in Poland,' she said and ran embarrassedly out of the room. Although she was my age, she acted like a kindergarten child. When we were invited to eat with her family, she didn't dare look me in the eyes.

We lived for about two weeks in Reb Shmuel's house. In keeping with his high station, it was one of the few in town to have a real toilet and taps in the kitchen with hot and cold water. Shmuel-Zalman was a small man with an imperious soul in his thin body that not even hefty Shura dared gainsay. I never understood how his consumptive-looking chest could emit such loud, frightening noises. The only member of his family to speak anything but Yiddish, he was its sole link with the Gentile world. In the streets of Zdolbonow he answered the greetings of the passers-by with a slight nod, taking for granted the deep bows of the peasants whose grain he bought and to whom he lent money. Although his debtors grumbled about the steep rate of interest he charged, they dared accuse him of usury only in private. He had a seat of honour in the front pew of the synagogue and the rabbi was sometimes his Sabbath guest. On the hottest summer days he wore a long, custom-made black silk coat and round fur hat. My mother didn't hide her loathing of him. 'He stinks of sweat,' she said.

Years afterwards, when nothing was left any more of the Jewish shtetls of eastern Poland, their pathetic world would be remembered with sentimental longing for a lost culture. Their poverty, their filth, and their backwardness all forgotten, they would be honoured for the charm of Peretz's stories, the legendary jokes of Hershele of Ostropolye, Chagall's airborne fiddler, the spiritual heritage of Hasidism. Can I have failed to see the hidden beauty of this heritage and gone astray after my surface impressions? In any case, there are no rich Jews left in Zdolbonow today. No poor ones, either. I think of Reb Shmuel, seated like a king on his throne, as of a romantic wax figure at Madame Tussaud's.

18

At 3.15 a.m. on Sunday, 21 June 1941, the Germans launched an offensive against Soviet Russia. Stalin was taken by surprise. The Kremlin dictator had refused to believe until the last minute that Hitler would renounce their treaty. Reports from Soviet spies that contradicted this assessment, which was based on the assumption that the Germans would not open a second front while they were still fighting in the West, were thrown into the wastepaper basket. A Wehrmacht soldier who crossed to the Russians' lines with a warning on the night of the attack was summarily shot as a provocateur.

That Saturday evening my father and some friends sat at a café in downtown Lvov discussing the impending defeat of Germany in the West. It took a generous helping of naivety to believe in such a thing now that the fall of France, Belgium, Holland, Denmark, and Norway had been followed by the occupation of Yugoslavia and Greece, and Rommel's North African corps was nearing the Egyptian border. My father's café friends, however, were busy planning the coming peace. The Nazis's surrender seemed just a matter of time to them.

It was in such an atmosphere of incorrigible optimism, over a cup of ersatz coffee, that my father managed to escape a grey reality of hard physical labour. Since our arrival in Lvov, he had earned a living as a wagon driver for the father of my old Bielsko friend Erik. Erik's father had also settled in Lvov, where he had established a Soviet-style cooperative for the manufacture of jams and preserves and appointed himself general manager. An adaptable man, he liked to say that while all Russians were bribable, the trick was knowing which to bribe. With the blessings of the local Soviet officials, he had appointed my father his head distributor. Others of my father's old friends – ex-lawyers, doctors, and industrialists – made do with lesser jobs as street sweepers, construction workers, or porters. Yet even when joking that his training as a cavalry officer was the perfect preparation for driving dray horses around Lvov, my father was clearly in low spirits. I did my best to comfort him, never dreaming that this was but the start of his humiliations.

The nights were not kind to us either. Our rented room was under the occupation of an army of bloodthirsty bedbugs that refused to yield an inch to the war waged against them by my mother. Every night she awoke covered in bites, turned on the light, and flung herself into the fray, seeking to crush the bugs before they took shelter behind the wallpaper. They made a sound like torn paper when they died and filled the air with a sickeningly sweet smell. We counted the dead in the morning by the bloodstains on the wall. It was a hopeless battle in which two of the enemy were born for each one killed. My mother, however, who was fighting for her human honour above all, refused to give it up for lost. There was something symbolic in her struggle with the little bloodsuckers. It was the last line of defence before the deluge.

If there was one thing she hated more than bedbugs, it was Bolsheviks. Worse even than the physical hardships to which they subjected us was their lack of etiquette. She loathed their sloppy appearance, scorned their bad taste and table manners, and refused to accept their barbarous ignorance of the basics of Western civilization. Disdainful of the wives of the Russian officers and officials who bought her nightgowns and wore them to social occasions, she thought no better of their husbands, who drank vodka from the bottle, smoked bad tobacco, smelled of sour sweat, and boasted about their primitive homeland. The theories of Marx, Engels, Lenin, and Stalin with which we were brainwashed were, as far as she was concerned, an intellectual return to the dark ages. Had she been able to, she would have kept me out of school entirely to keep me from being infected with 'those nasty Communist ideas'.

I personally did not suffer from the Bolsheviks. Children had a special place in the Stalinist empire, where they represented the first generation of Socialist Man. Although at home I ate rotten potatoes and watery soups, our school lunchroom fed us meat and fresh vegetables. I quickly learned Russian and Ukrainian, and, forced by no one to read *Das Kapital*, consumed Pushkin and Lermontov while remaining happily unaware of the mind control objected to by my mother.

Choosing the lesser evil, my parents registered me for the sixth grade of an elementary school run by Mrs Makowiecka and Mrs Fylska, two ageing women who had turned their institution into a bastion of Polish nationalism. Busy with more important things, the Soviet commissars had not yet gotten around to purging the school system of its imperialist influences, and the white Polish eagle, the symbol of a defunct country, still decorated the walls of the teachers' room. This exemption lasted until the start of my second year when our school was integrated into the Soviet system and Mrs Makowiecka and Mrs Fylska were sent for advanced pedagogic training to the gulags. The new principal, a Communist Party member, quickly set things right.

By a stroke of luck I was assigned to share a desk with Erik. However, our parents were sadly mistaken if they thought that that they had found a safe haven for us. Erik and I were outsiders. The other students, nearly all of them from old Polish families, did their best to torment us. Of the nasty names they took pleasure in calling us, *zhid* was far from the worst. Despite an official Soviet ban on religious discrimination, we were not allowed in the classroom when the school day began with a prayer to the Virgin. Yet when the Soviet commissar of education discovered pictures of Catholic saints hidden in the books of students, we were immediately accused of informing. Our punishment was severe. We were ostracized like lepers and talked to by no one during recess.

All this happened under the eyes of our home-room teacher, Mrs Bronislawa Piela. This slender, stern-looking woman also taught us geography and stubbornly insisted on using old maps of an independent Poland. Instructing us on the country's eastern provinces, she explained that: 'Until last September these were controlled by hostile minorities. Now they are in the hands of the Russians and their Jewish collaborators.' All eyes in the class-room turned towards us. I stared guiltily at the floor, feeling like a pariah. Although I wanted to be transferred to another school, I feared my parents would not understand.

In this atmosphere of hostility it came as a surprise one day when Mrs Piela stopped Erik and me as we were entering the cafeteria to ask:

'Are the two of you willing to serve a patriotic cause?'

'Of course, Mrs Piela,' we answered.

She told us to follow her to the teachers' room. Carefully closing the door behind us, she looked around as though checking for eavesdroppers. Then she enquired:

'Tell me the honest truth. Do you love our country?'

'To our last drop of blood, Mrs Piela,' Erik was quick to reply.

'That's what I was hoping to hear from such good students. I expect great sacrifices from you.'

Certain that we were about to be entrusted with an important underground mission, I regarded her with anticipation. Had she asked me to sneak into the principal's office and murder him, I would have done it without hesitation. There was no length to which I would not have gone to demonstrate that I loved Poland as much as the next student. But our home-room teacher had different plans for us.

'I'm sure you've heard of the Pioneers?'

Who hadn't? The Pioneers were the Soviet scout movement, a first step towards joining the Komsomol and the Communist Party.

'Well,' she sighed, 'we've been told to pick the best candidates for the Pioneers from each class in our school.'

'What does that have to do with us?' questioned Erik.

'It has to do with my wanting you to volunteer.'

I didn't get it. 'Why us?'

'Because it's your patriotic duty.'

I had no objection to joining the Pioneers. Its members were allowed into the 'Palace of Youth', a magnificent club with games and athletics, and could participate in special lectures, dances, and outings. But Mrs Piela's mysterious manner made me suspect that she had something up her sleeve.

'What's patriotic about that?' I asked. 'I still don't see –'

'I'll explain it to you, Roman,' said Mrs Piela in a silken voice. 'And to you, too, Erik. You're clever boys and will understand. We have to convince the principal that we are obeying the authorities' instructions. Surely you realize that I can't ask such a thing of any of the other students. You're Jews. It doesn't matter to you. You can save us all from terrible disgrace by agreeing.'

The cat was out of the bag. Erik shrugged. 'I don't know if that's the best solution, Mrs Piela. You know how things are. Our classmates will never forgive us. They'll say that only Jews could –'

'Don't worry about that. I've already spoken to them about it.'

'In that case,' I declared, 'we won't let down our country.'

'I knew I could count on you. After classes tomorrow you'll go to the gymnasium. There will be a Pioneer representative there to interview candidates.' She opened the door to indicate that the conversation was over. As we left Erik said:

'I'm not sure what your father will say about this. I can tell you one thing, though. He's not going to like it.'

The red neckerchief given me by the Pioneers looked extremely well on me. 'Oh my God!' exclaimed my mother when I arrived home with it around my neck. 'Take that rag off before your father comes home. He'll kill you.'

Although my father did not kill me, I was given my first spanking since the start of the war. It was not delivered in cold blood, as was his habit. This time he lost his temper and hit me so hard that I could barely sit down for a week. It was the last spanking he ever gave me. Perhaps this is why I remember it especially from all my experiences under the Soviets.

I didn't stay a member of the Pioneers for long. A week after Hitler launched Operation Barbarossa, his army controlled all of western Ukraine. The Bolsheviks retreated from Lvov without a shot. In the brief interval between their withdrawal and the arrival of the Germans my mother had time to burn my red neckerchief and throw it out together with my membership card. The previous day she had turned down the generous offer of a Soviet air force lieutenant to take us on a truck that had come to evacuate him. His wife Larissa had bought many of my mother's nightgowns and the two women were friendly neighbours. As Russian soldiers were loading his belongings, the lieutenant repeated his offer:

'This is your last chance, comrade. The Germans will be here in a few hours.'

'They're not cannibals.'

'They may not be cannibals, but they're certainly murderers. Haven't you heard that they're killing Jews?'

'I've stopped believing in all that propaganda.'

'It's not propaganda. It's fact.'

My mother was unmoved:

'I appreciate your good intentions,' she said graciously, 'but we've decided to stay.' The lieutenant turned, descended half a flight of stairs, halted, wavered, and looked back over his shoulder as though to give her one more opportunity. She smiled and waved goodbye.

19

The groundsels waving in the wind were harbingers of summer. They grew wild along the unpaved road that formed the border between the estate and the fields of yellow woad grown by the Ukrainian farmers. Every day at 5 p.m. a convertible with an SS licence plate drove down the road to bring my mother home. I liked meeting her there. While waiting I blew off the fluffy heads of the groundsels and watched their seeds float in the air. The German driver knew me. He slowed down when he saw me to let me jump on the running board and hitch a ride into the farmyard. By the gate of the manor house he stopped.

It was a carefree summer full of sun for me. I never thought it would end. In the living room of our house I found a record album. Sometimes I put a record on the gramophone and listened to an old German disc on which an unknown woman sang *Nach einem Dezember kommt wieder ein Mai.*

We had been living on the estate, a twenty-minute drive from Lvov, since the winter. The large manor house had two storeys and was painted white. It stood on a hilltop and had a view of cultivated fields that ran down the hill like the coloured strips of fabric that the peasant women sewed their skirts from. At the bottom of the hill the fields abutted a railroad track. The air was perfumed with the scent of flowers.

The children from the nearby village of Suchowola kept their distance from me. I was not interested in their friendship. Since I didn't go to school, I had all the time in the world. I often went for long walks. The peasants tipped their hats to me, the young master, as I passed. I represented the power and authority of the conquerors to them. My father was known in the village as 'the German gentleman', my mother as 'the woman who works for the police'. I made no effort to analyse or understand such a strange situation. The war with all its horrors was far away, beyond the railroad tracks, beyond the horizon, beyond the range of my curiosity. Somewhere else.

Was I really so childishly innocent that I failed to see any further? It would appear so. I had cut myself off from the world and saw what I wished to see. Sometimes SS officers, seeking a peaceful weekend and fresh air, came to stay with us. They went for walks during the day and played bridge with my parents at night. These games must have been nerve-racking for both my parents. They kept me away from the guests and made me stay in my second-floor room until they were gone. Not even that could keep me from feeling free, though. It was all so natural that I completely forgot about the danger in my mother's working in the local SS headquarters.

The Suchowola estate was part of a leatherworking business expropriated by the Nazis after the occupation of Lvov and put under the management of the SS logistics corps. The German military had established a wide network of profitable enterprises that enriched its coffers over and above what it received from the state budget. Our estate, which was one link in a huge syndicate, grew saxifrage for the tanneries in Lvov. A Protestant minister named Paul Jocz had put my mother in touch with Kurt Brinker, a high-ranking SS officer and the syndicate's director. Unlike most of his colleagues, Brinker was religious and took the minister's opinions seriously.

My parents had met Jocz shortly before the Russians left Lvov. He knew we were Jews. 'So what? Jesus was a Jew too,' was all he said. I liked the man. There was nothing condescending or unfair about him. Lies and hypocrisy were foreign to his nature. Yet in introducing my mother to Brinker, he had vouched without a qualm for her pure Aryan background. Brinker was looking for a German-speaking secretary and Pastor Jocz promised that he would find no better one. All that he asked in return for this service was my baptism into the Christian faith. He was interested only in me, he said, because my parents' souls were beyond salvation. Even if circumstances forced them to the baptismal font, they would be living a lie. He had no desire to make them sin like that. I, however, might yet see the light and pure truth of the faith of Martin Luther.

My mother was employed as a stenographer. Her main job was

taking minutes of the syndicate's meetings. Brinker was so satisfied with her work that within two months she was running his office. Everything passed through her hands. She kept Brinker's secret documents in her safe and gave instructions to the junior staff in his absence. Whenever he travelled to Cracow or Berlin, he brought her back a present. Asked by her to make my father manager of the Suchowola farm, he agreed at once. 'Don't thank me,' he said when she expressed her gratitude. 'It's I who should thank you. So few people nowadays can be trusted.' When we moved to the countryside, he placed his automobile at our disposal. My mother was even invited to the syndicate's celebration of Hitler's birthday. She brought back a bottle of champagne and a leather-bound copy of *Mein Kampf*. The book was placed prominently on the desk in my father's office for the benefit of all who entered it.

The race to amass fortunes caused no little conflict among the different branches of the Nazi bureaucracy. Often one of these worked against the interests of another. In their conferences, the directors of the SS syndicate plotted against the army's quartermaster corps and other units. Whole trains were re-routed to transport hides instead of other, more militarily crucial items. Unbeknownst to Berlin, prisoners were transferred to camps that provided the syndicate with cheap labour. False documents covered the deception. My mother recorded these sessions scrupulously, using a special system of shorthand that no one else could read. Locked in her room, she typed these minutes for Brinker. Not even his assistants were allowed to keep them in their safes. Were they to fall into the hands of the Gestapo, the SS's great rival, he would pay with his career. His close association with my mother created a feeling of intimacy. He doubled her salary and broached an idea one evening as she was typing:

'Why don't I make you a folk-German?'

The authorities were empowered to grant German citizenship to *Volksdeutsche*, natives of Polish regions claimed by the Nazis who spoke German well and could prove their racial purity. The *Volksdeutsche* had various privileges, such as special ration cards and the right to apply for state jobs. Having *Volksdeutsche* papers would be an added life insurance policy for us.

'There's nothing I'd like more. But –'

'No buts, Frau Frister,' said Brinker. 'I've thought it through. I've even brought you an application form. Fill it out carefully. I don't need to tell you that *Ordnung muss sein.*'

'Are you sure I'll be OK'd?'

'My personal recommendation will guarantee that,' promised Brinker, writing on the application form: 'Frau Franziska Frister is known to me as a woman with National-Socialist views, a deep acquaintance with German culture, and absolute loyalty to the Reich.' He showed her what he had written. 'What do you think?'

'I think you're a godsend, Herr Director.'

Despite Brinker's promptings, the answer was slow in coming. When it did arrive, it was ominous. The Bureau of Racial Purity in Berlin had not merely rejected my mother's application. Its official response cast doubt on her Aryan background. A copy had been sent to the Gestapo in Lvov.

Brinker handed my mother the letter and said:

'Don't be upset. I know this is ridiculous. I recommended you personally.'

My mother turned pale as she read the document. Trying to cover up her shock, she said:

'What nonsense! Me, a Jew? Why, it's an insult!'

'Don't let it bother you. You know those fellows. They can't sleep at night unless they've gotten into someone's hair during the day.'

'What do you suggest I do? Maybe you should arrest me.' My mother held out her hands as though for handcuffs. Brinker kissed one of them.

'You know it's absurd,' he assured her.

'A copy was sent to the Gestapo. They won't just forget about it. They'll want to question me. Don't worry, though, Herr Director. I won't breathe a word about the management's meetings. I know how to keep my mouth shut.'

'I'm not worried. I have a sixth sense whom to trust. And I'm not prepared to see my employees humiliated. You needn't even go to the Gestapo office.'

'What then?'

'I've arranged for an interrogating officer to be here at four o'clock. That gives you three hours to prepare. He'll probably sniff around you like a watchdog. Don't let it frighten you. They like to play tough. The truth will out in the end. Just remember that I'm with you.' Brinker glanced at his watch. 'I have to go now. I'll be back at four. I'll keep my fingers crossed. See you soon, Frau Frister.'

'Goodbye, Herr Standartenführer.'

Before leaving the office, my mother took a pile of signed transport authorizations. These entitled SS officers and their families to travel on German trains. She took her things, went downstairs, waited for the front gate to open for a truck of hides, and walked through it without being noticed by the guard. From there she took a tram to the railroad station. (A taxi driver might have remembered her face and destination.) She boarded the one o'clock local and reached the farm at Suchowola by two. The success of her plan depended on our being gone before the Gestapo officer knocked on Brinker's door.

My parents didn't tell me what was happening. But though I only learned the details later, I knew we were in grave danger the minute I was told we were leaving at once. The Ukrainian servant was instructed to pack three small suitcases. 'Going to live it up on vacation, eh?' she winked at me. A worker was sent to summon the farm's agronomist, who was told that my father had received an order to report to Governor Frank's office in Cracow. The alibi had to be perfect. Any slip-up could cost us our lives.

The coachman harnessed the horses. For once I didn't ask to hold the reins. I sat on a woollen blanket spread out on the back seat with my parents on either side of me. 'To the railroad station,' commanded my father. The coachman whipped the horses. I threw a last, sad glance at a landscape I loved.

The bored, sleepy stationmaster was sitting in the little shack with white muslin curtains that served as his office. A one-legged table with an ashtray full of cigarette butts stood in a corner. A badly scratched desk was pushed against a wall from which a portrait of Adolf Hitler stared down. Flies had left their droppings on its glass frame.

The stationmaster rose from his chair, straightened his uniform, gave us a startled look, and saluted my father. We had disturbed his routine, for the few trains to stop at Sochowola were always announced in advance by a wood-and-brass telegraph that might have remembered the days of the Tsars. Its buzz sent him to the platform to flag the train down with a pennant, after which he stood stiffly at attention until the caboose was gone again from sight. Only then did he let out a sigh of relief like a man saved from misfortune. He knew that a single complaint, justified or not, would be enough to cost him his job. Having spent his whole life in the station, his great dream was to be pensioned off without mishap. Sometimes, having nothing better to do, I dropped by for a chat with him. Once he confided to me that the thing he feared most was neither Hitler nor the police. It was a long old age without a pension.

'Help us to unload the suitcases,' my father ordered him with unchallengeable authority. To the coachman he said:

'Pick us up the day after tomorrow.'

'Yes, sir.'

'And don't be late.'

'No, sir.'

'Ask at the station when the train arrives.'

'I will, sir.' The coachman touched a finger to the brim of his cap and gave the reins a tug. As the carriage rolled off my father told the stationmaster:

'Put our luggage on the bench.'

Three suitcases, made by the leather factory in Lvov, were placed on the platform's only bench.

'What shall I do with them?' asked the stationmaster.

'Don't tell me, my good man, that you don't know what suitcases are brought to trains for.'

'Of course I do.'

'Then don't ask foolish questions. What time is the Lvov–Cracow express due?'

'At three-seventeen.'

'Fine. We have a quarter of an hour. We're going to Cracow.'

The stationmaster's jaw dropped.

'From here?'

'Naturally. From where did you think?'

'But the express doesn't stop in Suchowola.'

'You'll have to stop it, then.'

'The German express?'

'Don't worry,' said my mother. 'My husband is on an official mission.'

'I can't stop the train,' said the stationmaster. Beads of sweat glistened on his forehead.

'Of course you can.'

'I'm not allowed to.'

'You're not allowed to disobey my husband,' scolded my mother. 'Would you like to see our authorization?'

She waved a form at him.

'I can't read German.'

'It's time you learned.'

'No,' said the stationmaster. 'I can't stop an express. It's never been done.'

'There's always a first time,' smiled my mother.

My father put a hand on the man's shoulder. 'I don't want to have to get you in trouble, my good man. You'd better do what you're told.'

'I'll be punished.'

'The responsibility is mine. You'll only be punished for refusing.'

The stationmaster thought of a solution:

'I'll ask the higher-ups in Lvov.'

'That's fine,' said my mother. 'Go and ask.'

Propped against the suitcases on the bench, I wondered why she had agreed. The stationmaster entered his shack. A minute later he slid open a grimy curtain. I watched him crank the telephone.

'What if he gets through?' asked my father in German.

'You know that telephone works once a year – if that often.'

'But what if today's the day?'

'Come on, Wilek. You've always been able to smile in times like these.'

The line was dead. The stationmaster returned to the platform and threw despairing arms in the air.

'There's no line,' he declared. 'I can't ask.'

'Ask God,' grinned my father.

The stationmaster walked to the signal switch. Slowly the horizontal red semaphore rose to a vertical position. The stationmaster looked exhausted.

'I did it,' he muttered, mopping his brow.

The train stopped. The passengers peered through the windows.

Most were in uniform. A conductor opened a door in a first-class car. We boarded it. 'Our luggage, quick!' cried my mother. The stationmaster pushed it after us. The officer in charge of the train went to the stationmaster's shack to ask for an explanation of the unscheduled stop. I couldn't hear the exchange between them. The stationmaster pointed at our car. The officer seized him by the lapel and shook him hard. The locomotive let out a nervous hoot. The stationmaster ran to the semaphore. The red arm lifted and the train began to move. It picked up speed and chugged off.

There was one other passenger in our compartment, an infantry colonel with his arm in a sling and an Iron Cross on the collar of his neatly pressed uniform. He rose to give us a left-handed military salute. It struck me as curious that it wasn't a Hitler salute. 'I'll be glad to travel for a change in female company,' he said. He was on his way to a furlough in Germany.

'Unfortunately, I myself am on official duty,' said my father.

'With a wife and child?'

'There'll be time for recreation, too,' said my mother, slipping into the seat across from the colonel. The officer in charge came to check our documents. My father handed him the authorizations. He studied them at length, returned them, and said:

'Everything is in order. I apologize for losing my temper with that idiot in the station. He kept blabbering in that damn language of his and expecting me to understand. Those goddamn Ukrainians! If you need anything, feel free to call me. We'll reach Cracow at 12.30 a.m. Have a good trip.'

We did not reach Cracow on time. The wounded colonel fell asleep. My parents conversed in whispers. I dozed off too. A light hand on my face awoke me. 'We're getting off,' said my father. The train was standing in a well-lit station. Przemysil, said the sign. We were only halfway to Cracow. No one noticed us make our way from the train to the terminal. It was humming with passengers, despite the after-curfew hours. Whoever was stuck here would remain until the morning.

'How come we got off?' I asked.

'To avoid the honour guard awaiting us in Cracow,' said my mother. 'Brinker must be wild with anger.'

'Where will we sleep?'

'With everyone,' said my father, giving me a nudge.

We spent the night in a horribly crowded third-class waiting room. At dawn we boarded the local. From time to time it was searched by police looking for food smugglers. My parents' look of respectability exempted us. We reached Cracow in the afternoon. A porter took our luggage and put it on a wagon. In a quarter of an hour we arrived at my grandparents' house at 20 Szlak Street. The old concierge, Zofia Sziwek, opened the door for us.

'Welcome,' she beamed. 'I've found you an apartment nearby. Two rooms and a kitchen. The worst, thank God, is behind you.'

20

I remember the day you came to our home from the railway station. Your mother took my mother aside and talked to her in private. You and your father sat on your suitcases saying nothing. My brother and I, both curious to know what was happening, were sent outside. It was early in the morning. A frightened cat jumped from a garbage can it was rummaging in. We tried to catch it and couldn't.

Afterwards, when you were living at 76 Dluga Street, your mother dropped by often. Then, too, I was not privy to the grown-ups' secrets. I believe that my mother helped your mother to hide your family's possessions. There was a Jewish informer named Diamant in the neighbourhood. He was like that alley cat in the garbage, poking his nose into everything. I remember one evening when he came sniffing around in that despicable way of his while your mother was visiting. Seeing a stranger walk in, she kept her wits about her and said: 'Please wake me tomorrow at six. I have a requiem at church for a friend who has passed away.' It wasn't easy to fool Diamant, though. The man had a nose like a bloodhound. As soon as your mother left he began asking all kinds of questions. I can't swear there was a connection, but a few days later I was standing with my mother on a street corner when we saw you led away by the police – apparently on your way to prison. My mother crossed herself as one does when seeing a corpse and said: 'They're done for.' Yet here you are, alive and well!

This letter came from Zofia Sziwek's son Julian after he identified me on a Polish television programme in the summer of 1990. It brought me reluctantly back to the day I was arrested in the streets of Cracow after a Jewish informer confirmed that I was circumcised. His job done, he vanished. The two policemen debated handcuffing me while I led them to where I lived. They decided against it. The short policeman asked:

'Who do you live with?'

'I told you. I live alone.'

'Don't give us that crap. Every Jew has a big family.'

I said nothing. The policeman kicked me in the stomach. I felt no pain and kept silent. He kicked me again and barked:

'I asked who you live with. Are you deaf?'

'I don't live with anyone.'

The door at the end of the hallway opened again and I glimpsed the woman in the house robe once more. Then it shut. The policeman kicked me a third time. I mumbled:

'I live by myself. At 76 Dluga Street.'

He glanced at my forged ID and slipped it nonchalantly into the broad fold of his sleeve. 'He's not lying about that,' he said to his companion.

'Why should he lie? He's a smart Jew.'

'Let's pay his family a visit,' said the short policeman.

'I have no family,' I repeated. 'You won't find anyone there.'

'Maybe we'll find the Holy Ghost.'

'The place is empty.'

'Seeing is believing. Come on, you little kike, move! We're wasting time. Your family must be worrying about you. Just walk ahead of us. And don't get any bright ideas. We have live ammunition.'

I nodded submissively. What else could I do? Our address was clearly written on my ID. Yet for years afterwards I was haunted by the question: why did I agree to guide the murderers to our home? Why didn't I try to grab my ID and make a run for it? There were all kinds of excuses I could think of. That I was paralysed by the humiliation of having to drop my pants. That I was crushed by the realization of being turned in by a fellow Jew. That I had no chance of getting away anyway. Deep down, though, I knew the truth. I was quite simply afraid to die.

The policemen walked behind me. I heard their footsteps. *Tuk-tuk*, *klap-klap*, went the soles of their boots on the cobblestones. *Tuk-tuk*, *klap-klap*, my heart telegraphed the news of my impending death to my brain. The knowledge that the slightest careless movement on my part could squeeze the trigger was intolerable. Instinctively, I knew the great difference between a bullet in the heart and one in the back. The danger that was invisible, that came from behind with no knowledge of how and when it would strike, or of whether it could be escaped, compounded fear with uncertainty. For the first time I understood the meaning of the phrase 'a minute as long as eternity'. It took fifteen eternities to reach Dluga Street. I walked slowly, like a man in a timeless world. And yet it was time I was stalling for, although all I stood to gain was postponing the inevitable.

The policemen did not ask me to walk faster. Perhaps they enjoyed their game of cat and mouse. Although I wanted to turn around and see their faces, I was afraid the sudden movement might make them shoot. I walked as though I had swallowed a pole, my eyes straight ahead of me. It would have been easier if they had cursed or taunted me, even beaten me. Their silence only made me feel more helpless. *Tuk-tuk, klap-klap*, beat my faltering heart. Who would pity me? Who would lend a helping hand? A crucified Christ looked down silently from a church. I doffed my cap as Poles did when passing a picture or statue of a saint. It was a habitual movement that I had taught myself.

'Cut the crap!' said a policeman.

A voice at last. I felt better. I nodded and replaced my cap back on my head. An elderly couple stepped out of the church. The husband paused to regard us curiously. The woman tugged at his sleeve. 'Come on,' she said. 'Are you looking for trouble?' They turned left while we bore right. The street was like a deep canyon. No feelings could penetrate its high walls. The shutters on the windows were closed. This was a way for those behind them to turn their backs on their occupiers and say: *The street may be yours, but the houses are ours.* I looked up at them. What would you do, you good people, I wondered, if I suddenly knocked on one of your shelters and asked to be hid? I didn't need to ask. I knew the answer. I would hear the bolt slide shut on the door. And what right did I have to condemn them? Why should they risk themselves and their families for a Jewish boy they didn't know? Would I have behaved any differently? I knew the answer to that, too. I wouldn't have lifted a finger. Everyone was equally intimidated.

Sunk in thought, I hadn't noticed that we were already at the little market opposite our house. Peasants from nearby villages were selling pink amaryllis and blue cornflowers. There was a great demand for wild flowers. Both the occupiers and the occupied were hungry for fresh colours and scents. A policeman poked me in the back. 'Stop,' he ordered.

I halted. The other policeman went to buy a small bouquet of cornflowers. The woman selling them stuck his money in her apron. 'Put an aspirin in the water, they'll last longer,' she advised. The policeman didn't understand Polish. The woman repeated her remark in broken German. 'Very good,' said the policeman, rejoining us.

'It's for my girlfriend,' he said.

'You'll have a flowery fuck,' said the other.

Both laughed.

It was barely a hundred paces from the marketplace to our house. I glanced at the windows of our apartment, hoping that my father had seen us coming and would get away. Looking back on it years later, I felt doubly sorry that he hadn't. Even if he had made no attempt to escape, he would then have been to blame, too. But he did not see us. The blame was all mine.

'It's here,' I said.

Did I have a choice? Of course I did. I could have been sprawled on a distant pavement, my spilled blood cleansing my conscience. And yet what good was a clean conscience when you were dead?

'It's here,' I repeated.

'Very good,' said a policeman.

We climbed to the second floor. I said again:

'It's here.'

'Good.'

The policeman drew his pistol. The flowers were in his way. He set them down on the stairs.

'Ring the doorbell,' his companion ordered.

I tried imagining the moment my father opened the door. What would I say to him? How would I explain what had happened? Would he understand? Could one comprehend the incomprehensible? Forgive the unforgivable?

A metallic sound came from inside. It was followed by the shuffle of my father's slippers. The door opened. His glance slid from me to my two escorts and lingered there. I could see the blood drain from his cheeks. 'Oh, no,' he murmured, taking a backward step. My mother was looking over his shoulder. Usually she worked late. Why on earth had she come home early today? A policeman pushed me through the doorway. We entered. His companion shut the door. The trap was sprung.

'I think we can bribe them,' were the first words I uttered. It was the only thing I could think of saying. Perhaps I was trying to convince myself that all was not yet lost.

'Please come in,' said my mother as though the two needed an invitation. She was keeping calm. The policemen looked curiously at the apartment.

'Sit down, please,' she said, pointing to the chairs by the table. A vase with fresh amaryllis stood on the embroidered tablecloth. The policemen remained standing.

My mother took her purse from the couch, rummaged through it with steady hands, and took out a document testifying that she worked in the Wehrmacht Officers' Club. She smiled at the Germans.

'I'm afraid you've gone through this trouble for nothing. This is all a regrettable mistake.'

They didn't bother to look at the document. My mother had no way of knowing that it was hopeless. She tightened the belt on her dress and asked:

'Aren't you going to look at it?'

'You can show it at the police station.'

'I'll file a complaint at the club.'

'Shut up, you dirty yid,' said the short policeman. 'That's enough out of you.'

'We're not Jews. We have –'

'Mother,' I whispered. 'They made me take down my pants.'

My parents exchanged glances.

'We're not rich, but we do have some money and valuables,' my father said. The short policeman turned to him angrily:

'You shut up, too! Get your coats.'

'You'll have a hot time even without them,' joked the tall policeman.

'Where are you taking us?' asked my father. Not even he expected an answer to so pointless a question.

The policemen weren't brutal. They waited for my father to put on his shoes and even looked away gallantly while my mother changed clothes, although they did not allow her to go to the next room. Then they handcuffed both of them. Lacking a third pair of cuffs, they tied my hands with some cord found in the kitchen. On our way out the short policeman took the flowers from the vase.

'The keys!' barked the tall policeman.

My father handed him the house keys. He switched on the stairway light, shut the front door, checked that it was locked, and put the keys in his pocket. No one else was on the stairs. The short policeman combined the two bouquets, stuck his nose into the flowers, and said:

'What a smell.'

We reached the street without being noticed by the neighbours. The flower vendor was gone. The marketplace was behind us. We walked to the police station. The people we passed looked the other way.

The police station was in an old quarter of the city. My mother asked to telephone the Officers' Club. The desk sergeant tapped his head as though she were crazy. We were taken to a detention cell in the basement. The sergeant searched our pockets, took my mother's purse and my father's cigarettes, and locked the iron door. 'At least we're together,' my father sighed. My mother was as practical as always.

'Go over your Catholic prayers,' she said to me.

'What good will that do?'

'They run all kinds of tests. We're Catholic, aren't we? Every Catholic knows the Ave Maria by heart.'

I knew it, too. But no one except my mother wanted to hear it. There was no interrogation that night. I was the only one to sleep. In the morning we were handcuffed again. A green police van of the kind the Germans called a 'Bertha' took us to the detention centre in the former ghetto. We were greeted there by Wilhelm Kunde.

For fifty years I have blamed myself for my parents' death. Julian Sziwek's letter brought me some relief. It was tempting to think that Diamant realized we were Jews and followed me home from the public library. If it was he who brought about our arrest, I had nothing to do with it. My hands were clean. Thank you, Julian Sziwek. You have added one more alibi to the thousands I already have.

21

The television programme 'The World Next Door', transmitted every Sunday at peak viewing time, was watched by fifteen million people throughout Poland. I appeared on it for fourteen months, provocatively raising many issues that were widely considered taboo, such as Polish xenophobia and anti-Semitism. The programme made me a celebrity. I would be lying if I denied that I enjoyed it. Strangers said hello to me in the street. Waiters fawned on me. Even customs control let me through without a check.

The more popular I became, the higher grew the pile of letters on my desk. Some of these letters agreed with my views while others argued with them angrily. These unknown correspondents offered me a glimpse of another Poland, a country staggering beneath its burdens and venting this on foreigners. The chilling ferocity of their Jew-hatred, whether open or covert, turned their letters into poisoned barbs. Most began politely, even admiringly: 'If only all Jews were like you, sir, it would never cross my mind that . . .' This was followed by a long list of Jewish 'crimes' from the crucifixion to the imposition of Communism on Catholic Poland and the misdeeds of a next-door neighbour. A woman from Cracow complained bitterly that her dark hair and complexion made strangers call her 'dirty Jew'. A woman from Czestochowa wrote in illiterate Polish that a Jew in the market was underselling her. 'You tell me,' she asked. 'Is this how the Jews thank us Poles for putting up with them bloodsuckers for a thousand years?' A pensioner from Radom sent me a copy of *The Protocols of the Elders of Zion* and asked why the Jews wanted to rule the world. A provincial clerk was for Israel because 'You Jews want a country just for Jews the way we want one just for Poles.'

I never tried to argue with such people. It was enough to be taught a painful lesson in the Polish mind. Its human mask seemed suddenly stripped away. Or were, in fact, these opinions the most human thing about their holders?

In any event, I didn't spend too much time worrying about them because another pile of letters offered sympathy and encouragement. I was particularly pleased by those from old friends seeking to renew the relationship that they broke off when I left for Israel. Women from long ago whose faces I could no longer remember, no doubt grandmothers by now, invited me to visit them and their families. Some of these letters were bizarre. Loszia from Wrocław wrote: 'I'll never forget the times we spent together. I'd like you to meet my daughter so that she can see what a real man is like.' My male ego swelled like a balloon. When Loszia's daughter, however, an attractive married woman in her late twenties, turned up in my office one day, I baulked at pressing my advantage.

Apart from the note from Julian Sziwek, my most special mail was a letter that led to a moving meeting with Krystina, my daughter from my marriage to Gita – a marriage so brief that I only met its offspring when she was forty-two. First, though, I had better explain what made me return to the country of my birth after leaving it at the age of twenty-nine.

In 1990 I was introduced to Robert Maxwell, one of the titans of the media world – the owner of daily newspapers, weekly magazines, television stations, publishing and print houses, and dozens of businesses and holding companies the labyrinthine intricacies of which he alone could unravel. In the City of London, where he was based, he was a highly controversial figure. Listed as one of the twenty wealthiest men in Britain, he remained an outcast in British society. The doors of the nobility were shut to him and his rivals took pains to remind him from time to time of his true origins. Maxwell, who never missed an opportunity to mention his World War II British army service and the medal awarded him by Field Marshal Montgomery, was born Jan Ludvik Hoch to a poor Jewish family in a remote village in the Carpathians. Although he denied for decades that he was a Jew, married a Frenchwoman, and raised seven children as Christians, British conservatives never ceased to regard him as a foreign bone in the throat. Only in old age, some two years before we met in the Tel Aviv office of a well-known lawyer, did Robert Maxwell return to his Jewish roots.

He was welcomed almost as a national hero in Israel, where he symbolized for many the ability of a simple Jew to reach Olympian heights. Investing tens of millions of dollars in Israeli industry, he also conducted a successful takeover of the tabloid *Ma'ariv*. In his hotel suite in Jerusalem, he received the local Who's Who like a Turkish pasha. The president of Israel delivered the eulogy in the presence of the entire Israeli cabinet when Maxwell was buried on the Mount of Olives in November 1991. This was shortly before his empire collapsed, leaving the world to discover that a large part of his wealth was acquired by means that not even his most fervent admirers would have deemed kosher.

For twenty-five years I had been a senior editor and reporter for the liberal Hebrew daily *Ha'aretz*. Despite the professional esteem I was held in, I felt there was no more to be gotten from journalism. I had three years left until my retirement and the certainty that these would be unexciting. There was nothing I disliked more than routine. I was ready for a change. Yet in my wildest dreams I never imagined that this would make me one of Robert Maxwell's executives.

The rather flustered secretary of the Tel Aviv lawyer whispered in my ear that Mr Maxwell had decided to give me five whole minutes. Opening the door of the large conference room, she hurried off. I had no idea at the time of the awe in which Maxwell was held by those around him. He was sitting behind an empty desk, a tall, broad-shouldered man with a golf hat. The lawyer, whose offices occupied half the floor of a luxury building, served me tea with a flourish and sat down on my right. On my left was Dov Yudkovski. The editor of *Yedi'ot Ahronot*, which he had built into Israel's biggest daily, Yudkovski was now going over to its main rival, *Ma'ariv*.

'This is the man we were talking about,' Yudkovski introduced me.

Maxwell greeted me with a cordial smile. Although in time I would learn from his associates that irrational transitions from

friendliness to anger, and from ego-stroking to deliberate humiliation, were a stock-in-trade of his mercurial personality, I myself
never fell victim to his moods. During the two years that I
worked for him I was apparently the lucky exception.

In preparation for our first meeting I had been asked to prepare
a curriculum vitae. 'Make it short,' I was warned. 'He has no
patience for long documents.' I wrote:

I was born in Poland in 1928. After finishing fifth grade, I was
prevented by the war from continuing my education. Both my
parents were killed in the Holocaust. I myself was in Nazi
concentration camps. On 5 May 1945 I was liberated from
Mauthausen and returned to Poland, where I worked as a
journalist. I left for Israel in 1957, learned Hebrew, and began
to work in the Hebrew press. Today I am a member of the
editorial board of *Ha'aretz* and a newscaster for Radio Free
Europe. I am also the author of five books and chairman of the
journalism department of Bar-Ilan University. I have received
two distinguished prizes for my professional accomplishments, I speak Hebrew, German, English, Polish, and Czech,
and I am married and the father of children.

I didn't bore Maxwell with the details of my long struggle for a
place in the sun of Israeli journalism. Upon my arrival in Israel, a
former friend of my parents had volunteered to use his connections in order to get me a position as a bank clerk. He thought I
was crazy to turn down a job with security and a good starting
salary. 'How are you ever going to become a journalist here?' he
asked. 'You don't know a word of Hebrew or anyone with pull!'
When I decided to work nights as a cab driver while my wife
waited on café tables he dropped me entirely – which didn't keep
him from complaining angrily that I had become a socialist after I
landed my first part-time newspaper job on the left-wing daily *Al
Hamishmar*. Not until I won first prize in a competition of the
Journalists Association did he take me up again. Five years later,
when I was promoted to a senior post at *Ha'aretz*, he even began
to boast about knowing me. But in the CV I gave Maxwell, these
and other tedious details were omitted.

He glanced at the page in front of him and nodded with

satisfaction. 'When can you go to Poland for me?' he asked. Without waiting for an answer, he told Yudkovski:

'Cover his expenses. I want him in Warsaw tomorrow.'

'I'm afraid that's not possible,' I said.

Maxwell looked surprised. It wasn't what he had expected. He believed that where there was a will there was a way – as long as the will was his own. For a moment the friendly smile vanished.

'What's the problem?' he asked brusquely.

'I work for *Ha'aretz*. I can't just get up and walk out. I have to give at least a month's notice.'

'How much do they pay you?'

I quoted a sum twice the real one.

'I'll double that.'

'That still doesn't solve the problem.'

The lawyer squirmed. Bumper stickers saying 'Maxwell, I'm for sale' had been appearing on cars in Tel Aviv. Thousands of Israelis dreamed of joining the communications tsar's kingdom – and I, offered the opportunity on a silver platter, had the impudence to set my terms.

Maxwell, however, did not look put out. In fact my answer seemed to please him, perhaps precisely because I refused to grovel. Surrounded by sycophants, he held them in contempt. Instead of showing me the door he began a long conversation. We exchanged opinions about political developments in Eastern Europe and the status of the press in a post-Communist world. My grasp of the subject impressed him. We agreed that I would take a leave of absence from *Ha'aretz*, go to Poland for a month's survey, and write a position paper on the possible acquisition of newspapers, print houses, and 'anything else worth investing in'. I would, he assured me, be well compensated for my labours. He did not say by how much and I didn't ask.

Although Maxwell worked by intuition, I had no illusions about being wanted because he liked me. For years, while serving on the presidium of the International Association of Journalists in Brussels, I had been responsible for maintaining secret contacts with clandestine groups of Polish journalists. Many of these journalists had gone underground to edit the banned publications of the Solidarity movement after the liberal Polish press association was disbanded by the military regime of General Jaruzelski that seized power in December 1981. As a rule, I met them in the private apartments of Solidarity activists, or else in a little bar in downtown Warsaw staffed by opponents of the regime. With the latter's collapse in 1989, these people rose to political prominence and our old ties developed into friendships. As a result, I now held the key to doors still shut to other investors. Maxwell had a keen sense of my worth.

My trip to Poland was a success. I had no difficulty renewing old acquaintanceships. The report I sent to Maxwell contained inside information that few people had access to. Impressed, he suggested that I join what he liked to call his 'general staff'. The salary was tempting. It was not an offer to refuse. The one cloud on the horizon was the frequent rumours I had heard of highly placed executives, lured by the prospect of fame and fortune, who had resigned their positions to become part of Maxwell's team only to find themselves out in the cold, their former jobs gone, and Maxwell no longer interested. His employees were pawns on a chessboard, abandoned by him as soon as the game was over.

I was afraid of such a trap. 'I'm willing to work for you in return for a three-year contract that covers me until my retirement,' I wrote to him. My non-negotiable demand annoyed him. The battle of unequals between us was decided unexpectedly during our third meeting, which took place at Jerusalem's Laromme Hotel. Maxwell did not hide his irritation.

'I have no patience for stubborn mules like him,' he said to Samuel Pisar, who had accompanied him on his trip to Israel. 'Take him into the next room and cut a deal.'

A Holocaust survivor like myself, Sam Pisar was one of the leading corporate attorneys in all Europe and the United States, so much in demand that Congress had even passed a special law granting him US citizenship when Jimmy Carter sought his services as a consultant. Both of us still remembered a late-night discussion in my home when I had interviewed him upon the Hebrew publication of his book *The Phoenix*. Now, in the bedroom of Maxwell's royal suite, he sympathized with my position but was not persuaded of its justice.

Our talk dragged on. On the other side of the wall Maxwell went about his business, receiving important visitors to the buzz and whirr of phones and fax machines. Suddenly his bulky frame filled the doorway.

'Are you done?' he wanted to know.

'No,' said Sam Pisar. 'I know Frister. He's definitely a man you can trust. But what will you do with him if Poland doesn't pan out? You'll be stuck with him for three whole years.'

Maxwell lay down on the bed. The mattress springs groaned beneath his weight. He fixed his eyes on me. My chair became uncomfortably hard. I braced myself for an explosion. He yawned. Pisar said nothing. There were a few nerve-racking moments of silence. Then, as though from the pit of his stomach, Robert Maxwell's bass voice said:

'The man's no schmuck. What's wrong with being stuck with him for three whole years?'

Two weeks later I was invited to London to sign a contract. Maxwell and his son Ian were waiting for me in a little room off his main office. It was 8 p.m. On the ninth floor of the Maxwell Building, a few hundred feet from Fleet Street, work went on as usual. The private security force would not have shamed Fort Knox. No one but the boss and his close associates ever made it to the ninth floor. The wall-to-wall carpeting bore Maxwell's commercial trademark, a big M against a globe. Ian handed me the contract. A ballpoint pen lay on a round table.

'My father has already signed,' he said. 'Put your signature on each page.'

I picked up the document and began to read it. The text was in legal language. I couldn't understand some of its clauses and reread them. Maxwell grew impatient.

'What are you reading there? Don't you trust me?'

'I trust you completely, sir,' I said. 'But do you really wish to hire a man who doesn't read what he signs?'

Maxwell laughed. I was his type of person. Three long paragraphs of the contract comprised a secrecy clause as ironclad as if I were about to join MI5, the British secret service. Although there were several discrepancies from what we had agreed upon, I did not make an issue of them. I didn't want to push my luck, especially since the changes did not surprise me. I knew that Maxwell always expected to have the last word. I signed.

If the ninth floor was the summit of Maxwell's empire, the tenth was the Holy of Holies. Above it was only his private helicopter pad. His family mansion was in Oxford, where his wife Betty lived; here the taste was his own. The next morning I was invited for a visit. Maxwell's Portuguese valet Joseph poured us wine. 'Château Lafitte Rothschild,' Maxwell declared, sizing up my appreciation. I took a sip. The full red wine was superb, even if it was early in the day for it. I finished my glass and set it on the edge of the table, which stood in the middle of a huge room furnished like a Roman emperor's. Joseph cleared the glasses expertly. Maxwell's two sons and executives, Ian and Kevin, had left their wine untouched. Kevin sat facing me, obviously unhappy with his father's new employee. It became more obvious when he asked frostily:

'And what, may I ask, is your business experience?'

'I don't have much,' I answered drily. 'Mostly it comes down to having bought and sold the cars that I've driven.'

Kevin, who lacked a sense of humour, made a face. His business degree from a prestigious English university had not taught him to tell or listen to a joke. His father grinned broadly.

'You surely haven't forgotten all the Harvard and Oxford graduates we've hired and fired,' he told Kevin, listing some names.

'Of course I haven't.'

'And do you know what those chaps lacked? What this one has: common horse sense.'

Kevin nodded. 'I understand. Common horse sense is what we've been missing.'

Maxwell overlooked his sarcasm.

Thus it was that I joined the Maxwell Communication Corporation as its specialist in horse sense. The honorific bestowed on me, international director of communications development, was Maxwell's own inspiration. The corporation provided me with business cards to impress the gullible, a white Mercedes, and an open expense account. Before long I had suitable offices, too. My first move, which was to retain the president of the Polish bar as my legal adviser, met with high praise from Maxwell, who liked big names. Within two months I had his agreement to opening a Warsaw bank account for which – against the strenuous objections of his financial managers – I needed no co-signer.

But I was wrong if I thought that my path to business success would be strewn with roses. The end of Communism had not ended old work habits and patterns of thought. The heavy hand of government ministries on the Polish economy had remained the same. Bureaucracy was still everywhere. No one wanted responsibility for making decisions. The privatization bills brought before parliament were stalled by political rivalries in one session after the next. Ministries kept changing tax and customs regulations. Senior officials lost their jobs with each new government coalition. Worst of all, the trade unions fought all attempts to import foreign capital.

Populism was rampant. And besides the general chaos, there was a wall of hostility towards Maxwell himself. Captain Bob, as he was called by his friends, had neglected to inform me that back in the 1980s, while I was secretly meeting with Solidarity, he had visited Warsaw as a guest of General Jaruzelski. Nor did he tell me that he had published Jaruzelski's biography as part of a series profiling such world leaders as Bulgarian Communist boss Yuri Zhivkov, Rumanian president-for-life Nicolae Ceausescu, and East German dictator Erich Honecker. The Poles had not forgotten. Our main competitors, the media syndicates of the Australian Rupert Murdoch, the Italian Luigi Berlesconi, and the Frenchman Michel Hersant, added fuel to the fire by feeding to the Polish press stories of Maxwell's political and commercial blunders. This smear campaign reached its height with publication of an article about Maxwell's having worked for Soviet intelligence.

'Now go prove that he didn't,' I muttered to myself as I read it. It was a fine day. Standing on the fifth-floor terrace of my office, I folded the newspaper and looked around me. From my vantage point I could see the official mansion of the president of Poland, the parliament building, and the huge tower of the Ministry for Economic Cooperation with Foreign Countries. The new government had inherited its love of pompous buildings from the old one. Key figures in the former regime were now high-ranking executives and directors of private companies. They often did very well, having established valuable connections in Poland and the world while holding their previous positions.

Slawek Lipowski was not one of this fortunate group. After long years spent in the Polish intelligence and security apparatuses, he arrived in my office crestfallen and dejected. Like a derelict, he was ready for any job at any pay, even working as a messenger boy if necessary. He was a man in his fifties going mad

THE CAP

from having nothing to do. The decision to hire him was not an easy one. I had no idea of how completely he was ostracized and in need of a new life. I was still holding the article about Maxwell the Soviet spy and the last thing I needed was for the next exposé to accuse us of sheltering ex-secret police agents. This was not a story I wanted to star in. Still, Slawek Lipowski was not someone I could say no to. Slawek was a friend.

In the early years of the merry 1950s, Slawek talked me into renting a room in the large villa that he lived in on the outskirts of Wrocław. He was an economics major and an outstanding student, tall, blond, handsome, and with nerves of ice. His impeccable manners put him light-years away from the poor working-class family he grew up in.

I myself was as young and ambitious as Slawek, an editor on a mass-circulation local newspaper who drove a convertible sports car and had a head of curly black hair that was not the ugliest thing around. We soon became close friends. Indeed, our friendship withstood the test of time even when Slawek was asked to join the Public Security Service. The PSS offered to pay for the continuation of his studies in return for a commitment to work for it after graduating. Although I suspected that even then Slawek was working as an informer, I didn't make a point of looking into it. We had a silent understanding not to discuss the organization that was feared by every citizen of Poland.

Not that his belonging to it wasn't obvious. An ordinary Pole in those days stood no chance of obtaining a gun licence. Yet although the illegal possession of weapons was a severely punishable crime, Slawek had a pistol, a Soviet TT that he carried as proudly as a new toy. Once he almost shot me with it.

It was the middle of a harsh winter and we were being given a hard time by a girl we had picked up on the dance floor of the Polonia Restaurant. Best friends that we were, we shared everything, women too. The girl, however, did not wish to cooperate. Through the open door between our rooms I could hear her sob as Slawek ordered her into bed with me. She loved only him, she swore. 'Leave her alone,' I told Slawek. I had no ambition to be a rapist. I didn't want any woman who didn't want me.

But Slawek's authority was at stake. He could not stand being challenged, a trait aggravated by the gun he now carried. In a temperature of twenty degrees below zero he threw the girl outside without her clothes and made her stand naked in the garden, weeping silently. I begged him to let her stay with us until the morning. 'Absolutely not,' he insisted. I waited for him to fall asleep, took the girl's clothes, opened my window, called to her, and was about to toss her things down to her when I felt cold metal in my back. Woken by my voice, Slawek had tiptoed barefoot into my room. 'I'll shoot,' he said menacingly.

That was Slawek. To this day I don't know if he would have gone ahead and pressed the trigger.

After graduation he was posted to Warsaw. Then I was arrested. I did not seek him out after my release. I had no desire to embarrass him with a relationship to an accused counter-revolutionary. Perhaps, too, I did not want to put our old friendship to the test.

In 1963 fate brought us together again. Slawek was appointed first secretary to the Polish embassy in Tel Aviv. I believe it was his first posting abroad. (Later he was to serve in Washington and in Tokyo, where his job was to obtain access to restricted technologies.) Although officially he was a cultural attaché, he did not appear to pay much attention to culture. Our renewed friendship, he explained, was to be on the same no-questions basis as before. 'I need one place where I can get plastered without being afraid that I'll be made to blab,' he told me. 'A quiet spot I can bring a woman to without being photographed in compromising positions. You can count on me in return never to ask you to do anything improper.' We shook hands and drank a toast. As usual, neither of us kept his promise.

The rupture of diplomatic relations between Poland and Israel in the wake of the Six Day War once more cut the link between us. Apart from a brief meeting in New York, we did not see each other again until I came to Poland in 1978 for Ha'aretz to cover the opening of the Jewish pavilion in the Auschwitz Holocaust Museum. It was the first time since 1967 that the Poles, seeking to fend off American-Jewish protests, had issued visas to Israelis. Slawek came to my hotel in an official car with a chauffeur. He had just returned from Morocco, he told me, and was bound for

Algeria the following week. As always he radiated self-confidence. 'Any time you want a visa, just call me,' he said. I was to take him up on that twice.

During the fourteen months that Slawek worked for Maxwell Communication in Warsaw I gradually learned of his activities in the 1980s. They were nothing to be proud of. Involved in the anti-Solidarity campaign, he was part of a never-executed plot to murder Adam Michnik, one of the movement's leading intellectuals. He was also responsible for surveillance of various American-Jewish organizations.

I received no satisfactory explanation of these facts when he was confronted with them. Slawek simply appealed to our old friendship and to my compassion. I felt disgusted by him. I far preferred the man who had stuck a pistol in my back to the one now snivelling for mercy. Still, I didn't fire him.

Robert Maxwell took no interest in my office staff, although I kept him informed of whom I hired. On one of my many trips to London, I let him know how bad his image in Poland was. At once I regretted it, for if the *Guinness Book of Records* had had a section on libel trials, Maxwell would have topped it. He employed an entire battery of lawyers for the sole purpose of flooding the courts with suits against journalists who impugned his good name and I feared that doing that in Warsaw would turn the entire Polish establishment against him. To my surprise, however, he answered disdainfully: 'You do your job and I'll do mine. I'll send Sir John to Warsaw. He'll clear the air there.'

Before becoming Maxwell Communication's foreign policy director, Sir John Morgan had served as Great Britain's ambassador to Poland. An amiable English aristocrat, he was hopelessly lost in the maze of Maxwell's businesses. Moreover, all the VIPs he had known in Poland in the 1980s were now has-beens. The British ambassador who had replaced him was not a particularly gracious host when we called on him for high tea. Stirring his Earl Grey with a silver spoon, he informed us coolly that our Polish business affairs did not concern him. His Excellency, it appeared, maintained a strict separation between British diplomatic interests and the private commercial activities of British citizens. Any doubts I may have had about London's attitude towards my new boss were dispelled by these remarks.

Sir John was a fine fellow. Never averse to a glass of good wine, he hit it off with me from the moment I picked him up at Warsaw airport. That same evening we conferred over an excellent Bulgarian red and a Bulgarian white; exchanged opinions of Polish women; and reached the conclusion that we had to make the best of things. After a polite round of calls on Prime Minister Mazowiecki and a few ministers and politicians involved with communications, Sir John finished the official part of his visit and set about writing a report. Only now were his full talents revealed. Not only did he know Maxwell well, he was a wizard at finding the phrase to warm Captain Bob's heart. 'Take a pinch of fact and a generous helping of VIPs, throw in a pot, add statistics, season with a hint of profits, stir well, and he'll love it,' was his recipe. I learned a great deal from him about the art of survival on Maxwell's general staff. Unfortunately, none of this helped Sir John himself. Several months later he was fired without warning.

The first goal I had set myself upon arriving in Poland was to purchase *Warsaw Life*, an established daily with a large readership. Together with five or six regional papers that I also had my eye on, it would give us a Polish newspaper chain with a circulation of one and a half million. By joint management of these publications via consolidated purchase of ink and newsprint, and a single advertising bureau and printing press, we could ensure their efficiency and profitability. Maxwell approved of my plan, which called for exploiting a new law that barred the Communist Party from owning media and mandated an auction of its holdings. Special preference was to be given to the bids of workers' cooperatives.

I commenced a series of long trips across Poland to search out newspapers worthy of acquisition and convince their staffs of the advantages of a Maxwell partnership. After forty years of Communist enslavement, Polish journalists feared going from the fire to the frying pan. No sooner, it seemed, had they been given a taste of freedom than they were facing a takeover by a foreign tycoon. Much effort was needed to reassure them. Moreover, although Maxwell had empowered me to sign whatever agreements I saw fit, I had no confidence that he would honour my decisions. Even in writing, his word was never to be relied on.

This was something I came to realize in the course of acquiring

Sigma, a Polish house that published seventy professional and scientific journals. Maxwell, who owned Pergamon, the world's second largest academic periodical press, had appointed me its executive manager while urging me to add the Polish listings to its roster. A group of consultants hired by me had put the worth of the Warsaw company at four million dollars, an insignificant sum in Maxwellian terms. During our negotiations, Sigma asked for exclusive translation rights into Polish of all articles appearing in Pergamon's four hundred worldwide publications. Since I could not agree to this without making sure that Pergamon owned the copyright to these articles, I phoned its president in London.

'Excuse me,' he answered warily. 'With whom do I have the honour of speaking?'

I explained to him that I was his executive manager and was negotiating for seventy new publications. There was a long silence at the other end of the line. Then came the reply:

'I'm sorry, but I've never heard of you or of your acquisitions project. I suggest you speak to the chairman directly.'

The chairman was of course Robert Maxwell. I phoned him. His London office, which had a standing order to transfer my calls to wherever Captain Bob was, hooked me up to Gulfstream-4, his private jet that was then on its way from France to Italy. Maxwell told me not to worry. 'The president of Pergamon doesn't have to know whom I've appointed to the management. Give the Poles the rights they're asking for. I want that company.'

His answer rang a warning bell. Clearly, he hadn't the foggiest notion of who owned the copyright. I knew that any slip-up would be blamed on me. Since my friends on the ninth floor of the Maxwell Building had taught me to do nothing without written approval, Captain Bob having a well-known tendency to forget his backing of misbegotten projects, I faxed Gulfstream-4: 'As per your instructions, I have added a clause to the agreement with Sigma promising translation rights for all Pergamon publications.' The pilot confirmed the fax's arrival. I felt reassured – but not for long.

In May 1991 I was asked by Maxwell to come to Jerusalem for the opening of *Vremya*, a Russian-language weekly. The mass emigration of ex-Soviet Jews to Israel had created a market of three hundred thousand potential readers and an impressive ceremony was planned with the participation of the prime minister and senior cabinet officials. On my way I stopped in Frankfurt for a brief conference with a high-ranking executive of Berlitz. Not long before this I had opened the first branch of a Berlitz language school in Warsaw and I was anxious to learn about the operations of a company that, founded in the late nineteenth century and numbering over three hundred branches worldwide, was bought by Maxwell in 1988 as part of Macmillan Publishers in New York for the legendary sum of two and a half billion dollars.

'What do you say to the sale of Pergamon?' the German director of Berlitz asked me.

'What are you talking about?'

'Haven't you read today's *Financial Times*?'

He handed me a newspaper and pointed to a headline: 'Maxwell Sells Pergamon to Elsevier for £240,000,000.'

I was shocked. The Sigma contract was now with a public notary in Warsaw. Its unilateral abrogation could cost Maxwell four million dollars – and me, my credibility. I couldn't understand why he hadn't told me of the sale of Pergamon. He had already shared greater secrets with me, even used me to channel secret funds from one company to another. He knew I could be trusted and counted on to keep quiet. What had gone wrong?

My plane landed at Ben-Gurion Airport an hour before the ceremony. I changed clothes in the taxi to Jerusalem and got there on time. The distinguished guests were just arriving in the King David's Blue Room. Maxwell was standing to one side, chatting with Prime Minister Shamir. While waiting for him to finish I put out the cigar I had lit, since I knew he could not abide smokers. The conversation with Shamir ended. Maxwell was in high spirits. Smiling and bantering, he clearly felt like a fish in water. I went over and told him of my problem. He put a fatherly hand on my shoulder and said:

'Forget about Pergamon. Go back to Warsaw and buy Sigma for Robert Maxwell Holdings. The Poles don't give a damn where the money comes from.'

'But what about the translation rights?' I enquired. Maxwell remembered nothing about them. He asked his secretary for his mobile phone and talked to someone in New York. It was four o'clock in the morning there. Then he gave a stirring speech about Mikhail Gorbachev and his brilliant future, and disappeared.

The next morning my assistant was waiting for me at Warsaw airport. We went straight to the office. My secretary called our legal adviser. The contract signing, we were told, would have to wait for Sigma's agreement to a new buyer.

Sigma's agreement was obtained. The notary's, however, was not. He had no authority, he protested, to act on behalf of Robert Maxwell Holdings. Furthermore, since Robert Maxwell Holdings was not legally registered in Poland, it had no right to conduct business there.

It was a major complication. Not only would the foot-dragging of the Polish bureaucracy make registering Robert Maxwell Holdings a long process, I hadn't the vaguest idea what kind of company it was, where its home base was located, or who its directors were. I opened my desk drawer and took out an inner directory of the Maxwell empire. Among three hundred companies scattered from Tokyo to California and from Alaska to Beijing, Robert Maxwell Holdings did not appear.

Later that evening I got hold of Maxwell in London. Within forty-eight hours a courier arrived in Warsaw with documents authorizing me to register the company in Poland. Our legal adviser used his connections to short-cut bureaucratic procedures. At the last minute it turned out that we lacked a foreign account permit from the National Westminster Bank in England. After a few abortive attempts to contact Captain Bob, I called his son Ian. 'I don't understand what this is all about,' Ian said. 'My father knows we can't buy Sigma. Our agreement with Elsevier forbids us to engage in academic publishing for the next fifteen years.'

I slammed down the receiver. Ian wasn't offended. He understood me perfectly.

My plan to establish a newspaper chain had also run aground. Under the old regime, the Communist Party had controlled nearly all print media. Although parliament had ordered the government to dismantle the giant publishing company Prasa, which put out hundreds of dailies, weeklies, and monthlies, the whole operation was phoney: rather than auction these publications to the highest bidder, the national privatization commission was giving them away on a pre-arranged basis. Under the pretext of decentralization, one hand was washing the other.

Various parties and lobbies were being awarded the loot in return for their support on election day. Now, my friends in high places advised me to distance myself from the camp of Prime Minister Tadeusz Mazowiecki, which I had spent much time cultivating, and to place my bets on President Lech Wałesa. As this was not an expensive proposition, I advised Maxwell to invest a quarter of a million dollars in Telegraf, a new company established by Wałesa's cronies, and in some other projects close to the president's heart. Maxwell objected, telling me:

'You're too close to things and have lost your perspective. I know Polish politics better than you. Stick to the course you've been following.'

It didn't surprise me when our investment group in Warsaw, which consisted of Maxwell Communication plus several banks, government companies, and local entrepreneurs linked to Mazowiecki, lost every single newspaper auction. Our bid of four and a half million dollars in cash for *Warsaw Life* was passed over for an unknown consortium from Italy represented by a local Catholic politician. Only later did I discover that standing behind this mysterious bidder was Luigi Berlesconi. It did no good to promise another ten million dollars for the modernization of the paper, or to have gained the support of its editors and reporters, to whom I had promised nine per cent of all profits, or the backing of the Journalists Association, to which I had donated ten thousand dollars for professional training. The fix was on. The auction committee's explanations left no room for doubt that the presidential palace was involved. We had fallen victim to a political vendetta between two former anti-Communist comrades.

My mood was not improved even by our occasional successes, which included a contract with Polish television for an instructional series in American English (a project sponsored by the American Information Agency); the purchase of fifty per cent of Channel 2 of the Bulgarian television network; the creation of partnerships to publish local Yellow Pages in several East European countries; and our first inroads into Russia. I was on the verge of resigning when a new development took place. At a private party I met Andrzei Gelberg, the editor of *Solidarity*, the movement's official weekly. It was, he told me, in serious trouble. Dozens of glossy magazines were outselling it. Gelberg said:

'As an underground publication, we were the only game in town. The message was more important than the medium. Now the rules have changed. We have to roll up our sleeves, become more professional, and invest in infrastructure. The problem is that we have no money.'

'Would you take it from Maxwell?' I asked.

'From the devil,' was the answer.

Solidarity was still aligned with Wałesa, its first leader. A joint venture would be the seal of approval on all of Maxwell's activities in Poland. If Gelberg wasn't just talking a lot of hot air, I was holding the winning ticket.

'Let me sleep on it,' I said. I didn't want to show him how eager I was.

Maxwell gave me the go-ahead. I began travelling to Gdansk, Solidarity's stronghold, to muster support and prepare the ground. I liked these trips. A humming port, Gdansk had one of the loveliest old quarters in Europe. The details of the deal were worked out over the tables of its restaurants. My ability to match my fellow negotiators vodka for vodka was no small help in creating the desired atmosphere. A draft agreement was brought before Solidarity's central committee. After a fierce debate, the tie-in with Maxwell was approved.

It was decided to establish a joint publishing company called Tysol. An English copy of the agreement was sent to London via courier and three consultants arrived from Maxwell's staff to prepare a business programme. I was especially happy with Solidarity's willingness to reduce the magazine's political content to fifteen per cent of each issue. While the movement retained the right to choose its editor-in-chief, Maxwell was assured of a seat on the board. As the leasers of the magazine's new equipment, we would effectively be in control of it.

In late September I travelled to Solidarity headquarters in Gdansk for the signing. Not all of the movement's leaders were in favour. The debate in the central committee had developed into a conflict between Wałesa's loyalists and an opposition group. I had to work behind the scenes to clear away the minefields, weaken the opposition, and strengthen the hand of our supporters. The signed agreement in hand, I sped back to Warsaw in order to forward it to London before Solidarity could change its mind. Maxwell's signature was now all that was needed to put it into effect. At last I had made the major breakthrough that I had been looking for. Our legal adviser promised to draw up the documents for registration of the partnership within twenty-four hours. On 4 October Maxwell telegraphed:

'Sorry. Cancel deal.'

There wasn't a word of explanation. It was the last straw. I submitted my resignation then and there. By 26 October I had paid off my office's debts, arranged for compensation for its workers, and locked its doors. I had also shipped two trunks of confidential documents to London, loaded my things into my car, and set out for Frankfurt. I was accompanied on the three-day trip by Elisabeth, a forty-year-old linguist and theatre scholar. We parted in Germany with no idea that two years later we would reunite as a couple.

I parked my car in Frankfurt airport, brought the keys for safe keeping to the director of Berlitz, and flew to Israel the next day. Another chapter in my life was over. Robert Maxwell died on 5 November. His bulky body sank to the bottom of the sea, weighed down by billions of dollars of debt.

22

My wife Shulamit was part of my Warsaw experience. She spent half of each month in Poland, where she turned Suite 700 of the Victoria Intercontinental Hotel into my second home. I probably could never have survived without her, even if I didn't always share with her the details of my business dealings. She had the rare talent of being there when she was needed. And yet, absorbed in my work and in the book that I was writing, I allowed myself to grow distant from her without sensing that our marriage was headed for the rocks.

In our twenty-five years together, we had seen better times and worse. I was not an easy husband to get along with. Even now I can't predict the future of our relationship. The best and longest of my life, it may have been destined but it was never invulnerable.

We met on a drizzly day, in a petrol station. It was autumn, several months after my testimony at Wilhelm Kunde's trial. The weather was as gloomy as my mood. Shula's condition had gotten worse. For the past two weeks she had been in a sanatorium. That evening I was on my way to meet Rakhel, a young married woman who, like me, was looking to be distracted from her worries. We had arranged to meet in a café near her home. I had no compunction about this. It did not seem to me an act of betrayal. My wife was conducting her own romance with death and we no longer had a physical relationship.

Shulamit was driving a red sports car. She wore a gym suit, had short-cropped hair, and a problem. A loose screw in a windscreen wiper had forced her off the road. Did I happen to have a screwdriver? I glanced at my watch. I was in a hurry. Rakhel was one of the few women I knew who was always on time. Still, I heard myself answer:

'Yes. Here.'

'I'll return it right away. It won't take more than a few minutes.'

'I'm sorry, I can't wait,' I said.

My tank was filled. I switched on the ignition.

'Then how will you get it back?'

'I'll come to get it.'

'When?'

'Tonight.'

'Write down my address.'

She gave me a street and house number. I thanked her and gunned the car. The engine purred like a spoiled cat. I had a weakness for powerful vehicles, the kind that concealed their advanced technology behind an unpretentious exterior. I pulled out of the petrol station and headed down an avenue for downtown Tel Aviv. The radio played music from the fifties. The streetlights glittered in the wet asphalt. I slowed down. Why hurry? I didn't really feel like seeing Rakhel. I knew everything about her – or at least everything that seemed worth knowing. No matter what age we are, our toys eventually bore us. I pulled up by a public telephone booth on whose door an anonymous hand had written: 'Kiss my ass.' I smiled. A three-word challenge to the world. I found the number of the café in the phone book and apologized. 'I'm sorry,' I said. 'I won't be able to make it.'

'It's your loss,' said Rakhel. Her tone implied that I was not irreplaceable. Perhaps she too was ready for a new toy. The secret of such relationships lay in ending them in time.

I drove home to see if there was a phone message from Shula. Then I poured myself a drink, lit a cigar, and sat wondering how to spend the evening. At nine o'clock I drove to the address of the woman from the petrol station. Shulamit gave me a friendly welcome. I liked her. I thought I would spend the night with her and spent the next twenty-five years. After Shula's death we were married. Shulamit never returned the screwdriver. She keeps it in her bag as a memento. A worldly woman, she has her superstitious side.

23

My daughter Krystina lives in Jelenia Góra, in the green and peaceful mountains of Lower Schlesia. Her mother Gita remarried and had more daughters. In my neglectful absence, Gita's husband adopted Krystina, too. I barely kept up relations with her. For a long time we corresponded about once a year. Then Krystina married and changed her name and address, and I lost all contact with her. I never thought we would meet again.

Krystina recognized me on television and phoned the Israeli embassy in Warsaw in an attempt to get in touch with me. A young diplomat wrote down her telephone number and misplaced it. When he told me about this, I decided to find Krystina myself. It took me two weeks to track her down. We spoke over the telephone. She was highly emotional. I was less so. I didn't know what would develop between us or whether I wanted back in my life the child I had expelled from it before she was born. I promised to visit her the following weekend.

Shulamit agreed to come along. The drive took five hours. As usual, I didn't talk much on the way. The closer we came, the more curious I felt about meeting my oldest daughter at last. Although she was now a forty-two-year-old grandmother, I knew nothing about her. I had no way of knowing that, having cut her emotional ties with her mother at the age of fourteen, she had been longing for her biological father ever since. Twice she had run away from home as a teenager and tried in vain to locate me via the Polish-Jewish community. No one told her that I had left for Israel. Twice she was forced to return unwillingly to her mother.

As soon as she was old enough, Krystina fell into the first relationship to come along. It failed. Just like her father in his first marriage, she was too immature to share her life with anyone. Despite her repeated efforts to build a home and family, her yearning for a deep human bond went unfulfilled. When I met her, she was on her third marriage. Perhaps it was her gauntness that made me think of a wounded bird that could not fly. I had the awkward feeling one gets in the presence of the disabled. My neglect of her had clearly produced a maimed creature. Her efforts to conceal this behind a façade of self-confidence reminded me of myself. Her physical resemblance to me was even greater. 'You're as alike as two drops of water,' Shulamit marvelled.

This sense of sameness overwhelmed me from the moment I parked my car and she came running to greet me. She had been waiting by her window for hours. I don't know to this day what went through her mind while she sat there. I stepped from the car. We embraced as though we had just parted. Her body trembled. She gave me a searching look and said:

'You're all right.'

I took that to mean that she would accept me as I was.

'You are, too,' I said.

Shulamit stood off to the side, able only to guess what the two of us were feeling.

24

There was also a Jacek Frister in Poland. He was my son.

Jacek and Krystina had never met. Whereas Krystina wrote me letters and postcards, most of which went unanswered, Jacek was never interested enough in his half-sister and quarter-father to get in touch.

He was born in October 1952.

I was not a model parent. I hadn't wanted him at all. A justice of the peace in Wrocław made me acknowledge him.

Summoning me to his chambers, the judge asked:

'Why are you turning your back on your own offspring?'

'There's no proof that the child is mine.'

'I believe his mother's declaration.'

'On the basis of what, Comrade Judge? It was a casual acquaintanceship. His mother could have been sleeping with a dozen other men.'

'You had better face up to it, my young man. We live in a socialist society in which no child is illegitimate. Everyone deserves a father. Find Jacek another one and I'll shake your hand and send you on your way. But as long as you can't, you're his father. By the way, he's a very cute baby.'

'You haven't heard my side of it, Comrade Judge,' I protested.

'That will help you as much vitamins help a corpse. But if you insist, I'll hold a formal hearing. Your fellow reporters will be happy to write it up. You can give them my verdict as a scoop right now, because – begging your pardon – I do not intend to change my mind. Like it or not, the child's and society's welfare come before your private convenience ... Well?'

'You leave me no choice.'

'Quite right. Sign here and the case is closed. You'll pay two hundred zlotys alimony. That's less than a fifth of your newspaper salary. Not so terrible, is it?'

'Nothing is so terrible these days.'

The judge showed me where to sign. He had a crooked finger and ragged nails. I took a pen and wrote my name.

'Very wise of you,' he concluded, sticking the form in a green cardboard folder. I headed for the door. The judge cleared his throat. I turned around. He smiled contentedly and remarked:

'By the way, next time use a condom. I always do and I've never paid alimony yet.'

Czesia stood in the corridor, leaning on the sill of a high, narrow gothic window and gripping her bag as though it held a treasure. Her pale fingers all but crushed the clasp of it as she talked in whispers to her sister. A short, shapely woman of twenty-four, she had a pretty, mischievous face. She and her sister fell silent as I emerged from the judge's office.

'Well,' I flung angrily, 'you got what you wanted.'

'You needn't bother paying alimony,' she answered quietly. 'I don't want your money. But you have no right not to be the boy's father. Jacek is your son and should have your name.'

'He might have found himself a better one,' I replied, walking past her as if she were invisible.

I hadn't always felt that way about Czesia.

Czesia lived with her married sister in a small duplex house in a working-class neighbourhood far from the city centre. Her room was on the bottom floor, next to the kitchen; the upstairs belonged to her sister and brother-in-law. Her father, a horse trainer in a circus, had died when she was little, leaving her to manage on her own. Kept from continuing her studies past high school by the need to earn a living, she worked as a manicurist in a barber's shop. This did not prevent her from enjoying life, however. Czesia loved to laugh and dance. It took me years to realize how many tears were concealed by that laughter and how serious a person she was.

Some two years before my conversation with the judge, I had decided to spend a night at the Polonia. In the early fifties that was the place to go, mostly for its first-rate dance band. Although it was located on the ground floor of a shabby hotel near the Wrocław railroad station, a district unpleasant to walk in after dark, reservations were a must. Restaurants like the Polonia were good pick-up spots.

For that, though, I needed assistance. I not only had a bum ear, I had no sense of rhythm. The only dance I could do was the tango, which was largely practised in old-age homes at the time. My contemporaries were into more exotic things like the samba and the rumba, not to mention the boogie-woogie, the latest import from capitalist America. Now that its hops, steps and jumps had been declared 'decadent' by the Communist Party, it was a form of political protest.

With my clumsiness, the prospects of plucking a choice flower on the dance floor were slim. I was therefore compelled to make use of Robert, a carefree, vivacious fellow who worked as an understudy in Ida Kaminska's Yiddish theatre. Short, fat, and far from eloquent, Robert was a swinging dance partner. He was also hard up for cash, even though he lived with his parents. Our arrangement was a simple one. I paid for his meals and he brought his dance partners to our table. Since cutting in was acceptable in those days, he had his pick of the Polonia.

My attention was drawn by a blonde girl sitting with a bearded man. The man apparently had drunk too much, because he had fallen asleep among the empty glasses and plates of leftovers on the table while his date looked around for a knight-errant to rescue her. Our glances met. Mine sent a message of macho bravado. Hers replied: *Sorry, friend, but I'm not what you think.*

'Go ask her to dance,' I told Robert.

He looked her over professionally and declared: 'She's not worth it. There are better lookers here.'

Robert had his own system of evaluation. If he said, 'She's a ten,' he meant a woman was only worth taking home if no one better could be found by ten o'clock. His lowest grade was a two, which was his bedtime. The woman I pointed to was given a one-thirty. And it was only nine.

'It's a matter of taste,' I said.

'What's the matter? Feeling horny?'

'She turns me on.'

'You have a problem.'

'That's for sure.'

'I'll tell you what it is. The harder your prick, the softer your brains. It happens to some people.'

'Thanks.'

'Don't mention it. But I have a problem, too. I can dance with your shiksa all night, but how will I get her to this table? You see that guy that she's with. Drunks like him can be dangerous.'

'Tell her to step outside in ten minutes. I'll be waiting in my car.'

'My car' was a magic formula that few women could resist. In all of Wrocław there were three private automobiles, one of which I owned. Today you couldn't find the driver willing to take its wheel. It had a convertible Lancia chassis with a DKW engine that ran on a mixture of petrol and oil like a motorcycle and was equipped with an exhaust pipe to wake the dead. In 1951 in Wrocław, however, it was the ultimate status symbol.

My car was parked opposite the Polonia. I waited ten minutes. Czesia appeared at the end of the tenth. I opened the door for her.

'I'm Roman. I'm glad you came.'

'I know you are,' she smiled.

'Glad?'

'No. Roman.'

'How?'

'I saw you at the journalists' New Year's Eve party.'

'Are you a journalist?'

'No. I'm a manicurist. My name is Czesia.'

'Pleased to meet you,' I said. I leaned over to kiss her.

She pulled away. 'Not so fast. I'm the one who tells you when.'

'Don't count too much on my patience.'

'I wouldn't count on you for anything.'

'I'll teach you to trust me.'

'Where are we going?' she asked.

'To my place. It's not far. I've got –'

'I'll see for myself what you've got. And now take me home, please.'

We undressed, I a bit bashfully, Czesia as naturally as Eve in the Garden of Eden. Her bedroom was small. A bed by the wall, a closet, and a round table with two chairs were all its furnishings. On the table was a lamp with a pink shade. Its light gave a pleasant glow. Czesia stood uninhibitedly naked, letting her gorgeous body do the talking. I ran my eyes over the curve of her hips, feeling the blood pulse in every limb. As she bent to remove the bedspread, her firm buttocks tantalized me so that I gave them a hard whack with the flat of my hand. I had never done such a thing in my life and was sure she would be furious. Before I could apologize, she straightened up and said with lowered eyes: 'You're the boss. Do what you want with me.'

I couldn't explain it. How had this splendid creature, who half an hour ago had been telling me off, melted into such submissiveness? I didn't try hiding my desire for her. It was clear to see. 'Do what you want with me,' she whispered again. Those weren't just words. She really wanted me to give my imagination free rein. 'I'm your slave,' she added, looking straight at me. For the first time in my life I had a woman at my absolute beck and call. I had never known how pleasurable that could be. Together we set out on a long journey to the frontiers of intimacy. I learned things I had never known. I allowed myself to hurt her. 'More,' she pleaded. When we panted to our climax, she grasped my neck with all her strength and said softly: 'I love you.'

I wasn't looking for love. I never dreamed she might be telling the truth. She wouldn't have been the first to say she loved me without meaning it. The word was a cliché – a mere synonym for sexual desire, attraction, or excitation. It took me nearly forty years to understand that for Czesia it was more than that. I might have realized it sooner had I not had to clear out of Wrocław in a hurry two months after meeting her.

Just when nothing seemed more certain than my journalistic career, I was summoned again for interrogation by the Public Security Service. The accusation against me was more serious. I was charged with sabotage. Several hours of intensive questioning helped me to understand how the diligent PSS men were trying to frame me.

Although far from blind, I had failed to face up to reality. It was not by accident that the Communist regime wanted journalists to live the good life. Reporting on the world around us from our own privileged positions, we did not share its discontents. Our salaries were far above the national average. A journalist's card opened closed doors. The confidential information received by us, although selective, created the illusion of being a party to policy making. Blind and bloated with self-importance, I had never challenged the heavy sentences meted out in political trials nor the fact that these were held in military courts. And yet not only did I have no idea of what constitutional crimes were being committed, I didn't know what Poland's constitution even said.

'Sabotage' was a category of the criminal code that covered practically anything, from dealing in foreign currency to 'failure to perform one's public duty'. Almost anyone could be jailed for it. People were sent to prison for 'complicity in Poland's defeat in 1939', for 'seeking to undermine the regime by persuasion or bribery', for 'dissemination of false information'. Needless to say, information that the regime did not wish to be revealed was usually false by definition. We journalists were subject to a standing order of the censor's bureau that banned all political news not released by the official press agency. We were also forbidden any criticism of the Soviet Union; any mention of work accidents, natural disasters, environmental pollution, or foreign trade; any allusion to public wastefulness, low standards of production, food shortages, or scarcities. Most hush-hush of all was any illness in one of our leaders.

The list of unmentionables was generally updated every month. The censor told us which books to praise in the literary pages and which pointedly to ignore. Statistics concerning alcoholism, venereal disease, and Poland's exports to the Soviet bloc were forbidden, too. Only the chief editors and their assistants were even allowed to see the censor's directives. These were kept in locked safes; copying them was a criminal disclosure of state secrets. Censorship itself, of course, was perfectly legal. So were political trials. It never occurred to me to reflect upon the fact that they were legal in the Third Reich, too. I never sought to deconstruct a legal system written by the Communists for their own self-protection.

Compared to others, I was doing well on the eve of my arrest. I had a nice private house, a mistress I liked, a private car, good health, and what were considered to be good looks. The youngest of three assistant editors on the staff of *Polish Word*, one of Wrocław's two mass-circulation dailies, I had nearly reached the pinnacle of my profession by the age of twenty-three. The very top, of course, was for Party members alone. I took it for granted that the press was meant to spearhead the regime's propaganda efforts just as I assumed that the public had no right to know. Being part of the Communist system did not disturb me. Although I was not attracted by Marxist ideology, did not hold egalitarian views, and believed in individual enterprise and talent, I never questioned that I would eventually become a Party member. I even submitted my application, certain that it would be accepted within a year. I was no different in this respect from thousands of others who would one day be called crass opportunists.

Twice a week I was on duty as night editor. My job was to read every page laid out by the news editors and confirm by my signature that it was consistent with the principles of socialism – principles that had been defined by no one and that were interpreted differently by every official. Often I was nonplussed by the new winds that blew daily. Yesterday's green light was today's red one and vice versa. I failed to grasp that these about-faces reflected power struggles within the Party in which every faction was pushing for a different policy. I was serving a cause whose true nature I knew nothing of. All I did know was that, in case of doubt, I should consult with the head of the information department at regional Party headquarters. We all regularly passed the buck by sending him numerous articles and stories. He, too, however, was in no hurry to make decisions and tried to cover himself with OK's from higher up. In the wee hours of the morning, when the secretaries of the Politburo in Warsaw were unavailable, he preferred to return the ball to our court. 'Use your own judgment,' was his way of putting it.

Two days before my arrest Generalissimo Stalin had given an exclusive interview to a publication of the Chinese Communist Party in which he strongly attacked the production and use of nuclear weapons. By then the Rosenbergs had passed US atomic secrets to the Soviet Union and the Russians were acutely aware of the non-conventional arms gap between them and the Americans. Although this was why Stalin was seeking to mobilize world public opinion against 'the West's atomic conspiracy', I could never have dreamed that it would lead to my own political downfall.

It was nearly midnight when Gerd Grendziak, the editor of *Polish Word*'s front page, showed me the interview. Stalin's remarks, complete with a headline and a subhead, had come straight from the government press agency in Warsaw. In such cases, we knew, not a comma could be changed.

The original headline sent by the telex ticker said:

Generalissimo Stalin Issues Declaration on Banning A-Bomb Production.

I had no way of knowing that Grendziak had made a small change in it.

He himself had thought nothing of it. The problem was that the banner headline we were ordered to run could not accommodate that many words without reducing the size of the print, an inconceivable step when it came to Stalin's name. Grendziak, therefore – the Lord only knew what devil got into him – decided to omit the word 'Banning'. Since the caption still made perfect sense to me, I signed the page without a second thought and forwarded it to the censor. The latter, relying on my signature, OK'd it for print.

We knocked off at 2 a.m. In the café behind the Opera House two ballet dancers were waiting for us after appearing in the season's hit, Glier's *The Red Poppy*. The best-looking girls in the corps had been picked for it. Since every night shift was followed by twenty-four hours off, we spent the next day and night with them in a small town outside Wrocław. Leaving the change from a hundred-zloty note on the counter of the hotel kept the desk clerk from asking any questions. We returned to Wrocław at eight in the morning. I went straight to the newspaper. Gerd, who only worked nights, took the keys to my apartment for a few more hours with the girls.

My secretary looked flabbergasted to see me. 'What are you doing here? Everyone thought you'd escaped abroad.'

'Abroad? Why?'

'Because of the sabotage.'

'What are you talking about?' I said angrily. 'Are you out of your mind?'

I started to open the door to my office.

'I wouldn't go in there. They're waiting for you.'

'Bull,' I said and stepped inside.

On the third day of my arrest, I was offered a tempting deal: I could go free if I agreed to pin the rap on Gerd Grendziak. All I had to do was sign a statement that the night editor had gotten me drunk and made me sign the page while I was under the influence. 'We'll emphasize that you never meant to harm Comrade Stalin's image,' I was told.

I refused. Although I was young, I was not stupid. Such a confession would have been self-incriminating. Getting drunk on the job was as bad as sabotage. Eternal vigilance was the price of socialism. 'You're making a bad mistake,' my interrogator warned me. He opened a desk drawer, took out some keys, and laid them in front of me. I recognized them as my own. The hint was clear. Grendziak was under arrest, too. The poor bastard, I thought, taken into the cold from his warm bed. In the friendliest of tones, the interrogator tried again:

'What's it to you if you send him away for twenty years? He's not worth sticking up for. He's a Schlesian of German origin. His family lives in Düsseldorf. You can't have forgotten what the Germans did to your people, your parents, your family.'

I said nothing.

'Your nobility of soul will get you nowhere. You're endangering a fine career, a brilliant future, all possible chance of promotion. Grendziak has already admitted his guilt. He'll serve you up to us on a platter, roasted and ready to eat. Would you like to read his statement?' The interrogator waved a sheet of paper. 'No? You're under no obligation. But here, let me read you what it says. It says that you planned the whole thing. You bought a bottle of vodka before Grendziak's shift began . . . Just a minute, I'll even tell you where you bought it . . . Well, the little details are unimportant. What matters is that you forced him to drink. You told him that a glass or two would fortify him for the ballet dancers and saw to it that he drank half a litre. When he was pie-eyed – he remembers it despite being in a daze – you took the front page and crossed a word out. We have proof of it. We found the half-empty bottle with your fingerprints.'

I listened with growing incredulity. How could my prints have been found on the bottle? I had never been fingerprinted in my life. Besides, I didn't believe that my friend Gerd would play such a dirty trick. As though reading my mind, the interrogator said:

'You were drinking buddies. But Grendziak was no buddy. He took advantage of you.'

'He's not like that.'

'You bet he is. He's a low type.' The interrogator pushed the keys towards me. 'Sign here and the keys are yours. Those two beauties are probably still there.'

'I'm not signing.'

'I wanted to make it easy for you. But you're stupid and you're stubborn. You'll pay for it.'

I wasn't called for questioning again. After a week I was released. No explanation was given, just as none was offered for the fact that Gerd Grendziak was jailed for nine months without a trial.

Although free, I no longer had any rights. Having seen the inside of a Public Security Service cell was enough to brand you for life. I wasn't surprised to find a dismissal notice from the newspaper waiting for me when I returned home. I wasn't allowed to take the personal articles from my room. Even my coat remained behind.

I had no savings and no money. Telling no one, not even Czesia, I sold my car and moved to Warsaw. In the big city, I thought, I could lie low, disappear in the crowd, and find a haven. To say nothing of the fact that Mira was waiting for me there with a warm bed and a roof above my head.

Suffice it to say that our relationship did not turn out to be a great source of joy to her. When I moved into her country house outside Warsaw, I had every reason to believe that my motives were sincere. I was convinced that I had finished sowing my wild oats and was ready to settle down and start a family. Mira struck me as the perfect mate. She was pretty, Jewish, and practical. Today, years later, I realize that I was wrong. She was simply a lifebuoy. But the price paid for this realization was high and it was she who paid it.

Mira worked for the Party's central committee. I was unemployed. No newspaper was going to hire me. Since the Party controlled the media, all my job applications ended up on the desk of the same man, who turned down each one of them. I worked at odd jobs and did translation and ghost writing. A friend who edited a transportation journal asked me to write an article about a railroad car factory in Wrocław. I jumped at the opportunity. I still had a soft spot for the city in which I had experienced so much and was glad to visit it at someone else's

expense. I imagined coming back to it as though the year I was
away had been but a day.

The city had not changed. But I had. Wrocław no longer
inspired the warm old feelings. I rented a room in the Hotel
Polonia. It was a winter day. The heating was on the blink. The
mattresses were filthy. The wallpaper was peeling. The bathroom
smelled unpleasantly of disinfectant. The muffled sounds of the
dance band reached my room from the restaurant on the ground
floor. I thought of Czesia. I didn't have to shut my eyes to see her
before me. Her telephone number was in my address book. There
was a public phone in the corridor. I dialled. Bracing myself for an
onslaught, I thought of ways to mollify her. But Czesia sounded
glad to hear from me, as though she had been waiting all along for
my call.

'What are you doing in a hotel? Grab a taxi and come to my
place.'

'I've got some urgent business right now. I can come in an
hour.'

'If I waited a year, I can wait another hour,' she joked. 'Do you
remember the address?'

'What a question!'

'Then come.'

I had no urgent business. I was simply embarrassed to admit
that my merry bachelor days were over and I had to watch every
penny. Rather than take a cab, I preferred buying Czesia flowers –
even the cheapest were expensive in winter – and taking the tram
to her house. She was waiting for me in the entrance. We went
right to her bedroom. Instinctively, I reached for the light switch.
She seized my hand. I could feel the warmth of her own.

'Wait,' she said.

'What is it?' I joshed. 'You always liked to make love with the
lights on. You haven't put on weight, have you? . . . Well, say
something!'

'You'll understand in a minute.'

The curtains shut out the glow of the street lamps. I could
barely make out Czesia's profile in the darkness. Her dress
rustled as it fell to the floor.

'What's the rush?'

'Get undressed and don't talk so loud. I want to feel you close to me. The night is long. We'll have plenty of time to talk. There must be things you want to tell me.'

'I owe you an explanation of –'

'Shh. Don't talk so loud.'

'Why whisper?'

'I want to hear you whisper "I love you".'

She pulled me to the bed.

'I missed you,' I said, searching for the nipples of her breasts.

'I don't need to be missed. I need to be loved.'

I touched her flat stomach. Czesia took my hand. 'Do what you want with me,' she murmured, her body as taut and yielding as always. I pulled her towards me. An infant's cry filled the room.

'What's that?'

'That's your son. His name is Jacek.'

'Oh, no,' I groaned.

'Oh, yes,' she laughed, getting up to turn on the light. 'Look at him. He's a sweet baby. He hardly ever cries or makes trouble.'

In August 1973 I went to meet Jacek at Ben-Gurion Airport. I would never have recognized him without a full description. A bearded young man of twenty-two strode out of the Arrivals building. We embraced like old friends. He had come for a month's vacation, part pleasure and part getting to know his father. Since Poland had severed diplomatic relations with Israel after the Six Day War, his trip had been semi-clandestinely arranged by Yitzhak Patish, the Israeli ambassador in Vienna. Jacek was a law student at Wrocław University and could have gotten into trouble had the authorities discovered that he had journeyed to the Zionist state without permission.

Although I was determined to make his stay a pleasant one, I felt that we were not communicating. He aroused no fatherly feelings in me. We were strangers to each other. Only our mutual desire to avoid a rupture kept things on an even keel. In the evenings, after a day's touring, we often talked about his mother. The more Jacek told me about her, the more my admiration for Czesia grew. At the age of thirty she had finished accountancy school and successfully competed for a senior position in a government food marketing firm. Some time after this she married Janusz, a gentle, sensitive man with whom she had another son.

And yet when Janusz offered to adopt Jacek and give him his last name, Czesia objected. 'The boy comes from my love for another man,' Jacek heard her tell his stepfather. She had wanted him to grow up knowing that his real father lived in Israel and was irreplaceable. Jacek found himself in a difficult position. In public school he was called 'the Jew-bastard'. The high school girls wouldn't go out with him. More than once he came home in tears and begged his mother to bury her past for the sake of his future. She refused. Jacek was condemned to bear the name that a justice of the peace had given him against my will.

I saw Czesia again during my stay in Warsaw for Maxwell Communication. Twelve years earlier, when Jacek visited Israel a second time, I had asked him to bring her photograph. 'She wouldn't give it to me,' he told me when he arrived. 'She wants you to remember her as she was.' Now I understood why. Time had not been kind to her. Her hair was white. Her face looked shrunken. The lustre was gone from her eyes, the shapeliness from her body. Yet she never complained or criticized me. Her rented apartment was always open to me and Shulamit. Both she and Janusz had retired early because of poor health and lived in semi-poverty. Nor did they have a chance to enjoy the small apartment that they bought with a modest sum that I gave them. Czesia died of heart failure on 16 January 1991, the day before my sixty-third birthday. I was in my hotel suite. A bottle of wine was chilling in the fridge. We were expecting dinner guests. Suddenly the phone rang. It was Jacek. 'My mother is dead,' he told me. After a long silence he asked:

'Will you come to the funeral?'

'Of course.'

I felt a deep grief. That night I ran a fever. The next day I drove for four hours through a snowstorm to pay Czesia the respects she had never gotten from me while she lived. I arrived just in time. Friends and relations filled the small neighbourhood church. I knew no one beside Jacek and his wife. No one greeted me. I felt out of place. Czesia's coffin stood on a polished marble platform in the nave. The air smelled of incense. Many of the mourners had brought flowers. Czesia's made-up face was pale, almost white. I stepped up to the coffin for a last look. Her eyes were shut. I bent and kissed her lightly on the cheek. At that moment I realized for the first time that she had never stopped loving me.

The priest gave a sign for the funeral procession to set out. The gravediggers shut the lid of the coffin. Members of the family bore it on their shoulders. With no feeling of belonging, I followed it to a grave dug in the frozen earth. My mind was a total blank. The cold cut through me. The priest mumbled the words of the requiem. Czesia's sister was crying. Her husband kept crossing himself. I was so frozen in body and soul that I didn't even notice the ceremony end. Jacek touched me on the shoulder and said:

'I hope you won't mind if I don't walk you back to your car, Father. The family is going to my aunt's for the wake.'

'Of course I won't,' I said. I turned up my collar and headed for the gate. The snow was still falling. The feeling of not belonging was mutual. With Czesia gone, there was no more place for me in Jacek's world. It was my last farewell not only to her, but to our son and everything between us.

25

The sight of Czesia's pale face in her coffin made me resolve to give up the search for the past. Each time I found a piece of it, the result was disappointment and bafflement. The road leading to the places that had meant so much to me took me back not to my youth but to an empty theatre I did not wish to visit. The actors had changed. The drama was over. Behind the curtain was an empty stage with scattered props, faded colours, wilted flowers. Only what was shielded from all contact with the present survived intact in one's memory. This was why I never looked for Monika, although I could easily have traced her. She was the woman I most wanted to protect from the corruption of time. Perhaps she felt the same, since she never revealed her presence all the time I was in Poland. We both kept our old love stored safely in our souls, away from the test of a reunion.

If I had thought the Holocaust years had extinguished my capacity for true love, it was Monika who taught me I was wrong. She was the first woman in my life towards whom I behaved with more than cool calculation or momentary impulse. She made me feel that my heart was not just a pump for driving the blood through my veins; that there were fires that did not have to scorch me; that the closed person I was could open up. Until I met her, my way of relating to others was through my work as a journalist; I was like the stuttering actor who can only speak normally when impersonating someone on the stage. There is an entire psychological literature on this trait, which characterizes me in some measure to this day. People interviewed by me, or approached in connection with my work, find me warm and friendly without realizing that this is merely a technique. The only people I have been able to communicate with truly, without deception and without posing, are the women who have uncorked my passion, revealing hidden lusts that were new to me.

Monika was a year older than myself. Although she was educated in an Ursuline convent, her strict Catholic schooling had not dampened her fiery temperament. At the time I met her, shortly after parting from Gita, she was studying law in Wrocław while I still lived near Jelenia Góra. Every day I travelled a hundred kilometres on my motorcycle to spend the evening with her. I memorized whole Socratic dialogues to make myself her equal and have something to talk to her about. I desired her without daring to touch her. This went on for long months until we finally tasted the forbidden fruit and immediately regretted having wasted so much time.

Monika's mother was the editor of the local edition of *Polish Word*, the newspaper I eventually began my career with. While still living with Gita I had begun writing essays and stories that I filed away in a drawer because they did not seem good enough to print. This was not, however, the opinion of Jozef Muszkat, who worked for *Polish Word* in Jelenia Góra – or so he said one evening when I brought him some material to read. Impressed by his spacious home with its telex machine in the study, I was grateful for being treated as an equal rather than as a pupil by a teacher. Muszkat brought me a glass of orange liqueur, sat in an armchair facing mine, put on his glasses, and turned to the manuscript I had given him. I studied his face impatiently as he let page after page fall to the floor. Now and then he refilled my glass. I was not used to alcohol. My legs felt heavy. My head spun.

'Thanks, I've had enough,' I said.

'You'll never be an author,' he teased. 'All the great works of literature were written by men who were drunk.'

He filled my glass again. I gulped its contents and felt sick to the stomach. Excusing myself, I went to the bathroom, leaned over the toilet, and puked. I flushed the water, embarrassed to think that Muszkat had heard everything. He took off his glasses for a moment when I returned, gave me a fatherly look, and said with a smile:

'Don't be upset. You'll grow older and learn to hold your liquor.'

'I think I'd better go home.'

'Don't you want to hear my opinion?'

'Very much so. But I don't feel well.'

'Lie down while I finish reading.'

'I think I should –'

'No, you shouldn't. You're in no condition to ride your motorcycle. You're my guest and I'm responsible for you.'

'If you say so.'

'I do. Get into bed and forget everything. Tomorrow you'll feel like a new man.'

Muszkat rose, took me by the hand, and led me to the bedroom. I sat on a corner of the bed. 'Permit me,' he said when I had trouble with my shoelaces. I noticed his bald spot as he bent to untie them. My head ached. I undressed. With a feeling of relief I slipped beneath the blanket. The sour bile in my mouth made me fear I would throw up again. Before I could apologize, I was asleep, the last link to reality snapped.

I was dreaming. In my dream Muszkat's damp body was clinging to mine.

Slowly consciousness returned, as though from a distance. No, it was no dream. I could hear Muszkat's breath come in spurts. He was groping at my behind. I tried to move to the edge of the bed. He gripped my waist.

'Don't move,' he said like an adult commanding a child.

'Take your hands off me!' I yelled.

He let go of me. 'Don't be afraid,' he whispered. 'I won't hurt you.'

The alcohol evaporated at once. Stone-cold sober, I jumped out of bed. Muszkat lay there naked. Only now did I notice how thin he was. His ribs stuck out. His skin was clammy, repulsive.

'I disgust you,' he said sadly, reading my mind.

'What have you done to me?' I burst out. 'What have you done? Yes, you disgust me! I hate you!'

I was distraught. Muszkat drew the blanket over himself. 'You're not a child any more,' he said. 'Surely you can understand . . .' He never finished the sentence.

Yes, I was not a child. I could understand. I just couldn't forgive. An hour ago he was a man on a pedestal, a prominent journalist, a role model. My greatest desire was to be like him. Now, in one fell swoop, he had shattered everything. I pulled on my clothes, furious to be cheated of my ambition. I wanted only to get away, to disappear.

Muszkat turned on the light. I gave him a furious look. Why, damn it, had he spoiled it all? 'Where are my manuscripts?' I said. 'I'm going home.'

'Don't,' he said with sudden mildness. 'And don't be afraid. I was carried away. It won't happen again, I promise.' He stood facing me, wrapped in a sheet. He put his glasses on and sat down. 'You were too handsome to resist.'

'That's a lie. You planned it all in advance. Every detail.'

'Handsome and intelligent, too. Suppose I did. What's wrong with that? I didn't mean any harm. The love of a man for a man can be as beautiful as for a woman. Have you never had such an experience?'

'I have.'

'Then why am I any worse than the man you had it with?'

'It's a long story.'

'Tell me about it.'

'No.'

'Why not? The night is still long. We're not going to be able to sleep. Tell me.'

'I can't. Not now.'

'Then write about it.'

'Some day.'

'Why some day? Write it now, while you're angry. While the experience is still there and you're on fire. I read your stories. They're good. They're very good. But they have no soul. No passion. Go to my study and write. Now!'

'You're not serious.'

'I'm as serious as I'll ever be.'

'It's madness.'

'With a method,' he grinned.

It was two o'clock in the morning. I hesitated. Muszkat got into bed and turned out the light. 'Wake me when you finish,' he said.

I knew he was right. If I didn't write it now, I never would. I shut the bedroom door and went to his study. His desk light was on. The liqueur bottle stood on some files. I threw it in the wastepaper basket. It made my hands sticky. I took a pen and wrote.

Everyone called him Arpad Basci. He had been in more prisons than schools. He began his career as a pickpocket in the Budapest railroad station. As he grew older he took up burglary, an uncommon profession among Hungary's Jews. He was in jail so often that he became a king there. But for the German conquerors of his country he was a petty criminal – and a Jewish one at that. Long before Eichmann's deportation of Hungarian Jews, he was sent to Auschwitz. From there he was transferred to the work camp in which I met him.

Arpad Basci had a special status in the camp. An expert sculptor of chess pieces, he carved them from a rare material: bread. The camp guards who coveted his work brought him as much bread as he wished. Arpad Basci liked young boys; the young boys in the camp liked bread; and so the world went round.

He had a keen eye for spotting his new victims. The day after my arrival in the camp I was assigned to his crew of bread chewers. At night, after work, he sat five or six of us on the floor of the barracks and handed us lumps of bread. Our job was to chew them slowly, rolling them between our tongues and our palates until our saliva made them soft and malleable. From such bread alone, he explained, could he model his immortal creations. Once hardened it would withstand for ever the ravages of time, humidity, and bugs.

The bread tasted divine. Anyone swallowing a crumb would regret it. Arpad Basci was merciless. Seated opposite us, his eyes staring at each of our Adam's apples in turn, he warned that he would choke to death whoever fell into temptation. He knew how starved we were and he knew our tricks.

We spat the chewed bread onto a white linen cloth, where Arpad Basci inspected it as carefully as a jeweller grading diamonds, prodding it lightly for viscosity. Anything failing to meet his standards was scraped off the cloth and returned to the chewer. By the time I received the crust of bread that was my pay, my jaws ached.

Lights-out came at ten. At that hour we were supposed to be in our bunks with our uniforms folded and our shaven heads visible for counting. Only the kapo and Arpad Basci were allowed to move about at night. The kapo slept in a private little cubicle. Arpad Basci had his own habits.

I chewed Arpad Basci's bread for about two months before the time came for my final payment on his bread crusts. My bunkmate said nothing when Arpad Basci ordered him out of our shared bed and slipped into his place behind me. Even before he touched me I knew what was going to happen. His hand roamed my body, a shaky finger searching for the entrance. Smeared with lard, it easily found my anus and corkscrewed into it. Although I tensed my muscles to prevent him, the old man got the better of me. As soon as his finger was withdrawn his penis rammed into me with a single quick thrust. The pain was terrible. I wanted to scream. As if knowing my reaction, he covered my mouth with his hand. In it was a slice of bread. I stifled my cry and ate the bread from his hand. When I finished the first slice, a second filled my mouth. I swallowed it quickly in the hope of a third before he ejaculated. An expert rapist, he drilled into me with short, rhythmic strokes. My body felt torn apart. The sharp pain became a burning ache. I was bleeding.

He fell back. I swallowed the last crumbs. Only then was I overcome with humiliation and shame for having sold my honour for his bread. No, I wasn't raped. I hadn't resisted. I hadn't called for help. I hadn't even told him to stop. I had said nothing when he gave me a good-night slap on the rear and went off to sleep in his bunk.

He didn't go empty-handed. Two hours later I awoke from a draining, nightmarish dream to discover that my cap was gone. A prisoner without his standard-issue cap was as good as dead. At morning roll-call the kapo and SS officer regularly killed anyone not having one. Sometimes they played a game in which the kapo seized a cap and flung it across the parade grounds. If the owner of it stayed where he was, he was shot for being capless. If he ran to retrieve it, he was shot for 'attempting to escape'.

The son of a bitch! I cursed Arpad Basci under my breath. I had two, at most three, hours left to live. Cold sweat covered my back. I felt it drip down my spine. Arpad Basci's intention was clear. He wanted to get rid of me because I knew too much. I had never paid much attention until now to the fact that his bread chewers had a way of dying or disappearing under mysterious circumstances. The last one had drowned in a tank of excrement in the camp's outhouse.

I restrained myself from going to Arpad Basci's bunk and demanding my cap back. I could identify it easily. It had bloodstains from the time I was clubbed on the head by a kapo. But what good would that do? Arpad Basci would say it wasn't mine. He would laugh or call for his friend the kapo to punish me. In the Kingdom of Evil proof or evidence meant nothing. No word was more ridiculous than 'justice'. Arpad Basci was an old and privileged prisoner while I was just a number with an arm attached. I stood no chance in an open confrontation.

I slid quietly down from my bunk. My bare feet touched the concrete floor. Its chill surface felt good and cooled my feverish brain. I looked to the left and the right. A naked bulb above the door gave the only dim light that there was. The barracks resembled a dark tunnel. I heard the breathing of the sleeping prisoners. Somebody snored. I walked down the narrow aisle between the bunks, stopping every few seconds to listen, then move on. With cat's eyes I looked for the careless prisoner who had not hidden his cap beneath his blanket. I was scared. I would be lynched if I were discovered. No one would defend me. The theft of a cap was an unpardonable crime.

My anus was burning. Someone coughed. I froze. The cougher fell silent. I took a few steps and halted, racking my mind for an alibi in case I was caught. I had once witnessed the catching of a cap thief in Auschwitz. His fellow prisoners hanged him from a rafter. They left his body hanging all day as a warning. Involuntarily, I glanced at the ceiling. That was what led me to my victim.

He was lying in a top bunk, his face covered by his blanket. The tip of his cap stuck out from the crook of his arm. I tugged at it gently. He didn't awake. The cap was in my hand. I stuck it under my shirt, its rough cloth scratching my chest. I was overjoyed.

I started back to my bunk. I musn't hurry. I listened. Silence. The pounding of my heart was the only sound I heard. I tiptoed slowly. It took me ten minutes – or was it only one? – to regain my bunk. The man on the bottom mattress turned over in his sleep. Had he seen me? I held my breath. Weary, he slept on. We all were weary. No sleeping pill was as strong as our exhaustion. I clambered up to my mattress and stuck the cap in my pocket. I couldn't sleep. I stayed awake until reveille.

Roll-call was at five. Spotlights lit up the parade grounds. A light snow was falling. The cold cut to the bone. "Ten-tion!" shouted the kapo. We snapped to attention. The count began. I was in the second row. It was always good to be in the middle, neither too prominent nor too exposed, as far as possible from the officer's glance. In front of me, at the end of the first row, was the unassailable Arpad Basci. I recognized him by the back of his neck. It was the only one to have folds of fat on it. It belonged to a man who ate well. I recognized my cap, too, by the bloodstains.

Somewhere behind me was a man waiting to die. Only he, Arpad Basci, and I myself knew it was about to happen. Arpad Basci would be disappointed. I had no idea what the man without the cap felt. I had no qualms. I refused to think about it from his point of view. His existence didn't matter. Mine did.

The officer and the kapo walked down the lines, inspecting our uniforms, our posture, our ability to work. I counted the seconds as they counted the prisoners. I wanted it to be over. They were up to row four. The capless man didn't beg for his life. We all knew the rules of the game, the killers and the killed alike. There was no need for words. The shot rang out without warning. There was a short, dry, echoless thud. One bullet to the brain. They always shot you in the back of the skull. There was a war on. Ammunition had to be used sparingly. I didn't want to know who the man was. I was delighted to be alive.

I had finished. The pages lay in front of me. My handwriting was clear. Although the lines marched across the paper like prisoners on parade, the letters reared back, reluctant to make a word and yet another word. I ran my hand across the first page as if to brush away a speck of dust. I had done it! I had looked at what had happened without flinching, unvarnished by half-truths or half-lies. All that remained was to edit it. For that, though, I lacked the strength. I feared the text would turn on me, forcing me to tear it up to avoid judgment. I pushed it to the edge of the desk. Muszkat entered the room and picked it up.

'Are you going to read it now?' I asked.

'We're both waiting for an answer,' he said cryptically.

I watched him as he read. I had never before noticed the grey hairs in his moustache, the palpitation of his eyelids behind his horn-rimmed glasses, his manicured nails. His light wool suit concealed the thinness of his body. He rested his left leg on his right knee, then reversed position and crossed the right leg on the left knee. His hand drifted across the desk, its fingers drumming. This annoyed me. An undefinable tension filled the room. Muszkat reached the last page. He removed his glasses and looked at me as if doubting that I was the author.

'Is this all true?' he asked after a long silence.

'Every word of it.'

'I suppose you want to know my opinion.'

'Yes.'

He cleared his throat. 'It's a good story. We'll publish it in the Sunday supplement.'

'Never.'

'What?'

'It's not for publication.'

'Then why did you write it?'

'I don't know. Because I had to. Maybe because . . .'

'. . . of what happened tonight?'

'Maybe.'

'You're still angry, aren't you?'

'Yes.'

'The best works are written in anger or pain.'

'I'm not Dostoyevsky.'

'That's true. But there's a moral in your story for everyone.'

I didn't know what he meant. He laid a hand on my knee. Although this time it was the innocent gesture of a teacher in a tutorial, I pushed it away firmly. Muszkat understood. He thought for a moment, moved his chair so that he faced me, and said:

'I look at you – and what do I see? A handsome, personable young man with curly hair and a dark complexion, the typical product of a good family. But that's all an optical illusion. Every person has an outer shell that hides his inner self. It takes a surgeon to cut through that shell and bare the guts. The words you wrote were your scalpel. You ran it right through the wound.

You've demonstrated what honesty means. There's no going back on that. You can't repair the shell and crawl into it again as if nothing has happened. Think about that while I make you some coffee.'

We drank coffee and ate yeast cookies that stuck to the mouth like Arpad Basci's bread. Muszkat put up with my refusal to publish the story. We parted as friends. Before I left he bared his heart to me. He told me about his own concentration camp experience, his attraction to men, his fear of discovery. 'I envy you,' he said. 'To my dying day I'll lack the courage to slice open my shell and show what's inside it.'

His dying day came in a dingy basement apartment in Ramat-Gan, on the outskirts of Tel Aviv, where he died of an illness undiagnosable by modern medicine: homesickness. In March 1968, caught up in a wave of anti-Semitic purges, he was forced to leave Poland. The authorities had known of his homosexual tendencies and arraigned him for seducing a minor. A young plain-clothes agent testified that he had had sexual relations with him in return for the promise of a military exemption. Muszkat, he said, had lured him to his apartment, held a long telephone conversation with an officer at an army induction centre, and then made love to him.

In his cross-examination Muszkat asked the young man where the telephone in his apartment had stood and what colour it was. 'It was black and on your windowsill,' was the answer. The next day he surprised the judges with an official letter confirming that no telephone had been installed in his new apartment. But although the case was dismissed, he lost his job and was given the friendly advice to emigrate to the Zionist state. He never came to terms with the injustice. In Israel he was taken no notice of. Even I only sat by his deathbed to repay an old debt.

He never tried touching me again after that first night. His feeling of spiritual closeness to me held him in check while he steered me with a sure hand into the closed world of Polish journalism. It was his recommendation that got me a job with *Polish Word*, first as a reporter and then as editor of the Jelenia Góra edition. When I was fired because of a madcap stunt, he had me transferred to the paper's staff in Wrocław. He was even proud of me.

As befitted a socialist newspaper, *Polish Word* had a stable of proletarian stringers, mostly factory workers and officials who sent in news of the workplace in return for a modest fee. Their articles and payment were handled by me. I edited their crude prose, prepared it for print, and sent them their money once a month.

Everything would have been fine had not my financial needs soared. Needing money to buy petrol for my frequent trips to see Monika, I began phasing out our proletarian contributors, writing their articles myself and sending the remuneration meant for them to a list of 'dead souls' composed of my acquaintances. Within a year I had tripled my income.

The editors of *Polish Word* were surprised by the improved quality of the material they were getting. So great was their satisfaction that they decided to hold a conference of proletarian writers in Jelenia Góra at which certificates of merit would be awarded. At this point my dead souls, who included several doctors, lawyers, and even one police officer, refused to cooperate any further. I went to Muszkat, who had meanwhile moved to Wrocław, and told him the truth. Roaring with laughter, he promised to take care of the matter.

I was severely rebuked and transferred to the local editions department of the Wrocław office as 'a talented young man in need of careful supervision'. This department was headed by Maria, a woman who came from the extinct Polish petty nobility. Not only did she receive me kindly, she, too, was amused by my caper. She was already acquainted with me, because I was a frequent visitor in her house and had been the source of much aggravation there even before moving to Wrocław – all on account of Monika.

Monika was Maria's daughter and Maria had planned Monika's future; the plan, to which Monika had agreed, was for her to finish her law studies and marry the man of her mother's choice. When I met Monika, as Maria explained to me during my first dinner in her house, the bridegroom was still waiting patiently. Maria knew why she was telling me this, for she wanted me to realize that I had nothing to look forward to – other perhaps than her home-made cake for dessert. She overestimated her daughter's straightlacedness as badly as she underestimated my desire for her daughter.

These dinners became a regular institution. On special occasions they came with vodka. Christmas Eve was one of these. By the time we had reached the last course, the bottle on the table was half-empty. As I still could not hold my liquor, I was reeling. 'I'm not letting you ride back through the snow in your state,' said Maria, overruling my feeble objections and making a bed for me on a folding cot in the kitchen.

Monika slept in a room across the hallway. It was all of ten steps away. Had it belonged to anyone else, I would have covered this distance as soon as Maria went to bed. But my love for Monika misled me. She was a mystery to me and I was afraid of being rejected. We would never have gotten together if she hadn't made the first move.

I heard the hinges creak. The door opened. I moved over to make room for her. Then I touched her. She touched me back. We made love silently. I took my time. I wanted the river to flow for ever and not reach the sea.

In the nights to come we trysted in Monika's room. A framed photograph of her fiancé stood on her night table. Before undressing she turned it face down. What the man in the photograph did not see, however, Monika's mother did. Aware of the shenanigans beneath her roof, she reacted with typical tact.

'Did you notice how dry it was last night?' she asked me over breakfast one morning. 'I had to go to the kitchen three times for a glass of water.'

I turned red. She could not have failed to notice that the cot there was empty.

'I'm happy to see you still can blush,' she remarked, biting into her slice of bread and butter.

'Mother, I'm a big girl,' Monika said.

'I suppose you're in love,' Maria persisted.

I nodded.

'Well, then, permit me to clarify your situation.'

'Mother, not now, please.'

'If not now, when? When it's too late?' Maria turned to me. 'Monika is indeed a big girl. You're a big boy yourself. I'm not giving away any secrets if I tell you that I'm not thrilled by what's going on in this house. But I'm not going to preach to you. I wouldn't waste my time. I was once young and in love myself. Every generation thinks it has invented sex, but that's not exactly the case. Believe me, I have no trouble understanding you. That's why there's only one thing you need to know. Do what you like, but have no illusions about the future. Have I made myself clear?'

When you are twenty-two the future is not a well-defined concept. It is too distant and abstract to be grasped rationally. The present, on the other hand, seems simultaneously concrete and infinite. We think that it will never end, that it will continue to accompany us for ever. Monika and I overlooked the barrier ahead of us. We did not believe in cul-de-sacs.

Upon being transferred to Wrocław, I rented a room from Lydia, whom I had met in a district court. I was there to report on a trial for armed robbery. The defendant was sentenced to twenty years in a distant penitentiary. Even with time off for good behaviour, he would be forty when he returned to his wife, who was not yet twenty. That was Lydia.

She didn't refuse the interview I asked for. Girlishly innocent, she had married her husband a month before his arrest, mainly to get away from her parents' strict home. He was her first boyfriend and had made a good impression. He liked good times and had the money for them. She never asked where it came from and was in shock when the police searched their house. During the months of the investigation she had learned to be more independent. Friends found her a job in an impresario's office.

The interview over, I negotiated renting a room in Lydia's apartment. The path from there to her bed was a short one. We didn't discuss feelings. My undivided love still belonged to Monika. I felt no inconsistency. To Lydia I gave only my male prowess. Monika knew nothing about her.

But Monika had a secret of her own. She hadn't told me that her fiancé had received his degree and that a wedding date had been set. One day she broke the news by kissing me and bursting into tears.

'What's wrong?'

'That was the last kiss. Tomorrow I'll be a married woman. I've made a vow never to cheat on my husband.'

I wasn't invited to the wedding. The heavens avenged me. Thick clouds rained down on the city all day. From Lydia's bed I phoned the newspaper to tell my secretary I wasn't coming to work. I dressed warmly, went to my car, drove to the town square, and parked before the marriage registry bureau. After the ceremony the guests began to disperse. No one noticed me except Muszkat, who was at his most elegant. He came to the car and signalled me to open the window. Rain splattered onto my face.

'You'd better not do anything foolish,' he said.

'Don't worry. I'm here strictly as an observer.'

I was telling the truth. I didn't plan what happened next. Things simply got out of hand. Monika appeared in the doorway of the building. Behind her was her husband – who, I was happy to see, looked distinctly unimpressive. He was wiping his wet hair with a white handkerchief. Monika descended to the sidewalk while he opened an umbrella for her. With no idea of what I was doing, I opened the door of the car. Monika gave a start.

'What are you doing here? I asked you not to come.'

'Get in,' I said.

'I can't.'

'Just for a second.'

'You're crazy.'

'Get in.'

'For a second. No more.'

I stepped on the accelerator. The car lurched away from the kerb. From the corner of my eye I saw Monika's husband wave his umbrella like a black flag. He shouted something that I couldn't hear. The windows were shut and the motor was roaring. I turned right. Monika said nothing. I turned left. The car picked up speed. I passed the last houses of Wrocław and came to the highway. We were doing one hundred kilometres an hour. Monika asked:

'Where are we going?'

'Anywhere you want.'

'Back to the town square.'

'Anywhere but there.'

She showed me her hand. 'Do you see this ring?' I kept driving. 'Have you forgotten the vow I made?'

'We're going to the journalists' country place.'

It had come to me in a flash. The Journalists Association had a big villa in the Karkonosze Mountains, a hundred kilometres from Wrocław. I had spent many a memorable weekend there. It had a lovely garden and thick forests all around. Monika opened her bag and took out a mirror. She examined herself and said:

'You're insane.'

'But magnificently so. Do you still want to turn around?'

'I don't know.'

This put responsibility for the future squarely on my shoulders. But the future, as I have said, was a vague concept for me. I borrowed three days from the present and donated them to my life with Monika – which ended with her husband coming to get her from a little railroad station in the mountains. The red lantern of the receding caboose marked the last page of our wonderful adventure like the wax seal that consigns a document for ever to the archives.

The next day I went back to Lydia.

26

Lydia was pregnant. Watching her belly swell, I grew tender. This time, being a father didn't frighten me.

Lydia had a nice body, blonde hair coming down to her shoulders, sky-blue eyes, and a warm heart. I knew she would make a wonderful mother.

She wrote to her husband to ask for a divorce. His consent came several days before her due date. The signature was notarized by the superintendent of prisons. Lydia took it to be a good omen.

She went into labour on a Sunday. I drove her to the hospital. The doctor advised me to come back in a few hours. I roamed the streets. The stores were shut. The city was deserted.

It was evening when I returned. The doctor looked sombre. He asked me to follow him. We walked down some long corridors. In his office he offered me a seat and said drily: 'I'm very sorry. The strain was too great for her.' He glanced at his watch like a man in a hurry. I was shocked. I didn't know what to say. The doctor continued:

'It was impossible to save her. An old blood clot worked its way loose, went to the heart, and killed her.'

'What about the baby?'

'The baby? It had no oxygen, you see. We were trying to save the mother. What would you have done with a baby?'

'Yes. What would I have done?' I repeated. The doctor shook my hand. On the stairs it struck me that I should have asked if it was a boy or a girl.

Lydia was buried on a Tuesday. I thought of my mother as I looked at the waiting grave.

27

I do not know where my mother's grave is. After the war, a monument was erected at Plaszów for those murdered there. When I returned to Poland from Czechoslovakia in the spring of 1947 I placed a bouquet of purple lilacs on it – the flowers of my childhood. Green grass grew reassuringly on the surrounding hills. Nothing was left of the camp, its barbed wire, watchtowers, or anything else that I remembered from my arrival there the day after Wilhelm Kunde murdered my mother. Alone with my father, I broke the bitter news:

'Mama's dead.'

I hoped he wouldn't ask for the details. I didn't want to relive them. But he needed to know it all: how Kunde had done it, and how he had looked, and what my mother had said, and did she suffer, and how did I know she didn't, and who else was with us, and what Ritschak had said, and what the Jewish policemen and my cellmates had said, and when was the body removed, and where was it taken, and who took it. 'Father,' I begged. 'Stop. I can't take any more.' He persisted until I reached breaking point.

A column of marching prisoners behind us began to sing 'Lily Marlene' on command. Nothing could have sounded more horrible. I wanted to shout at them to be quiet, to show some respect for my mother. None of them would have known what I was talking about. So many mothers had been killed that the norm was not life but death. My father embraced me and wept silently.

'Papa, don't cry,' I whispered. 'Not here.'

He clung to me as though to a lifebuoy. His voice shook.

'Yes, Romek, cry. That's all we can do. When there are no tears left, that, too, will be impossible.'

My dry eyes shamed me.

'At least you're alive, Papa,' I said.

'Yes,' he said. 'I suppose that's the best revenge.'

As I grew older I began to understand that the self is formed by the layering of experience. Generally, we are no more aware of this process than the earth is aware of the plants and weeds taking root in it. There is something mysterious about the recombination or reappearance, unmonitored by consciousness, of long-forgotten memories. Each is an element in the periodic table that composes us. Each is compounded with all the other people, places, things, events, moods, smells, harmonies, discords, yieldings, resistings, that we are made of. Even if there is a logic running through this chemistry that we can miraculously grasp, there is no way for us to control it. How frustrating to be unable to command our inner selves! A muscle that fails to respond to the brain is considered palsied or atrophied, but we take it for granted that our thoughts and feelings do not obey us.

This is why I can accept the most absurd contradiction as perfectly normal. How is it possible that whilst I failed to shed a tear for my murdered mother, not even when describing her death to my father, my eyes grow moist at the most sentimental movie? Why do I risk my life by jamming on the brakes to avoid a stray dog when I have been merciless towards the suffering of my fellow men – towards my own suffering, too? There are emotions, it would seem, that are kept defensively locked in the depths of our souls, remaining there like caged birds until some outer shock sets them free and they sound their call.

Although Plaszów was an introductory course in survival, I never found out my exact grade. Now and then the camp was swept by a rumour of the Germans' impending defeat; just as quickly, it petered out. The only rumours to come true were the bad ones. Our lives were compressed into the brief intermissions between one brutal blow and the next. We grasped at every straw of hope, rationalized the most intolerable situations. My father sedated himself by chain-smoking. A hopeless nicotine addict, he exchanged his daily bread ration for shreds of tobacco that he rolled in strips of newspaper. At first I worried about his losing weight, not looking well, and seeming lethargic. Then I grew furious. Tormented by my first taste of hunger (yes, hunger has a taste, a sour burning in the belly), I was enraged to see my father casually trade away his bread. If he didn't need it, why not give it to me?

Our meetings were on the run. During the day we worked in different places, he in the upholstery and I in the metalworking shop. At night we slept in different barracks. The only visiting time was the evening, in the brief minutes between the end of work and the start of the curfew. My father refused to discuss our situation. It was as if he thought he could erase it by his silence. He wanted only to talk of the future, to paint scenes of the new, post-war world. They were really just scenes from the old world. The same house. The same work. The same friends. The same life.

My mother alone was not in them. My father never mentioned her. I could see he did not want to think of her. 'You're too young to judge,' he would say whenever I challenged him or criticized his triteness. I learned to keep my opinions to myself. He needed someone to listen to him. I listened. Sometimes, not noticing that he had gone on talking into the curfew, I had to steal back to my barracks unseen. Luckily, I always made it. One night I didn't.

I was more than halfway back to my barracks when a golden dot swept across the velvet heavens like a single huge photon of light. I stopped in my tracks to marvel at it, a comet from a far galaxy, a symbol of a freedom whose limit was the sky. Our housekeeper Paula always said that a wish made on a shooting star came true. Now, though, I couldn't think of any wish fast enough. There seemed nothing worth asking for. A fraction of a second before the light disappeared I exclaimed:

'Please let me live!'

'You goddam Jew, what are you doing here?' replied a voice from a passage between two storerooms.

I had not gotten my wish. Coming towards me was the camp commander, Amon Goeth. It was only the second time that I had seen him. The first was in our barracks, late one evening during my second week in the camp. He appeared then with Chajlowicz, the chief Jewish kapo, who ordered us to descend from our bunks and stand at attention. Speaking in Yiddish, Chajlowicz came straight to the point: we were to hand over at once any money or valuables in our possession. Goeth, who seemed to know the speech by heart, placed his officer's cap on the table and said:

'I want to see this cap full of gold coins. I don't care who they come from, but anyone holding anything back will be shot on the spot.'

He turned his back to us and started to count: 'One, two, three, four . . .'

Up to twenty-five.

To my surprise, the cap filled in half a minute. Goeth ran his hand expressionlessly through the coins and valuables. 'Are you sure nothing has been forgotten?' he asked sardonically. Without waiting for an answer, he ordered Chajlowicz to search an elderly prisoner. He had a sharp eye: the man was hiding a twenty-dollar bill in his sock. Goeth shot him through the throat. Blood spurted from the artery with each heartbeat until the man crumpled and it stopped. Goeth looked around for his next victim. I was standing close to him. The barrel of his pistol passed over me. He killed another prisoner, took his cap, and left.

Goeth was a tall man with impeccable Viennese manners, a former book editor. Intelligent and well educated, he was also a greedy, trigger-happy, charismatic sadist who killed his victims with the same alacrity with which he had turned the camp into his private fief. The wild parties that he threw were common knowledge, as was his having killed his Jewish chambermaid for shaking the hand he held out to her after coming home drunk one night. Another Jew who raised thoroughbred horses for him was shot for disparaging the riding skills of Goeth's mistress. His two watchdogs, Rolph and Ralph, were trained to bite prisoners to death. He had once personally shot eight Jews for hiding a single roll and some sausage. Orders to kill, torture, and humiliate were given by him all the time. Stories of his brutality were everyday talk at Plaszów. At his trial after the war by a Polish court, it was revealed that he had killed hundreds of prisoners with his own hands and tortured thousands more. He received the death sentence.

I stood before him helplessly. I knew the rule. Curfew violators were hanged.

'Attention!' Goeth bellowed.

I couldn't have moved even if I had wanted to. My feet were

rooted to the ground. In a state of paralysis, I watched his right hand move to his holster. He drew his pistol and aimed it at me.

Now began a game of cat and mouse. He didn't press the trigger immediately. He wanted to savour his power over me, to enjoy my terror of death that would only be ended by the bullet he fired. I could not have said how much time passed before he grew bored with this. The trigger clicked metallically.

Nothing happened.

Goeth swore at the jammed magazine of his pistol and tried reloading it. For whatever reason, he didn't succeed. His irate curses were the only human thing about him. They brought me out of my trance. I turned and ran wildly. Behind me I heard him shout:

'Stop, you goddam Jew!'

I stopped and flattened myself against the wall of a barracks, trying to blend with the darkness. My panting breath sounded to me as trumpet blasts. I tried in vain to force it back into my lungs.

Goeth didn't hear me. I heard him. His curses grew more distant, then faded. I had thrown him off my trail.

I fell to the ground and lay there. The comet was long gone. My wish had come true.

Amon Goeth came to Cracow from the Lublin district, where he received his training in murdering Jews. This was several months before our arrest. Although the Plaszów camp was established in the autumn of 1941, it was only under Goeth that it expanded into a huge establishment. Its expansion took place at a literally murderous pace. Seizing hostages from the families of the Jewish engineers who built it, he threatened to execute them for any delay. By the time the Cracow ghetto was liquidated, Plaszów was ready for its deportees. At first, classed as a forced labour camp jointly run by the SS and the Cracow military police, it took in Polish prisoners as well. In 1944 it was reclassified as a concentration camp and the Poles were moved to separate quarters. By then, however, my father and I were gone from it.

We were shipped out when the authorities decided to reduce the camp's population. Hundreds of prisoners were shot and thousands sent to other camps, mostly to work in armaments factories. By sheer chance, my father and I were put on the same train to Starachowice. I was glad that fate had kept us together. I didn't know that he hadn't long to live.

My father bequeathed to me neither his illusory hopes nor his half a loaf of daily bread that I coveted. All he left me when he died was his lice, which deserted his body for mine. At first I refused to admit that the epidemic had infected me, too. I attributed my weakness to overwork and malnutrition and thought I felt hot from the open hearths of the Starachowice steelworks.

I couldn't fool myself for long. The typhus fever overruled my denials. I collapsed and was taken on a stretcher to the same shack in which my father had died. Fortunately, I had passed out and was spared the shock of entering it. For a week, I was delirious. Fredek Minz stood by my side. His face greeted me when I emerged from my fog, coming slowly into focus as I ascended from my dive to the grottoes of death. I wanted to thank him but my tongue wouldn't move. My cracked lips were too dry to make a sound. I was thirsty. Fredek gave me some boiled water to drink. The next day he brought me half a loaf of bread and hid it under my mattress. As soon as he was gone I bit into it uncontrollably, swallowing whole chunks without chewing. I was afraid the orderly would take it.

But the orderly had had enough to eat that day. He stood by my bed and mocked:

'Eat, eat, before the lice eat you.'

I returned to work a few days later.

At night I heard distant thunder. At first I thought it was just me. Having lost the hearing in one ear from my illness, I believed the sound to be that of my own deafness.

But the thunder came from afar, from somewhere beyond the horizon. Rumours spread of fierce battles being fought on the east banks of the Wisla. The booming of the artillery was music to our ears. Some prisoners claimed they could distinguish between the outgoing and incoming shells. A Russian offensive was said to be imminent. All this was pure guesswork, of course. Still, the Germans were clearly worried. Having evaded combat until this moment, the SS officers now faced its overtaking them. They feared a prisoners' revolt as well. A company of Latvians was brought in to strengthen security. New watchtowers were built along the stockade. The spotlights illuminating the inner, barbed-wire fences were now switched off only by the wails of the sirens announcing an Allied air raid. There were more and more of these. They didn't frighten me. I was sure all their bombs would land on the Germans.

During one alert, five prisoners escaped through the front gate as it was being opened to let in a truck. Their absence was discovered at morning roll-call. The entire camp was restricted to barracks. We did not go to work. The Germans were openly nervous. A successful escape might inspire more. A campaign of disinformation was begun. Prisoners close to the Germans, some known informers, spread stories of special Storm Trooper units combing the area for the missing men.

'They don't stand a chance,' we were told by Shmul, who worked in the food warehouse. 'Sit still and watch out for your asses,' he advised us. 'We'll be free soon. Why risk your lives now? Even if you make it out of the camp, you'll be hunted down like wild animals.'

We listened with silent mockery. The forests surrounding the camp were controlled by partisans. The Germans didn't dare enter them. Even the roads were travelled only in heavily defended convoys. We knew from the Polish workers in the steelworks that these too were frequently ambushed with heavy casualties.

We were taken down a peg a few days later. The five men, we were told, had been caught. 'You'll have the chance to meet them personally at the execution,' taunted the roll-call officer.

The scaffold stood in the middle of the parade grounds, built overnight by a crew of prisoners. They were supervised by Yoske the carpenter, who had also recently constructed the additional watchtowers. Two hours before our normal wake-up time we were herded outside and surrounded by Latvian guards. Yoske gave the scaffold a last check, testing the posts with a hammer and pulling at the ropes to make sure they didn't break. He put his tools back in his toolbox.

We stood facing the rising sun, the blinding light of which now made Yoske invisible. A green police wagon drove through the main gate and stopped by the scaffold. Twelve hand-picked prisoners unloaded a large cage with five men in it. The light kept us from getting a good look at them. They were singing. The song was the popular German song *'Alle Vogel Sind Wieder Da'* (All the birds are here again). It was staged. Nothing had been left to chance. We were a theatre audience of a thousand prisoners. I could only wonder what threats of torture could make five men sing for their own deaths.

'All escapes lead to the hangman's noose!' trumpeted the camp commandant over the loudspeaker. A thousand throats shouted back:

'All escapes lead to the hangman's noose!'

It was time for Act Two. The prisoners were removed from the cage. Their hands were bound and they were dressed in standard Starachowice uniforms, their civilian pants and jackets painted with indelible red-and-yellow stripes. A Latvian guard slipped brown bags over their heads. The commandant read out their names. Each answered 'Present!' and took three steps forward. They were standing at the foot of the scaffold now.

'Mount!' ordered the commandant.

Although the men knew the scaffold was there, they couldn't see it. As courteously as though helping an old woman board a bus, a Latvian helped them onto a plank balanced across two poles. The hangman tightened the noose on each neck. An SS officer took photographs. A kapo walked up and down the lines of prisoners, striking anyone averting his glance.

The sun was in my eyes. I looked straight ahead.

'Proceed!'

The command was given to two Jewish prisoners, who pulled on ropes tied to the poles. The plank fell, leaving the five men dangling. The silence was absolute. None of the hanged men made a sound. A uniformed physician confirmed their death. The cage was put back on the truck. The German officers departed. Curtain.

And encore: we, the audience, were required to stand looking at the bodies for another hour. We were late for work that day.

In the evening the five corpses were gone. The scaffold remained on permanent display.

A few days later the first doubts began to circulate. At first they took the form of gossip that few believed. Once its source was authenticated, though, we understood that we were the victims of a hoax. According to the undertakers who had buried the five men, none was from Starachowice. In a small camp like ours, in which nearly everyone knew everyone, there was little chance of error. Moreover, the hanged men were uncircumcised.

After another week the truth leaked out. The Nazis had brought five prisoners from the city jail in Kielce and hanged them for our benefit. No one knew who they were. Most likely they were innocent Poles.

Realizing that its deception had been unmasked, the commandant's office switched to a more persuasive line. From now on, it announced, several prisoners would be executed for each escapee. The idea came from Wilczek, the chief kapo whose official title was 'The Jewish Elder'. 'To Wilczek,' the commandant was once said to have remarked, 'I would give the keys to the safe.' In it were deposited the valuables that Wilczek himself had collected and given the SS in return for various favours.

Among these privileges was being allowed to live with his wife and sons in a separate, well-furnished, well-equipped shack and to move freely about the camp at all hours. Sometimes, under the pretext of visiting the steelworks, Wilczek even left the camp without an escort. He was in charge of distributing the food, of which his lackeys had plenty while the other prisoners went hungry, and he was responsible for the work shifts, deciding whom to send to hard labour and whom to assign to easier jobs in camp. This power was reinforced by a network of informers who strengthened his position among the Germans, too. The dozen or so hand-picked prisoners who worked for him as kapos while taking advantage of the rest of us were completely loyal. They knew that on a whim they could be sent to work at the blast ovens. Hated and feared, these Jewish policemen obeyed all German orders. It would have been impossible to enforce discipline at Starachowice without them. Wilczek's son was their direct boss.

I sometimes wondered what made the Nazis pick Wilczek. A short, unprepossessing man who moved slowly and expressed himself with difficulty, his one striking feature was a long, aquiline nose. Before the war he had been one of the wealthier Jews in the nearby town of Wiezbnik, always ready – so it was said – to help a fellow Jew in need, a family man who didn't drink, never cursed, and would not have harmed a fly. What had made the Nazis choose him? Did they have a sixth sense for the monster's soul concealed in human form? Or was the same evil lurking in us all, waiting only for the opportunity to emerge from its cocoon?

It was Wilczek Junior who approached the Germans with his father's idea of dividing us into pairs to patrol the inner fences in shifts, each pair equipped with a whistle and white smocks that would enable the tower guards to identify us in the glare of the searchlights. Any attempt to approach the fences would be instantly punished. Each thwarted escape would earn the patrol a loaf of bread. Each successful one would cost it its lives.

Hats off to you, Mr Wilczek, for your brainstorm! But sometimes even geniuses miscalculate. You failed to allow for the fear factor cutting both ways. The louder the boom of the cannon, the more rumours there were of camps close to the front being liquidated. The Nazis were said to be destroying the evidence as they pulled back. Starachowice would be no exception. They would murder us all and blow up the steelworks before abandoning it.

Our fear made us close ranks around our common fate. Men stood whispering in groups, falling silent when one of Wilczek's informers drew near. Youngsters like myself were excluded from these conversations, which I naively thought concerned emergency plans in case of a German retreat. I was wrong.

The alert started at 2 a.m. I didn't hear the sirens go off. With my good ear pressed against my mattress, not even a bomb could wake me from my sleep. What roused me was the stirring in the bunks around me. The sound seemed to reach me through the pores of my skin. At first I didn't know what was happening. The same exhaustion that put one to sleep in bare seconds caused one time and effort in emerging from the fog. Even once awake, I was too tired to open my eyes. Someone stepped on me. I cried out more in anger than in pain, my voice driving away the last of my sleep.

'Idiot! Where are you running?'

This time the voice was Fredek Minz's. His unanswered question travelled the length of the barracks. I sat up. The front door was open. Silhouettes of men were slipping through it. They halted for a moment as they reached it and vanished in the darkness. The sirens had stopped. So had the noise around me. In the disturbing silence, the truth dawned on me.

'It's a breakout!' I cried excitedly.

Fredek disagreed. 'We'd have heard the whistles.'

I put on my shoes and began to tie the laces.

'What are you doing?'

'What everyone else is.'

'Not me.'

'Why not?'

'It's too risky.'

'Don't be silly. Get dressed.'

'Count me out of this game.'

'Would you rather die in your bunk?'

'Since when are you such a big hero?'

'I just don't want to be left behind.'

'Then go, you jerk! I'm staying put. At least you'll have someone to mourn for you.'

'To hell with your mourning. Are you coming or not?'

'No.'

Fredek pulled the blanket over his head.

The argument was over. So, I thought, was our friendship. I didn't ask who was deserting whom or what a friendship was worth if it couldn't cope with such instinctive reactions. There was no time to waste. The all-clear might sound at any moment.

Yes, I was acting on instinct, not rational analysis. Jumping down from my bunk, I ran outside without a backward glance. It took a while to get used to the darkness. Muffled voices came from my right. I ran towards them and saw a large opening in the inner fence. In the stockade beyond it, several boards had been pried loose. People were battling to crawl through the gap. It was every man for himself.

I joined the fray. Someone kicked me. I yanked someone aside. He lunged forward, leaving his sleeve in my hand. I clung to him, allowing him to block the path of others. The barbed wire tore at my clothes and hands. I reached the stockade. Someone tried to get ahead of me. I shoved him out of my way. He swore. To hell with him. One more push and I was out of the camp.

The Jewish kapos had double-crossed Wilczek. Sensing that the end was near, they had joined the carefully planned escape. Zero hour was set for the first air-raid alert on a moonless night. As soon as the fences and watchtowers were blacked out, the white-smocked patrols cut the barbed wire and pried boards from the stockade in four places. Each of the four groups breaking out had a pre-arranged escape route. It was the unexpected joining in of prisoners like me that caused the jam at the bottlenecks.

A thousand tomtoms pounded in my ears. I ran across a ploughed field, staggered, fell into the furrows, rose, ran on. Men were running on either side of me. I heard them panting. Two hundred more metres. One hundred and fifty. The dark strip of the forest loomed closer. I was almost there when the sirens wailed again. The all-clear could be our death knell. How much further to the tree line? How long for them to realize what was happening? . . . They already knew. The beams of the searchlights played over the field. Heavy machine guns opened up. *Ta-ta-ta-ta-ta-ta-ta-ta!* Men were hit, fell. How many more metres between life and death? Thirty. Twenty. Ten. I had made it!

'Follow me!' shouted someone, taking command. I fell in behind him. We fought our way through a wild blackberry patch. The bullets were landing further away now. We pushed into the forest. A carpet of pine needles cushioned our footsteps. The only sound was the voice of our guide. It was Zelig the Dwarf's. A stunted man who had worked as a camp undertaker, he came from this area and knew every inch of it. By the bank of a stream he let us take a short break.

'You have ten minutes. It's a half-hour's walk from here to our rendezvous with the other groups. From there to the partisans' base is no further than you can spit.'

I sat on a bed of damp moss while Zelig counted us. There were twenty-three of us. From now on we were to walk in single file, each man in contact with the man ahead of him. 'Try keeping your hand on his back,' Zelig advised. 'The forest is thick. You don't want to get lost.' He spoke Yiddish, a language I had trouble understanding. The man beside me translated. 'How come you don't speak *mame-loshn*?' he wondered. 'We didn't talk it in Bielsko,' I explained. He couldn't believe there was a town in Poland without Yiddish. 'You and I didn't live in the same Poland,' I said. He was telling me about his shtetl when Zelig gave the command to move on. I tried to rise and collapsed. A sharp pain shot through my left leg. I probed it with my hand. My pants were wet. My hand was smeared with blood. I rolled up my pants. There were two wounds in the side of my calf. I hadn't even felt the bullets. I didn't understand how I had managed to walk so far.

'I've been hit in two places,' I murmured.

The man talking to me moved away.

'What's the matter, kid?' asked Zelig.

'I'm wounded.'

He examined my leg and said:

'It's nothing. Superficial wounds. Your mama isn't here to help you, so move your ass and let's go. The partisans will give you first aid.'

The partisans were so sure of their grip on the forest that they had not even posted sentries. We spotted them from afar, eating and drinking around a campfire. They didn't see us until we approached their clearing. Even then they reached for their guns calmly, without haste. We halted and Zelig called out:

'Don't shoot!'

'Velcome to our zoup kitching,' a partisan called back, mimicking Zelig's comic Polish. 'Tell the others to stay back,' he added, instructing the dwarf to step forward. There were some one hundred and fifty of us. Zelig walked bowleggedly, his hands in the air and his head bobbing from side to side as if to convey that he couldn't possibly be dangerous. He and the partisan stood conferring halfway to the fire. They shook hands and Zelig came back with good news.

'Everything is arranged. We'll be given food and drink tonight. Tomorrow we'll get organized. It's quiet here. There are no Germans. We're out of danger. Sit beneath these trees, in one row ... Why in one row? Because that's what you've been asked to do. If you don't like it, you can go back to Starachowice and sing "Alle Vogel Wieder Sind Da".'

I rolled up my pants again. Although my leg hurt, the bleeding had stopped. But the partisans would not want a boy who couldn't fight. I had to bandage myself and wash my pants.

Zelig was in high spirits. He told Yiddish jokes that made everyone laugh. I hadn't heard such loud laughter in years. More than anything, it told me we were free.

I should have been in high spirits myself. But I was not. I could only think of my bad leg. Using my arms as oars, I dragged myself slowly into the trees. No one noticed me except for a little squirrel-like animal that leaped in fright from the hollow of a tree. It was amazing, I thought. There were still creatures on this earth that were frightened of me.

I got to my feet. Although that made the pain worse, I could walk. I headed back the way we had come, hoping to find the stream. The further from the campfire, the darker it became. Not even God could see in such blackness. Or could He? If a squirrel could, why not God?

The stream was knee-high. The water cooled my burning skin and brought relief. I removed my shirt, ripped off a sleeve, and bound my wounds with it, tightening the improvised tourniquet until I felt my leg pulse. I felt proud. I had beaten back misfortune.

A volley of shots ripped the silence. I threw myself on the ground and listened. The shooting stopped. So much for all the brave talk about the Germans keeping out of the forest! The shots started again. This time there were more. There was a third burst and then a fourth. The sound echoed off the trees, coming at me from every direction. A few last, single rounds rang out. Then the forest grew quiet again with its own noises: the ripple of the brook, the sighing of the breeze, the distant cry of an owl.

What was I supposed to do? Which way was I supposed to go? *Easy, Roman. Take your time. Don't make any dumb moves . . .* But how long could I wait? I started to count. At first to one hundred and twenty. That meant two minutes had gone by. It wasn't enough. I counted to a thousand. Then to two thousand.

I decided to head back towards the partisans' camp, hobbling on my good leg. My wet shoes made walking difficult. I took them off. The pine needles jabbed my bare feet. I walked slowly, stopping to listen to the forest. But the forest did not tell me its secret. When I discovered it for myself, it was the most horrible sight I had seen yet.

Near the camp, I took cover in some bushes. They were a good vantage point. A sixth sense, if there is such a thing, told me to take a careful look before rejoining my companions. By the light of the campfire the silhouettes of the partisans, moving behind a screen of smoke, looked like ghosts. At first I couldn't tell what they were doing. Why were they bending and digging in the earth? A bearded man threw branches on the fire. A thousand sparks leaped like fireflies into the air. The wind shifted, blowing away the smoke. Now I could see the dead Jews clearly. They had been taken by surprise. Most were killed beneath the trees where I had left them. Some still leaned against the pine trunks. Others were strewn over the ground. They had been shot begging for their lives, as uncomprehending as I was.

The partisans dragged the bodies like sacks of potatoes and threw them into a pit at the edge of the clearing. I hugged the damp ground, afraid to move and give myself away. The mass grave was covered with earth. The partisans returned wearily to their campfire, bundled up in their blankets, and went to sleep without posting sentries. The fire died slowly. Only when it was out did I dare creep from the bushes and walk off into the unknown.

I couldn't understand why the escaped Jews had been shot. Why murder a band of men who would have joined them in fighting the Nazis? I didn't know at the time that the forests between Kielce and Radom were controlled by the National Armed Forces, an extremist faction that put killing Jews and Communists ahead of killing Germans. In fact, it did not kill Germans at all, which let the latter concentrate on other underground organizations like the Armia Krajowa and the left-wing resistance. The Brigada Swietokrzyska, as the forces around Starachowice were called, sometimes even fought these groups together with the Nazis, who rewarded them by leaving them alone. When the Wehrmacht retreated from Poland, units of the National Armed Forces pulled back with it.

I knew nothing of this. Alone with my fear, I had no idea what to do. My faculties were paralysed. I didn't want to think. I wanted a miracle that wasn't about to happen. It was only in nursery tales that fairy godmothers helped little boys and girls in the forest. And I was not a little boy. I was sixteen and a half. If only I could have frozen time, stopped the earth in its orbit, revoked the law of gravity – anything so as not to have to act. I had never felt so lonely in my life. And so lost. I had never realized how great was my need was for human company – anyone's, even the enemy's.

I lost all sense of time. In Starachowice I had learned to tell time by my fatigue, or by the growling of my stomach, or by the play of light and shadow on the walls. Ten less centimetres of sunlight meant that so many minutes had gone by. Now, in the dark silence of this unfamiliar place, time had ceased to exist. Yet I felt its pressure. Coming from nowhere, it produced a sense of urgency.

I began blindly to put distance between myself and the partisan camp, taking the paths of least resistance through the thick undergrowth of ferns, berry bushes, and brambles. At dawn I reached the forest's end. Ploughed, brown fields lay ahead of me. I followed their furrows. A small village on the horizon lay deep in the early morning sleep that was said to be the best sleep of all. I headed for a little cottage that stood apart. The creak of its wooden gate aroused no one. I peered through a window. There was no one there. I walked to the back. A wagon stood in the yard, its harness blocking a half-open barn door. I ducked past it into the barn. A bored cow went on chewing its cud. A milk can stood on a stool in the corner. There was milk at the bottom of it. I drank it.

'What do you think you're doing?'

The woman's voice came from the far corner. I hadn't noticed her. She didn't seem startled. She must have spent the night in the barn and been woken by me. She brushed wisps of hay from her apron.

'Who are you?' she asked.

My shaved head and striped uniform did not leave much room for doubt.

'Let me have some food and I'll go,' I said.

'You're hungry?'

'Yes.'

'You're a Jew?'

I nodded. It was pointless to deny it.

'You'd better clear out before my husband gets up,' said the woman with sudden adamance. 'If you value your life, clear out!'

'Where? Where am I supposed to go with these clothes? Look at me. Maybe you could give me an old shirt and some pants.'

'Do you have money?'

'No.'

'Gold?'

'Nothing.'

'Nothing will get you nothing. That's life, boy. Don't you know that?'

'Yes, ma'am. I do.'

'I'm not a ma'am. I'm a peasant. Sweet Jesus, what a babe in the woods you are! Hasn't life taught you anything? Where have you been, in a feather bed with your mama? There are no handouts here. It's dog-eat-dog. These villages are poor. We barely have enough for our own mouths. The damned partisans rob our fields and the Germans take what's left. Do you think I sleep here in the barn for the fun of it? I have to guard this poor old cow. The Germans will make us pay if the partisans take her. They'll say we're in cahoots with them. But there are good Germans, too.' The woman's smile bared two rows of yellowed teeth. 'They'll give me a kilo of sugar or five of flour for a Jew like you. You don't know your own worth . . . Calm down. Calm down. I'm not going to the Gestapo. Let others do that. I once had a son your age. He went to the forest and never came back. Clear out, boy. Git! My husband won't take pity on any kike. He'll turn you in for sure. We haven't seen sugar in half a year. He'll be up and around any minute. Go on, git!'

She pointed to the door.

'But . . .'

She raised her voice. 'Do you want me to call him?'

'You don't have to. I'm going.'

I tried my luck at another, less run-down-looking cottage. Its angry owner tried to stab me with a pitchfork. 'Get out of here, you devil!' he cried. The neighbours' dogs began to bark. I ran, pursued by the peasant's shouts. When I was out of breath, I turned around and looked back. The peasant had returned to his house. The dogs had stopped barking. But there was no place in the bucolic serenity for someone begging for his life. The ploughed fields, pretty houses, and brightening dawn sky were the mask of a cruel world. Not even the forest was friendly. If I could avoid the partisans, I might hide out there. For how long?

The wild berries tasted sour. Although there were mushrooms in the moss at the base of the pine trees and the fir trees, I couldn't tell the good ones from the bad ones. The hours went by. The sun rose overhead. It was pleasantly cool beneath the sunlight-tousled tops of the trees. Despite the pain in my leg, I walked on until I dropped from exhaustion.

The situation called for a decision. The one I made may have been insane. Nevertheless, returning to the camp in Starachowice seemed the most sensible thing to do.

I let out a sigh of relief when I found myself facing its stockade. The familiar sight cheered me at once. Here was where I belonged.

I still had to cross the open stretch between the forest and the camp. I cocked my ears like a wary rabbit. There was not a sound. Three canvas-topped army trucks were parked by the stockade. I waited for it to get dark. The lights came on in the watchtowers. No beams combed the darkness. I studied the shadows of the guards. They looked relaxed. All the signs were that the camp had returned to normal.

I plucked up the courage to leave my hiding place and run limping towards the stockade. The gaps made on the night of the escape were now plugged with barbed wire. Despite the soft ground beneath me, the sound of my footsteps seemed to carry for miles. I halted. Silence. I touched the bonnet of the last truck. It had SS licence plates. The engine was cold. The truck had been standing there for a while. The driver's cabin was empty.

I climbed onto the bonnet and from there to the tarpaulin. Gripping its lashing for support, I peered into the camp. One window, the commandant's, was lit. Although I couldn't see the front gate, I knew it must be locked. My first plan was to wait for the night shift to change. That way I would avoid running into soldiers on their way to the gate or the watchtowers. Then, however, fearing to lose my nerve if I waited, I bounced on the tarpaulin as though on a trampoline, flexed my knees, and went soaring into the air higher than I had thought possible. I flew over the stockade and the fence and landed with a thud. A bolt of pain shot from my leg to my brain. I shut my eyes and waited for it to pass. I opened them. From where I lay, I could see the guards without being seen. I sat up and felt something warm. The wound in my calf was bleeding again. I looked around. No white-smocked patrols were in sight. Perhaps they had been called off after the breakout. The commandant's door slammed. I heard German voices. Then there was silence. I limped towards my barracks, doing my best to walk naturally. If caught I could always say I had had an attack of diarrhoea. But no one saw me.

I groped my way through the dark barracks. I came to my bunk. There were signs by which I recognized it – a protruding nail, a rough board. I climbed to my place, my eyes growing accustomed to the darkness. Many bunks were empty. I wondered how many of their occupants had made it to the forest and how many had been killed there.

Fredek woke. 'Is that you?'

'No. It's the Holy Ghost.'

'You're shivering.'

'I'm cold.'

He lifted the blanket. 'Get in,' he said, moving over to make room. I touched him. I wanted to touch someone alive. He held my hand.

'So the bird's back in its nest,' he teased.

'Just don't preach to me,' I whispered back.

Morning roll-call was at six as usual. The day before, Fredek told me, no one had gone to work. The dead and wounded were laid out on the parade grounds and the roll-call dragged on while the Germans counted the prisoners. Fifty-four men had been missing.

Now only fifty-three were. The officer on duty counted us again and again. Wilczek and his son had no explanation for the extra prisoner. Although I was afraid that someone would point at me and say, 'Hey, he wasn't here yesterday,' no one seemed to have noticed my absence.

After several hours the Germans gave up and went to the commandant's office, leaving us still undismissed or sent to work. Wilczek came over. Hands on hips in his favourite posture, he told us that the camp was to be dismantled. He was still talking when a company of SS troops marched into it.

'There's no need to panic,' Wilczek said. 'Preserve order. We'll be going to the train station in a few minutes.'

'Where to?' asked a prisoner.

'To hell,' said Wilczek's son, bursting into loud laughter.

28

We choked Wilczek's son to death on the train to Auschwitz. I say 'we' even though I took no part in it. My leg hurt too much to push my way into the lynch mob. I watched the fingers wrap themselves around his throat. I was for them. It was natural justice. Not every criminal could be tried by an impartial court. Wilczek's son paid the price of his vileness.

His father sat within arm's length of me, looking on with glazed eyes. He never let out a peep. He didn't lift a finger to defend the issue of his loins. Perhaps he rejoiced that the mob made do with his first-born. Although I would have liked to take away a memory of his expression as his son writhed his last, his face was a blank slate. His back was hunched. His head trembled slightly to the rhythmic rattle of the wheels.

A sign in French on our cattle car said that it had the capacity for a dozen horses or two dozen cows. Now it held a hundred men. In the heat of the summer day it reeked of sweat, excrement, and urine. We relieved ourselves where we stood, indiscriminately. The congestion made it impossible to move.

Wilczek Senior had removed his boots at the journey's start. They were the high, military kind worn by ranking officers. I wanted them. They would enable me to hide the bloodstains that were seeping again through my muddy pants. No one ill, wounded, or crippled stood a chance of making it past the sharp eyes of the SS men who would be waiting for us. Such cases were doomed.

My chance came while Wilczek stared at his gasping son. I reached out and seized the boots. Their soft leather took me by surprise. I patted them with pleasure and pulled them on.

Not until the lynching was over did Wilczek notice that his boots were gone. He looked around. I didn't try to hide a gloating smile. Wilczek looked down at the floor. I felt reborn. The omnipotent master of our fates was afraid to meet my glance. I handed him my filthy, misshapen wooden clogs. He accepted them submissively.

We didn't know the train was bound for Auschwitz. It wouldn't have meant anything if we did. It was not yet a name in the history books. Back in Cracow Grete had told me that the Nazi death factories were in the east. We were travelling west. Someone had managed to read the names of the stations through the wooden slats of the car. Wilczek's boots gave me confidence.

There was talk of escaping. I wasn't interested. I had already been there and knew how it ended. Three men gave it a try on the first night. Two more bailed out on the second. They ripped some planks from the floor, waited for the train to slow down on a curve, and dropped to the tracks below. You couldn't do it without help. The other prisoners had to make room for you to lie on your stomach and had to push you at the right moment with your head forward and your arms pinned to your sides. Your life depended on the impetus they gave you. The slightest delay in lying prone on the gravel bed between the tracks was fatal. It just took a second for the rear axle of the car to catch up with you and rip you to pieces.

The doors of the car were opened on the third day.

Armed guards surrounded us. We were on the notorious 'ramp' of Birkenau. The camp was covered by a milky mist. As the hours passed the white curtain lifted to reveal hundreds of barracks and thousands of prisoners, freshly risen for the morning roll-call.

Dr Mengele must have had the day off. We were marched straight to the showers without a selection. Wilczek was the man ahead of me. Unused to wooden clogs, he kept stumbling. The guards beat him with their rifle butts. A blow to the head knocked him to the ground. He hurried to rise and get back in line. He fell again. He rose. He said despairingly:

'I'll never make it.'

So what if you don't! Your death couldn't matter less to anyone. No one will mourn it. Fuck you, Wilczek, pay your debt ... Those were my thoughts. That's why I'll never understand what made me help him. Without breaking stride I took off the shiny boots, handed them to him, and kept marching barefoot. The same man who had been on the verge of collapse slipped his bloody feet into the boots with an acrobatic speed that did not seem possible. He did not thank me or give me back my clogs. Fredek saw it all. 'Schmuck!' he said.

In the shower room we were ordered to undress, fold our clothes, and lay them neatly on the floor at our feet. We stood naked, our backs to a concrete wall. A junior officer with a whip inspected us. He took his time, bored by the job and the tiresome need to decide men's fates. Wilczek stood on my left, breathing heavily. The prisoner on my right saw my leg and moved away as though I were a leper. My bloody bandage had written on it: *This boy dies*.

I prayed for a single, painless shot. For no shot at all. For a miracle. At the rate the officer was approaching me, I had half a minute to live. What does one do with the last thirty seconds of one's life? I refused to believe in what was about to happen. The officer halted. A shiver ran down my spine to the bottoms of my feet. Only my wounded leg felt hot. The officer signalled a kapo to join him. The kapo came and stood at attention.

'Do you see that?' asked the officer. It was not really a question.

The kapo nodded.

Was this it? My terror yielded to resignation. I had crossed the invisible threshold of death. I was standing on the other side, where nothing mattered any more.

But things took an unexpected turn. It wasn't my wounded leg that the officer was staring at. It was Wilczek's polished boots.

'Are these yours?' he asked.

'Yes, sir.'

The officer bent to examine the boots carefully.

'Who gave them to you?'

'This boy.' Wilczek pointed straight at me.

'Don't lie to me!' yelled the kapo.

'I swear it's true, sir. Don't blame me. It was the boy.'

'Do you know that these are the boots of a German officer?' asked the SS man.

Wilczek said nothing. The kapo slapped his face.

'Answer when an officer speaks to you!'

'It was the boy,' he repeated.

The German ignored him. His mind was made up.

'The Jewish impudence of stealing a Wehrmacht officer's boots! Do you know what happens to thieves?'

'I was the Jewish Elder of the Starachowice camp. I'm allowed to –'

'Precisely. You're allowed to die,' said the German, who finished Wilczek's sentence with a bullet to his brain.

Wilczek fell at my feet. There was no blood. The officer and the kapo continued down the line. I had been saved once more – for the moment.

PART III

The Taste of Freedom

The men of old are not remembered, and those who follow will
not be remembered by those who follow them.

Ecclesiastes I, 11

29

Happy and sad at once, the sweet, sentimental music was as out of place as ragtime at a Jewish funeral. It brought back nice memories, though, its tunes reminding me of the days when it was still permissible to be a child. Less than five years separated my last childish prank from my landing in Auschwitz. But real and subjective time were two such different things that the music could just as well have come from another incarnation.

In the Gypsy Forest outside Bielsko, at the foot of the hill climbed by me and my father, stood a wooden restaurant with a glassed-in balcony that was famous for its Gypsy bands and Hungarian goulash soup. Although these bands changed every month, each new one was publicized by large billboards like an important cultural event. I was so little able to distinguish between their styles that I suspected them all of consisting of the same musicians in different clothes.

On Sundays the place was mobbed. It was a different way of spending the day than by dining in one of the fancy restaurants in town. Pretty Gypsies in bright scarves and kerchiefs circulated among the guests, telling their fortunes for twenty groszy. One of them predicted that I would have 'an exciting life that will end happily ever after'. Another foresaw 'a long sea journey'. This cost me two weeks' allowance.

Sated with goulash and sweet music, the diners appreciatively tossed coins into the musicians' hats. Generally, Gypsies were treated with suspicion and disdain. My parents would never have permitted me to talk to them under ordinary circumstances. Bielsko's mothers warned their children that a Gypsy woman could cast a spell on their souls; its fathers watched their wallets when Gypsies were nearby, it being common knowledge that they were born pickpockets. The concierge drove them away when they came to play music in the courtyard of our building. The police often picked them up for questioning. Many did not have ID cards. Decent folk kept away from them.

Although I can't say that I liked Gypsies myself, it was for a different reason. Once, entering one of their encampments with my friend Erik, I saw young bears being trained to dance. I had always felt sorry for these animals, forced to shuffle on listless paws to the rhythm of drums and bells. I knew they were snatched from their native habitat and cruelly kept in chains. Now, my aversion to their captors grew as I watched the bears forced to stand on hot tin and hop up and down to music in an exercise in Pavlovian conditioning.

And yet in the restaurant I set these feelings aside and enjoyed myself like everyone else. In my childish daydreams I imagined touring Europe in a covered Gypsy wagon, pulled by a team of Gypsy horses, while Gypsy dogs yapped at our heels and my heart throbbed to the music of Gypsy fiddles.

Now these same melodies floated across the barbed wire that separated our barracks from the Gypsy block. On the recommendation of the Nazi Institute for Racial Purity, the Gypsies, too, had been classified as social parasites destined for extermination. They and the Jews shared a single fate in Auschwitz.

Although they may never have heard of racial institutes and knew even less about biology or politics, the Gypsies were well aware of what was happening. Nevertheless, their violin strings still sang as if life went on as usual. Their flutes continued to wail their way into the heart and the little bells of their tambourines tinkled merrily.

Auschwitz–Birkenau was not a family institution. Only rarely did the camp's commanders let men, women, and children stay together. Why they permitted it with the Gypsies (who like us were imprisoned within a fenced block in which they worked and lived, officially known as B/E/II) was something I never understood.

A bird's eye view of the camp would have shown a treeless plain stretching over dozens of square kilometres and divided into rectangular strips, each surrounded by its own fences and all sharing a common perimeter. These subdivisions, consisting of some twenty barracks and an outhouse apiece, were designed (not entirely successfully) to prevent contact between different groups of prisoners, thus making organized resistance impossible.

If the Gypsies thought of anything besides food, however, it was certainly not of resistance or escape. Each day they sat around for long hours, waiting to see what would be brought by a tomorrow that no one wanted to think about. In the evenings, as darkness fell, they gathered in the space before their barracks to while away the time with music. The children danced barefoot. Strange as it may seem, soon after my arrival in Birkenau they had begun to attend a Gypsy kindergarten complete with a brightly painted carousel whose strains carried as far as 'Canada', an area where prisoners were employed in sorting the looted property of their fellow inmates.

Auschwitz–Birkenau was a musical place. The Auschwitz Orchestra, composed of some of Europe's best-known Jewish musicians, played marches and arias for prisoners going to and from work and even serenaded those headed for the gas chambers. Although I was never certain whether these concerts were meant more for the morale of the murderers or of their victims, they were a natural part of camp life. They, however, were not as bizarre as the Gypsy melodies that drifted over us like a sentimental cloud. The German guards even let the Gypsies go on singing and playing during the curfew, when the rest of us had to be in our bunks. Their music put me to sleep like a lullaby, its notes laying a silken road to a different world in which there were no crematoria, electric fences, or death. As long as it flowed on into the night like a river of life, it seemed that nothing bad could happen.

But this too proved an illusion. On the muggy, airless night of 1 August, the Gypsy musicians fell silent.

The carousel had revolved for the last time. I was awoken by the stillness. Even before regaining full consciousness I knew what had happened. The merry Gypsies had been taken to the gas chambers. No one wept. No one protested. No one resisted his fate. I wondered if their fortune tellers had predicted it. And had they kept the terrible secret to themselves or shared it with the others? The sudden quiet was like writing on the wall.

In Birkenau, too, I shared a bunk with Fredek Minz. Since our arrival in Auschwitz, Fredek had been in a dark mood. His face fell and grew longer, his lips pursed tightly together. He was stingy with words and warded off my attempts at conversation. I was not surprised to hear him say laconically the day after the Gypsies were killed:

'There's nothing to hope for any more. This is the last stop for all of us.'

'All the more reason to get off in time,' I tried to joke.

'Very funny,' he said angrily. It was his standard reply to remarks that annoyed him.

'Who says that you have to wait for the last stop?'

'Spare me your humour.'

'What would you like instead?'

'To be left alone.'

'What's the problem? Tired of life?'

'Tired of waiting for it to end.'

'Then why not fry yourself on the fence? Some nut does it every day.'

We had seen many such cases since coming to Auschwitz, often involving people our age. Most ran at the electric fence as if amok, perhaps fearing that the will to live would bring them up short at the last moment. The slightest contact with the high-tension wires put an end to such apprehensions. A fraction of a second was all it took to knock you senseless. Sometimes the guards had to switch off the current before removing a carbonized corpse.

Fredek sighed like an old man.

'I wish I had the courage.'

I didn't respond. He seized my arm and said agitatedly: 'Can't you see what's happening? Whoever stops working dies. Yesterday it was the Hungarians. Today it's the Gypsies. Tomorrow it will be us.'

'Tomorrow is still twenty-four hours away.'

'Do you believe in miracles?'

'I believe in luck.'

Did I really, though? What was luck, anyway? Could it be defined scientifically? The luck of winning a lottery was different from the luck of slipping unscathed on a banana peel. And was it luck when a cancer patient died quickly without suffering? I had seen people spurned by luck because they failed to realize that it had to be cultivated like a delicate plant. It was Paula's belief that you had to talk to plants to make them grow well. But how did you talk to luck? Did you say: 'Hello, there, Mr Luck, please be nice to me'? Or perhaps: 'Why don't you help me to help myself?' That seemed the smarter choice. My luck, I was convinced, would hold out as long as I did.

But luck did not grow on trees. It hid in the shadows, like moss. Although it was under the noses of most prisoners, sometimes in the garbage cans outside the kitchen and sometimes even in their own deaths, few were able to see. They let the potato peels rot in the cans and they rotted themselves. It was true that sneaking out of your barracks at night to fill your pockets with the leftovers from the officers' mess meant risking your life. Most prisoners were afraid to die. And so their teeth fell out from malnutrition, their stomachs swelled from lack of protein, their bodies were covered with sores, and they died anyhow. The kapos collected them like wormy fruit and marched them to the gas chambers with the last of their strength. From there they went up the chimney to heaven, as our gallows humour had it.

The days went by. I felt my strength giving out. The potato peels I stole could not keep me going for ever. And the weaker my body, the less effective my psychological defences. As gradual as all this was, I saw it happening. I began to fear the moment when the resistances developed by me since childhood would crumble, leaving me to sink into a lethargy that no longer struggled to live. I had seen hundreds of physically and psychologically determined prisoners yield to such apathy overnight. Long before their final collapse, they had stopped being human. All that was left of them was a number on their arm, a striped uniform, and their infinite debasement.

I sometimes ask myself whether there was a formula for survival in the camps. American Rangers took survival courses in the jungle. British soldiers in North Africa learned to live off the desert. Allied pilots were taught to forage for food when shot down over enemy territory. What would I say if asked to write a handbook on staying alive in a concentration camp?

Would I have any practical advice to give? How to grovel before a Nazi officer? Make the prisoner ladling out the soup fish a bone for you from the bottom? Elude the barracks kapo looking for an amusing victim? Stay calm when a line of prisoners marches past you to the gas chamber? Remain serene amid the devastation all around you? What experiences did I have that might help me to cope with a similar situation in the future?

None. None at all. All my experience is worth nothing for the simple reason that there can be no similar situation.

Not everyone who left Birkenau went up the chimney. Now and then skilled workers needed for the Nazi arms industry were requested to step forward at morning roll-call. Anyone meeting the requirements was transferred to a labour camp appendaged to a munitions factory.

Our own barracks, however, were populated by shoemakers, doctors, tailors, rabbis, clerks, lawyers – all types the Nazis didn't need. And I myself wasn't even a shoemaker. Who could need me? No one. But that was no reason not to volunteer. I was determined to get out of B/E/II at any cost.

'The next time they ask for experts, we'll step up,' I told Fredek.

'You will. Leave me out of it.'

'Why? What's there to lose?'

'Everything.'

'You just told me that you're tired of everything.'

'What will you tell them? That you learned a skill in kindergarten?'

'In my mother's womb, if they'll believe it.'

'You're crazy. The only thing I'd volunteer for is iron casting. I learned that in Starachowice. I'm good at it.'

'I'm ready to be a pilot, a locomotive engineer, or a pimp. All that matters is getting out of here.'

'Bullshit. You're not a pilot, or an engineer, or even a pimp. You're a dreamer.'

'Fine. I'll volunteer as a skilled dreamer.'

'The one thing they're always looking for is skilled lathe operators.'

'Good. That's an excellent profession.'

'You'll tell them you're a lathe worker?'

'Why not?'

'Very funny.'

'That's all you have to say?'

'What do you have to say?'

'That it's the only chance ...'

'There is no chance. They're not idiots. How long can you fool them? An hour? A day? Two days?'

'Two days is two days.'

'You can have them here, too.'

'Here? Didn't you say this was the last stop?'

'Right now you're alive, aren't you?'

'Right now. How about after right now?'

'Go bother someone else with your questions.'

'Fredek, where are your fighting spirits?'

'I saw yours in Starachowice. You came crawling back from that forest on all fours.'

'All right. Let's not argue. You'll decide when the time comes.'

Deep down I hoped he didn't mean it, that given an opportunity he would grab at it. I didn't believe he would break up a partnership that had lasted this long. That was not how it turned out, though.

The morning roll-call that day took longer than usual. Generally we stood at attention for one to two hours. This time, clocked by my stomach, it took till noon. And the same thing was happening elsewhere in the camp. Something out of the ordinary was going on. I couldn't guess what it was. SS officers came and went, looking tense and nervous. Our kapo was jumpy, too. At such times the mind of a prisoner began to imagine all kinds of things. Perhaps the war was over. Perhaps Hitler was dead. Perhaps an anti-Nazi revolt had broken out.

Or perhaps it was just my imagination. After two more hours our kapo told us the reason for the delay. Two Polish prisoners had tried escaping and been caught. Both had worked on the farm that grew vegetables for the German staff. This was in an area beyond the electric fence, ringed by watchtowers and ordinary fences that were manned only by day. At night, after the prisoners coming back from the fields were counted, the guards left until the next morning. Only if someone was missing were they expected to remain at their posts.

Very few of these escapes were successful. In the early 1980s I met a man in Tel Aviv, an aeronautics executive, who had been one of the few to pull it off. He, too, had worked on the farm, from which he planned his getaway with two Polish companions. The three dug a pit in a potato field and crawled into it, after which their fellow prisoners covered it with dirt and branches on which they poured kerosene to throw the dogs off the scent. For three days the men waited until the Nazis gave up and withdrew the night guards. On the fourth they crossed the fence, walked to the home of a Polish underground member, were given civilian clothes and false papers, and went their separate ways. The Jew managed to return to his native town in Slovakia.

This was in 1942, when Slovakia, although a Nazi puppet state, was not yet deporting its Jews. That began in 1944 – when, finding himself on a speeding train back to Auschwitz, this same Jew tried to persuade his fellow passengers to jump from it to their deaths. He had no takers even when he showed them the number on his arm and told them of the horrors in store for them; indeed, when he tried jumping himself, he was beaten unconscious. 'My fellow passengers were afraid of collective punishment,' he told me. 'But it worked out for the best. I was dragged senseless onto the platform at Birkenau and left there for dead while the others were marched to the gas chambers. When it was dark out I came to and located friends from the camp underground who found a place for me in a barracks. That was how I was saved.'

On that day in 1944, the two Pole escapees were less lucky. SS dogs sniffed out their hiding place. Most likely they were shot. In any event, once the manhunt was over and the camp calmed down, we were visited by a group of officers and civilians. The kapo snapped to attention and gave the roll-call count. One of the civilians, dressed in an olive-green leather coat and a felt hat with a feather, declared:

'If there are any lathe workers here, take one step forward.'

Silence. I knew that in half a minute it would be too late. They would proceed to the next block.

'Let's go,' I whispered to Fredek, who was standing on my left. My whisper seemed loud enough to be heard at the far end of the world. Fredek shook his head. I grabbed his hand and stepped forward, trying to drag him after me. He dug his legs in and baulked. His hand slipped from mine. I didn't dare turn around or urge him again. The slightest false movement or word could be my undoing.

One of the Germans surveyed my skinny figure.

'You?' he asked incredulously.

'Yes, sir.'

'What is your profession?'

'A lathe operator, sir.'

'How old are you?'

'Eighteen,' I lied.

'He looks like a retarded child,' said another German.

'That's because of malnutrition, sir,' I hurried to explain. 'I'm a skilled worker. Give me food and I'll be as strong as an ox in no time.'

The officer looked at me sternly. I had talked too much. Prisoners were supposed to speak to the point, answering only the questions asked them. But the German in the leather coat had formed a better opinion of me.

'If you can work as well as you can talk, you'll get your food,' he said. 'Where have you worked before?'

'I graduated from vocational school and worked at the Hermann Goering plant in Starachowice.'

'What did you make there?'

'Artillery barrels, sir.'

The German nodded. The kapo nudged me with his club and ordered me to stand to the side. I tried to catch Fredek's glance. He wouldn't look at me. *Fredek, Fredek*, I wept in my heart, *what have you done to me?* In a world where man was a wolf to his fellow men, Fredek Minz had been a ray of light. Even when he brooded or said, 'Very funny,' or nothing at all, I knew I had a friend. Now, as the officer dismissed the prisoners, I watched him walk slowly, wearily away from me until his slim, stooped figure disappeared into the barracks. I wasn't concerned with what would happen to him. I felt betrayed.

But there was no time to think. The officer jotted down the number tattooed on my arm, the man in the green coat signed for me, and I was told:

'Go with him.'

I followed the man along a path that wound between the blocks of barracks. Two other, older prisoners joined us on the way. They spoke French and had red triangles on their uniforms. That meant that they were politicals.

I had never realized before how big the camp was. It took us a quarter of an hour to reach the front gate, an innocent-looking structure of red brick. Only those who had passed through it knew it was the entrance to hell. A sentry barred the exit. The factory official handed him a slip of paper.

'Three prisoners!' called the sentry.

'Three prisoners,' echoed a soldier in a watchtower.

'Outward bound!' called the sentry.

'Outward bound,' repeated the echo.

'Proceed,' said the sentry, returning the slip of paper to my escort. A small truck stood opposite the gate. Two armed soldiers guarded it.

'Get in!' barked one.

The factory official sat in the cabin. The soldiers climbed into the back with us and rolled the canvas top over the tailgate. The driver started the motor and we set out. The truck bounced over the bumpy road. The soldiers sat on a folding bench with vacant faces. Where were we going? I didn't give it a moment's thought. Nothing could be worse than Auschwitz. I would never have believed I would change my mind a few months later.

30

The camp near the Brotherhood Steel Plant was one of dozens, known collectively as Auschwitz III, erected in Schlesia. It stood across the road from the mill in a huge industrial zone on the outskirts of Swietochlowice. Like much of Upper Schlesia, this city was permanently covered with a pall of grey soot and smoke.

For generations the men in this place had been coal miners, iron piggers, alloy smelters, steel casters, builders of automotive and ship engines. Accustomed to dirty air and a rarely seen sun, they nevertheless found refuge after work in the little vegetable and flower gardens attached to each house. As in Bielsko, chronic friction between Germans and Poles was the rule here. For hundreds of years the region had passed back and forth between the two peoples, leaving Upper Schlesians with an identity and dialect of their own that outsiders did not easily understand. Many felt more Schlesian than Polish or German. One such man was Kurt Kolonko, who held out a helping hand when all backs were turned.

In a sense, the plant was a symbol of Schlesia. Founded by Germans in the early nineteenth century, it had passed to Polish ownership after the German defeat in World War I and had been returned to German hands following the Polish collapse in 1939. As the Nazi arms industry geared up for wartime production, the plant was retooled to produce Flack-88 anti-aircraft cannon in place of the diesel ship engines it had made previously. The industrial cities of the Third Reich were being carpet-bombed by the Allies in retaliation for the London blitz and the German high command was desperately seeking to strengthen its air defences. Our camp was one of six maintained by the Nazis to supply the plant with workers. The other five housed prisoners-of-war and forced labourers. Ours alone was a concentration camp.

The plant was still there when Shulamit and I visited it at the behest of its management in the spring of 1992. The invitation was extended following a television programme in which I told of my acquaintance with Kurt Kolonko. To my surprise, my hosts presented me with Swietochlowice's medal of honour. The attendant publicity, they hoped, would not only better the city's standing in history but lead to a brighter future.

It was only when taken on a guided tour of the workspace in which I had served my Nazi jailers that I began to understand their logic. The German lathes, dies, and rotary hones had been dismantled and shipped east to the Soviet Union in 1945 and the old diesel production line had been resumed. Most of its workstations, however, were now idle. Three-storey-high engine blocks stood on the floor waiting for some use to be found for them. During the Communist years the plant had sold its products to Soviet shipyards, which had paid for them via the Moscow-run clearing system of the East European economic union. Such bureaucratic centralization spared the managers the need to worry about such things as markets, profits, and suppliers. All decisions came from above.

The demise of Communism put an end to all this. Although the mill remained nationalized, it now had to find its own customers. The East European market had collapsed and its old trade pacts were inoperative. Whereas the Poles, flaunting their new economic independence, now demanded hard currency from the Russians, the Russians had discovered that the same dollars bought better engines in the West or Far East. Two-thirds of the plant's workers had been laid off and a similar fate threatened the remaining third in the absence of massive investment in new equipment and Western markets. Moreover, although there were German companies willing to buy the firm and rescue it from bankruptcy, the Schlesians wanted no part of their money. A German minority demanding national rights still lived in the region and the Polish government feared an increase in German influence. All the offers were turned down. 'It's the triumph of politics over economics,' the plant's manager lamented to me.

I took advantage of my brief trip to Swietochlowice to burrow through archives from the war years. I learned from them that on 4 May 1943 the plant's management had turned to SS headquarters with a request for more skilled workers. Brief negotiations led to an agreement that the SS would supply a thousand workers from its concentration camps and receive two marks per day for each of them. Any proving to be unsuitable would be exchanged for others at no extra cost. The SS also agreed to erect a branch of Auschwitz–Birkenau in which the workers would be housed. Construction costs were to be covered by the armaments ministry; the camp would be administered by the SS; and the soldiers guarding it, senior officers excepted, would be provided by the air force, the plant's main customer. All this was approved by the Head Office for Reich Security – as a result of which, I stepped out of our little truck in the summer of 1944 to be greeted by the head kapo:

'You have come, gentlemen, at a most auspicious time, seeing as we have just returned to Auschwitz three corpses of idiots like yourselves.'

It was all thoroughly familiar: the same bunks, the same barracks, the same electric fence and watchtowers, the same brutal regime of daily humiliations, watery soup, twice-daily roll-calls, and death in the gas chambers. The latter, however, were no longer so menacing. The clouds above us were the smog of heavy industry, not the smoke of crematoria. This small difference rekindled in me the illusion that human life meant something even to the Nazis as long as they could profit from it.

But exactly how were they going to profit from me? *Vanity of vanities, saith the Preacher, for what advantage hath a man from all the labour that he laboureth beneath the sun?* Dr Kalter, my old Bible teacher from Bielsko, had permanently installed that verse in my memory. Not that I agreed with its teaching. What good were all my attempts to survive if it was true? Why struggle if our fates were decided in heaven and our only power lay in prayer? And yet prayer was something that God seemed not at all interested in. Pious Jews went up the chimneys; sinless infants were cruelly murdered; and I, a godless infidel, remained alive.

No, divine justice was definitely unreliable. It was every man for himself. Who else would be for him? All I thought about that night was how little my life would be worth in the morning when I was asked to operate my first lathe. Although I still existed in a breathing, seeing, hearing, functioning body, no sane person would have bet a penny on its getting through the next day. Had Fredek Minz seen me sweating in my bunk, and not from a fever, he would have mocked:

'What did you expect? You made your bed, now lie in it!'

I lay there wishing morning would never come. If only the hands of the clock would stop, the dawn refuse to break! I might as well have been a goldfish for all my wishes mattered. As the first pale, hesitant rays of light trickled into the barracks I tried picturing the moment I would stand facing my fate, that many-headed creature that would have the form this time of a machine. My powers of imagination failed me. All I could visualize was a shapeless expanse as black as my future.

The Germans' efficiency surprised me anew each time. At the morning roll-call the kapo read my ID number and informed me that I was in the first work shift. I had no idea why he proceeded to kick me in the behind while declaring:

'You're a lucky bastard.'

I joined the line of men for work. The two Frenchmen who had travelled with me to Auschwitz did not appear to be among them. Not that I would have recognized them. Anyone not of immediate use to me was filtered immediately out of my consciousness. Before I could file away a face in my memory, it was blurred. I saw the forest, not the trees; mankind instead of men.

We walked from the camp gate to the factory, passing some workers in overalls, a woman with a shopping basket, an old man leaning on a cane. He regarded us without interest. Pedestrians waited patiently for us to pass so that they could cross the street. Prisoners in uniform were not a sight to arouse curiosity.

At 6 a.m. sharp I was facing a lathe. While it bared rotary teeth as though to tear me apart, I stared at it like an object from outer space. The foreman brought me a blueprint.

'Do you read German?' he asked.

'Yes, sir.'

German! What German! The technical language could have been ancient Chinese. I didn't understand a word of it. I didn't even try to understand the vertical and diagonal lines of the drawing it accompanied, or the numbers that resembled algebraic equations.

I looked around me. The work floor was huge. Dozens of

machines stood in ruler-straight lines. By every lathe, die, and hone was a prisoner. In the middle of the floor rose a tower crowned by an octagonal office. Metal stairs spiralled up to its glass windows. From a vantage point three metres above us, its occupants kept us under surveillance. The engineer in charge was a bespectacled man with a roundish face that gave him a good-natured look. I watched him rise from his desk and go to a window like an exotic fish in an aquarium.

It didn't take long to discover that his appearance was deceiving. The engineer's favourite pastime was wiring the spiral stairs, summoning a prisoner to his office, and watching him tumble epileptically down again as he sent a non-lethal shock coursing through him. Twitching on the floor like a fish out of water, the wretched prisoner would hear a voice calling his name and asking him to please climb the stairs faster. He had no way of knowing when his jolly tormentor would tire of the game.

All this, of course, I only learned later. For the time being, having failed to engage the lathe in conversation, I was trying to work my charms upon the blueprint. It was hopeless. The drawing stared hostilely back at me like a criminal indictment. I was still trying to make head or tail of it when the foreman stepped up behind me. His voice made me jump:

'Are you having trouble with that blueprint?'

'Me? Not at all, sir,' I said, hiding my dismay.

'You're sure you don't need any help?'

'I'll manage, sir.'

He still hadn't seen through me. Not yet. I put the blueprint down. He explained:

'We insist on precision work. Your daily quota is eighty-four parts. For every ten over the norm, you'll get an extra one hundred grams of bread. For every ten under the norm, you'll get ten strokes of the whip. Is that clear?'

'Perfectly, sir.'

The foreman went off. I took a metal rod and fastened it to the lathe head. Although the German would become suspicious if I didn't turn on the machine, I hadn't the foggiest notion of how to do it. I pressed a black switch. Nothing happened. I pressed a red one. The unresponsive lathe mocked me. I looked around helplessly. A few lathe operators looked back. They had seen types like me before. They knew what happened to them. My fate was written in their eyes.

My glance met the prisoner's on my left. A short, stocky man with ruddy cheeks and twinkling blue eyes, he was wearing a blue-and-grey-striped uniform like me. A red triangle with a P on it told me that he was a Pole. Pouring coolant on a cutting blade, he said in Polish:

'Hey, yid, how do you call that prayer for the dead of yours?'

'Kaddish.'

'I've never heard it. Have you been studying it?'

I shrugged. I was not about to give him lessons in Judaism.

'So what's it going to be with you.'

It was more of a statement than a question.

'God knows.'

'God sure isn't going to operate that lathe for you.'

'I don't suppose that He is,' I admitted.

'Not so loud,' he warned me. 'We're not supposed to talk.'

'Then why are you talking?'

'Don't be a kike, wise-guy.'

'All right. I'll shut up.'

'Don't you know who I am?'

'You're a lathe operator.'

The Pole laughed. 'Everyone around here knows me.'

'Everyone except me.'

'Honestly?' His surprise was genuine.

'Honestly.'

'My name's Kurt Kolonko.'

'Mine's Roman.'

'Don't you have a second name?'

'I had one. Now it's as phoney as yours.'

'You getting wise again?'

'I didn't mean anything by it.'

'Ever follow boxing?'

'No.'

'Before the war I was featherweight champ.'

'Of Poland?'

'Of Upper Schlesia, pal,' he corrected, not without pride. 'I was born a Schlesian and I boxed as one. You won't believe it, but I'm the fifth generation to put on gloves in my family. We're a dynasty. Every soul in town knew me. Even the kikes – if they've got souls. Not that I know what else they might have. I'm no doctor or priest. But ask if they was scared of me and I'll say: You bet. If they didn't cross the street when they saw me coming, they caught a good punch. I don't mean a jab, either. I mean a left hook they never forgot. Sweet Jesus, did I like to sock it to them! They're the reason we was so poor. They had all the businesses and jobs and women and we had the hard work. You guys sure know how to get along.'

'I wish we did,' I said morosely.

'So what's going to be with you? Smell the gas already?'

'They say Zyklon B has no smell.'

'You're dying to find out, eh? . . . Hey, that's some pun! I may not be a fucking intellectual like you, but I'm not so dumb either. I went to vocational school. I'll bet you studied literature or something, huh? Your father must be a banker or a lawyer, what?'

'He's dead.'

'And your mother went around in silk gloves, didn't she?'

'She's dead, too.'

'Yeah. Dying's the fashion these days. The sooner you do it, the less you suffer. You too. You're not the first or last to go from the frying pan into the fire. Tomorrow they'll make soap out of you. You know that's what they do with dead Jews, don't you?'

'At least we'll leave the world a cleaner place.'

That tickled him. He put a hand on my shoulder, pushed me aside, and stepped up to my lathe.

'What are you doing?' I asked. Kurt Kolonko leaned over the lathe, studied the drawing, and said:

'Stay out of this. Just tell me if the foreman's coming.'

He switched on the lathe and began working, talking all the time:

'Don't let it intimidate you. Everything here is automatic and very simple. Watch what I do and learn from me. These are vidia blades. They'll cut steel like butter. You tighten them in this revolving head, like this. Just be careful with them: they're expensive and the krauts go apeshit when you ruin one. You see this slot? Watch how I sharpen the blade and keep the coolant flowing over it. Vidia needs tender care like a woman. Ever get laid?'

'No.'

'Next to boxing, it's my favourite sport. Do what I tell you and you'll live long enough to taste some pussy.'

'But why . . .?'

'Why? I'm a man. A man needs a woman.'

'I mean why . . . this.' I pointed to the lathe.

'Oh. This? Because if I didn't do it you'd be soap that never got laid. You keeping an eye out?'

'Don't worry. The foreman's at the other end of the floor.'

'And the engineer?'

'He's got his back to us.'

'Good. I'm almost through. The blades are set. The lathe head turns them by itself. All you have to do is take out the finished part and insert a new one. Any dope can do it . . . Don't give me that goofy look! I told you to keep an eye out. You want to know why I'm doing this? First of all, because it kills me to see someone fucking up at a lathe. That's the main reason. I'll tell you something else, though. I may not like Jews, but I hate Nazis. You get me? Of course not. You're just a dumb, motherless kid. Well, don't be a dumb lathe operator. It's an honour to be given a toy like this one to play with. In my old workplace I never dreamed of a baby like this.'

'Maybe you'll have your own some day.'

'Maybe,' he sighed, the grin gone from his lips.

31

I met Kurt Kolonko's mother in the autumn of 1947.

How did I find her? It was simple. Kurt had told me where he was born and had spoken of a family business at the same address. His father had started out as a coal-mine smith and had invested his wedding dowry in two old lathes and some welding tools. The times, though, were hard for both welders and lathe operators. He barely eked out a subsistence living. The family lived in poverty. Kurt's father drowned his sorrows in drink. When this, too, failed to solve his problems, he was hospitalized in a mental institution. A year after the outbreak of the war he died, dragged down to an early grave by life's burdens.

Kurt and his twin brother Henryk took over their father's business. Things did not go well for them either. Although Kurt won praise and trophies in the boxing ring, where he spent most of his time, the family was penniless. One evening, he told me, his mother put a plate of medals in front of him for his supper. 'Here's what you've earned,' she said. 'Eat it.' Before he could react, Henryk took the plate and smashed it.

Henryk had a nasty temper and quarrelled with their customers, who took their patronage elsewhere. Before long their creditors went to court and obtained a lien on their equipment. Then the war broke out. Henryk was sent to a labour camp in Germany and Kurt was arrested by the Gestapo. His crime was taking to drink like his father. With no wartime boxing and no work, he passed his time in a local tavern that gave credit. The liquor went to his head. While drunk one night, he boasted that he could floor any kraut with a single punch, including Hitler.

The wrong person was listening. Kurt was hauled in for questioning. It did no good for his mother to stand sobbing in front of the Gestapo building, or for a lawyer to present documents attesting to his brother's devotion in the German war effort. When an electrode was inserted up his anus, Kurt admitted belonging to a non-existent underground organization. In late 1941 a military court found him guilty of hostile propaganda and sentenced him to a concentration camp. There he was classified as a political prisoner, a category that was treated harshly. He spent his first year in a punitive block that few people survived. By then, fortunately, the shortage of skilled workers in the German arms industry was severe. Kurt's imagined punch to Hitler's jaw was forgiven and he was sent to the Brotherhood Steel Plant.

'If you ever want to visit me after the war,' he once told me, 'exit the railroad station to the main street, turn left, walk five hundred metres, and turn left again. On the corner you'll see a street sign that says Narrow Lane. That's just what it is. It's pretty filthy, too, because there are open garbage pails on the sidewalk, but it's the place I was born and grew up in. Maybe they'll clean it up after the war. You'll have no trouble finding our business. Three Narrow Lane, that's all you have to remember.'

I found it easily. Five well-worn stone steps led down from the street to the basement of an old building. The door looked locked. I searched for a bell. There was none. The glass panes of the door had been smashed and replaced with plywood. Someone had scrawled on them: 'Lathe Work Done Cheap.'

I knocked. No one answered. I knocked harder. 'It's open,' called a woman's voice. I gave the door a push. 'Watch out,' the voice said, 'there's another stair.' The interior was dark. The only light came from a bulb hanging over a lathe by the wall. At the rear of the room stood a man. He looked like Kurt, although I couldn't make out his face.

'Kurt?' I asked uncertainly.

The man didn't reply. When I stepped towards him, the woman blocked my way.

'It's not Kurt. It's his brother Henryk. What might you want, mister?'

'I'm looking for Kurt Kolonko.'

'What do you want from Kurt Kolonko?'

'To talk to him.'

The woman looked apprehensively at the briefcase under my arm. She sounded suspicious.

'You have nothing to worry about, ma'am. I'm a friend of Kurt's.'

'Kurt has no more friends.'

'I'm one.'

She stood waiting for me to go on. She didn't offer me a seat. I introduced myself awkwardly.

'And who are you, ma'am?'

'I'm Kurt's mother.'

'I thought so,' I said, bending to kiss her hand in the best Polish manner. As though shrinking from me, she clutched the hand to her apron and took a backward step towards the lathe. She leaned against it and said:

'Who else could I be? Everyone knows I'm Kurt's mother. What about you, though? You're no client and you're no cop. Who are you?'

Her voice was cold, hostile. She looked much older than the woman of about fifty that I had expected from my conversations with Kurt. A shaft of light coming through the door fell on a weary, wrinkled face. There was no curiosity in her dull stare.

Henryk stepped out of the shadows and started to say something. With a firm gesture she silenced him. He obeyed her like a scolded child.

'Well, mister, what do you want?' she asked again.

'I don't know where to begin.'

'Then begin at the beginning.'

'It's a long story.'

'Try making it short.'

'The shortest I can make it is to say that I owe Kurt a great debt and have come to pay it, if there is any payment for such things. Does that make sense to you?'

'I didn't understand a word you said.'

'He never told you about me?'

She didn't answer. I stammered slightly, my discomfort growing:

'Let me explain. Kurt and I were together in the steel plant. You know about that because you once sent him a package there. He actually received it, although the kapos stole most of the packages. They didn't dare try that with Kurt. He had a special status. Everyone was his friend. You would have been proud of him. Of what he did for me, too. I've never stopped thinking about him. There I was, a helpless Jewish boy no one lifted a finger for, except Kurt ... Why Kurt? I'll never understand that. Not unless he explains it himself. Do you see this briefcase?'

'I see it.'

'There's money here for two new lathes, with Norton boxes and all the latest gadgets. It's not in payment for anything. You can't pay for a life with money. But it's the only way I know of thanking him. Does that set your mind to rest? Can you go get Kurt now?'

'No. I can't.'

I handed her the briefcase. She didn't take it. As though growing taller, she pulled herself up to her full height. Her mask of fatigue became a mask of anger. A muscle twitched in her face. She snapped:

'How dare you come to my house, you filthy Jew? How dare you live your filthy life when my son is dead? How dare you offer me your thirty pieces of silver? Get out!'

Henryk emerged from his dark corner to intervene. His mother waved him away, coming so close that I could feel her hot breath. We were forehead to forehead now, eye to eye. It was her anger against my consternation. 'May you rot in hell, you filthy Jew!' she hissed like a snake. She spat at me. I wiped my face with my sleeve. She spat again. 'Forgive her, mister,' Henryk said quietly. 'Kurt never came back from Auschwitz.'

I was shocked. Dumbstruck. As Kurt's mother started to spit a third time I threw down the briefcase – or perhaps I lost my grip on it – and ran away.

But no. I did not run away. It was nothing you could run from. The hard flame of those eyes, the fury in the face, the hatred of the voice, the venom with which she spat, the tremor of sorrow in the corner of her lips: all would haunt me as long as I lived. To this day, whenever I am rebuked for something, or provoke illogical, disappointing anger by being misunderstood, I run a sleeve across my dry face.

32

My story of meeting Kurt Kolonko's mother was a convenient way of explaining to my friends in Warsaw's Arkady Café why I had decided to leave for Israel. The confrontation, I told them, was so traumatic that I could not go on living in Poland. Ten years later I was still obsessed by the woman's hate-filled glance.

'That's a big lie,' my friends accused me. 'Why don't you admit it? Why don't you just say you want a more comfortable life?'

They were right. It was a lie. And wrong, because it was the truth. It just wasn't the whole truth. Although I hadn't forgotten Kurt's mother, no single thing was responsible for my emigration. It certainly was not characteristic of me to base a momentous decision on a ten-year-old incident. I wasn't a grudge bearer. And I hadn't lost my faith in humanity, either. I had a knack for seeing the other person's point of view and I did not think the world was against me for being a Jew. On the contrary. The world was being very nice to me.

There were twenty or thirty of us at the Arkady, young journalists, authors, playwrights, and assorted groupies, all brimming with energy, imagination, and the determination to get the most out of life. Some of us were well off, the beneficiaries of a regime that knew how to reward its faithful. Others lived on meagre salaries or odd jobs. But money didn't matter to any of us. We never allowed it to come between us. The only entrance ticket to our informal club was a good head, a quick tongue, and – not least – a way with women.

It was no accident that we chose to meet at the Arkady. We all laughed at the Communist Party's hypocritical puritanism and strove to outwit its Victorian morality. At the rear of the Arkady was a hotel in which, displaying the human face of socialism, the Party had allotted rooms to young couples who could not afford rented apartments. Anyone bringing a young lady other than his lawful wife to such a room, even in broad daylight, ran into the resistance of the desk clerk. While sometimes this could be softened by a hundred-zloty bill, the procedure was not always reliable, and we avoided risks by taking advantage of the fact that the Arkady's back exit led straight to the hotel's corridors. How the architects of socialist realism could have committed such a blunder was a mystery. But what did we care? The unspent hush money went to buy drinks and the girls liked the rear entrance better. They were more discreet about the casual quickie than we men.

New winds were blowing in Poland at the time, although they did not have much to do with sex. On 24 October 1956, in the central square of Warsaw, above which rose forty storeys of socialist-realist ugliness known as the Josef Vissarionovich Stalin Palace of Culture, hundreds of thousands of people cheered Władysław Gomułka, the new secretary of the Communist Party. Two weeks previously an angry Nikita Khrushchev, surrounded by a Kremlin entourage including Foreign Minister Molotov, Labour Minister Kaganovich, and Warsaw Pact commander Marshal Ivan Konev, had landed at Warsaw's military airport. While still on the airplane ramp, they had levelled at Gomułka the heinous charge of 'selling Poland to the Americans and the Zionists'. Gomułka had been Party secretary once before, right after the war, and was dismissed in 1948, following factional infighting, because of 'poor health' – for which he was sent to convalesce in prison as a nationalist deviationist. His crime had been to believe in a measure of independence from the Soviet Union and to call for 'a Polish way to socialism'.

In 1956, however, Poland's Communist leaders decided that the same Gomułka was the only man who could restore the Party's public image, which was at an all-time low. Khrushchev and his colleagues were reluctantly forced to accept this development and returned empty-handed to Moscow, thus signalling the onset of a political thaw. In a nationally broadcast speech, Gomułka promised to turn over a new page and to reduce Poland's dependence on the Soviet Union. The speech met with a euphoric reception.

It was only natural that our conversations at the Arkady were largely preoccupied with these changes. Although none of the café's clientele had taken an active role in politics, we followed them like an exciting horse race, placing our bets, cheering on the jockeys, and endlessly analysing their prospects.

The Israeli invasion of Sinai, which began four days after Gomułka's historic speech, was the furthest thing from anyone's mind. All my attempts to raise the subject at the Arkady were ignored. The Middle East was worlds away. Tuning in at home to the dispatches coming from there, I was surprised to discover that what meant nothing to the friends I had shared so much with concerned me greatly. Nor was I as enthralled by the events in Poland as they were. I already knew that I would not be around to enjoy the fulfilment of their hopes even if these came true. My decision to pack my few belongings and depart was final and unshakeable.

It was silly to accuse me of materialistic motives. I was doing very well at the time. A few months previously, *New York Times* correspondent Sidney Gruson had opened *The Times*'s first office in Communist Poland in the Bristol, Warsaw's fanciest hotel. In need of an English-speaking assistant who knew Polish politics, he had hired one of our gang, Tomas Atkins. Atkins, a Jew from Łodz originally named Pomerantz, was a colourful figure in the barren world of the Polish media. Soon to be arrested as a CIA spy, he was to escape from prison, make his way to the West, and turn up in Tel Aviv with an Israeli *laissez-passer*.

Shortly afterwards Gruson hired me, too. I began to be paid in greenbacks and – for the moment at least – my economic worries were over. But if I was good enough to work for the most important newspaper in the United States, I was still not good enough for the least important in Poland. My arrest in Wrocław continued to cast a shadow. Although permitted to work as a translator, I was forbidden to publish books, or even newspaper articles, and banned from all radio appearances. At first, I gullibly believed that the new atmosphere would change all this. Indeed, towards the end of that year I was given an opening when, without even asking for it, I was offered the job of Assistant Director of Foreign Relations at the large Polish tourist complex of Orbis. A government firm, Orbis enjoyed a monopoly on foreign tourism, international conferences, and hosting VIPs from abroad.

I was the right man for it. I knew foreign languages, had a good sense of how capitalist media and PR agencies worked, and could even handle a knife and fork – an ability far from common among Poland's proletarian executives. I didn't try hiding my arrest for 'sabotage' in my job interview. 'Don't worry,' I was told by my interviewers. 'Stalinism is dead and so are all those ridiculous charges.' My personal file was sent for approval to the manpower division of the Party's central committee. For weeks I waited to hear from Orbis. When no word came, I sent a registered letter; when this went unanswered, I telephoned. Orbis's managing director, I was told by the switchboard operator, was unavailable. Running out of patience, I appeared one day in his office. He told me sheepishly:

'I've been avoiding you because I was too embarrassed to tell you that the central committee has turned down your application. The reason given is that there are already too many Jews in high positions.'

It was a blow below the belt. Until then I would have adamantly told anyone asking about it that I had experienced no anti-Semitism in Communist Poland. Nearly all my friends were Catholic. So were nearly all of the girls I went to bed with. My Jewishness had never been an issue or an obstacle. I spoke like a Pole, acted like a Pole, thought like a Pole. I failed to understand that all the Poles who said, 'You're one of us,' simply meant that there was luckily nothing Jewish about me, since it was impossible to be both a Pole and a Jew at the same time. It took me years to absorb this fact. All the time I lived in Poland, I had felt that I was at home. It took Israel to make me realize that home had been a hotel. This was why it was so hard to put a finger on the moment when I first noticed the subtle boundary separating my friends' world from my own.

Today I see clearly that the decision to leave for Israel expanded in me like a yeast dough, slowly, layer after layer. In the end, all that was lacking was a catalyst. Such was the answer I received from Orbis. It had taken me years to appreciate the need to belong that others imbibed with their mother's milk. Those years were like water in an unused pipe. When I opened the tap at last, the first thing to emerge was a rusty stream. Only later did my cup of understanding fill with the pure elixir of truth.

33

Mira and her husband Jozef lived in a two-room, ground-floor apartment in a wooden dacha some twenty minutes from downtown Warsaw by express train. Although it was meant for Party workers – Jozef was the chauffeur of Politburo member Zenon Nowak – it was a rather shabby place. It did not even have a bathroom, its four families being served by a toilet in the yard and a sink that doubled as a tub. Still, having arrived from Wrocław jobless and penniless after my release from interrogation, I thought of it as more than just a temporary asylum. Not that I planned my invasion in advance or plotted Jozef's dispossession. Things ended up taking their own course. The only reason I called Mira from the public telephone in the railroad station was that I had no other number in Warsaw ... And perhaps, too, I still felt I had missed an opportunity when she appeared four years previously on my doorstep in Jelenia Góra.

We agreed to meet at an inexpensive restaurant near her office. Mira worked as a secretary for a clandestine shop that supplied high-ranking Party officials with luxury items. Not only did it have an unlisted phone number, but its name and address were secrets, too. It did not have display windows or customers departing with packages, either; all purchases were delivered by limousine. This system helped the 'red bourgeoisie' to keep living in the style it had grown accustomed to while the shelves of ordinary stores gathered dust. Many of these items, from Colombian coffee to Siberian furs, ended up on the black market. Those in the know kept their mouths shut. The censored press, needless to say, never dared run an exposé.

Although she could easily have cut herself in on this lucrative trade, buying cheap and selling dear, Mira never took advantage of her position. Deception of any kind repelled her. She was honest to a fault, a trait she had acquired from living with Jozef, who was himself a hopeless swindler. Not that she was rewarded by the Party for her loyalty. True, several months after I moved into her apartment she was promoted to manager of the assistant chairman of the Central Planning Commission's office. Ostensibly a super-ministry responsible for the centralized economy and run by Hilary Minz, popularly known as 'the Tsar of the Polish economy', this commission was an agent of the Politburo, whose orders it scrupulously carried out. The various economic ministries, some twenty all told, from the ministry of heavy industry to the ministry of coal mines, were under its jurisdiction. In order to give it a democratic patina, its assistant chairmen were appointed from two Communist-front parties, one supposedly representing the farmers and the other small artisans. Mira managed the office of Stefan Ingar, a member of the Farmers Party. Her real job was reporting on his activities. However, although such tasks were assigned only to the most highly trusted personnel, her promising career was ended by an incident that today would be considered grotesque but that was extremely serious in the Stalinist Poland of 1952.

Mira's office was in the west wing of a huge, new building in Three Crosses Square – one of the few squares in Warsaw not renamed for political reasons. A special pass was needed to enter it. On my rare visits to Mira there, I had to wait for an armed guard to escort me into an elevator and down long corridors, his hand on his holster as though I were Al Capone in Fort Knox. The entire building was super-mysterious and super-confidential. Not that the Central Planning Commission was any different in this respect from other government institutions or even from ordinary factories. Brainwashed by propaganda, we believed that Communism's enemies were lurking everywhere, waiting for our first lapse to spy, commit sabotage, or steal classified documents. (A category that included just about any scrap of paper.) Eternal vigilance was expected of us all.

I was unaware at the time that all totalitarian regimes create vague bureaucratic jargons in order to obscure the truth. The Nazis never spoke about exterminating the Jews; they only referred to 'the Final Solution'. So it was in the Soviet bloc, too. 'Vigilance' was a buzzword for informing, just as 'enemy' meant anyone thinking for himself. While none of us had heard of

George Orwell's *Nineteen Eighty-Four*, a 'subversive' book whose publication was not allowed in Eastern Europe, no place fitted its descriptions better. Not only did the Polish media use such contaminated language, they infected their readers with it. Between 'the labouring masses' and 'the world proletariat', no room was left for the individual. Although I never saved any of my pieces written before my arrest, it is a safe assumption that I composed them in the same horrid style, the full implications of which I was not conscious of.

Mira, too, was familiar with this style. She could never have developed a working relationship with her superiors if she weren't. As the manager of Ingar's lavish office, however, she was not overburdened with work. The assistant chairman was frequently away, leaving her with nothing to do. Her favourite occupation was settling back in her armchair behind the closed double doors of the office and reading. One day, as she was deep in Boris Polevoy's *The Story of a True Man*, the telephone rang. Absent-mindedly using her Party card as a bookmark, Mira shut the novel and stuck it in a drawer. For some reason she never returned to it. A month later she was summoned by her Party cell and asked to present the card. It was not in her wallet where it should have been.

The cell leader and his assistants stared at her. Mira returned to her office, went through her papers, looked in the closet and the safe, searched every drawer, even ransacked the bathroom – there was no card anywhere. 'So you've lost it?' asked the cell leader, raising an eyebrow. 'I must have misplaced it at home. Give me a day or two and I'll find it,' Mira pleaded. But a Party card was not supposed to be at home. It was supposed to be on one's person day and night, it being common knowledge that the enemy was waiting to lay perfidious hands on it. Mira was accused of gross negligence and transferred to the cookbook department of a government publishing house. Herself convinced of the severity of her crime, she accepted the sentence uncomplainingly. The cleaning woman who discovered her Party card in Polevoy's novel while conducting a routine search of the office was awarded a citation.

But in the restaurant in Warsaw that day – the shapely mother of two children, as beautiful as ever with Semitic looks that had always captivated me – Mira was beaming, at the height of her career. We ate potato dumplings, washed them down with buttermilk, and made small talk, ignoring the tension of a mutual attraction that could not be long suppressed. I was running a fever, having caught the flu in my interrogation cell. Mira casually suggested that I stay with her and her husband until I was well enough to rent an apartment. Neither of us mentioned the evening four years previously when she had agitatedly rung my doorbell and asked to spend the night with me. Her marriage to Jozef, she had told me, had run aground and she had made up her mind to leave him. I had talked her into going back to him. I was then taking my first steps as a journalist. Jozef, a Party cell leader in the military optics industry, was in a position to ruin my career.

Jozef and Mira met during the war in one of those situations that only war can create. Mira's parents, like mine, had fled the Nazis to the eastern part of Poland occupied by the Soviet Union after the Molotov–Ribbentrop Pact. However, unlike my parents, the Fremders continued their flight with the Red Army and eventually reached Turkmenistan, thousands of kilometres from the front. In their possession was an item more valuable than the Persian carpets the region was known for: a large box of insulin. Mira's mother was severely diabetic and needed a daily injection to stay alive. In a town by the Aral Sea, they prayed for the war to end before the insulin did.

In the summer of 1943 the Wehrmacht, although on the retreat, was still deep in Russia. Leningrad was besieged. Hitler had not abandoned hope of taking the Russian oil fields in the Caucasus. In Cracow, Gretchen was busy collecting the jewellery stripped by her brother from Jewish corpses. Wilhelm Kunde had forgotten my mother's murder. Amon Goeth was the scourge of Plaszów.

That same summer, the Russians organized the first Polish division to fight in the Red Army. Mira's father volunteered. She and her mother remained in Turkmenistan without means. That winter the insulin ran out. Between one bout of unconsciousness and the next, Mira's mother approached a terminal state. There was no one to help. She lost her eyesight and slipped into a coma. Mira dragged her corpse on a sled to the local cemetery in minus-thirty-degree weather and buried it herself in the frozen earth. She was fifteen years old and all alone. Perhaps something froze in her as well. Years later she paid her father back by having nothing to do with him as he lay dying.

Mira had an indomitable life force. Leaving behind a tombstone-less grave that she would never see again, she took a train north, hoping to find her father. The unheated, crowded, smelly wartime trains were a man's world. A woman boarding them paid for her ticket with a pitcher of home-made kvass or her body.

Although Mira did not find her father, the army became her new home. Lying about her age at an induction centre on the banks of the Oka River, she was conscripted by the Polish division – or, more precisely, by Corporal Jozef Wynszik. She was a friendless girl looking for a shoulder to lean on and he was a substitute father. Together they travelled a long way, fighting first on the German front and then on the home front, which was where I found them.

Jozef welcomed me warmly. He never suspected me of being the Trojan horse that would wreck his marriage. Calling me 'a wandering bird without a nest', he failed to grasp that the bird was a cuckoo. There was no problem laying my eggs, for I soon discovered that he had long ago crossed the thin line between excessive drink and chronic alcoholism. The sworn Marxist in him did not object when he and Mira placed their two daughters, six-year-old Frania and four-year-old Ala, in an educational institution run by the nuns of St Clara of Assisi, who preached asceticism, prayer, and silence. The more empty bottles he flung into the garbage pail, the less interest in his children he took. He disappeared often, hung out with drunks and whores, and came home at odd intervals to recharge his batteries for the next binge.

Mira and I had no complaints. The apartment was ours. Still, we played by the rules. Mira slept in her bed while I slept on a mattress on the living-room floor, where she joined me when Wynszik was carousing. We didn't think of the future. It was enough to seize the day. The last thing to cross our minds was my permanently taking Jozef's place.

Happenstance had other plans. Sozzled as usual, Wynszik came home late one night to find us in an unequivocal position. I braced myself for an explosion, accusations of betrayal, even blows. But Wynszik, a visitor in his own home, did not seem unduly perturbed. He sank into a chair, propped his elbows on the table, put his chin in his palms, and muttered apathetically:

'I knew it all along.'

I rose and joined him at the table. 'Try to understand . . .'

He interrupted me:

'What's there to understand? I may be drunk, but I'm not blind.' He took my hand and pumped it vigorously. 'Don't worry about it. I take no offence. There are a million women in this city, each with a cunt between her legs. Why live with the one who hates me most? Why? Tell me!'

'If that's how you feel,' burst out Mira, 'why don't you take your things and go live with your whores?'

Wynszik smiled shrewdly. 'I'll tell you why. Because I'm not giving away what can be sold.'

'Sold? What are you talking about?'

'You, darling.'

Mira was stunned. 'You're mad!' she shouted.

Wynszik paid her no attention. He released my hand, rubbed his thumb and forefinger together in the sign for money, and asked me:

'You tell me. How much is she worth to you?'

'What is this, a cattle market?' protested Mira.

'That's one way of putting it,' said Jozef cynically. He repeated his question: 'How much?'

'You can't be serious,' I said, embarrassed.

'I've never been more so. I'll tell you the truth. A friend is waiting for me outside in a car. We need cash. Give me four hundred zlotys and she's yours. I'll throw in the goddam apartment, too, with all its bedbugs and this crap they call furniture. Four hundred zlotys and you'll never see me again. How about it?'

The entire sum was a third of Mira's monthly salary. I was reaching for my wallet when she spoke again. This time she was cool and calculating:

'Don't be such a big spender. He'll settle for two hundred. I know him.'

Wynszik refused to come down, but he kept his part of the bargain. He left the house and never returned except when invited. When drink-driving cost him his licence, friends in the

Party found him a job as the political commissar of a government hospital in Rabka, a town in the Cracow district. Several months later, when Mira was due with her third child, he suggested she give birth there under the best medical conditions. It was a generous offer and she accepted.

We drove to Rabka in a BMW convertible that was as rare on the roads of Communist Poland as a stork in the Polish winter. Although we didn't own it, it symbolized the change in our economic situation. My friends at the Arkady Café had used their connections to find me work at the ministry of transport. My job was stopping drivers from using official cars for private purposes and reporting them to my superiors. I was also authorized to check the mechanical condition of vehicles and revoke their licence on the spot if they weren't roadworthy. Although I took the job reluctantly because we were no longer able to get by on Mira's meagre income, I soon discovered that I had fallen into a gold mine.

Every high-ranking official or Party functionary had a government car with a chauffeur. You could identify his rank by the vehicle. Ministers and Party leaders rode in American Chevrolets. Next came the possessors of Soviet Pobiedas. Lesser *nomenklatura* drove in Polish cars, often tin lizzies with old Fiat motors. It didn't take me long to find out that on weekends, when the chauffeurs had their day off, these officials used their cars for outings to the country, sometimes taking along their families and more often a pretty secretary out for a quick promotion. All I had to do was cast my net on the road leading north to the sea coast, or south to the mountains, and let it fill with fat fish. The fancier the car, the greater the bribe money; the higher the position, the more its holder paid to protect it.

It took a month to get on our feet economically. We even hired a housekeeper, a young villager who was given a sleeping corner in the kitchen. After a second month I suggested taking Mira's two daughters out of the institution and raising them ourselves.

As so often happens in such cases, however, our appetites grew as we ate. I had to look for additional sources of income. Once again chance came to the rescue. I was lying in ambush at Kilometre 120 of the Warsaw–Lublin road with the policeman authorized to stop cars for me, when an old truck came along.

The policeman flagged it down. You didn't have to be an expert to see it was overloaded. It was listing so badly that its front and rear axles weren't even lined up.

The cabin door opened. A man of about forty jumped out and said with a grin:

'I see you still haven't filled your daily quota.'

The policeman stepped aside and left the negotiations to me. He, too, had trouble making ends meet, and our arrangement was that he received one hundred zlotys for every transaction. This time, our victim was not just another palm greaser. He was an Open Sesame to magical riches.

Even in Poland's centralized economy, there were niches in which an able entrepreneur could make a fortune. Plumbers and other vital blue-collar workers, vegetable growers, abortionists, and private truck owners all made millions. The man we stopped on the road to Lublin had his own truck. Losing his licence meant losing an enormous income. We went to a ditch by the side of the road and sat down. He offered me a Chesterfield, the wealthy man's smoke, took out a wad of bills bound with a rubber band, handed them to me without counting, and said:

'There's more here than you earn in a year. And that's not all. If we cut a deal, I'll make you rich. Would you like to hear more?'

I heard more. We cut a deal. From that day on, I hounded the two trucks belonging to his main rival. It was easy to find mechanical faults in them. There wasn't a motor vehicle in Poland that didn't have air in its hydraulic brake system or something wrong with its steering or its lights. For every day that the competition's trucks spent in the repair shop, I received a fat sum. Better yet, during the harvest, when private trucks were mobilized to carry farm produce for sums of money that did not even cover their maintenance, I doubled my per diem. Then, in order that the government would not commandeer it for the harvest, I certified that it was my new employer's truck that was unfit to traverse the country roads.

Our work relationship developed into a friendship. We went out together on dates, generally with teenagers who were not to my taste. Eventually, he offered to take me in as a full partner. 'I need a Jewish brain,' he told me. It was not an easy offer to resist. However, I turned it down and settled for the use of his BMW.

This was the car in which Mira and I drove to Rabka. Jozef Wynszik was pleased to show us what an important man he was. His odd position of political director of a hospital had made him all-powerful. Mira was given a private room, attended by private nurses around the clock, and delivered by the best available obstetrician. In return, Wynszik took his revenge. When a bouncing boy, Mira's first, was born on 18 October 1952, her ex-husband issued a birth certificate with the hideous Teutonic name of Siegfried Wynszik.

'Why did you do it?' I protested. 'He's not your son.'

'I know,' said Wynszik gleefully. 'So what? You'll have a hard time proving it.'

He knew what he was talking about. It took months of running between government offices to change Siegfried's last name. His first name was decreed unalterable. For lack of a better alternative, we nicknamed him Witek.

Now that Witek was a fact of life – a noisy but very cute one – Mira and I decided to become man and wife. This time we needed no favours from Jozef. His Communist morality, it turned out, had never prevailed upon him to make Mira an honest woman. The mother of three was still unmarried.

We celebrated our wedding without the usual dance band. Two friends who were our witnesses at the marriage registrar's accompanied us home for a drink and that was that. All I remember from the ceremony is the old registrar's remark to one of these friends, Mira's old army buddy Bolek Schweigert, who answered proudly when asked for his profession: 'A colonel in the political police.' The registrar removed his glasses, gave Bolek a scornful look, and said quietly: 'That's not a profession. That's a gun for hire.' Such insolence could have landed him in jail for ten years and I told him so. 'I can afford to say what I think,' he answered drily. 'I have cancer of the liver.'

We stayed home for our honeymoon even though I had resigned from the ministry of transportation and had plenty of free time. My resignation was like the decision of a roulette player to swear off gambling after hitting a big jackpot. It was better to slaughter the hen that laid the golden eggs than to risk serving a sentence in the chicken coop. It was only later, indeed, that I found out that both my predecessor and successor had ended up behind bars.

When Witek was six months old we decided to invite his grandfather to Warsaw. Mira's father lived in Wrocław. Although I had spoken often to him on the telephone, I had never met him. We wrote him a warm letter and received no answer. By now I felt curious to get to know the man and understand why he had abandoned his daughter. I drove to Wrocław.

If I had expected to meet a monster, I was disappointed. Julek Fremder turned out to be a hospitable, warm, friendly giant of a man with a good sense of humour. His stomach spilled over the belt of his pants, his shirt was bursting at the seams from the sheer girth of him, and his hooked nose proclaimed his Jewish origins. He worked in an armaments plant, which – its existence being a secret, since only warmongers manufactured weapons of destruction – had a sign above its entrance declaring it a factory for water meters. The running joke in Wrocław was that its workers were incompetent, since each time they tried producing a water meter out came a machine gun by mistake. Julek Fremder liked this joke, just as he liked the young Polish woman he was living with. God only knew where he had found her. She was as gorgeous as a beauty queen, as stubborn as a mule, and as intelligent as a floor tile. She couldn't cook, wouldn't clean, and had no other virtues besides being younger than Fremder's daughter. Apparently, that was enough for him.

I visited him on 1 May. The streets of Wrocław were festooned with red flags. He, an ex-officer, was wearing his dress uniform. After a drink or two I observed that the many medals on his chest must testify to a heroic war career.

'Tell him the truth,' sneered the young beauty.

'I was a hero of the soup pot,' said Fremder.

'I don't get it,' I said.

'Go on, explain it to him,' urged Fremder's girlfriend.

'Why not? It's a good story,' said Fremder, fingering a silver medal hanging from a green ribbon. 'Do you see this little gewgaw? It's a medal for being in the battle of Lenino. Before you get too excited, let me assure you that I never fired a shot. All I did was make onion soup for the battalion commander. That may not have been as hard as a bayonet charge, but it wasn't easy, either. Go find fresh onions in the snows of Belorussia! It was freezing cold, everyone was starving, and the peasants guarded what little food they had with their lives. It took brains to find something that a man could put in his mouth without its ending in a stomach ache. I was good at that. I knew how to deal with those muzhiks. I found some onions hidden beneath a pile of branches. You'd have thought from the way the peasant's wife wept that I was kidnapping her newborn baby. But I had no pity on her. Pity in war is like syphilis in love – it ruins everything. I went back to the base and cooked the CO his favourite food. He wasn't a great gourmet, which was a fortunate thing, because what would I have done if he had wanted a cordon bleu meal with french fries or smoked salmon with capers? He liked my soup so much that he promoted me to battalion cook. That, too, was a stroke of luck, since I didn't know which end of the gun the bullets came out of and I was in no mood to charge the Germans with a hand grenade.

'Now look at this medal. Do you read Russian? It says "For Bravery" and it not only comes with a green ribbon, it comes with a funny tale. At one point there was a lull in the fighting. The CO was bored. He was the kind of man who thought that the only things worth doing in life were eating and shooting. In the farmyard where we were bivouacked was a horse that looked just as bored as he was. "I'd love to see a fat Jew like you ride it," he teased me. He even offered me a medal for bravery if I could stay on that horse for ten minutes. That was child's play for me. Back in Cracow before the war I hauled beer kegs on a wagon harnessed to Belgian dray horses, huge things that pulled two tons like a feather. Next to them that miserable Belorussian nag was like a hobby-horse. Even after I kicked it to put a little life into it, it didn't have a zloty's worth of ambition. But the CO was a man of honour. He gave me the medal. As for this one over here . . .'

My father-in-law had lots of stories, all amusing. When his girlfriend went to make us something to eat, I asked:

'Didn't you ever want to know how Mira was?'

'There was a war on.'

'She was your only daughter.'

'Why bring up the past? She's done all right for herself. She has a husband and children. What's the problem?'

'You're right,' I said. 'There isn't any.'

We sat talking and drinking until after midnight, when the young beauty announced that she was going to sleep. She made a bed for me in the living room and Julek Fremder wished me good night, laid a heavy hand proprietarily on her neck, and went off with her to the bedroom. I hadn't brought my pyjamas. A bit tipsy from all the liquor, I turned out the light, undressed, crawled under the blanket, and fell asleep at once.

I didn't hear the bedroom door open. I didn't even feel Julek's girlfriend get into bed with me. Nor did I ask any questions when she found an original and very pleasant way of awakening me. By way of explanation, she said:

'If I have to sleep with Jews, I like the young skinny ones better.'

I returned to Warsaw the next day. Mira didn't ask about her father and I didn't tell her anything. That was the last we heard from him until the 1960s, when we were already in Israel. Ill, he turned to her for help. Mira didn't answer his letter. He died a bitter, lonely man. When Mira revisited the Poland of her memories in the 1980s, her father's grave was not on her itinerary.

On Witek's first birthday I repeated my offer to take his two sisters out of the institution. The nuns refused to yield them. According to the law, they explained, the girls must be surrendered to the custody of the person who had committed them. I tracked down Wynszik. Having been dismissed from Rabka for the attempted rape of a new mother, he was now managing a state cattle-breeding farm in the north. While happy to see me, he refused my request.

'Isn't it enough that you've taken my wife away?' he growled.

'We visit your daughters every Sunday. You haven't been to see them in half a year.'

'A father's love isn't measured by visits,' he replied.

'That sounds wonderful. It's no help to Frania and Ala, though.'

'You want to be a big daddy, eh? Just like that, with no sweat. Make yourself some puppies of your own if you want more to bring up. What do you want with my daughters?'

'They're Mira's daughters, too.'

'That's so.' Jozef Wynszik thought it over. 'We should go half-and-half. Take the big one and leave me the little one.'

'Why separate them? Think of what that will do to Ala. She'll feel abandoned. She's not even five.'

'Spare me the proclamations. It's fifty-fifty or nothing.'

It was pointless to argue. I had Jozef sign a power of attorney and a week later we took Frania from the nuns. (Ala was brought by me to Israel after Jozef Wynszik's death, when Mira and I were already divorced.) Our relationship got off to a bad start. Imbued with the Catholic faith, she was not easily reconciled to Jewish parents. She missed the cross on the wall, the Christmas tree, the white confirmation dress, and, most of all, her religion classes and Sunday mass. Despite our best efforts, she clung to the teachings of the convent.

At this time – it was early 1953 – there was a strong current of anti-Semitism in the Soviet bloc. The Slansky trial, eleven of whose fourteen defendants were Jewish, had just ended in Prague. The year before that, twenty-five Jewish artists had been condemned to death in Russia. Six Jewish doctors were accused in January 1953 of plotting to assassinate Stalin and his associates. The American Joint Distribution Committee, so the government press claimed, was behind the conspiracy. Usually adept at controlling my emotions, I threw the newspaper on the floor and stamped on it in a fury. My Catholic friends liked to tell me that I didn't have a Jewish bone in my body. More and more, I felt only Jewish bones.

The campaign against the Jews was a masterpiece of planning in which the doctors' plot, the Slansky trial, the accusations against the Yiddish writers in Russia, and the planting of a bomb in the Soviet embassy in Tel Aviv were orchestrated by a single conductor. There is no knowing where it might have ended had it not been for the sudden death of Stalin on 5 March 1953. Within a few months the doctors' plot was declared a figment of overzealous imaginations and the anti-Semitic agitation subsided. The only ones to go on adding fuel to the languishing fire were the Jewish Communists in Poland. With genuine disgust I read the following in a book by one of them, Simon Zachariasz:

'Zionism and the Zionist government of Israel, with their ties to international imperialism, are aiding the revival of Hitlerism. For this purpose the Zionists have forged an alliance with the neo-fascists in West Germany. The builders of a new Wehrmacht and murderers of six million Jews are even now looking for additional victims . . .'

These words were originally written in Yiddish. I read them in a Polish translation. Even before finishing Zachariasz's book, I had made up my mind to get in touch with the Israeli embassy in Warsaw. Eventually these ties were to develop into a relationship whose full story cannot yet be told. Meanwhile, we had our own Jewish problem at home. Frania could not get used to living with us. It took Mira and me a long while to understand that the tensions between us had to do with religion and that Frania's bitterness, tantrums, and poor grades at school were a result of this unacknowledged factor. Our enlightenment came when Mira, going through Frania's schoolbag, came across hidden pictures of Catholic saints there. A closer look at Frania's notebooks revealed that she was regularly going for catechism lessons to a local church.

So this explained her frequent disappearances from home! We sat her down for a talk and were shocked by what we heard. Until she began going to the lessons like her classmates, she told us, she had been cursed at school for being a Jew. Her teachers were deliberately cold towards her. Even her friends refused to play with her during recess.

I could understand Frania's not wanting to be a freak. She lacked the strength to swim against the current – and, even more, the motivation. She had found a home not in our family, but in the Church.

It was pointless to try to talk her out of it. Mira decided on shock treatment. It wasn't her sense of Jewishness but her atheism that made her do it. She insisted that I go to the priest and have Frania excused from religion class. I did what she asked.

'Let's have a relaxed talk in my office,' the priest suggested, leading me to a small, dark room behind the altar. He apologized for its modest furnishings: 'We don't want to look extravagant.'

'So as not to attract the Evil Eye of the authorities?'

'Call it what you like. We've learned to coexist with them. But you haven't come to discuss Party–Church relations with me. Can I offer you a glass of wine?'

'No, thank you.'

'It wouldn't put you under any obligation,' he smiled, pouring himself a glass. 'You're here because of Frania, aren't you?'

'Yes.'

'She's a very intelligent and very devout girl. You musn't drive a wedge in her pure soul.'

'That's exactly what we wish to prevent.'

'Frania has found her way to God. She is determined to follow it.'

'She's not even seven. That's not old enough to think for herself.'

'Begging your pardon, Mr Frister, I must disagree. I wasn't talking about thinking. Faith resides in the feelings, not the mind.'

'You know that she's Jewish, Father. The Catholic Church is not for her.'

'That's a debatable proposition.'

'Not for me, Father.'

'Frania may be Jewish according to Jewish law, but not according to our beliefs. Her father was and still is a Pole.'

'He's a Communist who doesn't believe in God.'

'That's an optical illusion. We're a Catholic nation. Jesus Christ suffered on the cross for men like him as well. For all sinners; you too, Mr Frister. Please, don't punish your child for not being Polish.'

I lost my temper. 'What makes me less Polish than you? I was born in this country, too. So were my parents and ancestors. I'm as much a part of Polish history as you are, Father. Your cassock doesn't make you more of a Pole.'

'I didn't mean to offend you.'

'You did.'

'Please forgive me. Yes, you're a Polish citizen. You have a Polish ID and no doubt Polish nationality. But there is a difference.'

'What?'

'We and you have been living together for a thousand years. I don't make light of that, just as I don't make light of your contribution to our culture. But you have chosen to be Poles. That choice has been calculated and deliberate, which is why you can always change your minds. Your patriotism has no roots. It wasn't learned at your mother's breast. Poland is rooted in the eternal verities of Christianity. For better or for worse, we're Poles by blood and always will be. It's no accident that a Catholic marriage is for ever while you Jews permit divorce. To my way of

thinking, one doesn't choose a homeland as one does a mistress
. . . I hope I haven't insulted you. I speak without the slightest
prejudice. I respect Jews. I can never forget that the crucified
Christ preached love of one's fellow man, even of the non-
Christian. It is in the name of that love that I now turn to you,
Mr Frister. Don't stand in Frania's way. Don't prevent her from
joining the society she belongs to. Don't rob her of her faith, her
salvation . . .'

Whether he was being sincere and speaking as a true believer,
or simply playing a role, I had no intention of continuing the
conversation. The only thing that could make him surrender
Frania's 'pure soul' was the intervention of the authorities. It was
crucial for her to feel that it was he who was rejecting her, so that
her resentment would be focused on him. I said:

'I'm sorry to disappoint you, Father. The child is not a subject
for bargaining.'

'It's Christianity that is not a subject for bargaining. The
human soul is not up for sale,' he responded with passion.

'I'm afraid you still don't get it, Father,' I said, emphasizing
each word.

'The heart understandeth and the eyes see and the ears hear.
That's from the book of Deuteronomy. It's from your Bible, not
the New Testament.'

'Since you don't understand me when I speak tactfully, I'll stop
beating around the bush. You must know that my wife works for
the Party central committee and does not want her daughter to
have a religious education. If you don't end Frania's participation
in your catechism lessons, I'll have to file an official complaint. I
don't imagine that I need remind you that religious coercion is a
criminal act.'

'May the merciful God forgive your sin,' the priest replied. I
left. The key turned behind me. The sound of it told me that the
door of the Church was now closed to Frania, too.

I adopted Frania officially several weeks before leaving Poland.
She was eleven at the time and understood what was happening.
Our emigration to Israel seemed to her an exciting adventure to a
new world.

Mira was less enthusiastic. My rapprochement with Judaism
over the past several years had left her cold. Her main reason for

agreeing to part with the world she belonged to was her wanting us to stay together. A more mature person than myself would probably have convinced her that we should separate. But it wasn't rashness that kept me from doing this, even though I knew that our relationship was deteriorating and that a marital crisis was inevitable. Nor, I might say in my defence, was Mira blindly devoted to me. She understood the terms of our relationship as well as I did and was not above asserting her femininity with an occasional affair while away on vacation. What was the exception for her, however, had become the rule for me.

Whenever he travelled to Western Europe or the United States, Sidney Gruson left me the keys to the *New York Times'* suite in the Bristol. As he did this often, I was kept busy organizing lively debauches. The Bristol's waiters were accustomed to filling the elevator to our fourth-floor rooms with silver trays of Russian caviar, Hungarian salami, French cognac and champagne, and all kinds of pastries and desserts. A handsome tip kept them from advertising what they saw. Little islands of capitalist decadence in a Communist state, the parties I threw always had a 'sponsor,' generally a middle-aged black-marketeer who was happy to foot the bill in return for participating in our orgies. The most noteworthy of these was a paunchy Turkish arms dealer with a weakness for teenagers, particularly the tall, blonde, busty variety. If none of the girls wandering naked around the suite took his fancy, or were drunk enough to submit to such a tub of lard, I went down to the lobby and found him an 'amateur', someone ready to trade her young body for a fancy dinner with a foreign tourist. This was how I met Barbara, who was nineteen.

Barbara's long blonde hair drove our Turkish patron to distraction. She, on the other hand, the daughter of a sergeant in the air force, had a crush on me. Her parents had no inkling of the double life that she was leading and sincerely believed that their beautiful Baszia was spending her evenings taking singing lessons. Barbara, however, was busy acting out the Hollywood movies that she loved. It was in the Bristol that she met the Syrian pilots training on Polish-made Migs who used their monthly furloughs to seek female company in Warsaw. They generally found it in the hotel's lobby or one of its restaurants, where liquor loosened their tongues enough to give Barbara and the Turkish arms dealer much to talk about. Equipped with an excellent memory, Barbara enjoyed showing off her considerable knowledge of Soviet fighter planes; the Turk, for his part, liked to boast of the deals he had made between Poland and various Third-World countries. Netting this information like a lepidopterist, I passed it on to the Israeli embassy. My latest update reached it forty-eight hours before I left Poland. A few days later the chargé d'affaires who received it was declared *persona non grata*.

In June 1957 I kissed Mira and the girls goodbye, took the wheel of the *New York Times*' Plymouth, and set out. The plan was to spend two days in Wrocław, cross the border the next day, and – if all went well – phone Mira from Austria to board the next train for Vienna. From there we would proceed together to Israel.

It didn't quite work out that way.

Not only was Mira in the dark about my ties with the Israelis, but I had kept another secret from her, too. She didn't know that I had agreed to a proposition made by a Jewish manufacturer of cheap candies who was one of our regular 'sponsors' at the Bristol. A man of about fifty, which made him seem ancient to us, he, too, had decided to emigrate. Now he was looking for a way to get his property out of Poland. If it is true, as they say, that nothing brings two men together like a shared woman, we had shared dozens. During one of our shindigs, he asked me to smuggle two hundred kilograms of pre-war German silver coins across the border. My commission would be ten per cent of their worth, payable upon delivery in Austria.

The idea of taking a fling at smuggling appealed to me even more than the chance to make some money. I enjoyed the high tension of danger. Getting caught would mean long years in jail, but why get caught? Hadn't I been born with the lucky lottery ticket in my hand? I agreed and we shook hands on it. The coins would be waiting for me in Wrocław. Because of the risk, I preferred to leave Mira and the girls behind. They would await my phone call from Vienna.

In Wrocław I stayed with Robert, my friend from the jolly days in Wrocław, and his parents. A strange, elderly couple who lived in a world of their own, they never knew what to make of the dissolute son whom they had raised to be a conformist. His decision to come with me to Israel thrilled them. A Jewish state, they believed, would make an honest man of him. Although they could not have been more wrong, that chapter of Robert's life belongs in another book.

The fact was that going to Israel was simply one more of his many caprices. Although I was a good enough friend to know that he had no interest in Zionism, I was happy to have him along for the ride. I had told him what I was smuggling, not wishing to be responsible for any trouble he might get into, and he had replied that he was not concerned. After dark I drove to the garage where the coins were to be loaded. Robert decided to come along. I was already turning the key in the ignition when he stuck his head through the open window and said:

'I'll wait for you at home. And don't tell me where the money is hidden.'

'Why not? You're a partner.'

'The customs police are trained psychologists. They'll follow my eyes straight to the hiding place.'

The 1956 Plymouth station wagon had two hollow driveshafts running the length of it. Making a rectangular opening halfway down both shafts, the garage owner helped me fill them with the coins. The weight was distributed evenly on both sides of the car by a simple yet sophisticated method. The coins were packed in heavy woollen socks, five kilograms in each, and were stuffed into the shaft tied to strings that could be easily pulled out at the journey's end. Then we welded the shafts shut, tarred the bottom of the car, and drove it through sand. Not even the keenest-eyed customs official would notice anything.

I returned to Robert's home at 2 a.m. He met me in the hallway. His hands were shaking.

'Mira phoned,' he whispered.

'What does she want?' I asked worriedly.

'She was calling from a public phone.'

'Why?'

'The police searched your apartment. They asked where you were.'

'What did she tell them?'

'She was OK. She said you were abroad and out of touch with her. They took away her passport and said she would get it back only when you reported for questioning.'

'About what?'

'She didn't know. Why don't you call her?'

'Are you crazy? The phone will be tapped.'

'What will we do?'

'We'll head out at five in the morning. We'll cross the Czech border at seven, as soon as it opens.'

'They'll arrest us.'

'You remember that newspaper story we once wrote together? The one about the border police?'

'Sure I do.'

'We interviewed quite a few officers. What was it that they all complained about?'

'Faulty communications. I'm beginning to get it.'

'God bless old-fashioned technology. They put their telexes to sleep at night.'

'I still don't like it.'

'If you're going to pee in your pants, stay home. Mummy and Daddy will make you some hot chocolate.'

'I'll set the alarm clock for four-thirty. And I'll make us the hot chocolate myself.'

The policeman at the border crossing at Kudowa took our passports and disappeared for a long time into the shack that served as his office. Although it was indeed a moment of high tension, I'm not sure that I enjoyed it. My pulse raced furiously until the man returned, handed us our passports, and wished us a pleasant trip. I stepped on the accelerator. The police on the Czech side were polite. Towards evening we reached Mikolow, four kilometres from Austrian soil.

The town was empty. Later I learned that the authorities had evacuated all the peasants owning farms along the border. Two barbed-wire fences ran along the road, with a trench between them and yellow signs warning of mines. So this was what the Iron Curtain looked like! Too depressing for words, it brought home to me as never before how the 'peace-loving world', as it was called with infinite cynicism, was in fact a huge prison.

The Czech that I had learned in 1946 won hearts at the border. The officer studying the list of wanted travellers took a long time. I watched him from of the corner of my eye while striking up a friendly conversation with the police and customs officials. Journalists and literary men, they professed, were highly esteemed by them. Robert took from his suitcase a thriller he had been reading and handed it to one of them.

'This is about a gang of smugglers caught by the Polish police,' he explained.

A customs official laughed. 'Stick with us and you'll have enough material for another book. We catch smugglers nearly every month. Usually, they're moving money. The going rate in Austria is ten times higher than in the democratic republics. Silver ingots, coins, valuables, works of art – you have no idea of all the stunts we've uncovered.'

I asked for an example or two. He didn't need to be encouraged.

'There was a time when people got away with it. You wouldn't believe the things the human brain can think of. But today we have a sure-fire method. There isn't a smuggler who can outsmart it. We strip the car of everything, check the fuel, and put it on the scales. The vehicle's weight is in its registration papers. If there's a significant discrepancy, we take the thing apart. We haven't been wrong once. What do you say to that, Mr Detective Book Writer?'

'What can I say? Hats off to you fellows!'

When the officer came back with our passports, Robert was no longer by my side. He was standing ten metres away. 'We're off!' I shouted. He jumped into the front seat. Up went the barrier. I waved to the friendly Czechs and drove off in low gear to keep anyone from thinking we were in a hurry. The road was narrow and full of potholes. I drove carefully. If we broke a driveshaft now, God Himself couldn't help us. After some two kilometres I smelled something strange.

'They're fertilizing the fields,' I said. But they couldn't have been. 'No, that makes no sense. No one lives here.'

'It's me,' Robert said.

'What's your after-shave lotion?' I joked.

'It's not funny.' He sounded insulted. 'I may have crapped in my pants, but at least I had the brains to move away so that those fucking police dogs wouldn't smell that I was afraid.'

We kept driving past fields planted with mines. A few minutes later we saw the Austrian border.

'We're free!' shouted Robert. Both of us burst into hysterical, liberating laughter.

34

Freedom can mean different things. A lion in the green space of a progressive zoo feels freer than a lion in a cage. But how much freer does a hungry alley cat feel than a well-fed house pet? Does more freedom always mean more happiness? Where is the line between necessary limits and chains?

One could write any amount of philosophical essays on such questions, pitting theory against theory and experiences against experience. On the work floor of the steel plant, I had my own standards. Bent over my lathe, the freedom to travel to the moon did not interest me. I might even have said that I was happy where I was. The guards did not bother me. Neither did the cold nor the fear of tomorrow. I had become as good as any other lathe operator. Kurt Kolonko was proud of me. I was proud of myself. As absurd as it sounds, every precision part that met with a satisfied Nazi smile gave me a feeling of accomplishment. An aberrant feeling, you may say. But it never really occurred to me that I was producing for the German war machine. The war was too far off and nebulous. The metal curls pared away by my knives shone for me with a creative spark.

The illusion of freedom ended with the end of our shift. To the shrill of the kapo's whistle, we lined up to be counted and returned to camp. Was this also a return to reality? Or was the factory real and the camp phantasmagoric? I lived in both worlds. We went as routinely from one to the other as one goes from morning to night. Loath to accept mere appearances, I looked for hidden meanings in the transition.

The seasons of the year alone, which followed their own natural logic, reminded us that not all of life was lived by our laws. The summer died. Then the autumn. Winter came and lashed us with its frosty whip. While the factory was pleasantly warm, our barracks had no heating. We used their idle stoves for tables. After the evening roll-call, which went on for ever (or, more precisely, until the Germans grew tired of it), there was no place to escape the cold. We slept in our clothes and sometimes in our shoes.

The worst moment, though, was waking. It demanded the same decision every morning. As soon as the kapo's whistle blew at 5 a.m., I had to choose whether to fight or give in. It was a test of my own strength that I put myself to each time, feeling that the outcome was momentous. First I forced open my eyes. Then I rubbed their glued lids, counted to ten, threw off the blanket, and jumped from my bunk. There were thirty minutes from reveille to roll-call. Most of the prisoners used them to prolong the delusion of rest. The quicker ones needed three minutes at most to tie their shoes and get into line. I needed a quarter of an hour just to wash. That was something that no one else did.

The lamps were still lit outside the barracks, diffusing a yellowish light. Compared to the cold outside, even the freezing barracks seemed warm. An icy wind blew away the last cobwebs of sleep. I ran faster than I could think, flying across the space from our barracks to the washroom. 'You and your morning exercises!' I was taunted. Every morning I had to fight the temptation to stay in bed for those extra twenty minutes. I succeeded because I was convinced that the slightest lowering of my standards would start me down a slippery slope. I had a daily regimen of my own to counter the one imposed on me and I was almost insanely strict about observing it. The rules I made were the links that bound me to my own humanity. I knew that if even one of them snapped, all the others would weaken to breaking point. The ice water that I splashed over my naked torso from a tap-less pipe told me I was still my own master. It froze my blood and warmed my soul. As long as I felt the sting of the ice, I knew that I could prevail.

Maintaining my morale didn't make me any less cold. Although I took to wrapping my legs like Kurt Kolonko in the newspapers that could be found in the bathrooms used by the plant's officials, my shoulder blades hurt so badly that at times I could scarcely breathe. Not knowing that I had tuberculosis, I blamed the weather. Luckily, I found a solution for this, too. In a toolshed, left untended by some Russian prisoners-of-war who were working on renovations, I came across some empty sacks of cement. I waited patiently for the Russians to be marched away in a single file, looked around to make sure no one was watching, took a sack, and hid the others beneath some boards for future use.

I had to be quick. The foreman or an SS guard might peek in at any moment. If I were caught . . . But I didn't want to think about it. I stripped off my jacket and measured the sack for size. By making holes for my head and arms, I could get it to fit me like a woollen undershirt. I just hadn't counted on the thickness of the paper. It broke my fingernails and bruised my hands. It took a few nerve-racking minutes to finish. Lumps of cement still stuck to the sack. I was afraid to shake them off and make noise. I put the sack on beneath my striped uniform, tied my pants with the rope that served me as a belt, and returned to the work floor with measured strides. They concealed that I was shivering with fear.

'Where did you disappear to?' asked Kolonko.

'I was only gone two minutes.'

'You're not answering my question.'

I knew that I could trust him. I opened a button, bared my chest to him, and said:

'How's that for a mink stole?'

He slapped me on the shoulder. 'You're learning how to get along, yid.'

'I have a good teacher.'

'They'll cut your dick off if they catch you.'

'Not a chance.'

'What makes you so sure?'

'This.' I tapped my head.

'You think a lot of it, don't you?'

'Of what?'

'Your Jewish head. Haven't you ever seen a Jewish head in a hangman's noose?'

'Not mine,' I said.

There was one person in our camp who would dearly have liked to see that head in a noose: Arpad Basci. I was his last living rape victim. All the others had disappeared mysteriously. I had no idea how he had gotten rid of my fellow bread chewers. No doubt he had his methods. Arpad Basci was an experienced veteran, careful enough to leave no witnesses. Pederasty was a crime to which the Nazis showed no mercy even if the culprit was an important prisoner. I kept as far away from the man as I could, shunning all contact with his new circle of youngsters and evading his suspicious looks. I knew the old fox was waiting for me to slip up. Any mistake could be his golden chance. I couldn't afford to make even one.

I wondered why Arpad Basci didn't use his special relationship with the kapo or barracks elder to have me sent to kingdom come. Nothing would have been easier than bashing in my skull and claiming that I had been trying to escape. The SS never investigated such cases. It was simpler to bring another lathe worker from Auschwitz.

Had I told the truth to Kurt Kolonko, he would have taken me under his protection. His patronage was a guarantee of safety. The Schlesians were a rough bunch who intimidated everyone, even German collaborators. More than once the body of some kapo who had treated them badly was found in the cesspool of the outhouse. Despite searches, threats, and interrogations, the culprits were never found. A word from Kolonko would have made Arpad Basci think twice about risking his comfortable neck. Excused from all work to sculpt his chess pieces, he slept and worked in the little cubicle by the barracks' entrance and was even brought his own food from the guards' kitchen. No one interfered in his relations with his young catamites.

Why, then, did I not take Kurt into my confidence? The answer was simple: I was afraid of what he would think of me. Would he still have liked me had he known that I had saved my life by ending somebody else's? I doubted it. Kolonko was one of the few people in the camp for whom human life was a supreme value. As far as I could tell, this was not a principle he would ever compromise on. Behind the tough exterior of the ex-boxer and Jew-hater was a man who loved justice.

Only rarely do moments from the past reascend from the soul's depths to the upper layers of consciousness. This one still does. Again and again I feel compelled to analyse it. But by what standards of morality was my behaviour to be judged? By absolute or relative ones? By the former, I was guilty. By the latter, I was innocent, if only by benefit of the doubt. If life was a supreme value, was I not justified in remaining alive, even at someone else's expense? Who could possibly judge which life was worth more – mine or the nameless prisoner's whose cap I stole? Did I not have the right of self-defence implicit in the norms of the place and time?

I know the dangers in such a line of argument. It lays the foundation for an entire structure of rationalized atrocities. Still, when I was a boy of sixteen, the shot that killed that nameless prisoner did not echo in my conscience. Why should it do so now that I am fifty years older?

Arpad Basci's chance came inadvertently. When it did, he knew just how to exploit it.

I had no idea how he had learned about my paper undershirt. It was enough that the camp was crawling with informers who would stoop to anything for a crust of the bread he possessed in abundance.

Once a month we were given fresh clothes that had been deloused by steaming. The Nazis made use of this opportunity to inspect us thoroughly. Although I can't recall a single situation where they found anything of value, the procedure was rigorously repeated each month. The exact day and hour were kept a secret. Sometimes it was done in the early morning, before work, and sometimes before or after the evening roll-call. The kapos, who were the only ones with advance knowledge, had time to warn their friends to get rid of all food and smuggled mail. The rest of us had to depend on our own alertness. I had learned to rely on the Germans' love of routine and belief that *Ordnung muss sein*. The searches were always conducted in groups of ten bunks and my bunk was always in the fourth group. This would give me enough time, I thought, to slip out of my paper shirt and hide it in some corner. Even if it was found there, no one could pin it on me. And there were two more spare sacks behind the boards in the toolshed.

I failed to take one thing into account. God knows how he managed to arrange it, but Arpad Basci was told to line us up for inspection. The minute I saw him standing there with two kapos, his eyes glittering with malice, I knew I was in trouble. His eyes drilled holes into me. He pointed to my row of bunks and said in his Hungarian-accented German:

'You're first.'

The ten of us were made to stand at the far end of the aisle between the bunks. At a signal, we moved forwards in single file, keeping three metres between us and the next prisoner. The procedure was for us to undress, remove our shoes, and lay our things on Arpad Basci's table, which had been moved into the aisle. With practised agility the barracks elder went through our pockets, checked the seams, felt the collars, stuck a hand in the shoes, and told the SS officer 'Clean' or 'Dirty'. Sometimes, at the officer's request, a body search was performed. The 'clean' prisoners continued down the aisle and received a bundle of fresh clothes.

I placed my clothes on the table and stood standing in my cement sack. Too astounded to shout 'Dirty,' the barracks elder asked:

'What the hell is that?'

I said nothing. What was I to say? That I was sorry and wouldn't do it again? That didn't get you far in a concentration camp. Arpad Basci was merely stating a fact when he said:

'The kid's wrapped himself up in a package. Addressed to Auschwitz.'

He chuckled with satisfaction. Then the metallic timbre of his laugh stopped abruptly, as if a string had snapped in the instrument that sounded it. Arpad Basci looked straight into my eyes. He wanted to see the fear in them. Nothing is harder to hide than the fear in one's eyes. The old Hungarian could have written a doctorate about it.

'Take that thing off,' said the barracks elder quietly. His low voice was a hundred times more menacing than Arpad Basci's laughter.

I removed the paper sack and placed it by my clothes.

'Spread your legs.'

I did as told.

'Bend over.'

I bent over, my head down and my buttocks sticking up awkwardly. Waves of blood dashed against my brain. Black circles whirled before my eyes. My knees felt weak. I had to press my palms against the floor to keep from falling. The barracks elder circled me like a cattle dealer inspecting a cow. He stepped on a bare foot with his heavy shoe, raised my face with a finger, and asked:

'Did that hurt?'

I nodded. As my head was down, I wasn't sure he noticed. He kicked my bare rear and said to Arpad Basci:

'Search his body. Carefully!'

Arpad Basci didn't have to be told twice. I felt his finger touch the back of my neck, run down my spine, slip between the cheeks of my behind, and penetrate deep into my anus. It wasn't like the quick, knifelike thrust of his penis. His finger turned slowly inside me like a screwdriver working to free a rusty screw. He knew the pain was tearing me apart. Not many people had his expertise. I was sure his face had a big grin on it. Arpad Basci was a sadist. To finish me off with a flourish, he shoved my head to the floor and rammed his finger as far as it would go. I let out an uncontrollable groan. The finger dug into me. I fell silent. He withdrew it and told me to straighten up.

'Now open your filthy mouth.'

I opened my mouth as though I were in a dentist's chair. Arpad Basci's finger slid inside, slicing the gums with its nail and poking at my throat until I retched. 'Now lick it clean as a baby's prick,' he said.

'Well?' asked the SS officer.

'Clean,' said Arpad Basci with a trace of disappointment.

The barracks elder opened his notebook.

'Your number?'

'A-19818.'

He wrote something down, turned to the officer, and awaited a verdict.

'Do you work?' asked the Nazi.

'Yes, sir.'

'What at?'

'I'm a lathe operator.'

Arpad Basci had returned to his table, where he sat silent and grim-looking. From behind me came the heavy breathing of the prisoners in line. The officer and barracks elder conferred in whispers. My hopes rose with each passing second. I had often observed that the death penalty was generally meted out at once.

It was only clemency that needed to be debated. After a minute, my sentence was handed down: eight hours of 'guard duty'.

'Guard duty' was what we prisoners called being made to stand at attention between the wires of the electric fence. It was most draconian of all punishments and few people lived through it.

I felt like a man mounting a scaffold when I was brought to the camp gate and shown where to stand motionless for the next eight hours. How many hours of torture would go by before I stumbled and died? Stronger prisoners than myself had fallen against the wires and been electrocuted after an hour or two. The Nazis left their bodies on the fence for us to see on our way to work and back.

Darkness fell. The perimeter lights were switched on. The lights were also turned on in the administration building, a two-storey structure by the gate. I could see into an office where two Nazi officers were doing clerical work. They could see me, too. I was right outside their window.

The thermometer dropped below zero. The cold cut to the bone. Slippery snakes crept up from my feet and shed their icy skins on my stomach, along my back, on my neck. I hated snakes. Now, though, I regretted it when the repulsive feel of them vanished, for with it went all sense of time.

Not knowing if minutes or hours had elapsed was worse than the cold. It sapped my resistance. Keeping time now seemed the most important thing in the world. Exiled from Time's domain, I had no more existence. I tried becoming a clock. I counted to sixty to make a minute. I counted sixty minutes to make an hour. I lost track and had to start all over.

I grew terrified. The first link in the chain was about to snap. I had to find a way to stay awake.

I made myself think of my childhood. I tried to remember happy times, replacing the present moment with them. I thought of the Gypsy woman who had prophesied a happy life for me. I climbed into bed with my father, feeling his love and warmth. I marshalled my toy soldiers for battle, stole candy from Mr Hahn's store in Bielsko.

The stock of memories was soon depleted. I was exhausted. The grey cells of my brain felt full of fuzz. An enervating drone drowned out my thoughts. No, it was the current in the barbed wire. Hearing it meant that I was still alive. That the danger of electrocution was still there. That the enemy had been sighted and was being kept at bay. I now had a warning signal to help me maintain my clarity of mind.

The hardest part was keeping my eyes open. My eyelids kept shutting beneath their own weight. Each time I started to doze off I felt the life force within me clash with the urge to surrender, to yield to the peace of sleep. I was like a fly fallen into a jar half-filled with oil that kept climbing up the sides, desperate to escape, slipping back each time and climbing again. Now weakness attacked treacherously from the rear. It cast its heavy load on my shoulders, threatening to drag me down into the snow.

The snow! It was a blood-curdling trap. It cut off my circulation, drained my veins dry. I pinched my thigh and felt nothing. I wanted to stamp my legs, but was afraid the sentry would see me. The slightest failure to stand at attention would lengthen my 'guard duty'. I tried wiggling my toes. I couldn't tell if the message from my brain had gotten through to them. I had no sensation and could not see into my shoes.

The changing of the guard told me that the first two hours had gone by. An army truck drove along the road and spattered the new sentry with mud. He cursed the driver roundly. I was happy to hear a human voice. He leaned his rifle against the post of an overhang protecting him from the snow and cleaned his long army coat.

I had to relieve myself. The battle with my bladder became all-important. As long as I could hold in my urine, I controlled my body. The pressure grew. I squeezed my thighs together. The urine trickled down my leg to my foot, bathing me in its warm flow. The fact that I could feel it encouraged me. A moment later the warm wetness became an icy sludge. Waves of shivers rippled over me.

The lights went out in the administration building. I heard a door slam. A car started. A dog barked. Then all was quiet except for the drone of the electricity. I recited poems I had learned by heart in school. The words would not form lines. The lines would not rhyme. They went off in all directions, like bees buzzing away from a hive that was poked by a stick.

I tried playing chess. The results were no better. I had lost the capacity for abstract thought. The pawns, knights, queens, rooks, chess squares, stood for nothing. I could not remember how many times the guard had changed. Time was as shapeless as a watch in a Dali painting. No second of it was connected to any other. I was being sucked into nothingness. The heavier my limbs grew, the more I felt that I was floating helplessly in dark, hostile space. In some black hole of the cosmos, Death was waiting for me.

'Hey, you!' called the guard. His voice reached me from light years away. I could barely make him out. A white mist enveloped everything. At first I didn't notice the SS officer in a long winter coat standing behind him.

The officer signalled me to approach. The two or three metres between us seemed impossible to traverse. I tried to move, my shoes caked with mud and urine. I held my breath. Breathing might cause me to stagger into the fence, touching Death at the last moment.

I took a step. Nothing terrible happened. I took another. Time began to flow again, the seconds running into each other. I took a third step. The snakes were crawling down my back again. My wooden clogs slipped on the ice. I reached out to steady myself. There was nothing to grasp but the high-tension wire. I regained my balance, moved forward like a tightrope walker. The gate was near. Two more steps. One. I focused on the line that ran from my punishment box to the opening in the fence. It was a line without a parallel, because it existed only in my mind. The SS officer waited patiently. Perhaps he pitied me. Perhaps he was waiting for me to fall. I reached him. As if it were the most natural thing in the world, I asked:

'What time is it?'

'Two-thirty,' he said. Then, remembering whom he was talking to, he cursed me out loud.

My ears were clogged. I couldn't hear what he said, did not understand his curses. I fell asleep sitting on my bunk, in the middle of untying my shoelaces.

In January 1945 the plant was shut down. Its evacuation came as a surprise. We didn't know where we were headed. As we marched through the parade grounds to the Swietochlowice railway station, I felt sure we were being shipped back to Auschwitz.

The train was waiting on a side track. Russian POWs were throwing corpses from it onto the platform. They were still lying there when we pulled out.

There were eighty of us in the car. There was no room to sit. The doors were heavily bolted from outside and the transoms were boarded up. After a day, a night, and another day without even stopping to take on coal or water, it was clear that we were leaving Poland. We had no idea of our destination. We didn't know that the Red Army had launched an offensive at Upper Schlesia, that the 4th Wehrmacht Division had retreated in disorder, and that a furious Hitler had replaced its commander with Field Marshal Schoerner, a brutal general staff officer and dedicated Nazi. Nor did we know that Schoerner, too, had been routed and that high-ranking officials in the armaments ministry in Berlin had conceived an emergency plan for us prisoners to save the German arms industry.

Not that knowing this would have made it easier to stay on my feet. The stronger passengers fought for the places by the sides of the car, against which it was possible to lean. The weak were pushed into the middle, where they sank to the floor and were trampled. No one asked for help or consideration. No one would have given any to anyone wasting his last strength to ask for it.

I withdrew into myself, a stranger to everyone, alone in my world. I didn't want to know where we were going. We were crammed into a cattle car. Does a cow ask if it is being taken to new pasture or the slaughterhouse?

Twice during our journey the doors were opened for us to be handed bread and water. The dead were tossed out.

We arrived on the third day. The weather was gorgeous. The sun struck me in the face. The cold air made me dizzy. I read the name of the small station: Mauthausen. I had never heard of it. I looked around. I was dazzled by the white sheets of snow that shone with a phosphorescent silver.

When had I been dazzled by snow like that before? Six years previously, at seven o'clock in the morning. I was a fourth-grader, an only child with a childish childhood, neither happy nor deprived.

Our housekeeper Paula had dropped a copper pan on the kitchen floor. The noise woke me and drove away a dream that vanished before I could snag it for my memory. A no-longer-full moon hung in the sky like a pregnant belly. The snow-covered branches of the chestnut tree in the yard resembled the paws of a polar bear. I rose from my bed with its good smell of starch and indulgence and went to open the window. The air was clear and cold. It made me think of the lemon ice cream I had eaten the day before at the Italian ice cream parlour on King Chrobry Square.

As the moon dropped towards the rooftops, the sun came up. A first shaft of its rays, reconnoitring the new day, glinted off the snowy branches of the tree. Thousands of tiny sparks shot into the air.

I blinked. I didn't feel like going to school. The blinding snow gave me an idea. I shut the window, got back into bed, pulled the blankets over my head, and waited for Paula. Every morning she came to wake me at seven-fifteen, when I had to get up and wash. This time, when she pulled off the blanket – it was always done with a single quick yank – I didn't move. In a choked voice I announced that I couldn't open my eyes.

It was a cheap trick. But poor Paula didn't realize she was being had. She hurried to wake my mother; my mother woke my father; and soon I was trapped in my own deception. My parents called for the family doctor, the bald Dr Reich, who needed but a minute to accuse me of malingering. Well aware of whom he was dealing with, he threatened me with stinging eye drops and an injection unless I started to see. This only made me cling more stubbornly to my story. The truth was that I was more afraid of my father than of the medicines. If there was one thing he couldn't abide, it was being made a fool of. Dr Reich should do whatever he had to, I screamed. Injections, drops, bitter pills – I wanted to see again.

It did no good for Dr Reich to try convincing my parents that I was lying, that he had never heard of a muscular disease affecting the eyelids, and that the best cure for me was my father's leather shaving strop, which had more than once worked miracles in the past. My father was growing nervous. He was due in court at eight to represent an important client and the driver was waiting below. Paula began to weep from sheer concern for me and my father's uneaten breakfast. My panic-stricken mother, a hypochondriac in her own right, was already running through lists of famous physicians in Vienna. In the end my father decided to take me to an eye specialist in Cracow that afternoon. We would proceed to Vienna only if that failed.

I heard Dr Reich snap his case shut and leave in a huff. My father spoke on the phone to my grandmother in Cracow and called a renowned diagnostician in Vienna who was prepared to see me for a handsome fee at any hour of the day or night. Everything told me that I had gone too far. My father returned from the phone and tried to reassure my mother.

'Don't worry. It's all taken care of. That's what connections and money are for.'

'I'd give anything in the world for Romek to open his eyes,' said my mother.

The lazy little devil inside me awoke at these words.

'Even the electric train in the window of Milner's store?' I asked innocently.

'Even the train,' my father answered for her.

My father always kept his promises. I rubbed my eyelids, grimaced mightily, and slowly opened my eyes with a Herculean effort that any actor would have been proud of. I shut them and opened them again. What a performance!

'I can see!' I cried happily.

'So can I,' said my father. His voice was ominous.

That same day I was given the train, which cost twenty-eight zlotys, a sum equal to Paula's monthly salary. For a year, I was forbidden to play with it. Justice prevailed. To assist it, my father administered a double dose of his shaving strop, the medicine prescribed by Dr Reich. I couldn't sit on my school bench for a week. All because of the snow.

The white sheet of fields ran westward from the Mauthausen train station. Thousands of sparklers glittered in the sunlight. I squinted into the glare. The last prisoners stepped out from the cars. Alone on the platform with our guards, we stamped our feet like coachmen to warm up. The SS men stood to the side, apparently waiting for orders. They, too, were cold, their faces and ears red as beets. A cigarette advertisement on a billboard said: *Warum ist Juno rund? Aus guten Grund ist Juno rund.* The thought crossed my mind that I should take the ad with me. I could wrap myself in it for warmth. We were told to fall in for roll-call.

Today it is hard to believe that we knew so little about the kingdom of the SS. An army within an army and a state within a state, the SS had gone from being an elite unit, the strike force of the Nazi Party, to a vast political and economic empire. By the time of our arrival at Mauthausen, it controlled a large share of the German economy. All businesses confiscated from Jews had been transferred to its management. It was Germany's biggest manufacturer of furniture and mineral water, with an annual turnover of twenty-five million dollars. As the main supplier of cheap labour, it was a force to be reckoned with in heavy industry. By the end of 1944, the SS was providing German employers with 627,000 workers, 170,000 of them in the armaments industry. They were to be found everywhere, from subterranean Messerschmitt fighter plants to V-2 rocket production lines. Fifty thousand, mostly in concentration camps, worked for the SS directly.

Knowledge of what was happening in these camps leaked to the outside world slowly. Even then it remained largely confined to SS officials and the prisoners who worked in their offices. Although tens of thousands of people were continually on the move from camp to camp, they no more returned to tell their story than the dead return from the next world. This was why 'Mauthausen' was a new word for me. I never imagined that I was about to enter a place that would make me homesick for Auschwitz.

It wasn't the beauty of the Upper Austrian mountains that had made the architects of the death camps build this installation north of the Danube and near the Czech border. The site was picked for its granite quarries. On Adolf Hitler's drawing table at the time were plans for a monumental Führer's Square in Berlin that would memorialize the Thousand Year Reich. The job was given to Albert Speer, a young architect from Mannheim who had joined the National Socialist Party as far back as 1931.

Just as the Champs Elysées dramatically culminates in the Tuileries, so Speer had planned the Führer's offices, the Nazi Party building, and the headquarters of the Wehrmacht general staff as the crowning features of his project. Vast amounts of construction materials were needed. Following the annexation of Austria, the SS offered to lease the Mauthausen granite quarries from the municipality of Vienna for the annual sum of five thousand marks. Before the city of Johann Strauss had gotten used to the Horst Wessel song, it had already learned which side its bread was buttered on.

The SS offer was accepted, a contract was drawn up, and the Deutsche Reichsbank lent the German firm of Dest, which signed the lease papers, nine million interest-free marks. The SS logistics corps was highly pleased: since the quarry could be operated for next to nothing with political prisoners, and no investment in new equipment was necessary, the entire loan could be used to erect a slave labour camp. At first, in 1938, this camp housed but a few hundred workers, who were engaged as masons, dynamite drillers, and stevedores. Before long, however, Mauthausen and its sister branch at Gusen turned into two of the worst concentration camps in Europe. In 1942 they were reclassified by chief SS economist Oswald Pohl as penal installations for 'irredeemable prisoners'. In Nazi terminology, that meant only one thing. Such prisoners had no right to stay alive.

None of this was known to us as we climbed the winding path from the station to the concentration camp on the hilltop. The climb was difficult. The days in the sealed boxcar had sapped my strength and even the fine weather was against us, since the sun that melted the top layer of snow exposed the slippery ice beneath it. Each time I slipped, our escorts hammered me to my feet with their rifle butts. They were trained to strike at the base of the back, causing irreparable damage to the kidneys.

My prisoner's clogs made things worse. Their wet tops chafed my toes and the wooden soles refused to grip the ground. After a while I kicked them off, and continued barefoot. At first the frost burned like fire. Then I lost all feeling and could keep up. Months later, I was told during a check-up in an American clinic that going barefoot had saved me from the frostbite that many of the men I was with had suffered from.

Some four kilometres brought us to a T at the end of the steep trail. Here the path forked in two. On our right was a broad, snowy slope traversed by stone walls and watchtowers, a concentration camp that looked from a distance like a romantic castle. On our left was a farm.

A family of peasants stood by the entrance to the farmyard. The father wore a felt hat and a sheepskin coat. Two women wrapped in woollen shawls stood beside him. One was old and one was young. A girl of ten held one of their hands. They stared at us indifferently; caravans of slaves must have been a frequent sight. The man was eating a sandwich, chewing listlessly as only those who are not hungry can chew. Crumbs of bread clung to his moustache. A soldier waved to him. The peasant held up his half-eaten sandwich as if offering to share it. The soldier laughed. So did the peasant. His laughter was hearty, infuriating.

We turned right, towards the castle. The gate swung open. We entered an inner courtyard. Repair shops ran along its walls. At its far end was a second, locked gate. We were to find out that this led to the barracks and the gas chambers. Armed guards stood above us, pointing their rifles. The middle of the yard had been cleared of snow, pushed back in high banks of frozen slush.

All this took a second to observe. Life in the camps had taught us to photograph every situation, place, and movement at a glance. One's life might depend on these mental pictures.

What happened next was unforeseen. All at once a few dozen SS men fell upon us from nowhere with a barrage of blows and kicks. Panic broke out in our ranks. We scattered in every direction. The screams and curses of the beaten and those beating them combined to form a single wild din. The mêlée excited the dogs, whose terrifying barks made things worse. They strained at their leashes and bared their fangs. This was not my first concentration camp. I knew they were trained to attack.

'Let's go! Let's go!' yelled the Nazis. 'Clothes off and up against the wall! Face the wall, let's go!'

I was out of my clothes in less than twenty seconds. Hundreds of naked men were running about the courtyard. There wasn't enough room for them along the wall. The soldiers struck them savagely, knocking them down and stomping on them with cleated boots. Some of the prisoners were bleeding. The dogs would go for them first if unleashed.

Quicker than most of us, I already had my face to the wall. I couldn't tell if I was shaking more from the cold or from my fear. Gradually the tumult died down. Then there was silence. We braced ourselves for the unknown, always the most frightening of thing of all. As usual, I lost all sense of time. An officer shouted:

'Prepare for the shower!'

What shower? A chill ran down my spine. The showers in

Auschwitz had camouflaged the gas chambers. Was Mauthausen the same? I imagined choking on poison gas. But the Germans did not intend to kill us. Not yet. The 'shower' was their idea of a practical joke.

Ice-cold water sprayed from large fire hoses aimed at our naked bodies. A powerful jet pounded my back, jerked my neck, threw my head against the wall. Blood ran down my face and froze there. I couldn't move. The water had already turned to ice that was slicing my skin like hot knives. The pain brought me to my senses. *No*, I told myself. *I am not giving in. They can't make me.* The words had the power of auto-suggestion. I believed in them as if they had been uttered by a Supreme Force.

The joke went on even after the soldiers had tired of it. Although the hoses had been turned off, we were still not allowed to move. I stood hiding my private parts with my hands. *From what? From whom? The wall? The Nazis?* But clothing is not only a physical shield. It is a psychological one. The shabbiest pair of old pants creates the illusion of civilization. Without it we are vulnerable. I glanced at the man on my right. With his shaven, pear-shaped head, his hips sticking out like two wings, and the knobby sticks of his sore-infested legs, he looked as blue and wretched as a plucked chicken.

Suddenly the sticks snapped, right where the knees should have been. His hands slid down the wall, their fingers groping for something to hold onto. They didn't find it. The man crumpled to the ground. Someone grabbed him by the feet and dragged him away.

My eyes followed the progress of his body. Dozens of naked corpses were scattered about the yard.

Some SS men were chatting by the inner gate. An officer joined them. They opened the gate. Pursued by insults and blows, we were herded into a second square. Here we were grouped and registered. Everything took time. The kapos were in no hurry. My bare feet were frozen to the ground. A long while elapsed before I was given a tin bracelet with my new number on it. 'Guard this like gold,' said the kapo. 'You're a dead man without it.' He gave me a kick in the direction of the showers.

No, these were not gas chambers either. Real water came out of them.

I didn't notice that it was boiling. That night, however, my body broke out in painful blisters. Once out of the shower I was thrown a shirt too small to button and underpants two sizes too big. Jackets, we were told, were only for veteran prisoners. When the barracks elder struck me for not standing in line at roll-call, I couldn't protect myself. Both hands were holding up my underpants. He would have kicked me in the testicles if they had fallen.

Our barracks were Number 24.

From the outside it looked like any other barracks I had seen. On the inside, though, it was simply a large hangar. There were no bunks or mattresses. Our only bed was the concrete floor.

The SS stayed out of these barracks and left the daily intimidation to the kapos. They had chosen the right men for the job. No scientific study was needed to discover their motives. Like myself, they were guinea pigs in a giant laboratory of human survival. They ate well, had their uniforms custom-fitted by the camp's tailors, enjoyed the semi-privacy of their own alcove in the barracks, and indulged themselves by clubbing whom they wished. Those who were not born sadists soon became them, there being no surer way to stay alive. Their sense of security appeared justified, since their help saved the Germans tens of thousands of additional guards. They could not have been expected under such circumstances to remember that they were living in a fool's paradise, or that they would lose all their privileges as soon as they were transferred to another camp. The corpses of the kapos and barracks elders from the Swietochlowice camp were strewn over the yard at Mauthausen with the other prisoners. I say this not to comfort anyone, but merely to state a fact.

Of course, these weren't my thoughts while I ran beneath the rain of blows that drove us into our new barracks. All I wanted was to avoid getting hit. We fought our way through the narrow door, swarming inside like a colony of ants. The kapos herded us expertly. I never managed to understand how they were able to fit more than three hundred new prisoners into a barracks already housing seven hundred men.

The structure was windowless and dark. We were lined up in columns, one man's chest against another man's back, and ordered to lie down. The concrete floor became a squirming mass of humanity. There wasn't a square inch of space. The kapos and barracks elders made room by walking back and forth on us as though we were rugs. Anyone lifting his head was struck. Within a quarter of an hour everyone had a place.

Since our thin bodies did not retain heat, the floor failed to warm up. A mean winter wind blew through the open door. Exhausted and desperate to sleep, I now experienced an attack of hunger. As if it had waited until I had time for its suffering, my stomach began to burble and sour bile flowed to my mouth.

My bladder was full, too. The door was five metres away. I rose to go to it. In an instant, the space vacated by me disappeared beneath the sleepers. There wasn't a crack to put my foot in. I stepped cautiously on the nearest body. The only reaction was a sleepy murmur. Emboldened, I walked across the prone mass of men. They were too fatigued to feel me stepping on them. One alone seized my foot and tried to bite it. I squirmed free and kicked him in the head. He cursed and lapsed back into sleep.

I reached the doorway, feeling nauseous and wanting to puke. The space outside the barracks was empty. Lamps lit the nearby perimeter fence. I relieved myself in the snow. Then I kneeled, lowered my head, and stuck a finger in my throat. Nothing came out. The sour taste remained.

The frosty sky glittered with a hard, frosty beauty. The crystalline air made the cold more intense. I sucked it into my lungs. As it mixed with the vitriol inside me, my stomach acquiesced in my will. I doubled over like a punctured paper bag and brought up a smelly, greenish vomit that spattered over my underpants.

I felt better and returned to the barracks. The human carpet lay breathing on the floor. With no chance of finding a place in it, I stood in the doorway until reveille.

I had learned my lesson. From that night on I urinated where I lay. Everyone did. Within a few days we were one pestilent mass. The kapos woke us not with whistles but with water, hosing down the barracks while we still lay on the floor.

All day long we milled idly in the space outside. Having nothing to do was worse than the hardest labour, since Auschwitz rules applied here, too. If the Germans didn't need you, neither did life.

Even if we were not being shot or gassed, the Angel of Death could clap its wings happily. Unable to tell how I appeared to others, I could easily spot those next in line for the Great Vacuity. Well before their final collapse they were burned out, their blank stares betraying a doom they were not yet aware of. Intent on their outward functioning, they ignored the dying of the inner flame. The bodily husk did not know that the seed had rotted.

I learned to predict their end practically to the minute. The only thing I was not sure of was whether they were already dead when they hit the ground, or if the last spark was extinguished as they lay there, released at last from their long torment. Once a day we brought their bodies to the gate. They were counted by the barracks elder and an SS officer, who removed the tin bracelets with their ID numbers. These were returned to the camp registrar and more names were crossed off the roster.

The lighter from hunger I became, the heavier were the chains dragging me down. The earth's gravity had never been so tangible a force. In Mauthausen I gave up washing. As much as I regarded this to be a shameful concession to human weakness, I couldn't fight it any more. I had no more strength to force myself out of bed, run to the washroom that doubled as an outhouse, and splash myself with cold water.

Another link in the chain had snapped. I knew what this meant. But what was the point in struggling to maintain my wretched existence? What was the purpose of it all? To live another day? And after it, another and another? Three days still did not make a present, much less a future. Had I believed in a divinity, I would have prayed for a sign from heaven. For just a bare hint.

It was then, astoundingly, that I received one. Of course, one could just as well have called it an ordinary occurrence into which I read my own needs. Going to the outhouse early in one morning, I saw a corpse dangling from a rope that had been improvised from the dead man's shirtsleeves. Its hands were tied behind its back and its mouth was stuffed with a rag. The contorted face looked familiar. I came closer. The body was Arpad Basci's. I prodded it. It swung like a pendulum. It swayed back and forth while I peed.

Arpad Basci's death made me believe that reward and punishment existed even here. My glee was a sign of life. Although I had no idea who had strung him up, the thought that it was possible bolstered my spirits. I badly needed such encouragement, because my mood was black that morning.

The world was a dim grey when I left the outhouse. The winter dawn was in no hurry to break. The low clouds were stingy with the sunlight, which seemed reluctant to illuminate a hideous planet that was a cancer in the galaxy. Thick mist wreathed the watchtowers and stretched uniformly between the barracks like an undifferentiated, translucent muslin. The curious observation occurred me that it was my frame of mind that determined the colours of nature, not vice versa. These had seemed so dark because I had concluded that I couldn't go on. No tomorrow shone through the cloud cover. Yet just then it was torn by a voice.

'Prisoner One-Hundred-Twenty-Five-Thousand-Six-Hundred-Two!'

I had forgotten my own number. Only when an angry kapo called it again did I realize that it was mine. I pushed my way through the crowded barracks. Men pushed back at me. Someone kicked. Someone cursed. The kapo slapped my cheek.

'Do you have to be sent a special invitation?' he snapped. Still startled, I stammered:

'I'm sorry, I thought . . .'

'You're not here to think. You're here to obey.'

'You're right, sir.'

'The kapo is always right. Get that into your lousy head. The kapo is always right.'

'The kapo is always right,' I repeated.

'That's better,' he declared. With a look more contemptuous than angry, he surveyed my sorry appearance. I winced as he stuck his club beneath my chin and forced my head up.

'I swear, you belong in the ovens. It beats me why anyone would want a corpse like you.' He ran his club over my ribs as though they were a xylophone. I held my breath, not daring even to blink.

'Do you know who I am?'

'You're Kapo Franz.'

The kapo smiled contentedly. He enjoyed his renown. A privileged prisoner, Franz had been a prominent figure in the Berlin underworld before being sent to Mauthausen. The green triangle of the criminal offender was worn proudly on his freshly ironed striped uniform. My first encounter with him had been on the night of our arrival, when he had stomped me with his cleats. He could have killed me now, too, without owing anyone an explanation. The end of his club meandered towards my throat. One good whack would knock the life force out of me. I regarded him warily. The Green Triangles could be like wild animals. They had murder in their eyes. But Franz's eyes had nothing in them at all.

'Where are your clothes?' he asked. As if he didn't know that we had not been issued new uniforms.

'I'm wearing them, Kapo Franz.'

'All right. Come with me.'

I straggled after him. He strode to the central square, conducted me to the showers, and gave something to the attendant, who handed me a piece of soap and a rag for a towel. The soap stung my open blisters. Slowly the water washed the suds away along with the dirt and the pain.

Fresh underwear and a fresh uniform were lying on a bench outside. I put them on. Franz was gone. The attendant grinned:

'You look like a corpse on leave from Death.'

I said nothing.

'Why don't you say something?'

'I didn't think corpses could speak.'

'They can't eat, either,' he mocked, handing me a battered aluminium bowl and announcing grandly:

'La crème de sauerkraut soup.'

The soup smelled real. I scooped up its bits of brown jerky and half-cooked cabbage leaves, then put down the spoon and drank from the bowl as I had seen the Uzbek prisoners drink their *shorba*. My stomach, unused to so much food, swelled like a wineskin. I couldn't finish and pushed the bowl away with some soup still in it.

An SS soldier came to check the number on my bracelet and escorted me to the gate, where a small truck was waiting.

'Get in!' he ordered, jumping over the tailgate after me. 'Sit on the floor!' he barked. I sat next to four other prisoners.

The truck set out. The gate of the camp shut behind us. We drove down the hillside and past the farm. There was no sign of

the peasant or his family. The walls of Mauthausen receded and
vanished behind a bend in the road.

35

The Juno cigarette ad was still in the Mauthausen station. The waiting room was unheated. A few passengers, bundled in winter coats, were sitting there.

'When is she due?' asked our driver. An old woman said:

'She's long overdue.'

'It wouldn't have happened before the war,' said the SS soldier who had been waiting for us at the station. 'You could set your watch by the trains then.'

'Watch what you say,' said the driver, lighting the butt of a cigarette.

'You used to smoke Juno,' the soldier retorted. 'Now you're smoking straw butts.'

The driver took the butt's last puff and threw it on the floor.

'With a mouth like yours you'll end up where these characters are coming from,' he said, turning away.

There were five of us. I never knew their names and I don't remember their faces. It's the SS soldier's that I recall. Sombre and middle aged, he turned out to be – once our driver was gone – a mild-tempered man with none of the arrogance that characterized the younger guards. Perhaps this rare quality is what preserved him in my personal data bank. It did not take him long to let us know that he took no pleasure from his power over us; that he wished the war would end; that he hoped the Allied bombers would spare his house in Bad Wiesee and that his wife Elisabeth would take good care of their grandchildren. His two sons had been killed on the Russian front.

All this was imparted to us after we had boarded a local and taken our seats in a third-class compartment, the five of us on a bench facing him. The other compartments in the car were

347

empty. Although we could easily have taken away our guard's rifle and escaped, the prospect did not seem to worry him. Nor did it occur to us. It was probably no accident that he chose to tell us about an attempted escape of Russian prisoners from Mauthausen. It had started, he said, during a power failure, when the Russians seized their guards' weapons, stole some military vehicles, and raced toward the Czech border. It had ended with every last one of them being hunted down and shot by hundreds of SS soldiers and Austrian civilians.

He described these events dispassionately. 'The moral,' he concluded, 'is that you have to live with your situation. Rebellion gets you nowhere.'

He spoke with a heavy Bavarian accent, the smell of cheap beer on his breath. It was that smell that made him seem so human. In the SS's pantheon of values, ordinary humanity did not rank high.

Although he must have had orders not to tell us anything, he revealed that we were being transferred to a wing of Mauthausen near Vienna that supplied workers to the Saurer tank engine plant. He had escorted prisoners there before, but we were both his first Jews and his first ordinary train passengers. 'We're in luck,' he said, wrinkling his face in something like a smile. The 'we' made it sound as if he were one of us, an unheard-of form of speech for the SS. A garrulous man, he was glad to have an audience. For a brief lull in the war of extermination against us, we and our jailer found ourselves on the same side.

The train clacked along the tracks, its rattle accompanying his soliloquy. I looked out the window. Large ice floes lay on the Danube; across the river, on its north bank, brown grapevines peeked through the snow. Picturesque villages clung to the hillsides, their houses as bucolic as if there had never been a war. The calm landscape dulled my senses. The heat from the radiator dried out my sinuses and spread wonderfully through my body. I couldn't keep our escort in focus. His words became a meaningless buzz. Before I knew it I had lapsed into an inner void that dissolved my waking consciousness. For the first time since arriving in Mauthausen I enjoyed a real rest, covered by the invisible quilt of sleep.

I awoke to find us in the Vienna-East Simmering station.

The barracks smelled of sawdust and fresh paint. Built four

months previously, they housed the manpower needed to keep the Saurer plant running. The camp was near a working-class neighbourhood on the south side of Vienna, a half-hour's walk from the factory. Its prisoners had been assembled from every conceivable place in which skilled workers could still be found. There were fifteen hundred of us at morning roll-call. The kapos and SS guards treated us less harshly, having been instructed by Berlin that our existence had economic value. There was no gas chamber and no crematorium. Although our food was still meagre, our living conditions were vastly improved. Each of us had his own bunk with his own straw mattress and blanket. We slept by day and worked by night, leaving for our shift at 6 p.m., when it grew dark outside, and returning in darkness at six in the morning. As protection against Allied air attacks, production was carried on underground and camouflaged by an innocent-looking building. The workspace, warehouses, and offices were all several floors beneath ground level. An elevator took us down into the earth as though into the depths of a mine. In case of mechanical or electrical failure, it could be operated manually. A sophisticated air-conditioning system kept us supplied with fresh oxygen.

It was not difficult to get used to such conditions. Kurt Kolonko's lessons had paid off. The lathe and I were on good terms. It was now I who sharpened blades for the other prisoners. Now and then I was even praised by the floor boss. He was the only civilian on the night shift, the Austrian workers being employed by day. I never saw them and the only sign of their existence was that the work tools kept in a metal closet by my lathe were sometimes moved. All in all I had no complaints despite the twelve hours spent every night on my feet. The days, those of the last winter of the war, were getting shorter but clearer.

Prisoners everywhere share the custom of marking the passage of time with lines on their cell walls. The very sense of time, so taken for granted in ordinary life, is a problem in a place where the exact day or hour cannot be known. Calling the concentration camps 'another planet', as has sometimes been done, is appropriate if only because our earthly time-frames did not apply there. It was therefore a red-letter day for me when I opened my tool closet to find a folded newspaper in which extraterrestrials

from Earth had recorded their day, month, and year: 18 February
1945.

Even more exciting than the newspaper were the two slices of
bread and yellow cheese hidden beneath it. Since no one else had
access to our workplace, these could only have been left by the
worker from the day shift. The temptation was irresistible. I
wrapped the bread in the newspaper, stuck it beneath my shirt,
and asked permission to go to the bathroom. There, seated on the
toilet, I gobbled down my loot while glancing hurriedly at the
headlines. To my astonishment, I learned that the front was now
on German soil. All Poland had been taken by the Red Army.

For a moment I thought of Grete. What had happened to her?
Had she managed to flee with her brother the collector's items, or
had she been buried beneath the shelled ruins of her house?

The hell with her! What about Fredek Minz? Had he been
liberated from Auschwitz? Or had ... I could not go on sitting
there any longer. I flushed the toilet for the guard to hear and
hurried back to the work floor. Only then did I begin to wonder
about the motives of my anonymous benefactor. Had he forgotten the bread, whose theft he would complain about in the
morning? Or had he left it for a prisoner whose identity he would
never know?

I was never questioned about it. I never found any more food in
my tool closet.

36

A loaf of sticky black bread, a package of red beet jam, and a green army blanket: these were the provisions unexpectedly issued to us at roll-call one morning, scant minutes after returning from work. We were not permitted to return to our barracks. A kapo divided us into six columns, two hundred men in each. The camp commandant, rarely seen by us until now, climbed on a crate that served as an improvised stage and gave a short speech.

'Prisoners! The Third Reich does not desert those who serve it, whether willingly or under duress. The Bolshevik hordes, pressing a momentary advantage, are nearing Vienna. The Führer has ordered you to be transferred to a place where you will not fall into the hands of the barbarians. We will march on foot to our destination, where you will resume your work. Our route will take us along country roads, since the main highways must remain open for our troops to swing into action against the enemy and banish the Soviet threat from the heart of civilized Europe. The food you have received must last you for five days. Apportion it wisely, since no restaurants will be open on the way. Stay in formation. I expect iron discipline and your full cooperation. Any departure from orders will be punished severely. My men have orders to open fire at the slightest suspicion of an attempted escape. I hope this message is clear to you. And now – right face! Forward march!'

We marched out in perfect formation, turning right at the gate with the precision of a drill corps. I was in the second row of five men in the second column. Two hundred prisoners walked in front of me and another thousand behind. I didn't know a single one of them. Apart from Fredek Minz and Kurt Kolonko, I had never chosen to befriend any of the tens of thousands of men I had lived with for so long.

The four men marching beside me were strangers, too. I knew nothing about them, just as they knew nothing about me. Sharing a common fate did not create a common bond. There had to be mutual obligations and compromises as well. If none of us reached out a helping hand to the others in the whirlpool that was dragging us all down, this was because the loaf of survival was insufficient to go around. In the absence of a saviour to miraculously feed all the hungry, everyone hoarded every crumb he could.

We marched through an old residential area and cut through a wood in spring leaf. A flock of birds took off in fright from the treetops. We skirted the walls of a huge cemetery. A prisoner from Vienna said we were near Mödling. For a while we walked parallel to a railroad line that led nowhere, the tracks having been removed. Bombed boxcars stood alongside it. Two men tearing wooden planks from them ran when they saw the SS.

I looked around curiously. Yes, we were really in Vienna. But it was not the Vienna of my parents, or even of my own childhood. Nothing but a memory, one more dead butterfly under glass, remained from the city of St Stephen's with its grand shops on the Graben.

Sirens began to wail. The few passers-by disappeared into the basements of the houses. Our guards lost control of us. There was shouting, confusion. 'Run!' someone cried. We all ran, shattering our formation.

From far off came a dull thud of explosions. We made for the entrance to a railroad tunnel and crowded inside. The deeper into it we penetrated, the darker it became. *That's far enough, you can stop,* I told myself. I leaned against a damp wall, waiting to see what would happen. I couldn't see any soldiers. They must have been guarding the entrance.

There was a faint smell of smoke in the air. I folded my blanket, laid it on the ground between the railroad line and the tunnel wall, and sat down with my bread and jam. Suppose I stayed here when the all-clear sounded? The Nazis weren't likely to count us or notice who was missing. Even if they did, would they want to lose precious time searching the long tunnel? I calculated that my bread and jam would last for two days; four, if I ate as little as possible. How long would I have to wait for the Red Army? Less than that.

It could work. But I had thought the same about the breakout from Starachowice, during that wild dash for freedom that had ended – as Fredek Minz taunted me – with my crawling back on all fours. All that was left of it now was my fear. I still pictured the Polish peasant threatening me with his pitchfork; I still believed that my misery was better off having company; I still dreaded the utter loneliness of the escaped prisoner. Suppose the Russians took longer? Hunger would force me out of the tunnel. With my shaved head and uniform, I wouldn't last long in the hostile light of day. The first unfriendly stranger would turn me in.

I wasn't up to it.

When the command came to move out, I took my things and fell in dispiritedly at the entrance to the tunnel. The Nazis did not bother to count us. The sense of order had dissipated. Once again near the head of the column, I tied my blanket around my neck, stuck the jam in a pocket, put the bread under my arm, and set out with my aluminium bowl tied by a string to my pants.

We turned into a narrow street and then into a small plaza. Sarajevo Square, said a street sign. Sullen people were queued before a water truck. A prisoner in front me broke ranks and turned to the water distributor, holding out his bowl in a mute plea. The man gave a start and kicked the bowl. It clattered on the cobblestones. The prisoner ran after it. A guard fired. No one in the column reacted. The thirsty prisoner was still writhing as we marched past him.

37

In May 1991 I left my Warsaw hotel for a weekend excursion into the past. My time machine was Maxwell Communication's sedan. I crossed the Czech-Austrian border at the same point where Robert and I had done so in 1957. The customs officials were courteous. Passport control took less than a minute. The barbed wire and minefields were gone without a trace. The world had changed. Had I, too?

Nothing is more disappointing than revisiting a place whose image has been preserved in our minds like a pressed flower in the pages of an album. The flower has faded, its fragrance has vanished – and we refuse to recognize it. It is an illusion to think that we can travel through time and find old experiences waiting for us there.

During my years working for Maxwell Communication in Poland, I often hosted friends from Israel or America who asked me to accompany them to places where they were born or grew up. In their luggage was a bundle of memories taken from the cupboard of longing, that old storeroom that had not been opened in years. Wiser from my own experience, I tried talking them out of it. I never succeeded. I gave it up when I realized that my guests were looking not just for the graves of loved ones, houses they had lived in, streets they had walked in, or parks they had played in as children, but, most of all, for their own selves. The yearning to relive the past, no matter how harsh it had been, outweighed all logic. Mistakenly they thought that this act of ablution would wash away all the excess years from them. Not finding what they were looking for, they blamed the local inhabitants for vandalizing memories that were dear to them.

At bottom, it would seem, the lesson was lost on me, too. I have just finished reading a work by Søren Kierkegaard, a

Danish philosopher of the nineteenth century. A passage about the vicissitudes of economic change struck me by its wisdom. 'Human flexibility,' wrote Kierkegaard, 'can be measured by the capacity for forgetting . . . Forgetfulness is the correct expression for that fundamental adaptation to our environment that reduces all experience to the lowest common denominator. Nature is so tremendous only because she forgets that she was once the chaos of Creation.'

If Kierkegaard is correct, it was a grave mistake to drive all those hours to Vienna and its little Sarajevo Square. What drew me back there? What made me park my car and look for the water truck that had stood in the middle of the square? A flower stall was standing there instead. A ragged little dog warmed itself in the sun exactly where the prisoner had fallen. The pedestrians no longer looked dejected. Bright signs hung from the buildings. All had had a facelift.

I took a road map of Austria from the glove compartment and drew a line: from Vienna to St Pelten, from St Pelten to Melk, from Melk to Amstetten, from Amstetten to Steier, from Steier to Mauthausen. What made me do it? Surely it was not to relive what had happened to me fifty years ago, when I travelled this *via dolorosa* on foot. Even had I wanted to, how could I have felt the agony of that march sitting behind the wheel of a luxury automobile?

There was a time of my life in which I annually commemorated my liberation from Mauthausen by eating a bowl of turnip soup, which was a concentration camp staple. Eventually, I realized how absurd this was. The turnip soup, served to me between one lavish meal and the next, did not bring back the sensation of hunger. Nor did the narrow asphalt road running from the western outskirts of Vienna through unfamiliar fields and villages that could have been anywhere in Central Europe. Nothing was what it had been in April 1945. Don't ask me what I was looking for. I couldn't tell you.

It was a clear day. Now and then I stopped to take a picture. I like to photograph faces, landscapes, the play of colour and shape, because these do not distort the past like memory. The photographs from this trip are now arranged in sequence on my desk. One is of an innkeeper who drew a cold beer for me from the tap. I asked him whether he remembered, whether anyone had told him about those years. He gave me a queer look. My lens caught his puzzlement. '*Mein Herr*,' he said, 'I'm only thirty-nine.'

I wonder whether we have a duty to examine the deeds of our predecessors. What is the meaning of historical responsibility? What is a simple young Austrian who is neither a historian nor curious about the past – an innkeeper who wants only to be an innkeeper – required to know about such things?

I stood across the counter from him, a physically and by all appearances mentally hale sixty-three-year-old, sipping my beer. 'Real Pilsner,' said the innkeeper. I nodded. It hit the spot. I felt content. In the course of my life I had tasted my share of the sweet and of the bitter, but all in all, the balance sheet was positive. Life had not made me a misanthrope and I certainly didn't feel that it had been wasted. Given it to live all over again, I would probably have chosen the same path. Of course, there was always the element of chance: that path might not have led to the same places. But I had no regrets. I had been knocked down many times and had always learned from it. I had had small pleasures and big pleasures. I would not have wanted to pass any of them up.

For breakfast that day I ate two fresh rolls with butter and honey. In my carrying bag was a passport with the Israeli symbol of a seven-branched candelabrum. I was the free citizen of a free country. My credit card was honoured everywhere, I had no financial worries. I didn't suffer from a gap between my dreams and their fulfilment because I had never dreamed quixotically. Most of what I had wanted had been attainable. I had a suitcase with a stack of well-ironed shirts, a wrinkle-proof Italian suit, the latest fashion in ties, and a laptop computer. In Israel I had a home, run by Shulamit, that I always liked coming back to. Located in a central but quiet neighbourhood of Tel Aviv, it was filled with the mementos we had collected from our travels all over the world: sculpted gods from New Guinea, paper cut-outs from China, an Indian silk carpet, jewellery from the Gold Museum in Bogotá, brightly coloured masks from Nepal and Indonesia, African folk craft, Mexican silver work, art from Eastern Europe, a wall hanging from Peru. There was almost nowhere in the world that we had not reached together by plane, car, ship, even camel and elephant.

This time, however, I had wanted to be by myself. The engine of my car purred like a basking cat. The well-surfaced road drew the accelerator downward. It was a smooth and purposeless trip.

I took a curve too fast. The tyres squealed as I hit the brakes. Who could blame me for beginning to enjoy myself as I hit seventy miles an hour? The car gripped the road well. I pulled off onto the hard shoulder. On my right was a farm with a white house, a barn, and a two-storey silo that looked remarkably like a place we had stopped in for the night on our long march. I hesitated. I wasn't sure I really wanted to know. *Just a minute, Frister: isn't that what this is all about? Are you afraid to meet up with the past after all?* I parked the car, locked the doors, and walked to the farmyard. Pigsties ran along its sides. Was this it? I wasn't sure. Maybe. Maybe not. I knocked on the door of the house. A young woman opened it.

'What can I do for you, *mein Herr*?' she asked.

It was pointless. She was born at least twenty-five years after I had slept in this place. I returned to the car and switched on the radio. A newscaster's voice came over the stereo speaker. *Tomorrow's weather – more of the same.*

38

The night was chilly. We were so weary that the farmyard felt like a five-star hotel. About five hundred of us were put in the empty pigsties. The rest, including myself, climbed ladders to the top of a silo. The doors of the sties were bolted. The ladders were taken away. We could sleep until daylight.

I took off my shoes and burrowed into a pile of straw like a mole. My feet had swelled. I worried about their fitting back into their clogs in the morning. It felt good to clean the grime from between my toes. All I was missing was a basin of warm water.

I had no idea how far we had come from Vienna. We had been taken along partly unpaved country roads that passed through villages whose names meant nothing. I only knew that we had been on the road for four days. I had divided my bread into sections, one for each day. Now I finished the last of them.

Although the spring days were fine, the nights were uncomfortably cold. Like most of the prisoners, I had thrown my blanket into a ditch when we set out. In our debilitated state, even a feather felt like lead. When night came, it was too late to make up for our rashness. The first three nights were spent in the open air, on the ground outside military barracks. Now I thrust my feet into the straw and waited patiently for them to warm up.

It was already dark when I heard singing in Italian. A group of men was crooning 'La Plaloma', a sentimental tango I knew by heart because it was one of my mother's favourites. One man warbled grace notes while the others formed a chorus. Curious, I took my clogs and crawled to the window of the silo. The scene below could have come from an operetta. A company of green-caped Italian infantry sat harmonizing around a campfire. After 'La Plaloma' came more wonderful old tunes. The soldiers' supper was cooking in a tureen hung over the flames. Their rifles stood to one side, arranged in tripods. You would never have guessed from their easy manner that they belonged to the hastily retreating Axis armies.

The singing broke off. Suddenly the atmosphere felt charged. Some SS soldiers entered the yard. Their arrogant poses were an unspoken challenge. An Italian officer rose from the campfire. He went over to them. 'Welcome,' he said in broken German. 'Come sit with us.'

'Sit with you?' jeered an SS man. 'That's all you can do: sit on your asses and sing.'

'May I remind you that you're talking to an officer.'

The German persisted:

'May I remind you that this isn't La Scala.'

'What a bunch of guinea comedians,' said a second German.

'There's no need to insult our honour,' said the officer mildly. His lack of belligerence only spurred that of the Germans.

'What honour are you talking about?' This came from a third SS man, who had kept out of it until now. 'The honour of traitors?'

'We fought together. Why quarrel?' asked the Italian.

'We fought together,' mocked the first German. 'Big heroes! You duck for cover every time you hear a fart. One fucking Russian makes a whole company of you crap in your pants. With allies like you, we don't need enemies.'

The Italians went on sitting around the campfire. They didn't even react when one of the Nazis kicked their knapsacks and shoved the officer. Ladling their food into their mess kits, they ate quietly, took their things, and walked off to the taunts of the SS.

I had no idea what happened afterwards. Too tired to go on watching despite my curiosity, I returned to my bale of hay and fell into a dreamless, soundless sleep. Early in the morning the ladders were brought and we were ordered to descend for roll-call. The dead bodies of the Italians lay by one of the pigsties. One, a young soldier's of no more than twenty, lay on its back with an eye protruding from its socket on the stem of a reddish vein. The other eye was wide open, staring at the sky. Disgusted by the sight, an SS man flipped the body on its stomach with his boot. The Italians' rifles had not been touched. They had not tried, or had time, to defend themselves.

We were under way again.

At first the pain was mostly in my shoulders. After a while it crept down my spine to my hips, where it met a second pain creeping up from my swollen feet. The two joined to assail every muscle and tendon in my body. Somewhere beneath my brainpan an agonizing pressure was building up. My head felt gripped by a vice that tightened by the minute. It dimmed my sight and threatened to squash my skull. Yet its very presence helped concentrate my mind.

Despite our guards' efforts to maintain order, our column was in disarray. Those in the rear lost contact with the main body. Prisoners too weary to go on dropped by the side of the road. Most lacked the strength to rise again. They lay apathetically, unresponsive to the shouts of the guards. The latter had given up enforcing discipline. Whoever failed to rejoin the line after a few blows was allowed to stay behind. He hadn't long to live anyway.

Unable to keep up, other prisoners slowed down in the hope of catching up again. Few did. They fell further and further behind, drifting backwards through the column until they reached its end. The guards ignored them. At the rear of our formation cruised an Opel-Blitz army truck painted in camouflage colours, a heavy machine gun mounted on its tailgate. The gunner had orders to leave no live prisoners behind. An officer with a pistol checked the bodies, putting those still alive out of their misery.

None of this shocked me. The bloody corpses in the dirt simply strengthened my resolve to keep marching. And marching. And marching.

I found ways to outwit my pain, fool my exhaustion, cheat my fate. The trick was to take my mind off myself. I recited snatches of poetry that I had learned by heart as a child: two stanzas of Goethe, a stanza from *Mr Tadeusz*, a whole poem by Julian Tuwim, a few words from Mayakovsky's 'Left, Left'. My fund of literature exhausted, I began counting electric poles. My goal, I told myself, was to reach the third pole ahead of me. When I reached it, I set a new goal: the fourth pole. The fifth. The sixth. Without noticing it, I was nearing the front of the column. Soon I joined the strongest marchers and stuck to them doggedly for the rest of the way.

Our guards walked alongside us, automatic rifles dangling carelessly from their shoulders in what was the only outward sign that they, too, were beginning to go slack. Although the Red Army was breathing down their necks, they continued to behave as if the Wehrmacht were at the gates of Moscow. Today I wonder if they were aware that their defeat was imminent. Did they realize that Hitler's Thousand Year Reich was ending? Or had their brainwashed minds lost all power of judgment?

Hundreds of thousands of concentration camp prisoners trudged the roads in that April of 1945, driven towards enclaves in which the German army was holding out. In its final death agonies, the insane world of the Nazis still sought to drag us down with it. Contemporary Holocaust literature has called these treks 'death marches'. I have seen no statistics on how many died in them, nor do I know whose idea they were. The Nazi high command in Berlin was still subject to Hitler's whims. The mad dictator ordering non-existent divisions into battle may also have been marching us to factories bombed into ruins. No one dared tell him the truth.

On the eighth day we marched through Steier. On the walls of the houses were posters announcing in huge letters: 'The Great Swine Croaks'. A contorted face of Franklin Delano Roosevelt looked down from them. After the war this enabled me to date our passage through the town to 12 April 1945. Later I learned from the history books that the Nazi minister of propaganda Joseph Goebbels told Hitler over the telephone: 'My Führer, please accept my congratulations, Roosevelt is dead. It is written in the stars that the second half of April will be a turning point.' He was referring to a horoscope commissioned by Martin Bormann, the director of Hitler's office. Hitler believed that history was repeating itself. In the Seven Year War, too, the sudden death of the Russian Tsarina Elisebeta had saved Prussia and its Kaiser Friedrich the Great at the last minute.

At the Nuremberg Trials, Albert Speer, the Nazi minister of armaments in charge of hundreds of thousands of slave labourers like myself, testified that: 'From January on, it would have been possible to initiate and undertake any reasonable plan, even if opposed to official policy. Every sensible person in the country would have welcomed this. By acting in concert we had the capacity to delay and thwart Hitler's insane orders.'

Our commanding officer thought otherwise.

When we ran out of bread and our guards finished their battle rations, we were permitted every now and then to forage by the side of the road. We ate unripe barley, sucked the juice of bitterweed, and chewed nettle leaves first rubbed between our hands.

The Germans had different methods. At night, after locking us in a silo, stable or pigsty, they raided the nearby villages for anything edible. The Austrian peasants hid what they could. The few willing to sell their produce refused to accept German marks for it. This led our commanding officer to make an exceptional proposal.

'The fucking bastards,' he declared to us, referring to the Austrian family on whose farm we were spending the night, 'have a pig hidden in the woods. The fuckers want hard currency for it. This is itself a high crime for which they deserve to swing from the nearest lamppost. But there are no lampposts in this goddam hole, and what good would it do us anyway? The death of all these bastards isn't worth a single pig. Neither are you. You're fucking bastards, too. I'd gladly hang you from the first telephone pole and go back to fighting the Bolsheviks. But I'm a soldier, and soldiers obey orders. My orders are to bring you to Mauthausen and that's what I'm going to do.'

He gasped for air like a fish out of water. It was obvious that he had never given such a long speech before, certainly not to fucking bastards like us. Behind him two armed soldiers guarded the entrance of the shed housing us. Despite their officer's novel tone, our status was unchanged.

'I know you all. You've always screwed us by hiding diamonds and gold coins up your asses or in your ears or God knows where. I need two of those coins now. They'd best be Maria Theresa thalers, because that's what the fucking bastards want. We'll buy the pig and boil it. The soldiers will get the meat and we'll give you the broth. Half of you have already croaked along the way, thank God. How many does that leave? Five hundred stomachs at the most. There's plenty of water here. There'll be enough broth for you all. Don't kid yourselves. It's the only food you're going to get. The broth will be yours, I promise you. You have an SS officer's word.'

He gave us ten minutes to think about it. The guards shut the doors of the shed. A Frenchman of about thirty, nicknamed 'Petit' because of his short size, grabbed my arm and whispered:

'What do you think?'

It was the first time we had ever spoken. Why ask me?

'I stopped thinking long ago,' I said.

'Do you think we should give them the money?'

'It's not my problem. I don't have any.'

'You think they'll really give us something to eat?'

'Do you believe in God?'

'Yes.'

'Then ask Him. He knows everything.'

'I'm hungry. I can't keep going without food.'

'Do you think anyone else can?'

'What do I care about anyone else?' This got the Frenchman's goat.

'I have to make it back to France, don't you see? I have to. I was engaged the week before my arrest.'

'Congratulations. Now lay off me.'

'I know that Nicole is no saint. I can't help it if she has pepper between her legs. I can live with her grabbing a stray prick here and there. *C'est la vie*. What I don't see can't hurt me. But if I don't make it back she'll marry Roger. That's more than I can bear to think of. Roger . . . but what does someone like you know about Roger?'

'Get off my ass, Petit.'

'You know me?' he asked happily.

'You worked on my shift.'

'Yes. I'm a first-class lathe operator. Not bad in the sack, either. Ask Nicole, she'll tell you. Our last time in bed she gave me a sou to remember her by. "Never lose this, Maurice," she said. "It's our good-luck charm." She never called me Petit. It wasn't an ordinary sou. It was a gold medallion. I've guarded it with my life for the last three years. This isn't easy for me. Should I give it to them?'

Within ten minutes the unbelievable had happened. An enterprising prisoner collected several coins. Petit's sou was among them. How this money had been hidden – how it had eluded dozens of surprise searches – what stratagems had prevented its discovery by the kapos and guards – only its possessors knew.

Locked in the shed, we heard the squeals of the slaughtered pig. As soon as the door was opened in the morning, the Nazis pointed to four stone drinking troughs full of mouth-watering pig broth. The prisoners threw themselves on it, shoving and spilling it from each other's bowls. A prisoner fell into a trough. He was pulled out and beaten senseless. I behaved no better than the others. I pushed and kicked whoever I could. It was no time for table manners. The SS did not interfere. They waited for the orgy to be over before lining us up and counting us.

Deliberately or not, our commanding officer had revealed our destination: Mauthausen. This was a blow. We had deluded ourselves that there were still arms factories needing workers. The only work in Mauthausen was the granite quarries. Thousands had died in them. It was hard to believe that any quarrying was still going on. Berlin lay in ruins. Why bring us to a place in which they could do nothing with us? I fought against admitting the possibility that we were being taken there to be killed.

Our column grew shorter day by day. At morning roll-call the *Abgang*, the list of those fallen by the wayside, grew steadily longer. Hundreds of prisoners were missing, their corpses lining the roads like milestones. How many of us would last to the journey's end? There was no knowing how many days we still had ahead of us. I had no idea where we were, no chance to see a map, no one to ask. My only gauge was my power of endurance. Could I stay on my feet for another day – another two days – another week? It wasn't just a question of general exhaustion. The soles of my callused feet were covered in sores. These kept bursting like foul bubbles, their pus mixing with the dust of the road to form a thick paste in my clogs. At first I tried wiping this with leaves. Then I gave up. It was pointless. My body was an endless source of more. It leaked from every pore, the only substance I could still produce. My shirt was full of yellowish ooze that dried and caked. I and my clothes were a single stiff mass.

Although the pig broth I had fought for caused my digestion no problems, many of the prisoners came down with diarrhoea. Our systems had forgotten how to handle fat. Petit, who had been quicker than me and gotten two bowls of broth for his gold sou, had terrible stomach cramps. When we stopped for a break, which happened every two hours because our escort needed to rest, too, he unbuttoned his pants and scrambled into a ditch. I sat down on a road marker that said, 68 Kilometres, in black paint. But to where?

I sat idly watching Petit. A soldier smoking a cigarette watched him, too. What suddenly got into Petit, I'll never know. Perhaps the SS man's stare frightened him. All at once he grabbed his pants and darted out of the ditch for some bushes that were growing by the roadside. The white flash of his behind was comical. I grinned. So did the soldier. He kicked me lightly off the road marker, laid his cigarette on it, took his tommy gun from his shoulder, sighted, and squeezed the trigger. There was a short burst. He stuck his cigarette back in his mouth. *Adieu, Petit. The best of luck, Nicole. You can marry Roger now.*

39

'Herr Sturmbannführer! Obersturmführer Kietske reporting with the Saurer-Werke contingent from Vienna! Roll: one thousand and twenty prisoners. Struck from roll: six hundred and eighty-eight prisoners. Remaining: three hundred and twenty-two prisoners.'

We stood facing the locked gates of Mauthausen. The SS major who had come out to meet us spread his arms.

'I'm very sorry. This camp is not accepting more prisoners.'

'I have a written order, Herr Sturmbannführer.' The officer of our escort handed over a piece of paper. The major read it carefully, folded it in two, and handed it back.

'You're in a rum situation, my friend. But I'm afraid I can't help. This camp is full to overflowing.'

'That's none of my concern,' insisted Kietske. 'I have my orders.'

'Mine are the opposite.'

'What am I supposed to do with all these people?' Obersturmführer Kietske pointed at us.

'For all I care, you can march them back to Vienna.'

'That's totally illogical.'

'I'm not a logician. I'm an officer with orders.'

'So am I.'

'You can't change my mind. The camp is closed.'

'Then open it.'

'You're wasting your time.'

'My *time*? Do you have any idea how much time it's taken me to get these fucking bastards here? We've been on the road for nearly two weeks.'

'That is a waste.'

'I'll file a complaint!' Obersturmführer Kietske was losing his temper. The major looked suddenly amused.

'May I ask to whom?' he grinned.

'To . . .'

'Aha. You're beginning to get it.'

'I still don't get your refusal, though.'

'You want an explanation? All right. I'll give you one. I refuse to accept your three hundred corpses because we have no room for them, no food for them, and no one to guard them. Is that good enough for you?'

'No.'

'You're stubborn as a mule.'

'So are you.'

The two officers burst out laughing. The tension eased. Obersturmführer Kietske handed his orders back to the major. 'Why fight over it? All I'm asking is for you to sign this receipt. What you do with them afterwards is none of my business.'

'Sorry, but I have to disappoint you again. We're not only out of food, we're out of Zyklon B. I see you've got a heavy machine gun on your truck. Why don't you do the job yourself? Just don't leave the corpses by the gate. I've got no one to dispose of them.'

I understood every word.

Damn it all! Was it for this that my parents had forced me to take such pains with my German pronunciation and grammar? That I was made to read, besides the books that I liked, the classical German poetry without which – so my mother explained – no person could be considered cultured? That I laboured over the heavy volumes of the collected works of Heine? Had to learn by heart Mephisto's dialogue with the angels in Part I of *Faust* and recite them for the dubious pleasure of our dinner guests? I stood declaiming:

> *Die Sonne tont nach alter Weise*
> *In Brudersphären Wettgesang*
> *Und ihre vorgeschriebene Reise*
> *Vollendet sie mit Donnergang.*

The guests clapped as if for a show put on for them while waiting for my father to ring the bell that was Paula's signal to

serve the *digestif*. I hated it. Although the audience and programme changed each week, the performance was repeated like a
broken record. Sometimes, seeking to display my literary knowledge, my mother would ask me about the new play put on by the
municipal theatre (the German one, of course), or about my
opinion of some new book. These embarrassing scenes came to
an end one evening when, boasting of our intellectual compan-
ionship, she told the table how I considered her my best friend
despite all the talk of a generation gap. 'If anything bothers
Romek, or if he has some question, he always comes to me,' she
said.

I made Face Number Ten, a sweet innocent child's, and
remarked:

'As a matter of fact, I wanted to ask you about a new word I
heard in school today.'

My mother smiled with contentment. 'What word is that?'

'Fuck,' I said without batting an eyelash.

With a wiser child's hindsight, I regretted my behaviour. Now
that I was permanently banished from my parents' sitting room, I
began to miss these evenings, which had opened a window on the
adult world. As critical as I was of my mother, I had to admit that
the appearances I loathed had given me a sense of self-importance.

Although now and then my father liked the challenge of a
criminal case, most of his income came from civil law. It was
widely said that he had no equal at drawing up contracts and
finessing the thorny legal problems encountered by the banks and
large firms of Bielsko. Keenly aware of the importance of social
contacts for his career, he regularly entertained the upper crust of
the city in our home on Sunday nights. I enjoyed meeting them:
the textile magnates, the bankers, the top executives of commercial and investment houses, even the guests who were purely
decorative. My mother was a wizard at organizing these dinner
parties, the guest lists of which she put together like a florist
fashioning a bouquet. She would seat a politician beside a local
industrialist, an artist next to a snobbish collector, a much-
decorated colonel alongside the wife of a district judge, a would-
be investor with the manager of a bank.

Emil Zegadlowicz was the weed in her floral arrangements. To her great chagrin, he joined us every week. Not only did he irritate her by his very presence, but she was obliged to reserve for him the place of honour on my father's right. Zegadlowicz was a non-conformist, active in left-wing organizations, the author of books that no decent home would want on its shelves. In our own house his novels, most of them full of erotica, were kept hidden behind the volumes of *The Great Brockhaus*. My father supported him with a small monthly stipend that only infuriated my mother even more. Too young to understand this strange friendship between the conservative lawyer and the bohemian rebel, I later found out that they had been born in the same year, 1888; had studied in the same class in Wadowice, a town half an hour from Bielsko; and had in common their staunchly anti-fascist views. The one thing that recommended Emil Zegadlowicz to my mother and somewhat softened her opposition to him was his having translated *Faust* into Polish.

There was one iron rule at these dinners: all business talk was forbidden. Although this was a concession to my mother, who wished to preside over a cultural salon, her home was not exactly Gertrude Stein's, just as Bielsko was not Paris, nor even the most important city in the district. Invariably, the conversation drifted from the subjects she preferred to politics. It was the period between the *Anschluss* of Austria and the Nazi annexation of the Sudetenland, and all Europe was obsessed with Germany. Still, despite Hitler's growing appetite, German culture retained its lustre for my parents. Most of their guests, myself included, had been educated in it. I had an unchallenged respect for German-speaking civilization that my parents had inculcated in me. Like many others, I never imagined that the same people that had produced so many generations of titans would now produce a generation of murderers.

While the two SS officers argued loudly about what to do with the nuisance that we represented, my thoughts reverted to these childhood scenes. Perhaps it was a convenient way of blocking out the grotesque conversation taking place. The appearance of a third officer brought me back to reality. As in the Trial of Solomon, he ruled that half of us would be allowed to enter the camp and half would remain outside, 'no matter what'.

I did not wish to find out what this 'no matter what' signified.

My parents' dinner parties forgotten in an instant, I made a dash for the gate as soon as it opened. I never discovered what happened to those who didn't make it. At that moment they were my enemies, threatening to push me aside and enter the life-giving camp in my place.

I looked around. The same repair shops and watchtowers. Like one of Pavlov's dogs, I threw a frightened glance at the fire hoses. But the SS had no time for fun and games now. Perhaps they had run out of water, too.

For a while we aroused no one's interest. We lay about in the yard while the inner gate to the barracks remained shut. The guards regarded us with indifference. I was experienced enough to know, however, that all this could end in a volley of bullets at any moment. Instinctively I edged towards the back of a repair shop, where I wiped the pus from my pimples with a greasy rag. Even the most humane SS man would show no mercy to someone with acne like mine.

Towards evening the front gate swung open. 'Out! Out!' shouted the soldiers who rushed at us. I felt everything go black. 'Out' meant 'no matter what' – death on the spot or a long, insane march back to Vienna. God knows where I found the strength to rise and run. As everyone else was running with me, perhaps I was simply swept along like a driven leaf.

The thread of memory is broken at this point. An entire day has been obliterated for ever. When I came to I was lying on a cot in the 'sanitary camp', as the small infirmary outside the main barracks block was called. I have no recollection of how I got there. Although it was most likely under my own steam, I can't be sure of it.

'At least they have some peace.'

These were the first words to penetrate my consciousness. It took a while to make out their speaker. He was the man lying next to me, his face close to mine. His appearance was horrible. His eyes were sunk deep in their sockets. His nose was smashed. His cheeks were splattered with dried blood. He raised a hand and pointed to the open door. My glance followed his finger to a pile of corpses.

I was too weak to reply. There was nothing to say.

'Where are you from?' he asked. I couldn't place his German

accent. I didn't try. I didn't care if he was a Jew, Spaniard, or Greek. I wanted to be left alone. But the man was compelled to go on.

'Look,' he said. He tried to raise his skinny hand again, but this time it ran out of momentum and fell back.

'Cannibals,' he muttered.

Words and noises were taking a long time to reach me. It was as if the speed of sound, or perhaps my own hearing, had slowed down. When I finally understood the wretched man, I assumed he was raving. Hallucinations were nothing out of the ordinary.

But he was not. In the twilight I saw two figures approach the pile of corpses. They kneeled and bit into them.

'Canni—' said the man and fell silent. The two cannibals were joined by others. Hunger whipsawed my stomach. I felt too cold to think straight. In science fiction men are frozen and restored to life after hundreds of years. Yet lying there in a daze, taking refuge in non-existence, submerged in nothingness, I did not think of ever returning to this world. Lucidity and unconsciousness tossed me from light to darkness and darkness to light. Were it not for the sago distributor, I might never have re-emerged from my oblivion. The smell of food and the clatter of utensils brought me round like smelling salts.

The sago, a white, tasteless gruel, was distributed twice a day, in the morning and in the evening. A lifeline to hold onto, it helped shape the formless hours of the day.

That night my bunkmate stopped his groaning. In the morning, when I passed him his sago bowl, he didn't touch it. I ate his portion along with my own. It was only when he passed up his evening sago, too, that I realized he was no longer alive.

I said nothing. For three days I let his death go unreported, concealing it from the prisoners who came to collect the corpses that spread the dysentery raging through the camp. Six times I ate a double serving of sago. My stomach swelled like a balloon. It could no more digest food than my intestines could excrete it. I would have gone on with my deception had not the body beside me begun to rot and stink. I pushed it to the floor. Either it was as light as a feather, or I had gotten back some of my strength, because it did not even take an effort.

'Come on down, you idiot! It's over!'

Who was calling me? What was over? Why were the prisoners running outside? Why was the square full of cheering people?

Someone tugged at my arm. I rolled out of the bunk, fell, and got to my feet. Unfamiliar men helped me out of the barracks. I was bewildered. For years no stranger had offered me the slightest help. Two healthy prisoners dragged me to the open space between two barracks. A tank was parked there, a white, five-pointed star on its turret. Prisoners threw their caps in the air, a sure sign that there would be no more roll-calls. Cries of joy were uttered in every language of occupied Europe. A Babel of happiness. I wanted to cry that I was too weak, that I needed to be taken away from this place – where, I didn't know. I wanted my strength back. No cry left my throat. My desiccated vocal cords creaked like a rusty door.

The two men were still holding me up. I felt their strong arms beneath me. The tank turret swung round, its cannon describing a semicircle like a watch hand. The hatch opened. I saw the head of a black soldier. He waved at us. The full truth dawned on me. Yes, it was over.

It wasn't how I had imagined the liberation. Although I may never have had a clear picture of it, I was always sure it would be a moment of joy. Now I had no strength for joy. Perhaps I had forgotten what it was.

The black soldier removed his helmet and mopped his brow with a white handkerchief. It was a hot spring day. Armed guards looked down from the watchtowers. 'Hitler Kaput,' he called, signalling them to come down. They came at once. I later learned that the SS had pulled out of Mauthausen several days earlier, leaving the guard duty to the Vienna police. Such men were less cruel and certainly less eager to tangle with American tanks.

The black man said something again. I couldn't make out the words. The guards threw down their tommy guns and formed a line. A group of prisoners darted forward and snatched the guns. The cheers grew louder. 'Viva España!' someone shouted. French and Polish flags were being waved. The Soviet prisoners broke out in the Internationale.

I couldn't stand up any longer. My body felt as hollow as a mummy's. 'Please,' I said to the prisoner next to me. 'Help me back to the barracks.'

Although I didn't expect him to respond, he put his arm around me and dragged me to the barracks door. As soon as he let go of me, the last of my strength gave out. I fell to the floor and passed out again.

Reality came back slowly, at first as a wave of sound that grew louder from minute to minute, then as lights and shapes that gradually came into focus. I was lying on my back, looking up at the ceiling of the barracks. A pair of bare feet swung above me. They hung from the little stomach of a naked man who wore the cap of an SS corporal. It took me a few minutes to understand what was happening. The corporal was tied to a rafter by a rope passed around his wrists. Blood flowed from his body. A group of Soviet prisoners was using it for target practice, taking turns at throwing a long kitchen knife. Each time the knife pierced the suspended man's body, the Russians burst into wild cheers. A short, slanty-eyed prisoner turned to me. He put the knife in my hands and said:

'Make him bleed, son. Make him bleed. You can have my turn.'

I didn't respond. I lay there holding the knife. My eyes were open but unseeing. The vengeful shouts and joyful cheers made a single roar in my ears. Free to go where I wanted, I had no strength to stand up. I could kill a Nazi – and saw no point in it. I could shout, curse, sing, pray, but had no words. What good to me were my new rights? My clenched fist relaxed. I dropped the knife.

40

By any objective standard, my name should not have been on the list of surviving prisoners when the day of jubilation came. Luckily for me, objective standards do not determine the unwritten laws of chance.

A year or so later, at the trial of the medical staff of Mauthausen conducted in Dachau, Dr Eduard Krassbach testified with blood-curdling candidness:

'When I was appointed to the position of head doctor, I was given orders to kill all prisoners who were incurable or unfit for work. Prisoners pronounced unfit were exterminated in the gas chambers. A few were injected with gasoline.' Asked by the prosecutor whether it had not occurred to him that he was murdering human beings, Krassbach replied: 'No. Human beings are no different from animals. An animal born with a defect is shot. For humanitarian reasons, people must be treated the same way ... The state has the right to exterminate antisocial elements. Anyone unfit for work belongs to this category.'

Although not born with a birth defect, I certainly belonged to the category of the unfit. My weight, as I later learned from my American medical file, was down to thirty-seven kilograms. Apart from tuberculosis, running sores, intestinal spasms, partial deafness, and general debilitation, I was also suffering from an illness first diagnosed by a Polish prisoner who ministered to the sick in Mauthausen's sanitary camp, Dr Wladyslaw Fajkel. Not yet given the scientific name of Distrophia Alientaria, it was called by him 'the starvation syndrome'.

'Once the body has lost close to a third of its weight,' wrote Dr Fajkel in a medical paper, 'the expression grows veiled and remote, conveying apathy. The eyes sink deep into the sockets and the skin turns a transparent grey with a tendency to peel. In this state, the patient is highly susceptible to skin infections, particularly scabies. Breathing is retarded and speech is difficult and hushed. Oedema is common, appearing first in the eyelids and soles of the feet. If starvation continues, it spreads to other parts of the body, such as the thighs, the calves, the buttocks, the testicles, and the abdomen. At this stage diarrhoea sets in and the patient loses interest in his surroundings. He prefers to be alone and walks slowly, if at all, with no flexion of the knees. Due to a lowered body temperature of less than thirty-six degrees, there is shivering from hypothermia. Only the sight of food is capable of arousing the patient from his lethargy. Death is usually sudden.'

While fate was laughing at objective standards, Dr Fajkel was working for an underground group that tried to thwart the implementation of the policies so ably described by Dr Krass-bach.

Separate resistance units of Poles, Frenchmen, and Spaniards had been active in Mauthausen for several months, each looking after its own countrymen. We Jews had no such organization. The world's homeless cosmopolitans, we had no one to represent us. Indirectly, however, I owed my life to these other groups. Some two weeks before my return to Mauthausen, its German prisoners were given the chance to join the Wehrmacht. Many of them accepted the collapsing Reich's offer to exchange their striped prison uniforms for olive-grey. It was not patriotism or the illusion of a German victory that motivated them, but the desire to be elsewhere on the day of vengeance. Their jobs as kapos and clerical workers were taken by political prisoners active in the resistance groups. Well organized and cohesive, these prisoners were able to forge official documents listing the sick as healthy, report imaginary gassings, and play havoc with camp statistics. The SS lost its grip on what was happening and some three thousand condemned men were rescued.

According to German records for the first week of May 1945, congestion in the sanitary camp was intolerable. There were 8863 patients occupying less than two thousand bunks. Eight hundred critically ill prisoners were killed under the guise of being transferred elsewhere. When the Polish underground discovered plans to 'transfer' twenty-two hundred more, the camp's acting head physician, Dr Czaplinksi, courageously asked Mauthausen's second-in-command, an SS officer named Buchmeier, for an 'officer-to-officer' talk. Although normally Czaplinski would have paid for such insolence with his life, in the light of Hitler's suicide, which was by now general knowledge, and the imminent German surrender, Buchmeier preferred to save his own skin. The order was cancelled at the last moment. The Angel of Death missed out on me.

The lacerated corpse of the SS corporal swung from the rafter for two more days before being cut down by an American soldier. The barracks emptied out. The Russians – mostly political commissars in the Red Army who had been sent to concentration rather than POW camps – roamed the countryside, terrorizing the local Austrians. The American soldier picked me off the floor and called an ambulance.

I had lain where I fell for two whole days. The American dragged me outside by the armpits. Shortly afterwards I was taken to an American field hospital.

Two doctors and a medic in American uniforms stood looking at my file. I was lying on a stretcher. One doctor kneeled, put a stethoscope to my chest, and listened to the wheezing of my lungs. He plucked at my eyelid like a boy tearing the wings from a fly, shone a flashlight into my eyes, and announced:

'A classic case. We'll terminate treatment.'

'When, Captain?' asked the medic.

'Now.'

'Hasn't he been getting the right medicines?'

'There's nothing wrong with the medicines. It's the patient. He's had it.'

'Still . . .' said the medic. 'That's very cruel, Captain.' Still young and unjaded by war, his dedication to me had been boundless. Again and again he had cleaned my watery excretions and wet my dry lips. At night he sat at a small table in the middle of the tent, reading medical books by the light of a lantern. His ambition was to go home to Arizona and go to medical school. The doctor patted him on the back.

'Don't let it get you down. He'll depart this life peacefully. Death doesn't hurt.'

'Don't say that, Captain. The boy understands English.'

'I'm sorry,' said the doctor, proceeding to the next patient.

I listened to his verdict with perfect serenity. I was too exhausted to contest the ironic fact that, now that I stood in the light at the end of the tunnel, I was doomed. I had arrived at a point where not only death, but life, too, no longer hurt. I felt nothing. I was only dimly aware of those dying around me despite the wonder drugs they received, or of the others who took their place in an endlessly revolving door.

The days went by. Stubbornly, without the benefit of the Americans' medicine, I clung to life. After a month – or was it two? – I was transferred from the field hospital to a convalescent ward located in a former guards' barracks. My diarrhoea stopped. I began to enjoy my food and to take an interest in the world around me. My attacks of weakness grew rarer. Still bedridden, I sometimes listened to music. There was a radio in every room.

An International Red Cross delegation came to compile lists of survivors. I gave it my name. Several years later a Tel Aviv lawyer found it in some documents and tried convincing me to file a reparations claim. I leafed through the papers he showed me, looking for the name of Fredek Minz. It wasn't there.

I never filed the claim, even though West Germany allotted hundreds of millions of marks as compensation for the Nazis' victims. 'I'm sorry,' I told the lawyer. 'I couldn't accept such money. It won't bring me back my parents, my family, or the years that were lost.'

'You're being foolish,' the lawyer said angrily. 'There's no such thing as clean money or dirty money. There's only good money and bad money.'

I was about thirty at the time, still far from the age at which all things are measured by their material worth. Perhaps I was rash. I remained unconvinced even when asked by the lawyer: 'Would you rather the money stayed with the murderers?' No doubt he was right. So was I. There was no way of bridging right and right.

The army medics were gone from the barracks. We were attended by nurses now, all Germans or Austrians. Mine wore a grey smock and had an easily forgettable face. What I remember of her are pudgy fingers with a thin wedding ring; short, unpolished nails; and her moist, delicate touch as she daubed my sores with disinfectant.

I don't know how old she was. A seventeen-year-old boy thinks of all adults as old. There was something motherly and reassuring about her. Sometimes, when feeling weak, I longed to fall asleep in her arms. But my feelings were mixed, because as soon as I felt stronger I shrank from her as though from someone objectionable. Once I dreamed of her as Grete. I wanted to tell her about this when she came to make my bed that morning and ended up instead by insulting her for no good reason.

I was irritated by my dependence on this quiet woman who cleaned up after me without either taking advantage of my helplessness or condescending to it. I hated her eagerness to help; it spoiled my image of the overweening German. I fumed at her for putting up with my tantrums as if I were a child who didn't know better.

I lay in a small white room. Its other bed was empty. The nurse and doctor were my only visitors. One day the nurse surprised me with someone else.

'Sit up,' she said. 'This man will shave you.'

'Shave me?' I marvelled. 'What for?'

She brought me a little mirror. At least two years had passed since my last glimpse of my reflection. The face looking at me was a pale young man's. There were bags beneath his brown eyes. His hair had grown out, draping a first curl across the forehead. His lips were chapped and an ugly scar ran across his right cheek.

I didn't like my self-portrait. It gave me a strange feeling, as though it belonged to someone else. I ran a hand over my face and noted to my surprise that it was no longer smooth. I hadn't realized that I had grown a beard of prickly hairs. 'You'll be a man soon,' said the nurse in the same laconic tone with which she sometimes told me to turn over so that she could put ointment on my back. The barber lathered his brush. The razor scraped my face gently. I liked the feeling.

That day my doctor was pleased with me. 'A definite recovery,' he declared with some astonishment as he wrote in my file. VIPs – Washington officials and Congressmen – were brought to my bed to see the medical miracle. No one asked me about myself, nor did I inform anyone that I had been denied treatment because I was deemed a financially poor investment.

Early that summer some members of the Jewish Brigade, the Palestinian unit that had fought with the British army, came to Mauthausen. By then I was able to leave my room with the help

THE TASTE OF FREEDOM

of a nurse and lie on the lawn, or lean against a wall and let the sunlight drive out the chill that I still felt in my bones.

The Jewish soldiers in their British uniforms arrived in two trucks. Most spoke some Yiddish. A score of ex-prisoners clustered around them. They told us about their war and about Palestine, and urged us to come with them to Italy and sail from there to the land of Israel. Even had I wanted to join them, they were unlikely to have taken anyone in my condition. But the thought never crossed my mind. I felt no yearning for Zion. The land of my forefathers belonged to ancient history, not to the present. I still remembered my mother's visit to Palestine in 1935. She had taken a Mediterranean cruise on the *Polonia*, sailing from the Rumanian port of Constanza, and had returned to Bielsko to report that the Jewish National Home was no place for civilized people. Although this was the casual impression of a tourist, her verdict remained with me and shaped my opinion. Palestine might be fine for pioneers, not for someone serious like me.

The Jewish Brigade departed without me. I soon took a shorter trip.

A new frontier had been negotiated between the Western and Soviet armies. The Americans evacuated Mauthausen and withdrew to the south bank of the Danube. The Russians took over. The change of regime affected the medical care. My ointment was no longer available. Neither were the vitamin pills to build up my resistance. The food grew inedible. The Soviet doctors could not read English and ignored what was written in my files. I felt headed for a relapse and didn't need a doctor to tell me I was losing ground again. Since any change could only be for the better, I was glad when the Russians decided to move the entire ward. Put on a wagon pulled by a tractor, we were taken a short distance to Katzdorf, an Austrian village in the wine-growing region north of Mauthausen. There we were installed in an old-age home whose residents were forced to vacate it. The Red Army captain escorting us summoned the village headman, who appeared hurriedly, doffed a humble cap, and heard the warning:

'If you value your own and the villagers' lives, take good care of these people.'

The headman nodded. The major turned and left. We moved in. Each of us was given a large, clean, private room. On the table by my bed were two books, John Knittel's *Via Mala* and Georg Rendel's *Journey to Mother*. I didn't touch either. After a few days they were removed by my grey-smocked nurse, who had come with us. Although she continued to care for me, our contact was limited to the basics of food, medicines, and hygiene. The greater distance between us had its positive side. I did not feel offended when she brought me a toothbrush and said, 'You have bad breath,' or when she removed my dirty underpants with the remark: 'They smell of doo-doo.' I took it as it was meant.

There was an odd symbiosis between us. If I needed her, she, too, in a way I never understood, needed someone to need her. Yet there was no tenderness – not a smile, not an unnecessary word – in our relationship. She must have felt my lack of affection and not wanted to impose herself on me, an ex-prisoner who relished his privacy after years of unwelcome intimacy with strangers in shared bunks, crowded barracks, and electrically fenced camps. I wanted to be alone with myself and my thoughts. I was happy sitting behind closed doors, oblivious of what went on in the next rooms. I never strolled in the corridor. When I had the strength, I went to my window and opened it without permission. This illicit act gave me pleasure. I sat in a chair, leaned against the windowsill, and breathed the clean, fresh air as if it were the essence of freedom.

Beyond the window was life. I watched the Austrian grape farmers going to work, children playing hopscotch, women hanging out laundry, ordinary people living in ordinary houses – all things I had forgotten. I especially liked looking at people who could not look back at me. My time was my own, not some jailer's who divided it up for me.

Now that my sense of it had returned, I learned to value time anew. Once more there was a present, a past, and a future. True, the past was too much with me and the present was dull. But every morning, lying in bed while staring at the ceiling, I thought about the future. I didn't realize that even daydreaming requires a fund of available experience like the materials used in construction. As I had been deprived of five years of my life that I was too immature to process by reshaping and recolouring it into something usable, my imagination was undernourished. I knew nothing of these transubstantiations with their wondrous conversion of life into reflection that become the condensed wisdom of all we have been through. Having edited out the war years, I was left with no transition from my childhood to the years ahead of me. All I could think of was returning to Bielsko, where life had been good. But how return to a childhood that was no longer inhabited? That had no mother, no father, no Paula, no Nolek with his Leica, no bicycle won by blackmail, no toy soldiers on my bedroom floor, no school friends? How breathe in a vacuum?

The old-age home emptied out. The Russian major failed to make good on his threats. No one protested when the villagers cut down on our food. There was no one to protest to.

The two local doctors departed. Most of the nurses followed them. The farmer's daughter who cleaned my room every morning stopped coming to work. Those who didn't pull through were buried in the village graveyard, in a section of their own. The others packed their things and left. 'What do you think?' I asked my faithful nurse. She put her hands in the pockets of her grey smock and said: 'It's everyone for himself.'

Did that mean me, too? So far she had continued to take care of me. This had given me an unconscious sense of security. Now, I realized to my alarm, this was ending. I said:

'Tomorrow morning.'

She understood.

'Where?'

'Home.'

'You're lucky. I have no home.' It was the first time she had spoken about herself. 'Have you a family?' The first time she had asked me about myself, too.

I said nothing. She didn't ask again.

'I have some clothes for you. Have you any money?'

'Money?' I had forgotten that such a thing existed. 'I'll manage.'

'Transportation for repatriates is free. The westbound trains leave from Linz, the eastbound ones from Enns. Which do you want?'

'How do I get to Enns?'

'I'll ask the village headman. He'll get you a ride.'

That night I dreamed that I was lying on my left side several inches from an abyss. An unknown hand was pushing me into it. It was too dark and murky to see how deep it was, which only made it more frightening. My fear made me gasp. I couldn't breathe. I tried to push away the hand digging into my back. It remained there. I woke up in a sweat, seized by a coughing fit. My phlegm had blood in it.

The window was open. A breeze played with the curtain. Silver moonlight shone on the walls. The ceiling alone was black, a solid mass that bore down on my bare chest. I was cold. I pulled the blanket over my head. The dream resumed like a torn film that has been spliced. I was only saved from it by the nurse.

'Good morning. Are you ready?'

She draped a pair of brown pants, a white shirt, and a checked jacket over the back of the chair.

'I measured them. They're your size.'

I didn't thank her.

'The headman will be here soon. Get up. You need a bath.'

'A bath?' I rebelled. 'What kind of bath?'

I didn't need a bath. I needed someone to tell my dream to and utter a comforting word. She was not that person. Oblivious to how I felt, or simply refusing to acknowledge it, she yanked off my blanket and told me to hurry.

I reached for the clothes she had brought.

'Not yet.' She stayed my hand. 'First your bath.'

'But why?'

'Because you stink.'

'What do you care? You'll never have to smell me again.'

'Others will.'

I rose from my bed and followed her. The bathroom was at the end of the corridor. Its wall tiles were yellowed. Its fixtures had lost their gleam. The enamel was peeling in the sink. A bare bulb shone down on it.

'Take off your clothes.'

I undressed. I wasn't embarrassed to stand naked in front of her. I didn't think of myself as a man or of her as a woman.

She belted her smock and helped me into the bathtub, holding my arm to keep me from slipping. She smiled as she glanced at my thin body. It was the first time I had ever seen her smile.

'You should be scrubbed with sandpaper,' she declared. 'Stand still. There's not enough hot water for a bath. I'll give you a shower.'

I stood still. She opened the tap, shut it again to save water, and soaped my body. The soap stung my sores. She washed me expertly. Her hands ran along my thighs, joined between my legs, touched my testicles. She rubbed my penis. I felt no excitement. She held it and said:

'Don't worry. One day this will grow when touched by a woman. That will be a big day for you. You'll see then how beautiful life is.'

She turned on the tap. The warm water felt good. It was cleansing.

Epilogue

What happened to him, that child from a good home who shed the morality he was raised in and learned overnight to live by the laws of the jungle? What made him discard the ideals he was taught and think of life as a pure struggle for survival? To what depths of his soul did this penetrate?

These questions have preoccupied me ever since I began to think about them. *The Cap or the Price of a Life* is an attempt to answer them. Its story, I think, has a moral. Many people have felt the need to come to terms with the past and to understand how they have been shaped by it.

Fundamentally, I have sought to challenge the philosophy that there are universal truths valid for all times and places and capable of withstanding all criticism. To put it most simply: how can the acts of a time of blackness be judged by the values of a time of light?

I have not tried to write a work of history. The people in this book are presented subjectively. I have described things as I remember them. In a small number of cases, where it was a question of credibility, I made use of written documents. Needless to say, I have portrayed myself as I appeared in the mirror that I held up in front of me.

This book took me four years to write. Part was written in Tel Aviv and part in Poland. Everywhere I was accompanied by the encouragement and help of my wife Shulamit. The fact that our marriage foundered upon the completion of this book in no way detracts from my gratitude to her.